W9-BVY-462

"In a world where youth culture is becoming increasingly more dangerous, those who care about an adolescent need to be aware of the differences between youth today and yesterday. Walt's understanding of music and the media's impact on today's youth is eye-opening. He not only informs about the astounding undertones youth live with, he offers sound advice on how parents and loved ones can help youths manage the difficult challenges they face."

Dr. Brian Newman
Clinical Director, Minirth-Meier New Life Clinics

"[This book] goes far beyond offering parenting tips and ideas for preparing a child for the teen years. Not only will you learn how to do a better job as a parent, teacher, or youth leader; not only will you gain confidence in helping someone through the 'earthquake of adolescence,' you'll truly understand the world of today's teen."

David B. Jones
President, Scripture Union

"Walt Mueller writes with a keen eye for insight, a clear mind for biblical principles, and a compassionate heart for kids. His years as a youth pastor and a father come together to give this book its remarkable mix of careful documentation and pastoral concern."

Duffy Robbins
Department of Youth Ministry, Eastern College

"Walt Mueller has his finger directly on the pulse of America's youth and a heart for the problems they face. No person who cares about kids should be without this book."

Ken Davis
Speaker and author

Understanding Y

Today's
UTH
Culture

WALT MUELLER

Tyndale House Publishers, Inc.
Wheaton, Illinois

Copyright © 1994 Walt Mueller
All rights reserved

Cover and interior photos copyright © 1994 by Brad Baskin

Scripture verses marked TLB are taken from *The Living Bible,* copyright © 1971 owned by assignment by KNT Charitable Trust. All rights reserved.

Scripture quotations marked NIV are taken from the *Holy Bible,* New International Version®. Copyright © 1973, 1978, 1984 by International Bible Society. Used by permission of Zondervan Publishing House. All rights reserved. The "NIV" and "New International Version" trademarks are registered in the United States Patent and Trademark Office by International Bible Society. Use of either trademark requires permission of International Bible Society.

Scripture verses marked Phillips are taken from *The New Testament in Modern English* by J. B. Phillips, copyright © J. B. Phillips, 1958, 1959, 1960, 1972. All rights reserved.

Library of Congress Cataloging-in-Publication Data

Mueller, Walt,   date
   Understanding today's youth culture / Walt Mueller.
      p.   cm.
   Includes bibliographical references and index.
   ISBN 0-8423-7736-0
   1. Mass media and teenagers—United States.   2. Popular culture—
Religious aspects—Christianity.   3. Parent and teenager—Religious
aspects.   I. Title.
HQ799.2.M35 M84   1994   94-26142
261.8'34235'0973—dc20

Printed in the United States of America

00   99   98   97   96   95   94
6   5   4   3   2   1

To the Glory of God
with thanks to Him for
His special gifts to me:

Lisa,
my wife, partner in life,
and best friend.

Caitlin, Joshua, Bethany, and Nathaniel,
who are growing as fast as the smiles they
bring to our faces and the joy
they bring to our hearts.

CONTENTS

PREFACE

A FATHER ONCE asked me, "How can I expect my son to hear the still small voice of God with all those other voices screaming in his ears?" I wrote this book to help you answer this question.

For the last twenty years I have worked with teenagers and their families. During that time I have realized that there is a widening cultural-generational gap that needs to be closed. On one side stand parents and adults who are bewildered by the rapidly changing world of children and teens. On the other side stand children and teens who long for parents and other significant adults who are willing and able to help them through the confusing maze of contemporary youth culture, leading them to a spiritually and emotionally healthy adulthood. I'm convinced that it's a gap nobody wants. This book is for all of you who desire to close this cultural-generational gap and as a result, help the children and teens you know and love hear the God who still speaks.

This is a book for parents.

Parents, you need to read this book because you care deeply about your kids. Your love for them has motivated you to be the best parent you can be, and you would do anything for them. You want to counter the negative influences in today's youth culture by increasing your positive influence on your kids. Yet it's easy to feel out of touch and confused by their world. Maybe you've seen some MTV, listened to your kids talking with their friends, and heard some alarming stories about teenage behavior. If you need help making sense out of the mystical maze of today's youth culture, then this book is for you.

As you read, keep in mind that this is not a book on parenting. While I will share some parenting principles drawn from the combined wisdom of hundreds of parents who have already raised their kids through the teen years, this is primarily a book to help you understand the world of your children and teens so that you will be better able to understand them and thereby parent more effectively. In fact, as a fellow struggler in the parenting journey, I'll be reading along with you!

This is a book for youth workers, teachers, and anyone else who works with kids.

First, this book will help you to understand and address the complex interplay between the cultural forces that are molding and shaping the values, attitudes, and behaviors of the kids under your care. The information I have included will increase your ministry and teaching effectiveness by deepening your understanding of the issues facing kids every day, and your ability to address those issues with intelligence and relevance.

And second, this book will provide you with valuable information that you can pass on to the parents of the kids with whom you work. They are hungry for this kind of help! Use it as a text for a twelve-week parents-of-teens class. Place it in a parents resource library. Use it as you prepare to teach parents about the world of children and teens. Pass on bits and pieces of the information you learn from this book through your newsletters and bulletin boards. Because you share a concern for their kids, parents will eagerly accept any insights into the confusing world of youth culture that you pass on!

I hope this book will open your eyes to the real world of today's children and teens, a world that we often choose to ignore or simplify. My intent is not to shock and sensationalize but to paint a truthful picture of youth culture and its effects on kids as they grow through adolescence and into adulthood. Armed with that understanding and a growing, vital faith in the living God, we can work together to help them hear and respond with an emphatic *yes* to his life-changing invitation to "Come, and follow me."

Walt Mueller
Center for Parent/Youth Understanding
May 1994

ACKNOWLEDGMENTS

IF GOD HAD not allowed my life's path to cross the paths of many others, the pages of this book would be blank. As with everything that I am and do, this book reflects the investment that numerous mentors, influencers, and friends have made in my life. While I only have the space to thank a few here, there are many more who deserve recognition.

My deepest gratitude goes to my heavenly Father. The mystery of his grace and love still baffles me.

Second, I thank those he has brought into my life. My wife, Lisa, has endured many late nights, early mornings, and the good and bad that the labor of writing brings out in me. I am thankful for her constant encouragement and support for my work. More than anyone else, she has helped me to maintain good priorities and perspective since the day we began our life together. Thanks for loving me and being the person that you are. You are a gift from God! Caitlin, Joshua, Bethany, and Nathaniel, you are constant reminders of all that really matters. I treasure you!

And to my parents, Dr. and Mrs. Walter Mueller, thank you for the valuable inheritance of faith that you passed on to me, Mark, and Ken.

I am grateful to past and present members of the Board of Directors of the Center for Parent/Youth Understanding who have invested so much time and energy into making a truly profound impact into the lives of parents and teens across the country: Dr. Jeff Wildrick, Kim Seldomridge, Sue Dunswell, Bob Barit, Bill Rowe, Rev. Jeff Conway, Thom Keller, David Jones, Barry Ferguson, Doug Reed, Steve Myers, Georgia Myers, Dr. Mike Flavin, Mark Mueller, Don Musso, Dave Channing, Joan Baliban, and Rev. Bruce Griffith. You are more than a board . . . you are treasured friends.

The supporters and friends of the Center for Parent/Youth Understanding are to be thanked for their partnership and commitment to strengthening families.

To Ken Canfield, Lowell Bliss, Brock Griffin, and the rest of the staff at the National Center for Fathering, thanks for believing in what we are doing and your part in making this book a reality. Your work is extremely valuable and has made a tremendous difference in the kind of dad I am and the message that I am communicating to others.

I would also like to thank my good friend, Scripture Union President David Jones, for editing my initial manuscript and making valuable comments and suggestions during the early stages of writing. I am grateful to Kim Seldomridge, Sharon Seldomridge, Dr. Bill Piepgrass, Marcia Piepgrass, and Debby Jones for reading and responding to each chapter as they were written.

The folks at Tyndale House have been great to work with! Ron Beers, Carole Johnson, and Dan Elliott have made the process of birthing a book that much easier. A special thanks to Ramona Cramer Tucker for her many hours of diligent editing to make the manuscript stronger than when it left my hands.

With friends and mentors worthy of thanks but too numerous to mention here, I'd like to single out just a few of the people who have shaped my thinking through their teaching, example, and investment in my life. While I was growing through the difficult years of adolescence, there were four men who took an interest in me and modeled the redeeming love of Christ: Rev. Phil Douglas, Rev. Mike Barbera, Rev. Chuck Wiggins, and Dr. Lowell Meek. I hope that this book will enable thousands of other men and women to influence children and teens in the way that you did me! And my thanks to those thinkers who taught me a love for understanding the Word as well as the world: Dr. Russell Heddendorf, Dr. Dean Borgman, Dr. Dan Jessen, Dr. Richard Peace, Dr. J. Christy Wilson, Dr. Gary Pratico, and Dr. Royce Gruenler.

And finally, to the thousands of teenagers whom I have met and talked to over the years, thanks for allowing me the opportunity to have access into your world.

SECTION I

Understanding
Your Teen

CONGRATULATIONS... YOU'RE THE PARENT OF A TEENAGER!

▌▌

When I got to a point where I had been given all I could humanly handle, I never once doubted that God in his grace would give me all I needed to continue on and handle whatever was to come.
Mother of a rebellious teen son

REMEMBER THE ANTICIPATION you felt as you prepared for the birth of your first child? You wondered what kind of child you would have: what they would look like, what talents they would possess. And, during some sleepless nights, you also wondered what kind of parent you would be.

Less than one year after we were married, my wife, Lisa, informed me that she thought she might be pregnant. Surprise, surprise! We had anticipated spending three or four years together as a couple before the arrival of our first child. Someone had other plans.

We spent the next few months getting ready: reading books on pregnancy and childbirth, taking childbirth classes, watching a movie on the miracle of birth (Lisa's eyes were glued to the screen while I had to put my head between my knees to keep from fainting). Armed with a tape recorder, we traveled together to each prenatal appointment, anxious to hear and record our baby's heartbeat while the doctor told us about the stages of fetal growth. Baby paraphernalia began to fill a corner of our small apartment. We accumulated diapers, bottles, and clothes. I assembled a crib and other nursery furniture. The days, weeks, and months seemed to drag as Lisa grew, and we eagerly awaited the big day.

Finally, on a Wednesday afternoon that I will never forget, I was called out of a seminary class to meet my wife at the doctor's office. Lisa was in the early stages of labor. We were going to have our first baby!

The anticipation built through the night. Sent home until labor progressed further, we meticulously followed the guidance of our birthing-class instructor. In an attempt to make Lisa comfortable, I lowered the lights and put on soft music. Armed with a pen, clipboard, stopwatch, and flashlight, I timed Lisa's contractions while she tried to rest. It wasn't long before she turned to me and said, "Would you knock it off and go to sleep!" At three in the morning, the time was right and we headed for the hospital. After a long labor, Caitlin was born at 6:40 P.M. that Thursday evening! It was the most incredible moment of my life.

As I watched my first child enter the world, I was overcome with a wave of emotion impossible to express in words. My eyes filled with tears, my heart raced, and I laughed with joy. My first words to Lisa were, "Lisa, it's a little girl. And she's beautiful! She looks just like me!" (Lisa about fell off the bed with that last comment.)

For the rest of the evening, Lisa and I shared in the joy of God's gift to us. Every few minutes I would walk to the nursery window and stare at Caitlin. All I could think was *Thank you, God! Thank you for such a wonderful gift!*

What to Do When Your Child Grows Up to Be a Teenager

When a new baby is born, fathers, mothers, family, and friends all celebrate. For several days balloons, flowers, gifts, and cards flood the hospital and decorate the new parents' home. The new parents experience a kind of euphoria: giving birth to a new creation that is a bit of them.

But for many parents, it is only a matter of days, weeks, or months before being faced with any number of parenting difficulties. Sleepless nights, colic, crying, and a baby that won't settle down can wear a young parent's patience thin.

As babies grow into toddlers, they go places they shouldn't go and touch things they shouldn't touch. Little children with independent spirits, disobedient streaks, and an ability to talk back can be a nuisance when they are someone else's, but they are terribly frustrating when they are your own. Some parents say that as the years progress, the difficulty of the parenting role increases proportionately. At any given point, parents may be tempted to cry out, "What did I ever do to deserve this!"

The responsibility of raising four young children born within a six-year period had taken its toll on one young mother. To put it simply, she was *surviving*. One day when our paths crossed, she looked disheveled and out of sorts. With all four kids in tow, she resembled the mother chimp I had seen recently at the zoo. One kid was riding on her back; an infant was in her arm; one was holding her free hand; still another held tightly to her leg. Hoping to encourage her, I asked her how she was doing. She never looked up. Instead she shuffled past, mumbling, "I can't wait until they're all in college!" Frustrated with her responsibilities, she had succumbed to wishing the years with her children away.

Some parents of teens feel the same way. The brief time your child spends in the teenage years is filled with a complex and confusing mix of change and discovery. Neither fully child nor fully adult, a teenager's daily life is similar to paddling a small canoe through a hurricane. And for those of us who reside with a teenager, life can be difficult and trying. Even if we have done our best to prepare ourselves for all of the developmental changes that occur during the teen years, we may feel as though our child has just thrown us a curve by becoming a teen, and we might be tempted to wish away these teen years.

Good news: There is hope and help for parents of teenagers!

Let's face the truth: We are parents; they are teens. Although we may share a roof and a last name, a cultural-generational gap automatically *will* exist. And if we, as parents, don't make an effort to close the gap, it will continue to widen. What should parents do when they experience the highs and lows of parenting in a rapidly changing world? How can a parent avoid being overwhelmed by the normal feelings of confusion, frustration, and misunderstanding that go with the teen years? Is there anything constant that a parent can grasp onto when the earthquake of adolescence hits home? Yes, there is!

Finding Your Way through the Maze of Adolescence

As Lisa and I lead our kids from childhood into adulthood, we continue to be deliberate about taking the time to learn from those who have gone before us. Some of the most valuable lessons we have learned about raising children come from observing and listening to others who have already raised their children through the teen years: our parents, friends, neighbors, and older couples. Our desire to uncover the keys to enjoying, loving, and guiding our own children has led us to talk to a spectrum of teenagers. We've read about the lives of some long-gone biblical characters and have worked to understand their successes and mistakes. And we have prayed for God's guidance and wisdom.

The fruit of our search has yielded some distinct patterns and approaches that are present in those situations where parents and their teenagers have worked together well to understand and find their way through the maze of adolescence. As you read through the remainder of this book, I trust you will understand even more the unique pressures and issues facing our teens in the nineties. In order to be prepared to respond to these issues in a hope-filled, positive, and productive manner, it is important that you under-stand and claim five common truths for yourself and your family. If you accept them, they can radically transform your own life and the way in which you approach the valuable years that you spend with your children.

Some of you will find these truths familiar. If so, they will serve as a helpful reminder of things easily forgotten in the midst of difficulty. For others, these five truths may be radically new and different. Whatever your situation, I want to challenge you to read them care-fully, examine them, evaluate them, and put them to the test in your home. Don't write them off until you've put them to the test!

TRUTH #1: God gives us the gift of children.

The psalmist writes, "Children are a gift from God; they are his reward. Children born to a young man are like sharp arrows to defend him. Happy is the man who has his quiver full of them" (Ps. 127:3-5, TLB). It is a big mistake to think of our children as liabilities; they are a reward from God, given as a sign of God's favor. Because he values them so highly, so must we. They are never to be considered an inconvenience or nuisance.

As our little gifts from heaven grow up, though, it sometimes gets harder to see them as gifts. I am not proud to confess that when we have faced difficult times with our "quiver full" of children, I have been tempted to take the psalmist's analogy to its wrong conclusion. When my patience runs short, I sometimes feel like reaching back and pulling the guilty arrow out of the quiver, loading it onto my bow, and shooting it somewhere far enough away that it won't bother me for a while.

I must never forget that God has given me my children as gifts, whether they are four hours, four weeks, four months, four years, or fourteen years old. Once a gift, always a gift. We are to treasure the gift of our children!

TRUTH #2: *No one ever said that it would be easy.*

I learned a shocking lesson shortly after Caitlin's birth, and I've been relearning it ever since. No matter how much time and effort we put into preparing for parenthood, there will always be unexpected surprises. Raising and relating to children is difficult for everyone, and it tends to become more so as children reach the teen years. The situation grows more complex for parents who raise more than one child since each child brings to the home a unique personality and set of life experiences.

At the root of the problem is the sinful and selfish nature of children and their parents. While parents and children long to get along, it can be hard to live together peacefully. Parents must strive to be the best they can be while raising healthy, well-adjusted kids. But parents who hope and expect to raise perfect kids are unrealistic and will burden themselves and their children with the sense of failure that accompanies the albatross of not being able to measure up.

A quick overview of the Bible yields a realistic picture of how sin affects the home front. Rebelliousness and disobedience have been a fact of life since the first children, Adam and Eve, disobeyed and rebelled against their heavenly Father. Recognizing this fact is a big step in gaining a realistic sense of confidence in raising and relating to kids. Although God gives us parenting and child-rearing guidelines and commands, there is a conspicuous absence of any assurance that kids will always turn out OK and will never cause any problems. Rather, parents are told that discipline is necessary (Prov. 13:24) since a child's heart is filled with rebellion (Prov. 22:15). Kids *will* make poor choices that require discipline in order to steer them straight. At times, you—like other parents—will cry from the heart, "Help me! This isn't easy!"

One of the men who influenced me most in the early stages of my spiritual growth is a man I have never met, Dr. John White, a counselor and professor of psychology. As a young college student I longed to learn more about the Christian faith and found Dr. White's books to be helpful guides on my journey to maturity. But my high esteem for this man was almost shattered when I came across a book he had written for parents entitled *Parents in Pain.* As I read the first few paragraphs, I was shocked by what I read:

> I am a practicing father, one who has made mistakes, who has struggled at times with a sense of hopeless inadequacy and who has grappled with the shame and the pain about one of his five children who went astray. I have known a sickening dread when

police cars drew up to my house and men in blue walked up the path to the front door. I have known wakeful nights, rages, bitterness, frustration, shame, futile hopes being shattered and the cruel battle between tenderness and contempt.[1]

These words didn't sit right with my young faith because of my naiveté. I believed that good Christian parents always find it easy to raise good Christian kids. Therefore, the Whites must have done something wrong to have raised a wayward child (an easy conclusion for a young man who wasn't yet a husband or father). After all, this man, who in my estimation had it all together, had still failed by raising a rebellious son. My respect for Dr. White dropped several notches. But then I read on, and I'm glad I did! I learned that there are no guarantees. We can't take the credit for our kids when things go smoothly, although we may want to. And we can't take the blame when we work hard at parenting and they turn out badly. As Dr. White writes, "Genes, home environment, school and social environment, and the child's capacity to make certain choices all bear on the final outcome."[2]

All of us will experience a different set of highs and lows, jolts and joys, thrills and spills. But we can approach our parenting as a glorious challenge.

TRUTH #3: The world is more than happy to raise our children for us.

"Who's raising our kids?"

We all know what the answer should be. But we also know that *what should be* and *what is* can be entirely different. In recent years, adolescents have had fewer opportunities for interaction and communication with parents and other adults. One study showed that teens spent only 4.8 percent of their time with parents and 2 percent with adults who were not their parents.[3] When push comes to shove, American dads and moms are devoting less time to bringing up their sons and daughters, thereby allowing someone or something else to raise their children for them.

Recently I attended a presentation on a new reading program at our local elementary school. While I applaud the efforts of our school district in teaching kids to read, I was concerned at the social problems cited for the existence of the program, known as HOTS (Higher Order Thinking Skills). The goal of HOTS is to help children who consistently fall behind at school learn how to think for themselves through the use of computers and "controlled floundering." Dr. Stanley Pogrow, the founder, explains:

> Traditionally, we learn to think by sitting around the table, being questioned by parents, and talking as a family. Today, who has time for sit-down meals? Yet, this critical stage of development cannot be bypassed. . . . So what is the solution? . . . Bring dinner table conversation to school. That's what HOTS does![4]

Sadly, the HOTS program exists to fill a void left by parents who no longer see the importance of spending time together as a family. When parents give up these responsibilities, others take over. In this case, it's the school.

In the same way that God gives parents the gift of children, he gives children the gift of parents to love and nurture them. Scripture clearly states that we are to exercise our parental responsibilities by spending time with our children, including teaching them God's commandments (Deut. 6:6-7). Raising our children and teens requires a diligent and unwavering investment of *all* our resources.

W*ho's raising your kids? You or some-one else?*

Try viewing each of your children as distinct lumps of clay that have been entrusted to you by God. He has a plan for each one. Like the lumps of clay that find themselves spinning on a potter's wheel, no two start out alike. And by the time the potter is finished, each will become a unique cup, vase, or bowl.

I look at our four lumps of clay and often wonder what they will end up like when all is said and done. But I do know that God has chosen my wife and me to be stewards. We have the awesome task of molding and shaping those lumps under his guidance. If we choose not to mold and shape them, someone else will.

A potter is committed to shaping that lump of clay. If he makes a mistake, he reworks the clay rather than giving up on it. What would happen to the clay if the potter suddenly threw it out the window, deciding that he didn't want to work with it anymore? Its destiny would vary, depending on where it landed. It could land in the street and be run over, flattened, and forgotten. It could land in the grass, only to be pounded and eroded by the elements. It could bake in the sun until all of its pliable properties disappeared. Dried and hardened, it could never be worked again. All too often children and teens in America meet such fates due to parental neglect. It is as if they are thrown out the window and left to whatever may come their way.

But when the potter keeps the clay in his hands, working and reworking with tender care, it eventually turns into a beautiful piece of pottery. So it should be with our kids. They must grow up knowing that Mom and Dad are hands-on kind of people who eagerly fulfill their God-given responsibility to raise, mold, and shape their children.

The degree of influence that the world has on our children depends greatly on how involved we become in their lives. Media, peer groups, and a host of other influences are there to pick up the slack left by absent, busy, or indifferent parents. Parents used to have the luxury of knowing that the dominant cultural messages were nothing to be alarmed at because culture usually reinforced what was being taught in the family. Not so anymore. Today's parents are faced with raising children in opposition to the dominant cultural messages. In the struggle for the hearts and minds of our kids, parents should make an effort to spend even more time raising their children and teens.

TRUTH #4: We've been given a "punkas."

When my son Joshua was five years old, I took an extended ten-day trip to speak in the southeast. Sadly anticipating my departure, he started to get antsy the day before I left. As I sat in my recliner reading the morning paper, he ran in a circle from the living room, through the dining room, kitchen, and hallway, and then back to the living room again. Each time he passed, my paper would blow in the breeze. On one of his passes, I looked up long enough to see him stop, get down on his hands and knees, and look frantically under the couch. Not finding what he was looking for, he got up and continued running. My curiosity got the better of me, and I asked him what he was doing.

"I'm looking for something, Dad . . . something I want to give you before you go away on your trip!"

I went back to reading my paper while his frantic search took him upstairs. I heard drawers and closets opening and closing. "What are you looking for, Josh? Maybe I can help you," I yelled.

"The tire pointer, Dad. You know, that punkas. I'll find it."

I had no clue what he was talking about. A few minutes passed, and his search brought him back downstairs. Then he yelled with excitement; he had found the object of his hunt.

Seconds later he climbed up on my lap. "Dad, I want you to take this with you when you go on your trip." In his hand was a tiny dime-store compass set in a miniature tire.

"Why do you want me to have this, Josh?"

"Because, Dad, you are going away for ten days. I want you to keep my punkas in your pocket so that you know where you are from, where you belong, and how to get back home."

Tears filled my eyes. I wasn't scheduled to leave until the next day, and already I felt I had been gone too long. I kept that "punkas" in my pocket the entire time I was gone.

In many ways life is a journey. I've been on mine for almost forty years. And just when I begin to discover the answers to my questions, I enter a new phase of the journey with its own set of confusing choices and circumstances. The questions keep coming. Whether we are children, teenagers, or adults, we all look to some outside authority for answers. That authority, be it a friend, parent, spouse, writer, TV star, or even self, becomes our "punkas," directing our steps as we try to figure out where we are from, where we belong, and how to get there.

In a world where there are many "experts" sharing conflicting opinions on raising and relating to kids, it's good to know that there is a "punkas" we can trust, handed to us by the One who created life, children, teenagers, parents, and families. And his written Word, the Bible, reveals what we need to know about everything we encounter on the journey.

The words of the apostle Paul to Timothy, a young man who needed encouragement, apply not only to Timothy's life and ministry but to us today as we fulfill our God-given ministry in parenting: "All Scripture is God-breathed and is useful for teaching, rebuking, correcting and training in righteousness" (2 Tim. 3:16, NIV). In this verse, Paul lists four valuable uses for the "punkas."

First, the Bible offers sound instruction. It is a believable teacher and the only true source of knowledge. Like the instruction manual accompanying a complicated machine or appliance, God's Word helps us to understand the complexities of life, including our changing children and their confusing world.

Second, a growing knowledge of the Bible helps us to evaluate and test everything else that claims to be true. All other parenting philosophies, advice, manuals, and approaches should be measured against the blueprint of the Bible.

Third, the Bible serves as a diagnostic checkup and troubleshooting guide. As we look at our own lives and approaches to parenting, the Bible helps us to see where we have gone wrong while offering clear guidelines and instruction on how to correct our course.

Fourth, the Bible is a road map that helps us stay on course in all of our tasks and activities. It lays out a clear path for right and godly living. In a day and age when some kids grow up without parents or any other positive adult role models, our kids desperately need godly parents whose disciplined and regular study of Scripture pays liberal dividends in Christlike parental love and direction.

TRUTH #5: We've been given all we need!

Gilda Radner, the late *Saturday Night Live* comedian, had a repertoire of hilarious characters that included the television commentator Rosanna Rosanna Danna. Somehow Rosanna was always able to throw her trademark line into every weekly commentary. Maybe she was speaking for parents whenever she would say, "It's always something!"

Life with teenagers is never dull and boring. A parent's patience can be tried by adolescent moodiness, the drive for independence, foolish choices, school difficulties, laziness, peer pressure, an unwillingness to communicate, and a host of other situations. And if your experience is like that of other parents, you begin to overcome one problem only to realize that the light at the end of the tunnel is an oncoming train!

But in the middle of teen chaos, this fact speaks reassuringly from the pages of God's Word: Although his people often experienced great hardship and difficulty, they were always loved and provided for by a gracious God who never turned his back on them. Read the accounts of Abraham, Isaac, and Jacob. Examine the lives of Noah, David, Ruth, and Joshua. Look at the experiences of the prophets. Read the words of the Gospel writers and the apostle Paul. Peruse the records of Jesus' encounters with the people of his day. Then think about your experience as a parent. It is good to know that God is still active and that he makes available all of the resources we need to raise our children and teens according to his blueprint. If courage and wisdom are needed when the going gets tough, he gives it. If time and energy are needed, he provides it. The key is that we seek his will in his Word and then try to do it. It sounds so simple, yet it is so true. However, it's easy for us to forget that we are dependent people who are created and loved by a dependable God. This is why Paul, while talking about his "thorn in the flesh" and other hardships, could enthusiastically say that in the midst of weakness God's grace is sufficient to meet every need (2 Cor. 12:9).

And while God never promised that we would be immune to life's difficulties, he did promise that we wouldn't be overcome by them (Ps. 91).

■ IT'S YOUR TURN

Think for a moment about how you handle the trying times that parenting throws your way. Can you say like the apostle Paul: "We proclaim him, admonishing and teaching everyone with all wisdom, so that we may present everyone perfect in Christ. To this end I labor, struggling with all his energy, which so powerfully works in me" (Col. 1:28-29, NIV). What role do you allow God to play?

I know from my own personal experience that I sometimes fail to live in total dependence on God. I try to parent with my own effort and willpower and sometimes find myself tired, burned out, and defeated.

I have also made the mistake of "letting go and letting God." After all, if he's in control, what good will it do if I try to help? Let him raise the kids!

And who of us hasn't worked hard to manage our lives and families on our own strength, only to cry out "Lord help me!" when a crisis hits?

But true total dependence on God requires that we recognize our need for God's guidance and enabling every minute of every day. Studying his Word daily and seeking his will through prayer allow us to parent in faith with his strength.

Parenting is hard work and involves many struggles. But through constant, active dependence on the God who never changes, we can live through the teen years. And we can experience the joy of letting God work powerfully in and through us to affect the world—through our teens.

2 WHAT IN THE WORLD IS A TEEN?

▌▌

When a child turns twelve you should put him in a barrel, nail the lid down, and feed him through a knot hole. When he turns sixteen, plug the hole.

Mark Twain

"I REALLY LOVE kids, until they're twelve. After that, I can't stand them." There was a bit of seriousness in this father's tongue-in-cheek remark as he anticipated his oldest child's upcoming thirteenth birthday. He knew from watching others raise their kids through the teen years that there was a good chance life was going to change around the house.

What comes to your mind when you hear the words *teenager* and *parenting* together? Over the years I have kept a record of parents' responses, and they can be summed up in three words: *confusion, frustration,* and *misunderstanding.* What is it about these words that makes them the most appropriate to explain the feelings many parents and other adults have about raising and relating to kids in the nineties?

Well, let's face it. Kids can be very confusing. One day we hold our babies in our arms as they coo, cuddle, and look lovingly into our eyes. But before we know it, a major metamorphosis takes place. We have to remind our teenagers to "look at me while I'm talking to you." One man I know likened this transition to the story of the wolfman. He felt his easygoing son had passed through childhood to turn into a monster! The unexpected changes that come with adolescence are bewildering, and you may find yourself wondering what's going on.

It doesn't take long for confusion to lead to frustration. During childhood, your children were fairly predictable. Your parental instincts allowed you to know with some degree of certainty how your kids would respond and react to your comments, direction, and discipline. You knew what would make them happy or sad.

Then they entered the world of adolescence. You began to wonder,

What can I do to get through to these kids? It was this frustration that prompted my mother's daily threats to send me off to military school if I didn't soon shape up! Eventually, the confusion and frustration cause some parents to throw up their hands and say, "Would someone please help me understand my teenager!"

If raising teenagers could be reduced to a mathematical equation, many parents would write it like this:

$$\text{raising teenagers} = \text{confusion} + \text{frustration} + \text{misunderstanding}$$

Perhaps that is why Sigmund Freud once suggested that adolescence is a temporary mental illness and Anna Freud said that "to be normal during the adolescent period is by itself abnormal."[1]

As we raise the teens we love so much, we *will* experience the normal feelings of confusion, frustration, and misunderstanding at various times and levels of intensity with each child. But the fact that these feelings can be expected as normal should not allow us to let them go unaddressed. Parents should always be asking the question, How can I begin to break through the walls?

The starting point in this demolition process is to face the truth about who teenagers are. We must constantly seek answers to these questions: What is their world like? What makes them tick? Why do they think and act the way that they do?

In this chapter we will examine a simple but fundamental truth about teenagers: *There is a developmental difference between teenagers and adults.* Teens and adults are at two entirely different places in the life cycle. Much of the confusion, frustration, and misunderstanding exists as a normal part of living with a child who is growing up. Taking the time to gain insight into normal adolescent development will help us to overcome many of our concerns and to close the cultural-generational gap.

Your Developing Teen

Clinical psychologist Earl Wilson has defined an adolescent as "an adult trying to happen."[2] Adolescence is a transitional state; you are neither child nor adult. Everything begins to happen at once. You look in the mirror and see your body changing. The hormonal changes lead to feelings and drives you've never had before; members of the opposite sex become more attractive to you. Friendships and family relationships change. Emotional changes cause you to feel more but understand less. You start to think in new and different ways. You even begin to question things that you always thought were true. Adolescence is a period full of demands and changes.

The complexity of the teenage years is compounded by the fact that all of these changes occur over a short period of time. The eighteen years from childhood to adulthood go by very quickly. At the beginning of those eighteen years, the child is dependent on Mom and Dad for everything from feedings, to diaper changes, to rolling over. Eighteen short years later, that same child is officially classified as an independent adult. But normal developmental changes cause the dependent child to begin to crave adultlike independence about the age of eleven or twelve, leading to six or seven years of chaos for parents if they don't see it coming.

D *o you know who your teen really is?*

Knowing how their child will soon be changing can prevent parents from being blindsided. Armed with a working knowledge of normal adolescent development, parents can begin to interpret their children's behavior correctly while helping them through the difficult transition from childhood to adulthood.

What is normal when it comes to our growing and changing children? Developmental experts have isolated five areas of change with which parents and those who work with teens should become familiar.

Your teen is changing physically.

Kaboom! The physical transition from child to adult begins as the body produces and secretes hormones that lead to the onset of puberty. The physical growth and development that follows is rapid. While most kids experience puberty between the ages of eleven and fourteen, it can occur anywhere from the ages of ten to seventeen.

The most notable change for both sexes is the increase in height and weight. When John, a sixth grader, came to youth group for the first time, the top of his head barely reached the level of my chin. But one look at his feet (several sizes larger than mine) and I knew that he was going to be tall. Three years later, this five footer had grown to be six feet, four inches tall. I realized that I had better start calling him "sir," especially after eating his elbows several times on the basketball court. Like any normal teenager, John's growth spurt had some side effects. At times he was active and energetic; other times he was lethargic and exhausted. His sleep was heavy and his appetite ravenous.

It is not unusual for a parent to notice that their growing teenager is preoccupied, curious, and perhaps even alarmed about the many physical changes that are taking place. The appearance of acne can be confusing and scary. Underarm-hair growth, an increase in perspiration rate, and the appearance of pubic hair are all signs of growing up. Boys will experience the emergence of facial hair, a deepening of the voice, muscle development, and a broadening of the shoulders. Girls will become women as their breasts develop, waistlines narrow, and hips widen.

There is no question that the most exciting and confusing physical change occurring at puberty is the body's new ability to reproduce a child. The external genitals enlarge. Boys begin to produce sperm. Girls begin to ovulate and menstruate. The wonderful God-given gift of sexuality takes center stage with all of its newly discovered drives, feelings, and sensations. Boys become men, and girls become women. And it all happens so quickly!

Something to remember . . . You can help your child through this confusing transition of rapid physical growth by playing the following roles:

• *Be sensitive and affirming as your teen's body changes.*

Our children need parents who will openly explain and discuss what is happening to their bodies. We live in a world that constantly sets unrealistic standards regarding physical beauty, where only a handful can measure up. Teenagers spend hours in front of the mirror looking for facial and body flaws. Those who hate what they see are painfully aware that they don't measure up. They worry over what the end result of all the changes might be: Will they be too tall, short, skinny, or fat? Most of these changes occur during the junior high years when group acceptance is of utmost importance and when peers tend to be most cruel and insensitive. Life can be miserable for the boy or girl who grows too fast or too slow. A loving and sensitive parent can serve as a buffer in the midst of the type of ridicule that could scar a kid's self-image for life.

• *Offer your teen a godly perspective on the changes that are taking place.*

In addition to modeling the unconditional love and acceptance of Christ during the physically awkward years, Mom and Dad should temper the social pressure to be preoccupied with outward appearance. Take the time to teach your children about the inward qualities of godliness.

• *Understand the sexual temptation your teen faces.*

The newfound gift of sexuality can be corrupted by a culture that encourages its youngest children to "go ahead and do anything you want, with anyone you want, whenever you want." It is crucial that parents understand, teach, and model the biblical perspective of sexuality.

- *Communicate openly with your teen.*

Adolescence brings with it a host of confusing physical changes that place immense strain on the teenager and can cause friction at home. It is essential that parents take the time to understand these changes and encourage communication through open discussion with their kids. Not only will you help to provide a healthy transition for your teen, you'll also reap the benefits of growing family closeness.

Your teen is changing socially.

Meredith's parents eagerly awaited her arrival at the train station. Fourteen years old and their oldest child, she had been away at summer camp for an entire month. None of their kids had ever been gone from home this long. They couldn't wait to spend some uninterrupted time hearing about her experience at camp.

The train pulled in. With excitement and a big smile, Meredith ran off the train to greet her parents with a big kiss and hug. The short drive back to their house was hardly enough time to begin to talk about camp. They hadn't been home even a minute before Meredith was on the phone with her best friend, Tracey. Her parents waited patiently in the living room. After a few minutes, Meredith announced that she had to go see Tracey right away. Before they knew it, Meredith was heading to Tracey's house on her bike. Whatever happened to time together as a family?

With children from birth to age ten, playmates are important. But when it comes to social networks, home is truly where the heart is. Not so with teens. Adolescence is a time when teenagers begin to disengage from the family while building extensive and meaningful relationships with peers. This shift in social orientation from parents to peers is normal. But it can be painful for us as parents to see our children trade time with family for time with friends, especially when you see some of the characters they are spending time with! This is when we must remember that adolescents are on the road to becoming independent adults. They are beginning the process of breaking ties with family in order to establish an identity separate from their parents. They are developing an increased awareness of the important role that friends play in providing intimacy and emotional support. Neighborhood, school, and church friends will function as a kind of bridge between the dependence of childhood and the independence of adulthood.

In the teen years, parents are no longer all-powerful and all-knowing. Your children now see you as you really are—a human being with faults. In fact, they won't hesitate to point out those faults to you whenever they have a chance! Those same kids who wanted so badly to take you to show-and-tell might not want to be caught dead with you in public.

A few years ago I attended a high school football game on a day when they were honoring the team's seniors. Before the game began, each senior was introduced along with his parents. As they were introduced, the players walked from the end zone to midfield with their parent(s). The coach had instructed the boys to give their moms a kiss when they arrived at the fifty yard line. I'm sure they were all thinking, *How can he do that?! How humiliating! Doesn't he know that kissing your mother in public is illegal among teenage guys?* You should have seen these big, macho football players kissing their moms in front of bleachers full of hooting classmates. Every one of the guys got red in the face.

Was this abnormal? I don't think so. I'm sure that all of those guys loved their moms. Yet being an adolescent means that you want to build closeness with friends—and you don't kiss your mother in public anymore.

Something to remember . . . It's easy for parents to feel rejected as their teenagers give greater time to building friendships and less time to the family. Don't misinterpret this as rejection. Studies, observation, and discussions with kids have all yielded the same result: Parents remain tremendously important and significant in the lives of their teenagers. The evidence may lead you to believe that you are being taken for granted, but if you were suddenly removed from the family picture, you would be sorely missed. The changes in parent-teen relationships should not be viewed as a deteriorating situation but rather as a transformation in the type of relationship.

There are a number of steps that parents can take to help their teens' social development during adolescence.

- *Don't allow your self-image to hinge on how your teen treats you.*

While teens can be incredibly loving and compassionate, they can also be immature, rude, and insensitive to the feelings of others. Realize that many of their remarks are a result of the confusion they are experiencing as they change and grow.

- *Let your teen know they are loved.*

The social world of the peer group can be brutal and unforgiving. As children struggle to find a place to fit in at school, they need to know that they are always loved and accepted at home. Parents should continue to provide a secure home base from which teens can venture out into the stress-filled world of their peers. Studies consistently show that the better one's relationship with parents, the higher one's self-esteem.[3]

- *Look for opportunities to teach your teen about friendship and treating all people with dignity.*

Encourage obedience to the second great commandment, to love our neighbors, by providing a consistent model of that love. Your children should also be challenged to choose good friends who allow them to be who God created them to be, not chameleons who have to change colors in order to be accepted.

- *Encourage your teen's involvement in friendships with other adults who share your faith and values.*

Youth pastors, neighbors, a favorite aunt or uncle, etc. can all be listening ears when the kids want to talk to someone other than Mom or Dad. When your kids seek out people like this, don't be threatened. These significant others can play a valuable role in affirming and cementing the lessons you have already taught.

Teens need the parental care and love you'd give a child, but the respect you'd give an adult.

Your teen is changing intellectually.

During my own adolescence, part of my world shattered when I realized that while I was the one growing up, it was my parents who were changing. No longer were they intelligent. Suddenly they were ignorant about most of the issues that I was pondering. I began to wonder how they had survived so long in the big cruel world when they were so . . . stupid!

I remember numerous family dinner conversations about the problems of the world, boy-girl relationships, Christianity, and a host of other topics. My father would offer his insights while my younger brothers would soak it all in. They believed every word he said without question. My job, I felt, was to challenge what I thought was my father's inferior, off-base way of thinking. I was now able to imagine a perfect world, and my youthful idealism caused me to be critical of anyone who didn't share those same ideals.

My distrust of adult opinion and intellectual capacity extended to the halls and classrooms of my high school. My peers and I viewed all of our teachers as somewhat knowledgeable in the fields they taught. But when it came to talking about life instead of math or English, they were as ill-informed as our parents. We believed in the omnipotence of our own thought!

What was happening to me as a teen? We as parents can understand some of the intellectual changes in our teens by looking at the work of the late Swiss psychologist Jean Piaget, who pioneered some of the most significant research in the area of child and adolescent intellectual development. Piaget found that young children pass through three distinct intellectual stages by the time they reach the age of eleven or twelve.

The first stage in the development of intelligence (roughly birth to two years) is called the *sensorimotor stage,* when a child's intelligence is manifested through actions. Every parent remembers the joy of watching their child progress from acting solely on reflex to using their senses to solve problems like reaching for a toy or opening a door.

The second stage in Piaget's scheme is the *preoperational stage* (roughly two to seven years), when a child has the capacity to use language and play make-believe. The developing child uses imagination to pretend that a block of wood is a car or that two sticks are an airplane.

Piaget called the third stage during childhood the *concrete operations stage* (roughly seven to thirteen years). The child is now able to think, using limited mental logic to solve simple problems. Children in this stage see things literally and think in terms of facts. They see social problems and issues in terms of black and white, right and wrong.

The intellectual abilities of children are limited. Mom and Dad, along with most other adults, are viewed as being knowledgeable and correct on most matters. This makes life around the house fairly stable and comfortable. But things change when a child enters adolescence.

They certainly did for me when I was a teen. In hindsight, I realize that it wasn't my parents who had changed, it was me. Although I didn't know it at the time, adolescence had ushered me into Piaget's *formal operations stage.* I now had the ability to use more advanced logic to explore and solve complex hypothetical problems about the world on my own. I was becoming an adult.

Something to remember . . . While there may be marked differences in the ways that different teens view the intellectual capacities of adults, their newfound ability to think as an adult will make for some interesting conversations and confrontations at home. Sometimes the best approach for parents is to bite their tongue and understand that this is a part of normal adolescent development. Remember, your adolescent is not yet an adult. You can expect an interesting mix of adult thinking ability tainted by immaturity and inconsistent logic.

Wise parents learn that while it is important to continue to offer advice and explanations, they should at the same time give their children some freedom to make their own decisions. Some of the best lessons are learned through discovery. Your kids will appreciate this, and it will benefit them in the long run. Parents who continue to think for their teenagers will raise children who will have difficulty making vocational, marriage, educational, time-management, and other important choices later in life.

As parents, encourage the use of these new intellectual capacities by doing the following:

- Challenge your teenager to reflect on issues about which you might not see eye-to-eye.
- Encourage discussion, and be sure to listen before offering advice.
- Treat your teenager as an adult whose opinions you value by allowing them an increased role in the family decision-making process.

When I was fifteen, my parents allowed me to purchase a twenty-five-dollar car. Believe it or not, the thing ran well even though it needed some major work. I would spend hours driving it up and down the driveway and tinkering under the hood in preparation for the day when I would turn sixteen and could take it out on the road. One summer day I decided that it was time to replace the muffler. I grabbed my toolbox, crawled under the car, and began to work on removing that old muffler. It was so rusted that it wouldn't budge. I spent the entire day pounding with the hammer. Sensing my frustration, my dad would appear from time to time to lean under the car and ask if I wanted his help. Each of his requests increased my determination to do it myself. As the day came to an end, he appeared one last time. This time he suggested that I was hitting it in the wrong place. (This in itself seemed absurd since I had hit every square inch of the crazy thing.) If I would only let him take a shot, he knew he could get it. That made me more determined than ever to show him that I was right and that I could do it. It was one of those great father-son showdowns.

The next day I angrily went back to work. Several more hours passed. Not only was I steamed at the muffler, but my dad kept making those irritating appearances to offer his expertise. I finally gave in, hoping beyond hope that when he crawled under that car, he would be under there pounding for several hours. He asked me to hand him my hammer. There I stood, knowing that I was right. I heard him take one swing with the hammer. Then I heard the most terrible noise I had ever heard in my life—the sound of that rusty muffler falling off and hitting the driveway. I was so angry! I couldn't even bring myself to tell him that I had probably loosened the thing up for him. As my dad slid out from under the car, he didn't say a word, even though he was smiling from ear to ear. I looked at him and shouted, "Why do you always have to be right?"

Some years later, when I was a college student, an amazing thing happened. I returned home for a holiday break. As I sat talking to my parents, it dawned on me. They were no longer stupid! This seemed strange since I was the one who had gone off to college to get an education. They were now smart again. I had matured and honed my intellectual capacities enough to see that they were actually pretty wise. I was no longer young enough to know everything! I'm not sure if it was that day or sometime shortly thereafter, but I told my parents how I had regained my respect for them and their wisdom. My dad simply responded, "Remember the muffler!"

If you are struggling with an intellectually superior teenager, trust me, there will be a day when you will get smart again!

Your teen is changing emotionally.

Most parents would say that they experienced the easiest and most crisis-free years of parenting when their children were young. If children are raised in a loving home absent of stress-causing turmoil (death, divorce, abuse, etc.), children's emotions will be stable and predictable.

The emotional stability of most children parallels the stability of childhood in general. Because our children's days are filled with play, a routine school life, and relatively little pressure, they remain on an emotional even keel. Rarely is the boat rocked. As parents, we know what makes them happy or sad. When a child is angry, upset, or crying, a parent can find ways to calm and comfort the child rather quickly. Tears can turn to smiles in a matter of seconds. Children find it easy to forgive, forget, and move on like nothing ever happened.

Contrast childhood life with the words of this sixteen-year-old girl: "I never in my life want to go back and be an adolescent. I want so bad to get it over with."[4]

The adolescent years are filled with an onslaught of changes and milestones that are difficult for kids to understand and handle. If we could put a face on the toll this stress can take on kids during the teen years, it might look like the faces I saw on the news footage of the 1993 Los Angeles earthquake: some cried; others struggled to comprehend what had happened, often without a clue as to what to do next. In the same way, the "earthquake of adolescence" arrives quickly, passes quickly, and leaves the landscape of a kid's life radically altered.

What are the normal emotional changes you can expect when the earthquake of adolescence shakes the foundation of your home? The easiest way to answer is to say that when it comes to teenagers and their emotions, you might never know what to expect. Mood swings from the highest of highs to the lowest of lows can occur in minutes or last for several days.

Many of these mood swings are directly related to the physical and social changes that are taking place. A look in the mirror can trigger a quick ride down the steepest hill on the roller coaster of adolescent emotions. Self-criticism of what they see, or what they think their friends see, can lead to feelings of loneliness and worthlessness. Being an early or late developer has repercussions on a teenager's emotional well-being in a society that is preoccupied with appearance. Negative mood swings can also result from academic failure, poor peer relationships, family disunity, and the anxiety of perceived rejection by members of the opposite sex.

Periods of elation, excitement, and youthful exuberance are triggered in numerous ways. A young teenage girl gets a phone call from that special guy. She's up! In fact, she's so up that nobody in the world, especially Mom and Dad, can understand the depth of the love that she is feeling for this special guy. Climbs up the roller coaster also result from peer acceptance, academic success, making the team, and other achievements.

The bottom line is that when it comes to teenagers and their changing emotions, strange behavior is often normal!

Something to remember . . . Parents play an important role in helping teenagers to understand and handle their emotions in healthy ways. Here are a few suggestions on how to offer stability when those topsy-turvy teen emotions seem to be out of control.

- *Treat teen emotions as important.*

Don't ever become insensitive. The variety of emotions that teens feel are very real to them. Many of them stem from a preoccupation with self and the accompanying fear of rejection. Teens expect their parents will always love and accept them. To be written off by an insensitive parent is the type of rejection that can send a "normal" teen over the edge to clinical depression and even suicide. What teens need are parents who will hang in there and love them in spite of emotional ups and downs over what may seem to be trivial things. Even when we think our kids are overreacting, they are handling their confusion in the best way they know how. Listen sensitively as they share their joys and their fears.

- *Make every effort to ensure that your home is stable and secure.*

The teen's world can be ugly, full of rejection, and unforgiving. The home must continue to be a fortress of acceptance and love.

- *Look for and emphasize your child's positive qualities.*

Encourage them in the activities they do well.

- *Don't take rejection personally.*

Expect that some of your encouraging advances and advice might seem to be rejected. Consistently love and encourage your child.

Your teen is changing morally and spiritually.

Chris had been raised in a Christian home. A star pupil in Sunday school, he couldn't stand to miss a week. He grew up with a well-deserved reputation for having mastered the facts of the faith. But Chris knew even more than facts and figures, for at a young age, he had dedicated his life to loving and serving Jesus Christ.

As Chris entered the teenage years, his Sunday school teachers and youth leader began to notice a change in his attitude. Chris was becoming skeptical about the most basic facts and tenets of the faith that he had so readily accepted before. Gradually, his interest in spiritual things appeared to fade as he became more involved in sports. Before long, he was dating a girl who wasn't interested in church. He began to question the existence of God and the reliability of the Bible.

What had happened to Chris? Children from birth to age ten have a blind-faith tendency to accept without question the values and beliefs of parents. But it won't necessarily stay that way in adolescence. Armed with a newfound ability to think, evaluate, and solve problems, teenagers will begin to question the values and beliefs they had previously accepted. They will take what you have painstakingly and faithfully handed down to them, and put it to the test. But take courage—it's a step on the way to a real and vital personal faith.

Fortunately, nobody ever wrote Chris off as a hopeless spiritual rebel. His parents and youth worker allowed him to think and openly discussed his questions while challenging his changing values and behaviors. They understood that his developing intellectual capacity was leading him to think more deeply about theological concepts. They prayed hard.

As with all areas of adolescent development, teenagers will go through this transition in different ways and to varying degrees. Some will continue to cruise along the path of spiritual growth without any prolonged doubts or questions. A few teens will reject the Christian faith and grasp another value and belief system. Some will dabble with other worldviews in order to submit Christianity to a comparison test. Other teens will be like Chris. They will act, question, and talk like they have outgrown their childhood faith.

Experience has shown that, as a general rule, those teens whose parents have taught and modeled the Christian faith on a consistent basis will enter adulthood with a commitment to the faith they have been taught. And because they have gone through the process of personalizing that faith, their commitment to it is strong. It is theirs and they are ready to defend it!

Whatever happened to Chris? Now in his twenties, he serves as a youth worker. He has a special ability to communicate with kids whose age-related skepticism has caused them to doubt so much of what they had learned before. By loving them and answering their questions, Chris helps them personalize and cement the valuable lessons they learned as children.

Something to remember . . . The questioning attitude of a teenage child who has been taught the faith can be the most challenging and disheartening aspect of parenting for Christian parents. I know several parents who have weathered this storm to watch their children grow up with a faith that has become their own. When I ask them how they got through it, they consistently offer these simple and valuable suggestions to parents who are still facing this challenge:

- *Be diligent in teaching young children by precept and example.*

Talk about your faith. Spend time together learning to understand God's Word. And most important, allow your children the opportunity to see the fruit of that faith in your life. By doing so you will help your children build a strong foundation.

- *Don't be upset when your children start to ask questions.*

Rejecting the faith of your childhood is very different from asking questions and doubting. A teen's struggle to find answers is a step on the road to spiritual growth. It is difficult to understand complicated theological issues, and therefore, it is important to encourage questions. The teen years provide a good opportunity for parents to build relationships with their children by encouraging honest discussion about values, morals, and faith.

- *Encourage your teen to be a vital part of your church.*

A wise church family will seek to involve teens in a variety of leadership and service responsibilities.

- *Never stop praying for your kids.*

We can never be successful in force-feeding faith to our kids. We can only teach them and answer their questions. The rest is in God's hands.

Answers to Life's Big Questions

For our first three years of marriage, we lived just outside Boston. If you have ever had the opportunity to drive in or around there, you know what I mean when I say that traffic regulations accepted by citizens in all other parts of the country are totally disregarded. With apologies to all of my friends in Boston, I like to refer to the Boston driving experience as "Darwinian." You are surrounded by streets full of Neanderthal characters who abide by only one rule of the road: survival of the fittest.

Imagine coming from a normal, law-abiding community to drive in Boston for the first time. I remember it well. People weren't stopping at stop signs. One-way streets went everywhere, but always in the wrong direction! You'd get in the inside lane of a traffic circle, and nobody would let you out. Everyone is an offensive driver, and horn honking abounds. The sudden change in rules and driving environment shook me up. I never got used to it. Though I miss the city, I was happy to leave the streets of Boston!

Adolescence is not much different. A child cruises through the first ten or eleven years of life, only to arrive in "Boston." The changes are confusing and overwhelming. Suddenly the rules are different. And if the physical, social, intellectual, emotional, moral, and spiritual changes of adolescence aren't enough, there's more.

The rapid change and newness of adolescence is compounded by the fact that teenagers struggle during these years to find answers to three life-shaping questions: Who am I? Who are my friends? Where am I going?

Who am I?

During the late sixties, the stereotypical young person who was disenchanted with the world hopped into a VW bus and headed to California to "find themselves." This struggle to find oneself is normal, and it plays a role in determining who teenagers become as adults.

Perhaps you looked up to certain heroes during your teenage years: TV or music stars, people you knew. Your own sense of confusion about yourself and lack of self-acceptance may have caused you to emulate your heroes. Teenagers still dress, walk, talk, and participate in certain activities based on what they see in those that they look up to. What may seem like odd teenage behavior now was once normal to you as you tried on some different "yous" for size and feel. Feelings of worthlessness and bouts of self-criticism will come and go as they evaluate where they are as compared to where they think they should be.[5]

Teens are looking for answers to life's questions.

In the quest to discover and accept who they are, your teenagers will be looking for answers to questions, such as: Am I worthwhile? Do I look OK? How am I unique from others? What makes me special? As teens grow, they become new and more confident people.

Who are my friends?

Did you know that it is illegal for a junior high girl to go to the girls restroom alone? The law requires that at least twelve girls travel together in spite of the fact that only one has to go . . . or so you might think. As children move into the early stages of adolescence, peers become increasingly important. One feels more secure when accepted by a group of friends. Security is maintained by moving with that group of friends, even if it's to the girls restroom. An insecure and self-conscious teen feels safe when hidden in the group.

As teenagers move into high school and become more secure, the quantity of friends usually decreases while the quality and depth of friendships increase. Teens may try on a number of different peer groups for size until they find their place to fit in. Changes in attitude, behavior, and dress may accompany this experimentation, but this is also normal. Your kids are learning how to choose and develop friendships—a skill necessary for becoming a healthy adult and knowing how to choose adult friends and a lifelong marriage partner.

Where am I going?

When I was young, I thought that childhood would last forever and that, like Peter Pan, I'd always be a boy. Then I became a teenager. The high school years flew by, and relatives began to ask me what I was going to do with my life. I realized that soon I'd be responsible for myself. After all, my parents wouldn't let me live at home forever!

One of the most awesome tasks of adolescence is that of making decisions regarding the future. As teens begin to focus on a vocational choice, they ask many questions: What do I want to do with my life? How will I learn the necessary skills? Do I need to go to college? And if so, where? What will I major in? How will I get a job? Will I get a job? Will I earn enough money? Where will I live? Will I get married? The list goes on.

These questions can be difficult and overwhelming as teenagers cope with all the other changes taking place in their lives. Yet, to become a responsible adult requires that these questions be answered. Parents must be sensitive to their teens as they face the task of searching out God's will and deciding what to do with their lives.

■ IT'S YOUR TURN

It would be much easier for parents if there were a universal adolescent experience. If this was the case, someone would have come up with a formula for success long ago, and we would all be experts at understanding and parenting adolescents. But because each child responds uniquely to the challenges of change, parents will have plenty of surprises. The interdependency between all of the developmental areas simply means that changes in one area will cause changes in the others. For example, a child's slow physical development may cause social stress and rejection that could lead to a deepened faith in God or to an animosity towards a God who they think has ruined their life.

When asked about what was so tough about becoming an adult, a fourteen year old said this:

> Life. It's friends and people and the things that happen; the decisions, the changes, the newness of everything. Boyfriends and girlfriends and worrying about my hair and my schoolwork and parents and how I'm going to get out of the house on Saturday night and what my parents will do if they find out. For me the hardest thing is change.[6]

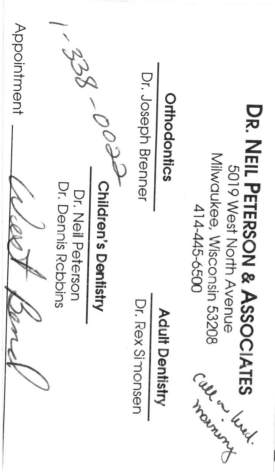

lves in our teen's shoes and
though times have changed,
back to your teenage years,
s, the day you were teased.

e all the guys were jealous
xt to a well-developed girl
ed girls in seventh grade, she
one day she was gone, and
ft school to have a baby, a
mprehend or understand.
sses, thinking that every eye
fections. I felt clumsy, and I
ation.
e time seemed to stand still,
b the rope while the entire
e locker room, where even
lance around the community
oping at different rates.
lescence is "a time of transient. The child has to learn to
body. You as parents have to
."[7] If you let them, teenagers
you crazy. If you understand
lace in their lives that they
u can fulfill your God-given
responsibility. You can help them pass safely through the mine-
field of adolescence that lies between childhood and a healthy
and productive adult life.

3

YOUR TEEN'S CHANGING WORLD

▮▮▮

Our young people are our nation's most valuable resource. . . . The America of today is far different from what it was when we were young. The challenges are different, the pressures greater, the poverty and despair more rampant, and the availability of drugs and alcohol more widespread. These things are tragic—and we must do everything we can to turn them around.

Former Surgeon General Antonia Novello[1]

"I CAN'T BELIEVE this is where you went to first grade," my first-grade daughter Caitlin exclaimed as we stared into the old classroom where I had spent a wonderful year with Miss Wallace. I was amazed that, twenty-eight years later, the alphabet choo-choo train was still on the wall!

But my amazement changed to puzzlement with Caitlin's statement. "Why not, Caitlin?" I queried.

"Because it's in color!"

Her answer made me feel pretty old. I remember growing up and thinking about what it must have been like in the old days for my parents. Somehow all the pictures and old eight-millimeter movies left me with the impression that anything that happened in the world before I was born must have been in black and white. Now my kid was thinking the same about me.

What Used to Be . . . Ain't Anymore

Although the visual colors of the world haven't changed over one generation, in a sense the world has.

On my parents' bedroom wall hang three Norman Rockwell paintings given to them by their sons on their twenty-fifth wedding anniversary. Mark, Ken, and I wanted to show Mom and Dad our appreciation for the loving home they had provided. Each of us carefully chose a Rockwell painting that said something about our experience in the Mueller family.

One of the paintings hanging over their bed shows a nervous young man ready to head off for college, sitting with his dad and his bag on the running board of the family pickup while waiting for the bus. That was me, the oldest of the boys. I was the first to leave home for college, and it hadn't been easy.

The middle painting on the wall was of a boy precariously balanced on and ready to tumble off a pair of stilts. That was my daredevil brother, Mark. Always trying my parents' patience with something new and dangerous, Mark spent countless hours on stilts, his unicycle, or the tightwire he had built in the backyard. One time my dad found him eating fire in the garage! Mark eventually went off to clown college.

The third painting was of an intelligent, bespectacled young boy who, with a diploma in his hand, was receiving pats of praise from his instructor. That was Ken's picture. He was the youngest. He reaped the benefits from having two older brothers by capitalizing on our school experience and doing better. This was the kid who read the dictionary while still in elementary school.

Every time I see those three pictures, I am reminded of my childhood and am thankful for the stable home, full of love, that our parents gave us. When Norman Rockwell painted America, he had painted our family.

I've always wondered, if Norman Rockwell were alive and painting the American experience today, what would his pictures look like? Maybe he would paint the family kitchen, with only half of the members sitting at the dinner table while the others were off doing other things. Or a picture of a third grader arriving home from school to an unsupervised house with several hours of unlimited TV viewing and Nintendo. Maybe it would be a picture of a tenth-grade girl walking to school with books under one arm, a diaper bag under the other, and her baby in a stroller. Sadly, Rockwell might paint students passing through a metal detector as they arrive at school.

Growing Teen Violence

The growing epidemic of youth violence extends beyond our cities into virtually every community, with no regard for socioeconomic status. In 1950 the rate of fourteen- to seventeen-year-old youths who were arrested was 4 per thousand. In 1985 that rate had increased thirtyfold to 118 per thousand.[2] And from 1988 to 1992 the arrests of juvenile homicide offenders climbed 93 percent.[3]

Most adults can remember walking the halls of their high school and coming across an occasional fistfight. But a recent survey by the Center for Disease Control found that one in five high schoolers (and nearly one in three boys) carries a weapon to school with the intention of using it if necessary.[4] More and more schools are installing metal detectors and implementing weapons policies in an effort to keep guns out.

Kids say guns are easy to buy and can be purchased on the street for as little as twenty dollars. Carrying a gun means that other kids will "respect me." Triggers are pulled for numerous reasons. It can be as trivial as someone "giving me a look" in the school hall or "saying something stupid." Kids are assaulted or killed for their sneakers or trademark clothing. For some teens a gun is "my bodyguard." One sixteen-year-old boy who carries a nine-millimeter pistol in his bookbag talks about protecting himself in a confrontation: "You've got to finish the job. . . . You don't kill him, he can come back and get you."[5]

A University of Michigan study found that, in 1991, 19 percent of this country's eighth-grade students had been threatened with a weapon, and 9 percent had actually been assaulted with a weapon in school.[6] Students aren't the only ones in danger. The National Association of School Psychologists reports that in a typical month, 125,000 secondary-school teachers (12 percent) are threatened with physical harm and 5,200 are victims of a physical attack.[7]

As violent behavior among children and teens continues to escalate, the statistics become more and more alarming. The National Center for Health Statistics reports that homicide by firearms is now the second-leading cause of death (after motor-vehicle accidents) for fifteen- to nineteen-year-old whites. It is the leading cause of death for African-Americans in that age bracket.[8]

There are several reasons for the rising rate of youth violence. The breakdown of the family has left many kids without guidance or support. Spiraling out of control, many seek refuge in gangs or an unorganized group of peers. These become outlets for kids who seek the unity and togetherness they aren't receiving at home. One common thread seen among offender profiles is the absence of a father and the male support bond. "If we want to learn the identity of the rapist, the hater of women, the occupant of jail cells," writes

David Blankenhorn of the Institute for American Values, "we do not look first to boys with traditionally masculine fathers. We look first to boys with no fathers."[9]

Many children with healthy, intact families are influenced by the rash of violent images in music, film, and television. The average child has witnessed eight thousand murders and one hundred thousand other acts of violence on TV by the time he has completed the sixth grade.[10] Some of the most violent movies, such as *The Terminator, Batman, Teenage Mutant Ninja Turtles, Total Recall,* and the *Nightmare on Elm Street* films, are targeted to children and teens.

And then there are the toys. Many of the more violent toys are based on movies and TV shows. One of the best-selling toy lines of the last few years is the Ninja Turtles. And it might not surprise you that another big seller, Nintendo, and other video game systems have kids spending hours in a world where killing is winning.

If this book had been written five years ago, there would have been little or no mention made of teen violence. But we live in the most violent of industrialized nations. And as parents, we must acknowledge and face that growing problem.

What Is Happening to Our Kids?

In the early 1980s, scholars and researchers on family and adolescent issues began asking the question, What is happening to our kids? Their answers came through a series of books, with discouraging titles such as *The Hurried Child: Growing Up Too Fast Too Soon,*[11] *All Grown Up & No Place to Go: Teenagers In Crisis,*[12] *The Disappearance of Childhood,*[13] *The Erosion of Childhood,*[14] and *The Rise and Fall of Childhood.*[15] Over the last ten years, the problems addressed in those books have snowballed, manifesting themselves in the negative teenage attitudes and behaviors that concern us so much. Things aren't getting better. Now parenting and family issues shelves in bookstores are expanded to help parents deal with drug and alcohol abuse, teen sex, violence, and all the other complex issues our kids face each and every day.

In chapter 2 we examined the first fundamental truth about our teens: There is a *developmental difference* between teenagers and adults. We live in two different stages of the life cycle. In this chapter, we will examine the second fundamental truth: There is a *cultural difference* between teenagers and adults. We live in two very different worlds.

Meet Sarah, an "Average Teen"

Several years ago I asked teens to send me a list, ranking the five greatest pressures that they face. The results opened my eyes to the way things have changed.

One of the kids who responded was Sarah, a sixteen year old from New York. Her list was representative of the other lists I received. As number one she listed the pressure for "looks." She was consumed with self-conscious worry about her hair, makeup, shape, and clothes. Next, she listed "grades for getting into the right college." Third was "drinking," with "sex" and "popularity" fourth and fifth.

Sarah's list was helpful, but the real eye-opener was what followed:

> Walt, I suffer from a combination of anorexia and bulimia. It is very hard to recover from these devastations, caused largely by the pressure to be thin and to be perfect. I hope that I have helped.

I had never heard of anorexia and bulimia until I was twenty-one years old. Even then, I only knew one person who had had anorexia. Most of today's junior high girls know at least one friend who suffers from an eating disorder. Sarah not only had both but also knew about their causes and the difficult road to recovery.

Sarah and I began to correspond. She greatly helped me understand the pressures facing teens these days. Perhaps her story in her own words will give you the opportunity to peek into the window of the pressures, fears, and choices facing today's children and teens.

> I come from an upper-middle-class home. I'm a straight-A student, class president, and an overachiever in every way. I don't really know why I am anorexic, but I think it's partly because I thought that if I got really sick, people would pay attention to me. The irony of it is that my father is a psychologist. He doesn't know.
>
> My mother always compares her life to mine, so much that sometimes I feel smothered by her. I cannot talk to my father at all about important things. I never could. My father is home every evening at 6 P.M., but my mother is never home. She recently opened a business so she has to work from 9 A.M. until midnight. Sometimes she comes home to see me in the afternoons, and sometimes she is around on weekends. Incidentally, my parents do not get along very well.
>
> My mom says that if I get therapy, it will go on my record and

may keep me out of Princeton or Amherst, the colleges to which I am applying.

I know my parents love me, but they think that I am so bright and capable that I don't need help or attention anymore. I just want people to realize that I do not have a perfect life and that I am lonely. I want people at school to notice me more and like me. Actually, I'm not at all sure what I want.

I have met many Sarahs over the years. I meet more and more as time goes by. Although their stories differ in terms of the places, dates, and details, there are common threads. Each is confused and frustrated by circumstances. Many of them cope. Others struggle to survive. Some self-destruct.

During the teen years, kids are like walking question marks, seeking answers to significant life questions. Today, there are many more conflicting voices, all screaming answers at our overwhelmed teenagers. The fortunate kids are those whose parents love them enough to take the time to understand the truth about the world and its bewildering mix of changing cultural trends.

What Forces and Trends Affect Our Teens?

There are twenty-eight million teenagers living in America. Many will get through adolescence with only a few minor nicks and bruises. Their worst crisis might be a bad case of acne, flunking a driver's test, or getting cut from the team. But for an increasing number of teens in America, the pressures of life can be overwhelming. If they are like Sarah, they will carry some severe scars and handicaps with them all the way through their adult years.

Those in our culture who study children and teens are concerned by the rising casualty rate. In February 1989 the National Association of State Boards of Education joined with the American Medical Association to call attention to the declining condition of children and teens in America and issued this statement:

For the first time in the history of this country, young people are *less* healthy and *less* prepared to take their places in society than were their parents. And this is happening at a time when our society is more complex, more challenging, and more competitive than ever before.[16]

Senator Dan Coats, a member of the Select Committee on Children, Youth, and Families, has concluded, through his years of observation and study, that the statistics point not to a crisis of teen behavior but to a deeper crisis of character:

> [This] is not a problem that will be solved with money or clinics or medicine. It has deeper roots in hearts and souls. In the mainstream of youth culture, it is deeply disturbing. It leaves a legacy of broken lives. But at the extremes, it is frightening—with children who seem drained of conscience.[17]

This crisis in character is manifesting itself in frightening ways. Over the last several years I have worked hard to listen to the Sarahs and the experts. I have observed teenagers and asked them lots of questions. There is no doubt that our kids are facing a whole new set of choices, expectations, fears, pressures, challenges, and problems. And they are facing them at younger and younger ages.

Today's teens face more pressures than we ever dreamed of.

In order to deepen our understanding of teens, we need to take a look at the major cultural forces and trends that shape their character, values, attitudes, and behaviors. I believe they are at the root of Sarah's cries and the experts' concern.

Families are changing

A recent *Newsweek* special edition asked the question, What happened to the family? Their answer bears testimony to the many changes that have taken place in the family over the last few years:

> The American family does not exist. Rather, we are creating many American families, of diverse styles and shapes. In unprecedented numbers, our families are unalike: we have fathers working while mothers keep house; fathers and mothers both working away from home; single parents; second marriages bringing children together from unrelated backgrounds; childless couples; unmarried couples, with and without children; gay and lesbian parents. We are living through a period of historic change in American family life.[18]

This radical shift in family patterns can't help but affect our kids, creating more stress and confusion.

What are some of the disruptions and changes taking place in the American family?

The first change is *the increase and acceptance of divorce.* In 1960, seven out of every thousand children under the age of eighteen lived in a family where the parents were in the process of being divorced. By 1982 that rate had increased to eighteen out of every thousand.[19] Fifty percent of marriages begun since the midseventies will end in divorce. For second marriages, the estimated divorce rate is 60 percent.[20] There are now 1.2 million divorces finalized each year in the United States.[21] Roughly three thousand children a day see their parents get divorced. It is estimated that up to 60 percent of the children born in the nineties will live in a single-parent home for part of their childhood.[22] All these statistics add up to this cold fact: The United States has the highest divorce rate and the highest proportion of children affected by divorce in the developed world! Perhaps it is TV's Mr. Rogers who has best testified to these changes: "If someone told me twenty years ago that I was going to produce a whole week on divorce, I never would have believed them."[23]

When I speak to teenagers about family issues, I often ask how many come from homes where Mom and Dad are divorced, separated, or in the process of splitting up. Typically, about half of the hands in church groups go up. One-on-one conversations lead to a deeper understanding of the toll that divorce takes on our kids. The family was created by God as the basic unit and building block of society. It is the unit into which we are born, find our identity, are socialized and nurtured. The increased incidence and acceptance of divorce indicates that, in many cases, the building block is falling apart.

In her study on the effects of divorce on middle-class families, Judith Wallerstein discovered that divorce hurts children deeply and for a long time. Nearly half of these children enter adulthood underachieving, worried, angry, and disapproving of themselves. Three in five of these children feel rejected by one or both parents. Forty percent set no specific goals as they entered adulthood. Many of the children (particularly females) enter adulthood carrying a load of guilt and anxiety that leads to multiple relationships and impulsive, early marriages that end in divorce. Her study also concluded that children of divorce are plagued by a variety of other problems, including rebellion, depression, discipline problems, grief, guilt, fear, an inability to concentrate, and an inability to trust.[24]

As our society changes, husbands and wives become more committed to being uncommitted. The result is that more children suffer.

A second change is that *approximately one-third of this nation's children will go to bed tonight in a house where their fathers do not live.* Sadly, more and more children don't even know who their fathers are. Millions of other children are growing up in homes where their fathers may be physically present, but spiritually or emotionally detached.

The consequences are grave. We now know that father absence is the greatest variable in the present and future well-being of children and teens. Children who grow through the difficult, challenging, and formative years of adolescence without their dads have a greater risk of suffering from emotional and behavioral problems such as sexual promiscuity, premarital teen pregnancy, substance abuse, depression, suicide, lower academic performance, dropping out of school, intimacy dysfunction, divorce, and poverty. It is no surprise to learn that 70 percent of the juveniles serving time in long-term correctional facilities did not live with their father while growing up.

A third change in the family that affects our children and teens is *the increasing number of mothers who work outside of the home.* In 1960, 39 percent of mothers with school-age children were working outside the home. In 1987, 70 percent of mothers with school-age children had such jobs.[25] While the figures are lower for mothers with infants and preschool children, still over 50 percent are working. More mothers are juggling the responsibilities of jobs and families. As a result, many young children spend a large amount of their formative years with someone other than Mom or Dad.

A fourth change is *the decreasing amount of time that parents are spending with their children.* Men and women in high-pressure careers often work more than forty hours a week and bring home work pressures and economic worries. Children are the ones who get shortchanged. The rise of the myth of "quality time vs. quantity time" is used to justify absence from the kids. One recent study found that working mothers spend an average of eleven minutes a day in meaningful activity with their children on weekdays, thirty minutes a day on weekends. Working fathers spend an average of eight minutes a day in meaningful activity with their children on weekdays and fourteen minutes a day on weekends.[26]

Carl Zwerner grew up in a home with a father whose life was his auto-parts business. Swearing that he wouldn't make the same mistake with his own family, Carl began a glass-import business:

> Like his father, he worked 10 and 12 hour days, with little time for his wife and three children. Home life was a joke, he says. "Can you picture changing a kid's diaper and all you're thinking about is the next day's paper work? How much caring can

happen there?" Even on drives to the children's camp in North Carolina, "I would stop and see customers on the way." After 19 years, Mr. Zwerner and his wife divorced. When it comes to business, the long hours may pay off. When it comes to family life, everybody loses.[27]

Fifth, *more and more children and teens are victims of family violence.* By the age of sixteen, one out of every four girls in the United States and one out of every ten boys has been sexually abused. Most of the abuse comes from the hands of a parent, sibling, or close relative. Violence is a part of life for fifteen million families in America. Some of that violence is a direct result of alcoholism.[28]

It is no coincidence that the increasing difficulty of living through the adolescent years parallels an increase in divorce, sexual abuse, violence, alcoholism, and the time parents spend outside of the home. Likewise, the decreasing quality of life for teens corresponds to a decrease in family time, two-parent families, and marital commitment.

Home used to be a place of refuge. I remember how great I felt entering the warmth of my house after battling the pressures and expectations of my peers at the war zone known as school. While my family was by no means perfect, I at least knew when I got home, I could open the door and walk into never-ending encouragement, acceptance, and love.

But many teens don't share my experience. Some time ago, after an exciting senior high retreat, I noticed that every kid on the bus was asleep—except for Meg. She was staring out the window. The tears running down her cheeks told me she was thinking about more than the passing scenery. I thought she might be disappointed that the retreat had come to an end. "Sure, I'm sad the weekend is over," she said. "But that's not what I'm crying about. My dad hasn't talked to me or my mom in weeks. He just sits in his chair and watches TV. My mom's an emotional basket case. Sometimes I feel like I'm her mother. And my brother—he yells at all of us. I don't want to go home." Meg's home had become a war zone.

Meg's sad story is only one example of how the changing face of the family is taking its toll on kids.

Outside influences are shaping teen values

After graduating from high school I took a summer job working on a construction crew. Shoveling steaming blacktop made an already hot summer the hottest summer I can remember. While my stint with the crew only lasted three months, most of my coworkers had been at the job all their lives. Several of them were rough characters who were a little "ragged around the edges." It was easy to tell that they had spent a lot of time with each other. Each day's conversation was filled with off-color jokes and language that would have made my mother turn green. I had been raised in a home where I never heard my parents utter a single profanity, and I was never tempted to let a blue streak fly. Unfortunately, I spent more time on the construction site than at home that summer. It wasn't long before I found myself thinking and saying things that I had never thought or said before. A stubbed toe, an impolite driver, or a poor call by an umpire brought out my new vocabulary.

While I realize that I was ultimately responsible for my words and actions, there was a sense in which I had been socialized and educated during my time spent with the other crew members. They had "worn off" on me.

The changes that I experienced that summer are an illustration of the larger-scale changes taking place in today's youth culture. Traditionally, the home was the institution that exercised the greatest influence on the values, attitudes, and behaviors of teens. The school and church

Is your home a refuge or a battle zone?

shared and reinforced the values that were taught at home. Today the changing face of the family and the pluralistic flavor of our society have weakened the positive influence of the home in the life of America's children and teens. In fact, the home, school, and church don't always agree on issues of right and wrong.

As the traditional influences weaken, the voices of other institutions become more powerful forces in educating and socializing teens in America. These voices grow ever louder, answering teen's questions and drowning out the voices of parents, school, and church. Although each of these voices will be discussed in the remaining chapters of this book, let this overview serve as an introduction. And then commit yourself, as a Christian parent, to grapple with the following forces and win!

Music and other media. This generation of children and teens spends an incredible amount of time watching television and listening to music. The media have become a source of information on everything from sexuality to politics to alternate lifestyles to issues of right and wrong. Many believe that the media, not parents, are parenting our teenagers. (See chapters 4–6 for further information on how to understand the complex world of music and media and for ideas on how to protect the eyes and ears of your teen.)

Peer group. Peer pressure has always been a part of the adolescent experience. While the pressure exists for people of all ages, it reaches its zenith during the teenage years. One significant difference between peer pressure now and twenty years ago is the form that it takes. Peer pressure used to manifest itself through an individual's or group's verbal encouragement to "go ahead and do it" when we knew that what we were being encouraged to do was wrong. Now the pressure is an unspoken expectation to participate in some type of behavior that is generally accepted as normal and right by the teen population and even many adults. So much of what teens think about themselves is wrapped up in acceptance by the peer group. Many will compromise and do what they know is wrong just to be accepted. (More on peer pressure and how to help your child put it in a realistic perspective in chapter 7.)

Changing influences are leading to new trends

Sex—no rules. Our teenagers live in a sex-saturated society. The media tells them that sex is something to be enjoyed whenever, wherever, however, and with whomever they like. We live in a country where 78 percent of all young people ages between eighteen and twenty-nine and 61 percent of the total population believe that sex before marriage is OK if both people are "emotionally ready."[29] Teenagers longing for love and acceptance buy into these images and look to have their emotional needs met through a few minutes of physical intimacy. As more and more teens adopt these attitudes, it becomes increasingly difficult for others to keep their virginity. Many schools add to the pressure by dispensing all the technical information and condoms that kids need without ever suggesting abstinence as a possible option. (Chapter 9 will help you understand more about the sexual challenges your child faces today and will give you some ideas of how to encourage virginity.)

Materialism—the desirable lifestyle. In the nineties, more and more teens are working, buying cars, and furnishing their rooms. Many have more monthly discretionary income at their disposal than the average adult. They expect that this is just the beginning of a life full of having what they want whenever they want it. But these teen expectations may not "materialize." All the signs point to the possibility that this generation may be the first since the Great Depression that can expect to live at a lower standard of living than their parents. Regardless of what happens in the future, the present situation indicates that today's teens are building their lives around the desire to possess things. (See chapter 9 on understanding and combatting materialism.)

The prevalence of substance abuse. Nine out of ten teenagers will experiment with alcohol because they are pressured, bored, depressed, or trying to relieve stress. And for many, it will become a lifestyle. Not only is drinking showed as enjoyable on beer commercials, but it's portrayed as normal. Never do kids get to see the consequences of drunken driving, alcohol-related crime, alcoholism, beer bellies, and death. Many grow up truly believing that the night belongs to Michelob. And even though alcohol is the drug of choice among teenagers, parents should be concerned about the use of many other illicit drugs. While several recent studies indicate a slight decline in drug use among teens, don't be fooled into thinking that drug abuse went out with the sixties. Three out of five teens will try an illicit drug. (Chapter 10 will give you up-to-date information on alcohol and drugs so that you can help your child hold his or her own against them.)

Rising rates of depression and suicide. If I had to isolate the one word that kids are using most to describe what it's like to be a teen in America, it's *stress*. Kids are stressing out over grades, schedules, family problems, weight, looks, popularity, violence, the future, you name it. As a result, more kids are now victims of depression, eating disorders, and suicide than ever before. The Center for Disease Control reports that suicide rates among American high school students have quadrupled in four decades, from 2.7 per 100,000 in 1950 to 11.3 in 1988.[30] Ten percent of adolescent boys and 18 percent of adolescent girls have made some attempt to take their own life.[31] Suicide is now the second-leading cause of adolescent death. Parents would be wise to be well aware of the discouragement and stress factor in their teens' lives. (Chapter 11 will help you learn how to guard your teen's emotions.)

Truth that's up for grabs. Half of America's adult public believes that "everything in life is negotiable." Sixty percent agree that "nothing can be known for certain except the things you experience in your own life."[32] Sadly, it is the younger segment of the adult population, those who are teaching and raising kids, that tend to hold these views. This explains the growing tendency of children and teens to reject the truth of the Bible in order to develop and build a value system based on a potpourri of ideas gathered from home, peers, teachers, and the media. One of the greatest responsibilities a parent has is to teach their children the difference between right and wrong. But the nature of our culture makes it difficult to instill a set of transcendent godly values when our children grow up learning to "choose to believe what you want to believe." (Consult chapter 12 for ways to point your teen to godly values.)

How Can We Help Our Teens?

Facing the truth about the way things really are isn't always pretty, comfortable, or reassuring. As a result, we often choose to cover up the pain and live in denial. But denial keeps us from addressing issues that must be dealt with and often leads to a more critical and costly situation. So it is important that you avoid two common responses to these feelings that are unhealthy and counterproductive.

- *Don't assume that everything will turn out all right.*

When I was a junior in high school, my chemistry teacher recounted a few class horror stories of experiments gone haywire and the resulting damage to people and property caused by explosions. I guess he didn't want anything to blow up in our face just because we carelessly assumed that we were invincible.

While parenting was never intended to be a haphazard experiment, some people live that way. Many years ago I met a mother who felt that her six kids would be able to weather the teenage years without any of her help. Fully aware of teenager developmental issues and armed with a working knowledge of youth culture, she felt they were good kids; they would turn out OK. Her approach was to let them make their own choices and decisions without the help of any unsolicited and informed parental input. "After all," she reasoned, "the apple doesn't fall far from the tree."

Unfortunately, that mother underestimated the power of the combination of forces that were shaping and molding her growing children. While she assumed that everything would turn out all right, she was wrong. Victims of an experiment gone awry, all six kids have continued to pay the price of the foolish decisions they were allowed to make without parental guidance. Two became unmarried teenage mothers. Others struggled with alcohol- and drug-abuse problems. One was in and out of trouble with the law. All of them turned their backs on the church. That mother's good intentions blew up in her face. Her carelessness and naiveté may have been the biggest factor that led all six kids to make a series of poor choices that will affect them for the rest of their lives.

Parents, don't make the mistake of understanding the pressures and dynamics of the teen years while assuming that your kids are invincible, immune, and able to weather the storm alone.

- *Don't think it can't happen to you.*

A frustrated youth worker who had worked hard to help parents by raising their awareness of the many pressures facing teens today called the parents together for a meeting. He wanted to inform them of some behavioral trends among local students in which many of their own kids were participating. Only a handful of parents showed up. It was too bad because the parents who had stayed home were the ones who needed to be there. These were good loving parents. But it was their kids who were sneaking around without their parents' knowledge. When he began to share with these parents sensitively on an individual basis, the majority responded in anger and disbelief. "Sure we know what's going on out there. But none of those things are happening to *my* children!" Their ignorance somehow made them immune. They refused to face the truth.

Your kids aren't invincible. They need you.

The following survey found that parents, in general, have little or no idea about what's really going on in their teenager's life. Many of the parents were clueless about the values, attitudes, and behaviors adopted by some of their kids. Although they thought that it couldn't happen to their kids, it did. Look at some of the results:

QUESTIONS	TEENS' RESPONSE	PARENTS' RESPONSE
1. Have you had one or more alcoholic drinks?	66% say yes	34% think they have
2. Have you considered suicide?	43% say yes	15% think they have
3. Have you ever smoked?	41% say yes	14% think they have
4. Do you tell your mom about boyfriends and sex?	36% say yes	80% think they do
5. Have you ever used drugs?	17% say yes	5% think they have
6. Have you lost your virginity?	70% say yes	14% think they have
7. Have you thought about running away from home?	35% say yes	19% think they have[33]

It is a mistake to understand the world of children and teens and respond to the various developmental and cultural issues by assuming your children won't be touched. No family is immune.

As you think about your kids and their adolescent experience, ask yourself, In what ways are my children being affected by the culture that surrounds them? How can I help them sort out all the influences on their lives?

The Widening Cultural-Generational Gap

It took the Fonz to show me how hopelessly out of touch my mother was with the real world. Barely into puberty ourselves, my brother and I squirmed with embarrassment while watching Fonzie help Richie Cunningham hide his first hickey from his parents. Our mom was in the room with us. Our nervous adolescent snickers turned to hysteria, however, when my mom naively asked, "What's the big deal? Isn't a hickey just a pimple?"

The chasm between adults and an apparently alien youth culture is very real. A few years ago, I was driving a van full of junior high students to a church function. While sitting at a stoplight, I noticed the older couple in the car next to us looking with curiosity and mild contempt at my cargo. A quick glance over my shoulder confirmed my suspicions. The kids were acting like kids. Granted, while their behavior could easily have been construed as immature, socially unacceptable, borderline criminal, and flat-out disgusting, they were really just being "normal." While the woman shook her head in repulsion, her husband prepared to speed away from us as soon as the light turned green. I couldn't resist. I rolled down my window, looked at the woman, shook my head with disgust while pointing back over my shoulder, and said, "Teenagers!"

Let's be honest. Kids and their rapidly changing world *are* difficult to understand. Everything changes so quickly. The language changes. What was once "cool" became "hot." What used to be "good" turned "bad." If it was "for real," it's now "bogus." I remember the ultimate cut was to be called "a dope." Not long ago even this became a compliment!

The world of music changes by the week. I used to listen to bands like Chicago, Kansas, Boston, and the Atlanta Rhythm Section. Now kids listen to music by House of Pain, Public Enemy, Fine Young Cannibals, Nine Inch Nails, Slaughter, Napalm Death, Suicidal Tendencies, and Cadaver.

Yesterday's heroes can't even stand the test of time. I feel old when

I confess that my heroes were George Washington, Patrick Henry, Abe Lincoln, and Batman. Now the only qualification for being a hero is not character or what you stand for but how much of a celebrity you are. Basketball players, TV stars, and whoever happens to be on the Billboard Top 100 chart are often mentioned as heroes among today's teens.

And how the styles change: A good gauge of how the times have changed is to watch your teenagers laugh hysterically as they look through your high school yearbook!

While we all share space on the same planet, the world of parents is drastically different from the world of teens. Sadly, for many parents and teens, their daily encounters with each other go beyond what is natural and normal to become like my encounter at the stoplight. There are a few quick uncomfortable glances, the light turns green, and both parties continue down the road of life separate from each other. In the process, parents and their children can grow farther and farther apart.

The recent glut of movies about the trials and travails of growing up as a teenager document this widening cultural-generational gap. *The Breakfast Club, Ferris Bueller's Day Off, Dead Poets Society,* and *Pump Up the Volume* are representative of the many films that portray the adolescent struggle to survive the teenage years. The teenage characters become an island to themselves as out-of-touch parents, usually portrayed as bumbling self-absorbed buffoons, fail to respond with any amount of sensitivity to their children's needs and cries for help.

While these movies usually overdramatize the gap that exists between most parents and teens, they do reflect the truth of our times: Over the last three years, changes in youth culture exceed the amount of change that took place in the ten years prior to that. Today's teens are "more complex, more sophisticated, more discerning than ever before."[34]

When the cultural-generational gap widens, relationships become strained as parents and teens begin to find themselves unable to understand each other. As communication breaks down, parental influence decreases. Children and teens, longing for someone who will listen and understand, may look elsewhere for guidance, love, and understanding. Even Christian parents may be left reeling by the fact that their kids have bought into a set of values, attitudes, and behaviors contrary to Mom and Dad's.

Certainly there are many teens who fare well on the road to adulthood. But it is alarming to see an increasing number of kids adopting narrow self-serving values and ungodly attitudes. Our kids need parents who constantly work hard to stay in touch with youth culture so that they can guide them through the maze of growing up.

Getting in Touch with Our Kids

How is it that so many parents—including well-meaning Christian parents—have found themselves "out of touch" with the real world of children and teens? Some make a conscious decision to avoid entering their child's world since the teen years "will soon be over anyway." Others make lifestyle choices that leave little time or reason for understanding their teens. But through these choices, parents are paving the way to stay out of touch with their kids.

What about you? Think about yourself as I describe the following six common reasons for allowing the cultural-generational gap to continue. Have any of these "excuses" found their way into your conscious or unconscious justifications for staying out of touch with your children? Have these obstacles to family growth opened the cultural-generational gap in your house?

I'm scared.

To put it simply, raising kids is a difficult task that scares the daylights out of us! The fact that we live in a rapidly changing world that often scoffs at our values doesn't make the job any easier.

A Christian mom and dad who love their children dearly were concerned that a sinful world could exercise a negative influence on them and their children. So while the kids were still young, the couple, guided by a lifelong conviction and practice of keeping themselves "out of the world," made a decision to do whatever was necessary to keep their little ones from harm. They sent them to a Christian school (and be sure that I am not biased against Christian schools!) and allowed them outdoors only when going to and from school or out on a family walk. Never did the children play with the neighbors. When they were in the house, the kids were not allowed to watch TV or listen to the radio. Like the "bubble boy" whose nonexistent immune system forced him to live in a germ-free plastic bubble, these parents provided a protective shield around their kids. They reasoned that, by separating themselves and their children from the world, the world would never influence or affect them in negative ways.

Granted, this is an extreme case. But even in less extreme cases, this unrealistic approach, rooted in fear and ignorance, can be counterproductive. While we might be successful in protecting our kids from the world's influence for a while, sooner or later the bubble will break, and the germs will rush in. Or our kids will decide to move out of the bubble and into the germs. Without the protection of a parent-instilled immune system strengthened by years of learning to understand the world and its potential influence, their spiritual, emotional, and even physical health could be in jeopardy. In fact, many sheltered kids venture out into the world only to find themselves curious about what they have never seen before. Then they are enticed into willing participation in the very things they were shielded from while growing up.

And what happens then? How can these parents respond to their kids when they don't have a clue as to what their kids are dealing with since they've spent years of living life in a protective bubble themselves?

A better approach would be to realize that, yes, the world is a scary place and that we are called not to be involved with obscene entertainment, pornography, sinful behavior, and anything that could be considered idolatry. But God has called us to be salt and light by learning how to live *in* the world while not being *of* the world. Observing youth culture helps us to understand and relate to our kids while equipping them to relate to the world around them.

Something to remember . . . Observing and learning about youth culture does not imply participation in or acceptance of the worldly aspects of youth culture. It simply means that we want to know as much as we can about our kids and their world so that we can understand them, help them develop a realistic framework for making good choices, and equip them to live as light in the midst of the darkness.

> **A**re you there
> for your kids,
> *emotionally*
> *and time-wise?*

Not now . . . I'm too busy.

Pushed by a father who is emotionless, busy, detached, dictatorial, and totally out of touch with his son, Neil Perry of the movie *Dead Poets Society* attends a prestigious prep school in order to fulfill his parents' dream of becoming a doctor. While at the school, Neil's father directs his every move. On the few occasions that his father visits, it is to remind him that "I made a great many sacrifices to get you here Neil, and you won't let me down." Neil cries out to a father who never hears him. He tells his classmates, "He's planning the rest of my life for me. He's never asked me what I want." The movie climbs to its tragic climax when Neil disappoints his father by finally discovering that he wants to become an actor. Dragged home by his father and removed from the school after giving an outstanding debut performance in a community theater production against his dad's will, Neil fights back in the only way he knows how. He takes his own life while sitting at his father's desk. On finding the body of his son, Mr. Perry cries out, "Neil! My son . . . my poor son!" Too little. Too late. One has to wonder what would have happened if Mr. Perry had only taken time out of his busy schedule to listen to and understand his son.

We live in a busy day and age. We get wrapped up in the demands of our work, house chores, social engagements, church activities, community affairs, softball leagues, etc. While many of our pursuits are important, could it be that we are letting even more important pursuits slip through the cracks—like taking the time to understand our kids and the changing world in which they live?

David Elkind, professor of child study at Tufts University and author of *The Hurried Child* and *All Grown Up And No Place To Go,* argues that one result of our busyness and the individualistic thrust of American society is a generation of parents who have become egocentric. They either forget or find it impossible to understand, nurture, and meet the needs of their children. In effect, they are out of touch and become more out of touch as time goes on.[35] If Elkind and others are right, then one consequence of parents shifting their energies from raising kids to a focus on "me, myself, and I" is the current cultural-generational gap.

Something to remember . . . The task of parenting requires a consistent and concentrated effort at listening, observing, and understanding your child and your child's world. It may demand major changes in your lifestyle and priorities in order to have the time to parent effectively. If you were to take an inventory of how you spend your time, what would you learn about your priorities? Are your kids getting the short end of the stick? Or are you taking the time to get to know them and their world? to help them grow into healthy adults?

I didn't know!

Several years ago a mother came to me and excitedly told of a "major victory" in an effort to nurture her fourteen-year-old daughter in the Christian faith. "I've finally gotten her interested in Christian music. She loves listening to that guy who wears a cross and who has made an album called *Faith.* In fact, she's going to see George Michael in concert tonight!" I wasn't sure whether to laugh or cry. All I know is that I almost had to pick the poor woman up off the floor after giving her a copy of the lyrics to his song "I Want Your Sex": "It's natural, it's chemical (let's do it), it's logical, habitual (hey, we're doin' it), it's sensual, but most of all, sex is something we should do. . . . I want your sex!"[36] I'll never forget what she said to me: "I just didn't know!"

This wasn't a parent who didn't care about her kids. She loved her children dearly and was a fine example of what a parent should be. Yet her naiveté about the unique youth culture in which her oldest daughter was steeped had led to a difficult situation. From that moment on, she committed herself to become an informed student of youth culture so that she could better understand and guide her own children.

More than one parent has been caught off guard. I recently read the obituary of a fourteen-year-old honor student who was found hanging in his bedroom. His mother told me that he had died while "scarfing" (autoerotic asphyxiation: masturbating while limiting the blood flow to the brain by constricting a rope around the neck), an activity popular among junior high boys to heighten the sense of sexual pleasure. Still grieving over the death of her son, she told me how she wished someone had warned her about autoerotic asphyxiation so that she could have discussed it with her son. In an open letter to other parents printed in a local newspaper, this grieving mother writes:

> People may not realize that they need to warn their sons about some very dangerous experimentation that may be going on. We are willing to share what little we know with any parent who wants to call us. A beautiful light has gone from our lives forever, and the only way to deal with the pain is by trying to prevent this from happening to anyone else. Information is the only weapon we have in our struggle to protect our most precious treasure—our children.

Something to remember . . . Those who don't understand the world of teens don't make a conscious decision to be naive; more often than not, it's a matter of circumstance. They are loving, caring parents. But all parents should take the time to become informed so that they can better help their kids sort through the many muddled messages that bombard them during the turbulent teen years.

Who cares?

One night when I was leading our youth ministry, I asked the high school kids to break down into small groups to answer this question: If you knew the world was going to end in five minutes and you had the opportunity to say one thing to one person, what would you say and who would you say it to? The kids were used to questions like this from me, so the discussion started rolling. One group of eight seemed to be laughing hysterically at the answers the group was giving, so I went over to listen. But when it came time for Janelle to answer, they all got very quiet. Finally, with an angry look on her face, Janelle shared her answer through gritted teeth: "I would walk right up to my father, look him in the eye, and say, 'Dad, you missed it!'"

Janelle was a beautiful young girl, gifted intellectually and musically. A straight-A student who had the lead in school plays, she was the kind of kid who would make any parent proud.

After youth group I asked her, "Janelle, is everything all right at home?"

"No," she said. "I'm not a bad kid, and I try really hard at everything I do. But all my father is concerned about is work and reading the paper. He never talks to me or my mom. He never comes to my plays or concerts. He has no interest in my life. He doesn't care!"

Janelle is not alone. There are lots of kids whose parents just don't care. Maybe it's a matter of messed-up priorities. Maybe they never wanted to be parents in the first place. Maybe they are so at odds with themselves and their own past that they have no time or energy to care for a spouse or children. Parental apathy can take many different forms. But there is one common thread: When parents don't care, there is no way to close the cultural-generational gap and grow as a family. Janelle's dad didn't even have time for a five-minute conversation. How could he find the time to discover what was going on in her world?

In the end, most of the Janelles fall prey to whatever cultural voices seem most inviting. A few kids, by the grace of God, will find a teacher, neighbor, or other relative who will guide them through the teen years and into adulthood. Regardless of how children of apathy turn out, most of them will carry the burden of animosity and hatred toward apathetic parents with them for the rest of their lives.

Something to remember . . . Think about your relationship with your children. Would they say that you are "missing it"? We can love our kids and care deeply about them, yet still be apathetic about getting to know them by not getting to know the world that they live in. We need to take the time and energy to say, "I love you. I care about you. I want to walk with you and guide you as you grow up. And in order to do my best, I'm going to take the time to get to know the world that you are growing up in so that when you need me to, I can help you to understand it."

It can't be that bad.

A few years ago I took up jogging in an effort to beat my body back into shape. While the lazy country roads near my home are relatively free from the danger of cars, they are full of another road hazard: dogs!

During one afternoon jog, I found myself overcome by terror and fear (while trying to look cool on the outside) as I rounded a bend just in time to see a very large Rottweiler charging down the hill and right at me. His bared teeth and throaty growls sent my heart to my feet and a shiver up my spine as I realized that there was no way I could reason with this beast. With no place to run and not a single tree to climb, I wondered what part of me he would eat first. I tried to act brave and conceal my fear by yelling something like, "Down, Satan!" The dog appeared to be deaf. Just as my life began to pass before my eyes and Cujo was only five feet away from a big supper, the dog's master appeared around the corner. With a loud and angry yell, the man shouted a command (it sounded like "No! I'm making you a steak!") that stopped the dog in his tracks. With his head down, the dog ran back up the hill to his master. I felt like running up and kissing the guy.

As I continued my jog, I thought about my surprising confrontation with the dog. At the initial moment of panic, my wisdom and experience had told me in no uncertain terms that I was in danger and that I needed to react. I could have stood there and denied that there was a dog running at me. I could have tried to convince myself that even though there was a dog, he wouldn't hurt me. If I was really stupid, I could have watched the dog take a chunk out of my leg while yelling to the owner, "Don't worry about it. He's not serious. He's just playing."

Contemporary culture is rushing like a hungry Rottweiler down the hill at our kids. Now, I will be the first to say that not all elements of contemporary culture are bad. But let's focus a minute on just the bad. As the bad runs down the hill with its teeth bared, inexperienced and uninformed young children and teens might not realize that they are in danger. They might even reach out to pet and embrace the dog. Fortunately, most parents fulfill their God-given responsibilities by acting on their wisdom and experience. They step in to protect their children from harm and provide for their well-being. But sadly, there are many parents who leave their children "to the dogs" because they have never gotten to the point where they themselves see the danger. They look at the rapidly changing world and say, "It's not all that bad; it hasn't affected me. And my kids are smart;

it won't affect them." But parents who deny the power of culture handicap themselves when they could be helping their children grow into healthy adults.

Something to remember . . . Contemporary culture has an incredible effect on our kids and their values, attitudes, and behaviors. How aware are you of your teen's world? Parents who get serious about understanding the influences on their teens equip themselves mightily in the fight to save their kids "from the dogs."

Times have changed—lighten up!

The last reason for the continued growth of the cultural-generational gap is perhaps the most frightening and difficult to deal with. It occurs when parents become so entwined in the prevailing cultural climate that they fail to see any need to deal with it. Unlike others whose apathy, busyness, and denial keep them from acknowledging and understanding the powerful influence of culture on kids, these folks know the culture too well because they are a part of it. It is as if they were hijacked by the culture so long ago that they are now enjoying the ride.

I was once speaking to a group of church parents on teenage sexuality. My presentation included an in-depth overview of contemporary teen sexual behavior, the reasons for an increase in sexual activity, the consequences of premarital sex, and some suggestions for how parents can begin to instill healthy sexual attitudes in their children based on God's design for our sexuality. During the question time, a woman, obviously puzzled and frustrated by what I said, raised her hand and asked, "You mean to tell me that God wants me to teach my fourteen-year-old daughter that she has to wait until she is married to have sex? After all, she's reached puberty. That's so outdated. This is the nineties!"

Sadly, this type of cultural accommodation has infiltrated the church. The Barna Group's research concluded that most Christians are living a "Christian facade" that does not demonstrate or reflect the spiritual depth and commitment required of Christ's followers. There is little evidence of an intense pursuit of faith.[37]

Some of us have become so much like the world that we don't see it as we should. We create for ourselves a comfortable mix of bits and pieces from the world and from our faith. Then we begin to enjoy the world and its culture. Author and cultural analyst Tom Sine says this:

> Until we recognize our captivity we cannot be free. To the extent that our secular culture's values captivate us, we are unavailable

to advance God's Kingdom. . . . We all seem to be trying to live the American Dream with a little Jesus overlay.[38]

If we fail to model and teach our children about true faith, we will only hurt our children. And the cultural-generational gap will continue to grow.

Something to remember . . . When we are honest with ourselves, we know we can't guide our kids through culture until we deal with the inconsistencies in our own lives first. We have two choices. We can take the easy way out (for now) and keep sailing along on the same course, preferring not to rock the boat. Or we can row vigorously into the sea of youth culture, striving to understand it. I'm thankful for all you parents reading this book because you have chosen the second option!

But before you read on, let me challenge you to conduct a personal inventory with the help of your family members and a few close friends. Do you fall prey to any of the following reasons for continuing the growth of the cultural-generational gap:

- I'm scared.
- Not now . . . I'm too busy.
- I didn't know!
- Who cares?
- It can't be that bad.
- Times have changed—lighten up!

Ask for your spouse's opinion. Ask your kids for their opinion and then really listen to what they have to say. (And remember you asked because you want answers that will lead you to make positive changes.)

If you find that you need to overcome one or more of the obstacles, develop a plan that is guided by prayer and the advice of family and friends.

Principles That Bridge the Cultural-Generational Gap

There will be times when you will feel overwhelmed with responsibilities as you go about raising and leading kids. When you do, keep in mind the following six facts. They'll encourage you when you need it most!

I. Understanding the world of kids is a parent's calling.

Youth workers, Sunday school teachers, and other significant adults all play an important role in the spiritual development of children, but Scripture is clear: The primary arena for Christian nurture is the home. Parents are called by God to teach the truth of God's Word by precept and example. An understanding of our kids and their culture helps us to prepare them for the unique challenges presented by the world. Only then can we effectively teach them to walk through difficult times by integrating Christian faith into all of life.

2. It's never too early.

Don't wait until your children are eleven or twelve years old to develop a working understanding of youth culture. Prevention is still the best medicine. We live in a world where youth culture doesn't just affect teenagers. Second graders talk about having sex; kindergarten boys cry if their hair doesn't look just right; third-grade girls go on diets; four year olds watch MTV while parents naively sip coffee in the next room; eight year olds carry guns to school. The innocence of childhood has been lost as young children face pressures once limited to the teen years. They desperately need well-informed parental guidance as they deal with an increasing set of choices and expectations.

Many parents would echo the thoughts and frustrations of a father who approached me after I finished teaching a seminar on contemporary youth culture. "This was really great. I learned so much," he said. "I only wish I had heard this ten years ago." *Now* is the time to begin to understand the world of children and teens. An early and ongoing understanding of youth culture will equip you to take conscious and informed steps to counteract the negative influences of youth culture while your kids are still young, minimizing the later effects of the cultural-generational gap in your family.

3. It's never too late.

What if your kids have already entered into the adolescent years? Every time I speak, I see war-weary faces of parents who feel they have failed. In spite of trying "everything," communication has broken down. Hurt and heartache rule at home, and they are haunted by guilt. Is it too late for you if this is your situation?

Several months ago, a man came to me with tears streaming down his face. "My son and I used to do everything together. But for more than a year he has shown no interest in church or Christianity. He won't talk to me. And when he is home, he shuts his door and just listens to music. He is angry. He has even pulled a knife on his mother. I have spent the last year trying so hard to understand him and figure out what has happened."

He looked at me, waiting for a response. What could I say to him? I wish I could have handed that agonizing father a ten-step plan guaranteed to correct complex problems in an even more complex world. But there is no such thing. Instead I told him that it's never too late. No situation in life is unredeemable because God is sovereign. In the midst of crisis, conflict, and turmoil these words can sound like a cliché. Yet, they are true! Hurting but not hopeless, this man has continued to pray about his relationship with his son. He has not given up. His hope is in almighty God. He continues to work hard to understand his son and his son's world in the hope that he might exercise a redeeming influence in the situation. And guess what? His work is paying off. He has since told me that his newfound under standing of his son has opened the door of communication. The slow process of healing has begun!

Whether your relationship with your teenager is full of heartache or extremely comfortable, it is never too late to increase your understanding of youth culture.

4. It's not going to be easy.

When you begin to study youth culture, it won't be long before you realize that there is only one thing of which you can be sure: Youth culture is always changing! This book will serve as a springboard on your quest. To stay in touch with the unique adolescent subculture, try the following:

- *Continue to read literature written about the world of your children and teens.*

  (See "Good Reading for Parents" at the end of this book for additional resources on the topics addressed during each chapter.)
- *Watch programs and videos that are popular with your children.*

  This will give you a window into your child's mind and heart.
- *Observe teenagers at a mall, church gathering, or at your house to help you gain insight into their attitudes, values, cares, and concerns.*

  Listen, watch, and notice what is going on.
- *Don't be afraid to ask your teen questions.*

Ask them about their heroes, fears, hopes, dreams, etc. Good questions can't be answered yes or no.

It is the wise parent who works hard to take as many paths as possible to understand the unique world of their children and teens.

5. Understanding youth culture equips parents to pass on the torch of faith.

Maybe you've heard your teens moan and groan about how boring and irrelevant church is. In many ways, kids have a legitimate gripe. Granted, the message of God's Word is as relevant and necessary as ever. But the problem lies in the package: We haven't taken into account the cultural context in which our kids live.

Maybe it's time we take a clue from the ministry of Jesus. His starting point with people was always an understanding of them and what made them tick. He wasn't a dispenser of pat religious answers and formulas. Rather, he spoke to the deep needs and hurts of people that he understood intimately. The God-Man took the time to know people and the world in which they lived. His communication was effective and relevant because he knew how to bring the light of God's truth to shine on the darkness of people's needs.

Christian parents need to see that it is difficult to pass on the faith apart from knowing and understanding the cultural context of their children. Modern-day missionaries don't stop with knowing the truth and talking about it; they are meticulous about adapting the gospel to their target culture. There are three steps to communicating the gospel to kids:

- Know the Word.
- Know kids and their world.
- Bring the light of the Word into their world.

There is value in knowing what our kids watch and listen to. There is value in knowing how they think, what they believe, what they value, and how they communicate. Those of us who have chosen to teach our children to follow Christ must be aware of the fact that culture is challenging our kids to get in step with the times and do whatever they think is all right to do at any given moment. But armed with a well-informed understanding of youth culture, parents can begin to present the never-changing truth about God in ways that our children, living in and influenced by an ever-changing world, can understand.

6. Understanding youth culture fosters family closeness.

When teenagers were asked to describe their relationships with their fathers, the majority of daughters described them as distant, uncomfortable, withdrawn. Sons most frequently reported that their fathers were judgmental, withdrawn, insensitive, careful about what they said, serious, uncomfortable, criticized, unwanted, and distant. Rarely were sons or daughters likely to be playful, relaxed, open, or to feel loved and accepted when around their fathers. The study concluded that, in comparison with other important persons in their lives, teenagers feel most distant from their fathers.[39]

Words such as "We just don't talk anymore," "I don't think they understand me," "We haven't spent time together for who knows how long," and "We've grown apart" are being spoken with increasing frequency by both parents and teens. In his classic book *The Five Cries of Youth,* Merton Strommen identified one of the five cries as the "Cry of Psychological Orphans" who "need to be part of a family where we love and accept and care about each other."[40] In his later book, *The Five Cries of Parents,* Strommen's research identified the parent's "Cry for a Close Family."[41]

Every year I lead numerous parent-teen weekends. In preparation for my time with families, I ask that a group of parents and teens gather to discuss what they feel their needs are as families. And every time, the parents and teens unanimously agree on three major needs. First, they want to relearn (and in many cases learn for the first time) how to communicate with each other. Second, they want to relearn how to play together so that they might enjoy laughter as a family again. And third, they sense that they are not functioning as a healthy family and want to discover what God is calling their family to be. Take all three of these needs, combine them into one, and what do you get? A desire among parents and teens to come back together, eliminate the gap, and be the family they were created to be!

■ *IT'S YOUR TURN*

A recent television talk show on parent-teen relations confirmed the need for closeness in families. Teen after teen shared stories of heartache about life at home with parents who were out of touch with their kids. As the show came to its conclusion, the host asked the audience for their comments. A fourteen-year-old boy stood up, with his mother standing beside him, and shared these words with a national TV audience: "This is my mom. She's the best! She knows me."

Closeness *can be* restored through loving and caring. Be a parent that closes the gap by taking a loving interest in your child and his world!

Understanding the Media and Music That Surround Your Teen

Warning to Parents: Because of the nature of today's world of music and media, chapters 4 and 5 contain explicit and graphic material.

4 MUSIC: IT AFFECTS MORE THAN YOUR TEEN'S EARS

▮▮

Although the purpose of "entertaining" is usually seen as mere amusement or just moneymaking, its real purpose is education. The teenager goes to the school of adolescence with entertainment as the friend and teacher.

Quentin J. Schultze, Dancing in the Dark[1]

DO TEENAGERS LOVE their music? You'd better believe it! Just try taking it away from them sometime. They will respond as if you were asking them to give up pizza for life.

The life of the average teenager is saturated with music. Popular music serves as life's sound track while they drive, do homework, dance, date, and play. Television shows and commercials utilize popular music as a device to grab and hold adolescent attention. School teachers and youth leaders find music to be an effective weapon in their arsenal of creative teaching tools. Kids spend leisure time listening to the radio and stereo or watching music videos on MTV. It's the teenage population's love for the ever-present sound of popular music that has earned them the well-deserved title the MTV Generation.

Any serious attempt to understand our children and teens requires an ongoing effort to comprehend popular music and the role that it plays in their lives. It is no easy task. A quick trip to the local record store can be overwhelming. Racks of cassettes and CDs are loaded with thousands of different albums featuring as many singers and groups. And the section labeled Popular is filled with varying types, genres, and subgenres of music that appeal to the varying tastes and preferences of teens. There is everything from pop to rhythm and blues to rap to alternative to heavy metal. To make matters worse, what's hot and what's not changes every week. A band or performer that was at the top of the charts might find themselves struggling for an audience in a matter of months. Just the mention of their name brings groans of disapproval from kids who may have been their greatest fans at the height of their popularity.

While groups and performers come and go and while the tastes of kids change rapidly, certain aspects of the relationship between kids and music remain static. In this chapter, I will attempt to navigate the confusing labyrinth of popular music. We'll examine the major components of the relationship between kids and music along with some general facts about the music that today's kids listen to.

The All-Powerful Sway of Music

In recent years a number of stories regarding the supposed power of music have received a large amount of press. While the names and details differ, the story is always the same: A teenager or group of teenagers are driven to kill either themselves or someone else as a result of listening to popular music. Heavy-metal singer Ozzy Osbourne and the group Judas Priest have appeared in court to answer charges that their music caused kids to kill. Stories like these are few and far between, but they make for good material on afternoon talk shows.

While the accusations may have some merit, they can steer those who are truly interested in understanding the power of music away from the real issues. *First, these accusations tend to equate power in music with heavy-metal music alone and blame it solely for youthful acts of extreme violence.* But as you will learn from our discussion in this chapter, *all* popular music has power and influence that can affect the sum total of the values, attitudes, and behaviors of children and teens.

Second, focusing on these isolated incidents of sensational behavior can sidetrack parents from understanding the role that music plays in cooperation with all the other socialization factors in a child's life. In other words, music can become an easy scapegoat to blame for rebellious teen behavior. But music does not act alone; it is merely one of many forces that shape adolescents. Music influences the life of the average teen, not just the deranged adolescent killer.

Music sways the lives of our teens in two powerful ways: It helps them define what reality and life are, and it affects their language, hair, and clothing styles.

Music helps teens define reality.

To fully understand how music exercises power in the lives of our kids, we must remember that teens are adults waiting to happen. They are in a tumultuous period of tremendous physical, mental, emotional, and spiritual change. They want to know what life is all about and how to approach it. Adolescence, like all periods of change, is a time of uncertainty. Most of us have experienced the process of evaluating and making decisions regarding a major life change. When we consider marriage, a job offer, a move, or having kids, we look outside ourselves for guidance. As kids go through adolescence, they are no different from the rest of us. Their uncertainty leads them to seek and process new information from a variety of sources in the hope of solving their dilemmas.

Popular music meets our children and teens where they are, answers their questions, influences their evolving world and life view, and plays a significant role in determining who they will become as adults.

Music and media's power to define reality is far greater than it once was. A synthesis of eighteen studies completed in the early 1980s compares the influence of various institutions on the values and behaviors of thirteen to nineteen year olds and how this influence has shifted over time. The study showed that in 1960 the family exercised the greatest influence on teen values and behavior. Other institutions of influence, in order, were the school, friends and peers, and the church. It can be assumed that, for the most part, these four institutions were in agreement on basic values, thereby providing a relatively unified voice in terms of their influence on teenagers.

The greatest power of the mass media is the power to define reality and, therefore, shape who our kids become.

By 1980, just twenty years later, friends and peers had jumped to number one as the greatest influencer of teen values and behavior. The family dropped to number two, and the media jumped onto the list at number three. The school dropped two notches to number four, and the church dropped out of the top-four list altogether.[2] In addition to the change in order and relative strength of the influences, children and teens were hearing mixed messages as these institutions agreed less and less on basic values.

What would this list look like if the data were gathered and evaluated for the nineties? The overwhelming acceptance and popularity of MTV (Music Television) would boost the media's influence to the top of the list. Friends and peers, immersed in and influenced by the same media voices, would drop to number two; the family to number three. School would stay at number four.

In the fall of 1988, a group of six college professors began an eleven-month study of this growing, changing, and powerful influence of music and media on youth. Their goal was to understand and evaluate the relationship between media and teens. Without any axes to grind or agendas to advance, their research culminated in what I believe is the most informed and balanced discussion of teens and popular music available today. The thesis of their book *Dancing in the Dark* is that:

> Youth and the electronic media today are dependent upon each other. The media need the youth market, as it is called, for their own economic survival. *Youth, in turn, need the media for guidance and nurture in a society where other social institutions, such as the family and the school, do not shape the youth culture as powerfully as they once did* [italics mine].[3]

In other words, music is raising our kids.

The authors of *Dancing in the Dark* suggest that the entertainment industry has developed the masterful ability to provide children and teens with "maps of reality" that serve to guide them through the maze of adolescence and into adulthood. Music interprets and defines life for teenagers. It suggests legitimate and proper responses to the different situations, problems, and opportunities that teenagers will face each day. It serves to define the meaning of life, values, attitudes, behavioral norms, and social and gender roles.[4] Music has become a powerful socialization authority for teens. It is as if music holds out its attractive and inviting hand while saying, "Teenager, I know that you are confused and full of questions. Come with me and I'll show you the way!"

A quick glance at youth culture shows that our children and teens have answered music's invitation with an enthusiastic "Take me. I'm yours!" Granted, few teens consciously decide to be socialized and nurtured by music and media. No study has ever shown that kids turn on the radio or CD player for the purpose of learning. This does not mean, however, that music doesn't teach or communicate information. Learning takes place even when learning is not the reason for listening. Although I have never turned on the TV to watch commercials, still I see them, and they influence me.

The changing values of young Americans on issues related to sexuality, politics, and personal and corporate morality are due in large part to the cranked-up volume of the voice of popular music and its principal players. The fruit of changing values and attitudes is seen in behavioral trends. It is no coincidence that teens are becoming more sexually active, violent, materialistic, and self-centered. Music has taught them that this is reality. This is what life's all about.

Music shapes our teens' language, hair, and clothing styles.

The ever-changing language of our kids is another evidence of music's power to shape a generation. Parents are often baffled by the strange slang terms heard in the course of teen conversation. For instance, 1992 became the year of "Not!" thanks to the movie *Wayne's World,* a cinematic ride through life with two rock-music junkies and their friends.

Hair and clothing styles are influenced by teen music heroes. Rap music's rise in popularity during 1992 led mainstream kids to adopt the look of rap star Marky Mark. Mothers tried without success to get their sons to wear a belt as they left the house with baggy pants riding almost below the hips. It was Marky Mark who popularized this low-riding, underwear-revealing look. The recent rise of "grunge" music has lead to a parallel rise in grunge fashion. Dressing like their heroes in groups like Pearl Jam, Soundgarden, Alice in Chains, and Stone Temple Pilots has led kids to rediscover the untucked flannel shirt, longer hair, and for those guys who can grow it, facial stubble. While the tendency to follow the fashions of the stars is nothing new, the visual bombardment of music videos allows even young children to keep up with the latest fashion trends like never before. The music industry has fueled and fed an obsession with clothing and style.

It is the family, school, and church that have turned up music's volume by choosing to walk away from the opportunity to lead and help children and teens.

Music has become one of the most effective teachers, preachers, and evangelists of our time. Its following is an entire youth culture. Its power lies in its ability to define reality and shape world and life views. And its messages are providing a sound track for a generation that is being molded in the image of music itself.

How Does Music Mold Our Kids?

When I was in elementary school, I often fell asleep listening to the

Philadelphia Phillies pursue the elusive National League pennant via my trusty nine-volt transistor radio. And that little radio also introduced me to the exciting world of popular music. It wasn't long before I was spending more time with the Beatles, Monkees, and Mamas and Papas than the Phillies. But in the sixties, our windows into the world of music were limited to a transistor radio, a few scratched-up 45s, and an occasional hour of *American Bandstand.*

Today, cassettes, CDs, personal stereos, car stereos, dozens of popular music stations, twenty-four-hour music television, fan magazines, concert tours, and a host of other music outlets have made music a powerful teacher. How does music shape our teens? Let's look at four ways: through the lyrics, visual images, lifestyles promoted, and concerts.

The lyrics

While many kids say that they don't listen to the words of songs, experience and observation prove otherwise. If you've ridden in the car with a teenager while the radio is on, you know that they usually sing along to their favorite tunes. After hearing the song only a few times, most kids know the words. Like childhood nursery rhymes and the ABCs, words and concepts are easier to learn and remember when put to music. Our kids come to popular music with dozens of adolescent questions, open minds, and a limited and undeveloped sense of discernment. They are like sponges, soaking up anything that fits into their pores without questioning its composition or the effect that it might have on them.

Singers and songwriters believe in what they write and what they sing, and their songs express different aspects of their worldview. By packaging their messages in music that is appealing to young ears, they become effective teachers.

I have often heard both parents and teens protest and argue that the singers "don't really believe or mean what they are singing. It's just a song." This is a faulty argument for a number of reasons. First, Jesus made it clear that our words betray who we really are and what we believe (Matt. 12:34; 15:18). Second, our own personal experience as people who communicate affirms Jesus' point. While we may say some things that we "don't really mean," it is the conviction of our heart that it's all right to say it, otherwise we'd be quiet. And third, the singers and songwriters admit their desire to express themselves through their songs.

Madonna has a reason for producing sexually explicit songs, videos, movies, and books: "With everything I do, I ask two questions:

Am I being true to myself, and does it say what I want to say? It's not about pushing limits, it's about expression."[5]

Red Hot Chili Peppers sing their world and life view in their song "Special Secret Song Inside," which includes the lyrics "Struck by lust in a telephone booth / Busted by a cop he said that's uncouth / He said he could hear my baby / Screaming to me—f___ me Anthony, Anthony." One of their members, bassist Flea, says that "all we ever want to do is play music that comes from our hearts."[6]

The tendency to think that many popular song lyrics, particularly those that are sexually or violently explicit, are intended as a joke and shouldn't be taken seriously is dangerous and naive. While this may be true in a very limited number of cases, on what criteria does one decide that the song in question is being sung in jest? If we are never told, we don't know. How can children and young teens, without the benefit of well-developed critical faculties, discern between the satirical and the serious? And even if the song is a joke, there is a good chance that the lyrics can lead one to laugh at something that isn't funny.

Today's teens are walking question marks. In your household, who's providing the answers?

The classic case of this lyrics-as-a-joke line of reasoning proves just how much this mind-set has permeated our way of thinking and clouded our good senses. Several years ago the rap band The 2 Live Crew took bad taste to its limits with the song "Me So Horny." The lyrics described the singer's insatiable appetite for sex along with violent descriptions of various and perverse sexual acts including oral sex, anal sex, and "busting" a girl's vagina. They were acquitted of obscenity charges in a Fort Lauderdale courtroom by six jurors who explained that they regarded the lyrics as "comedy," but certainly not as obscene. One juror stated that "in this day and age, this is the vernacular of the youth."[7] Assume for a minute that these lyrics are a joke and intended just to be funny. If children and teens grow up on this type of lyrical garbage without realizing that it is a joke (which I don't for one minute believe it is), they will assume that this type of sexual behavior is normal, acceptable, and laughable. Sadly, repeated exposure might lead to songs like "Me So Horny" actually representing the way kids talk and act. America would take several more giant steps down the ladder of cultural decline if everyday conversation was peppered with words that betrayed disgusting attitudes and beliefs about women, love, and sex.

Whether positive or negative, the lyrics of today's music speak loud and clear to a generation that is looking and listening for answers.

Visual images

My first exposure to popular music allowed my imagination to run wild. While I could hear the music through my trusty transistor radio, it was my mind's eye, fueled by my imagination, that allowed me to "see" the performers and create visual images to accompany my favorite songs. While I could visually identify each of the Beatles by name, the endless line of other popular recording artists was nothing more than songs and voices. I rarely saw them.

The impact of music videos. MTV's twenty-four-hour barrage of music videos has changed all that by adding another dimension to the world of popular music. This new visual dimension has not only smothered the use of the imagination and created a generation of passive viewers/listeners but it has increased the ability of popular music to shape children and teens. Researchers have found that "the marriage between television and music is powerful. . . . Multisensory input reinforces any message, specifically by enhancing learning and recall."[8]

The visual component of music videos serves many purposes. In some cases the video clarifies the meaning of a song. The hit song "Jeremy" took Pearl Jam's listeners into the ugly world of parental neglect and peer group ostracism, where viewers are offered a peek into Jeremy's young and difficult experience as he struggles to cope with his confusing circumstances. At other times, the surrealistic and dreamlike nature of many videos, enhanced with numerous special effects, can serve to confuse a song's meaning. U2's dizzying string of special effects and spinning camera shots in their "Even Better Than the Real Thing" video do more to facilitate sensory overload than enhance the song's message. Some video "stories" add meanings that are not obvious in the lyrics. If you listen to Nirvana's 1992 hit song "Smells Like Teen Spirit," you will hear a song combining driving guitar sounds and muddled marble-in-the-mouth lyrics that leaves most listeners wondering what obscure foreign language the group is using. The video makes it clear that the song is an angry anthem of teen angst.

In all cases the video content serves to teach. In one study, music videos were shown to middle-income seventh and tenth graders. Teens questioned after viewing less than an hour of MTV were more likely to approve of premarital sex and less likely to disapprove of violence. The results of this study confirm that values and attitudes often change to conform with what children and teens have seen and heard.[9]

The impact of album covers and artwork. Popular music's ability to teach kids visually extends beyond music videos to the world of album covers and artwork. The drawings, paintings, and photos that appear inside and outside cassette and CD packages are art forms that often serve to describe the contents inside the package. Although the following examples are rather sickening (and I chose not to include ones that were even more graphic), they will give you a realistic idea of the kind of messages available on album covers these days.

Guns n' Roses' hit debut heavy-metal album *Appetite For Destruction* contains a reproduction of a Robert Williams painting of the same name. In the painting, a female street vendor lies bruised and unconscious by the side of the road. Sexually assaulted by a pantless robotic creature, the young woman's clothes are disheveled with her panties around her knees, her shirt open, and a breast exposed. It is not surprising to note that the album contains several songs glorifying a mixture of violence and sex.

Red Hot Chili Peppers released a 1988 album entitled *Abbey Road E.P.* The cover photo parodied the Beatles' *Abbey Road* album and featured the four members of the band crossing the street entirely naked with the exception of socks strategically placed over their penises.

By the end of 1993, the biggest selling rap album of all time and perhaps the most talked about album of the year, Snoop Doggy Dogg's *Doggystyle*, had already sold two and a half million copies. The cartoon album cover features an almost naked woman, sexual suggestiveness, gunplay, violence, profanity, and drug and alcohol abuse. One reviewer commented that Snoop Doggy Dogg subscribes "mostly to the repugnant philosophy that labels women whores if they sleep with a man too soon and condemns them if they don't."[10]

These few examples don't even begin to tell the whole story. Record stores are filled with rack after rack of CDs and cassettes, each one with its own unique cover and story to tell. Whether good or bad, the images communicate messages to our kids.

The already powerful ability of music to educate and shape reality for our children and teens is greatly enhanced when it engages the mind through more than just the ears. The educational process is more effective when what is heard is also seen.

The lifestyles of music performers

When Madonna began singing and dancing her way to stardom in 1985, she was an immediate hit, especially with the preteen and young teen audience. Her songs were full of a strange mixture of schoolgirl innocence, sexual suggestiveness, and religious imagery. Her first hit song, "Like a Virgin," was not about Mary the mother of Jesus.

Shortly after she arrived on the scene, thousands of elementary schoolgirls joined the legion of Madonna wanna-bes. Their moms and dads were shocked to learn about the unwritten wanna-be dress code, which included everything from innocently teased hair held high in a scarf to wearing black lacy underwear as outerwear.

Her early concert performances were described as:

> A sweaty pin-up girl come to life. She wiggled her tummy and shook her ass. She smiled lasciviously and stuck out her tongue. She rolled around on the stage and got down on her knees in front of a guitarist. And when she raised her arms, her scanty see-through blouse also rose, revealing her purple brassiere. . . . What Madonna is really about is sex, and there was plenty of that.[11]

An entire subculture grew around Madonna, with preteen and adolescent girls imitating her look and admiring her lifestyle.

In the years since 1985, Madonna has continued to change her image and maintain her popularity while other singers have long since been forgotten. Her self-proclaimed one-woman crusade to change America has extended beyond the world of lyrics and video to include books, movies, and television appearances. She has allowed Americans an ongoing voyeuristic look into her sexually permissive and perverted lifestyle. She has played a powerful role in shaping the culture and educating a generation through her efforts to promote freedom of expression and sexual liberation.

An interviewer once asked Madonna if she saw herself as a "kind of sexual missionary." This was her response:

> I suppose that's one way to look at it. . . . Sex is the metaphor that I use, but for me really, it's about love. It's about tolerance, acceptance and saying, "Look, everybody has different needs and wants and preferences and desires and fantasies. And we should not damn or judge somebody because it's different than yours."[12]

One reviewer describes her most recent attempts to communicate her message (the album *Erotica* and the photo book *Sex*) in this way:

> She has taken her vision of sexuality—sadomasochism as a feminist power trip—completely out of the closet, stripping it of

any hint of romantic suggestion. . . . The Madonna who once celebrated sin as a heady, liberating force, a way of lovers opening themselves up to each other, now transforms erotic passion into something cold, forbidding, aristocratic.[13]

This describes not only Madonna's performances but her lifestyle. With so many glimpses into Madonna's life, kids can't help but know that she stands for total sexual freedom and perversion of every possible type. How effective has she been? While she represents the extreme, Madonna has stretched the bounds of the sexual values of many Americans, including our teenagers.

Madonna is just one example of how the public and private lifestyles of the stars shape young lives. Kids know more than the lyrics and videos of music's movers and shakers. Television tabloids, MTV specials, and fan magazines allow kids to see the lifestyles of their rich and famous heroes. And kids are dressing, acting, and thinking like and being shaped by these celebrities.

Teens also cannot help being affected by their heroes' values and attitudes. In *Details* magazine, Ice-T reveals his secrets on how to pick up girls when he writes, "Picking up a girl is a lot like robbing a store."[14] Pop star Rod Stewart openly discusses his embarrassment with being married and, in so doing, testifies to the entertainment industry's bias against the institution of marriage.[15] When asked what he would do if he was invisible for one day, rocker Jon Bon Jovi said he would "hang out in a girl's shower in the locker room of a strip club." And if he only had one week to live he would "stay drunk, eat like a pig and sexually abuse as many women as I could get my hands on. . . . I would overindulge in everything."[16] Preteen heartthrob Marky Mark, known for dropping his pants during concerts to sing in his underwear, released a photo-bio in 1992 that included a publication he dedicated "To My Dick."[17] And the three members of the popular all-girl group Salt'N'Pepa are vocal and seemingly proud about the fact that each of them chose to have children without getting married.[18]

Kids who struggle with spiritual questions are also able to gain plenty of spiritual counsel from their rock heroes. Guns n' Roses bassist Michael McKagan shares this about Christianity: "I think the Bible's a good story, you know? . . . Back in those times, the Romans were just squashing everybody, and here came this guy who had positive thoughts. I think that's all there was to it. . . . All of a sudden all of the people were going, 'This guy's f_____ groovy.' And the Romans were like, 'Not that groovy because he's f_____ taking over all of our people we're squashing, so we're gonna kill him.' And there's no such thing as the Immaculate Conception. His mom got f_____ to have him, you know? Come on. He was just a positive guy who wanted to spread love and goodness."[19]

The Black Crowes' lead singer Chris Robinson eagerly shared his views on Christianity in response to protests from a group of Christian parents who had heard of the Black Crowes' interest in voodoo: "Jesus Christ loved everyone. Jesus Christ probably loved Satan. I mean, I don't believe that God and Satan are real, but if you're a Christian, then you love everyone. And if you're a Christian and you think I'm f_____ . . . then f___ you."[20]

Our kids are being given more than a peek into the private and public lives of popular music's heroes. Sadly, the messages these stars communicate, which help define reality for our kids, are more often negative than positive.

The concerts

Another of popular music's educational avenues is the live concert. The concert is not just an opportunity for kids to see their heroes in person and hear their favorite songs performed live. Concerts include so much more, including elaborate sets, choreographed stage shows, and between-song chatter. Any adult who decides to attend a concert might come out saying, "Boy, did I ever get an education!"

Aging yet still popular rockers ZZ Top used laser lights on one concert tour to project a line drawing of a woman naked except for cowboy hat and boots onto a gigantic screen above the stage. One of their two-hour shows in San Francisco was reported as:

> full of expected nods to adolescent sexual fantasy, including taped orgasmic screams, soft-porn videos and the Demolition Debbies, a crew of five scantily clad young ladies who paraded about the stage during a roof-raising version of "Give It Up."[21]

While performing in New Jersey, Faith No More's lead singer, Mike Patton, known for his brash antics, "asked a prepubescent girl—with Dad in tow—if she'd ever seen a grown man naked."[22]

The current trend towards nudity and performing simulated sex while onstage is cause for concern. Pop star Bobby Brown was arrested during a 1993 concert for simulating sex on a bed with a female member of his group in front of an underage Georgia audience.[23]

Madonna's 1991 Blond Ambition tour featured a performance of her song "Like a Virgin" that included simulated sex on a bed with two of her male dancers and by herself. Numerous other stars have followed suit with various types of "dirty dancing," crotch grabs, etc.

Singer Jesse James Dupree of the group Jackyl felt that police were discriminating against him when they arrested him for exposing his buttocks to a Cincinnati concert crowd. Dupree justified his actions by saying that "it should be my right as an artist, as a musician, to express myself."[24]

In a July 1993 concert in Philadelphia, the four members of rock-rap group Rage Against the Machine stood naked for fourteen minutes with electrical tape over their mouths and *P.M.R.C.* written in big black letters across their chests, one letter on each band member's chest. They were protesting what they believe to be the Parent's Music Resource Center's efforts at music censorship.[25]

Grunge band Nirvana pulled out all the stops during a concert in Belgium when lead singer Kurt Cobain dove headfirst into the crowd (not unusual concert behavior, by the way), climbed back on stage, and proceeded to spit on members of the audience lucky enough to secure seats in the first three rows. Bassist Chris Novoselic stripped down to nothing before the entire band proceeded to smash and destroy all of their instruments.[26]

These are just a few examples of concert behavior that made it into the newspapers and magazines. For each of these, there are hundreds more incidents of simulated sex, profanity, pornography, and what most people would consider to be obscene behavior. The bad news is that, for the teenage concertgoer, it's a usual part of the show.

Rock Music—How Much Do Our Teens Listen and Watch?

There is no question that popular music, through numerous outlets, is impacting and educating our children and teens. Even when parents are present and the school and church are doing their jobs, music remains a powerful influence that must be recognized, understood, and dealt with. Bruce Springsteen recognized the power of music to define reality when he wrote his 1985 hit "Born in the USA": "We busted out of class / had to get away from those fools. / We learned more from a three-minute record / than we ever learned in school."

Part of the power of music lies in the large amounts of time our teens devote to listening to music and watching MTV.

Music with an ear: Listening to rock

In 1985, the Parent's Music Resource Center reported that the standard teenager listens to rock music an average of four to six hours daily.[27] In the six years from grades seven to twelve, the average teen will have listened to 10,500 hours of music, just slightly less than the eleven thousand hours spent in the classroom from kindergarten through high school.[28] Most adolescent listening takes place alone in one's room, through headphones, or while riding in the car.

Over 90 percent of U.S. teenagers tune in to the radio at some point during the course of a normal day.[29] While most teenagers have access to some type of radio or television, two-thirds of U.S. teenagers own their own stereo system, and slightly fewer own their own personal Walkman.[30] Eighty-eight percent of all teenagers listen to CDs and tapes.[31] In 1991 young people ages ten to nineteen accounted for 24 percent of all recording sales in the U.S. Of all types of recorded music available, rock, pop, and urban contemporary music accounted for 66 percent of total sales.[32]

Several studies and surveys point to the fact that teenagers who do homework without music are the exception. In one study, fewer than 10 percent of seventh through eleventh graders said they never study with music. Over half said they did so often or always.[33]

While music serves to fill the time and minds of kids, their interest fills the pockets of those involved in the business. In 1992 we saw numerous stars sign multimillion-dollar recording contracts. Aerosmith signed a $30 million four-album deal with Sony. Janet Jackson signed a $40 million three-album contract with Virgin Records. The aging Rolling Stones agreed to record three albums with Virgin for $45 million. Madonna's deal with Time-Warner had a price tag of $60 million and will net seven albums and her own entertainment company. Michael Jackson gives Sony six albums and a film in exchange for $65 million. Prince topped them all by signing with Time-Warner for $100 million![34]

Kids also spend big money to attend the concerts. The summer 1993 tour season took in $900 million in total receipts.[35] And once kids get to the concerts, even more money is spent on the large variety of merchandise available for sale. In 1986, kids bought over $250 million worth of T-shirts, posters, and other paraphernalia. One night's income from merchandising sometimes exceeds ticket sales.[36]

One thing is clear: Statistics on how kids spend their money and their time show that they like to listen to and watch music.

Music with a view: The MTV phenomenon

August 1, 1981, might be the most significant date in entertainment history. It was 12:01 A.M. when MTV came on the air with the Buggles' video, "Video Killed the Radio Star." Suddenly, the world was able to "watch music." It was the dawn of the video age and the beginning of a phenomenon that was to change the face of international popular culture.

The popular-music industry had hit rock bottom as record sales plummeted during the late seventies (blame it on disco!). Virgin Records chief Jeff Aygin recalls, "We [the record industry] were looking for a savior and it came in the form of MTV."[37] Record sales skyrocketed, and popular music found new life as exposure on MTV almost guaranteed a group's success.

In those early days, MTV reached only 1.5 million homes. Cable operators didn't want to take a chance on a channel that was programmed with round-the-clock music videos. In response, MTV launched a direct-marketing campaign using leaflets, television commercials, and other forms of advertising. Using the slogan "I want my MTV," the network had found its way into 10.7 million homes by 1982 and 18.9 million homes by 1983. MTV is now a fixture on virtually all basic cable packages across the United States. With 55 million American subscribers and about 194 million more in forty foreign countries, MTV has become a major commercial and educational force. The authors of *Dancing in the Dark* call it "one of the most powerful forms of contemporary propaganda."[38]

MTV founder and chairman Robert Pittman was the heart and soul behind MTV. His quotes speak volumes about the concept behind MTV, the reasons for its success, and its enormous impact on contemporary youth culture:

> We're dealing with a culture of TV babies. They can watch, do their homework, and listen to music all at the same time.
>
> The strongest appeal you can make . . . is emotionally. If you can get their emotions going, [make them] forget their logic, you've got 'em.
>
> At MTV we don't shoot for the fourteen year olds, we own them.
>
> The only people who can understand the new way to use that television set are the people who grew up with it. . . . They . . . will accept almost anything over that screen.[39]

MTV's programming is anchored around the music video. Almost all of the videos played on MTV are furnished free of charge by record companies. In effect, the network is a twenty-four-hour commercial. Yearly profits as high as $100 million have allowed the network to expand beyond the music-video format. A series of weekly and daily shows cater to those who prefer rap, heavy metal, or comedy. Other shows focus on political issues, fashion, sports, and sexuality. One of the most successful ventures in TV history, MTV has become a cultural institution.

The impact of MTV's innovative approach to programming and production led to wholesale changes throughout the entertainment industry. Record companies began to sign, develop, and market stars whose visual appeal sometimes eclipsed their musical ability. If they looked good and could dance, they could be taught how to sing. The great Milli-Vanilli lip-synch caper was an example of MTV looks and moves with no ability to sing. They were two handsome guys with great visual appeal and an ability to dance. Millions of kids bought their albums. Thousands attended concerts. Regular MTV airplay made them stars. A major uproar and numerous legal battles ensued when it was discovered that Milli-Vanilli weren't singing in concert and never sang on their recordings!

Prime-time broadcast television has felt the ripple effect of MTV. In 1983 NBC programming chief Brandon Tartikoff wrote the words *MTV Cops* on a piece of paper and handed it to TV producer Anthony Yerkovich. From that came the hit series *Miami Vice,* a slightly surrealistic police show with a sound track featuring some of the most popular rock singers and bands of the time. In many ways, it was a one-hour video. Yerkovich acknowledges that MTV "reeducated and expanded people's capacities and brought a new style of story-telling to the small screen."[40]

The movie industry followed MTV's lead with films like *Flashdance, Footloose, Pump Up the Volume,* and a rash of other productions with popular music sound tracks. Some of the films were actually extended music videos with the plot unfolding between the songs.

Advertising has also been influenced and changed by MTV. Phillip Dusenberry, chairman of the ad agency for Pepsi-Cola and Apple Computers, says that "MTV's impact, first and foremost, is as a teacher. It has educated people, particularly young people, to accept lots of information in a short period of time."[41] Commercials aimed at young consumers are like rock videos. Visual, aural, and technical trickery all reflect the influence of MTV. The constantly changing visual images, all in rapid-fire succession, make it difficult to distinguish between a music video and a commercial. A 1988 survey of two thousand television ads determined that 72 percent of them featured some sort of background music, up from 63 percent the year before.[42]

Much of that music was taken from well-known popular songs and sung by the original artists themselves.

Although there are no clear statistics available regarding daily music-video viewing among teenagers, studies indicate that the average teen watches somewhere between thirty minutes and two hours of videos a day.[43] As such, MTV is a reality definer, shaping our kids and the world in which they live. It is an effective teacher that keeps kids' attention. And it is the network, record companies, and advertisers whose pockets overflow with the bounty of an attentive teenage market segment.

What Your Teen Hears: Prominent Themes in Music

The following section offers an overview of the major themes prevalent in nineties music. Although music groups change rapidly (some may even become defunct before this book goes to press!) and the themes appear in the songs of different bands, singers, and songwriters with varying degree and frequency, I will attempt to give examples of the values and attitudes espoused through popular music. As parents, the more aware we are of the music scene as a whole, the more easily we can guide our teens through these influences on behavior and lifestyle choices.

Sexual promiscuity

Have you ever listened to the radio stations in your area or watched MTV? Most parents I know have never taken the time to make themselves aware of what's out there. Those who have done so know that our children and teens are being treated to an around-the-clock dose of no-holds-barred sexuality. Lyrics, videos, concerts, and the lifestyles of the stars all combine to send one clear message to anyone listening: When it comes to sex, express yourself! You can do whatever you want, with whomever you want, wherever you want, whenever you want, however you want! After all, this is the nineties!

In the world of music *love* no longer refers to the lifelong commitment made to each other by two people of the opposite sex. Rather, it has been reduced to the act of sexual intercourse. I'll be the first to admit that God's gift of sexuality is incredible! But God has provided us with sexual guidelines that, when followed, allow for sex to be experienced in the best way possible. But this is not the message of today's music. By reducing love to something that can be magically made between the sheets by two or more people who might not even know each other's names, the music industry has contributed to the moral confusion and emptiness of our children.

Our children's interest and involvement in popular music increases about the same time their hormones kick in. This is a crucial time when our kids need parents who will help them understand this confusing new mix of desires and teach them about responsible and godly sexual expression. They have many questions about what's happening to their bodies. They are inquisitive about the new and intense set of sexual urges that they feel. Too often, their openness and curiosity is answered by the voice of music, which teaches them that sexual pleasure is an end in and of itself.

My ongoing evaluation of popular music over the last few years has convinced me that sexual freedom expressed through a promiscuous lifestyle is the most overt theme in today's music. Pop star Neneh Cherry hit the charts in late 1992 with her second album, *Homebrew*. Her sexual views could have easily come from anyone in the music industry. She says that one of her songs was inspired by her frustration with America's uptight mores about sex.[44] Her song "The Pusher" is a "sexual celebration" and a means to express her outrage over the negativity of the media AIDS campaign. In her description of the song she complains about people who "live and sleep in the Middle Ages. The way they've dealt with [AIDS] is to promote this fear of sex and put this really ugly vibe over it. It's about scaring people into conforming. Men and women have got to be allowed to feel good about themselves—to feel sexy, to feel beautiful, to feel wanted, to feel horny."[45]

Those of us who are disturbed by the sexual images in lyrics and videos are considered prudes. We are labeled as living in the moral dark ages and accused of censoring sexual and artistic freedom. These accusations betray the prevailing attitudes of the entertainment industry. The videos do the same. One content analysis of two hundred concept music videos found that sexual intimacy occurred in 75 percent of the samples. Half of all women were dressed provocatively.[46] And when it comes to romantic relationships, today's music usually stresses the physical over the emotional aspects.

What are some specific examples of how this theme of sexual promiscuity is acted out on video and in the lyrics? The difficulty lies not in finding examples but in deciding where to begin. Following are just a few examples of what our kids are seeing, hearing, and learning.

The provocative female dance/rap trio TLC have been known to use their platform to speak to elementary school audiences about making good choices in life. But kids get a confusing mix of messages when they hear the group's 1992 hit "Ain't 2 Proud 2 Beg." The girls, who encourage safe sex, wear condoms pinned to their clothes, ask to be kissed on "both sets of lips," and sing about penis length.

Popular alternative band R.E.M., who consider themselves to be "moralistic,"[47] include the song "Star Me Kitten" on their album *Automatic for the People*. In the lyrics, the song is actually called "F___ Me Kitten." Why the name change on the album jacket? "They didn't want to court unnecessary fuss."[48]

Heavy-metal music certainly has more than its share of sexually explicit lyrics. Van Halen's song "Black & Blue" includes the lyrics "Baby, I ain't through with you / The harder the better / Let's do it 'til we're black and blue / The wetter the better." And Mötley Crüe has developed a reputation for loading their albums with songs encouraging sexual promiscuity. The album *Dr. Feelgood* is no exception. On the song "Slice of Your Pie," an account of a lusty encounter with a nineteen year old, the band sings, "So young . . . ever get caught, they'll arrest me / School girl, studied up well on hoochie coochie / Lick lips, kitten with a whip, so undress me, undress me."

Sex is a prominent theme in today's music. And it isn't married sex.

The sudden rise of the popularity of rap music among kids all over the country has increased the number of sexually explicit lyrics that kids hear from the most "innocent" mainstream rappers to the most hard-core rap groups. Vanilla Ice, who in 1991 was an "innocent" white rapper who developed a following among preteen girls and appeared in the movie *Teenage Mutant Ninja Turtles II: The Secret of the Ooze*, sang a song called "Havin' a Roni." What most parents didn't know is that in rap language, *tenderoni* is a young virgin.

One of the most successful rap groups of the last few years, Naughty by Nature, describes their MTV hit "O.P.P." as a "cheatin' song" without the guilt. In other words, have sex with whomever you want even if that person or you are committed to someone else. Their follow-up hit, "Hip Hop Hooray" (#8 on the 1993 MTV Top 100 Videos), continues the theme, justifying premarital sexual promiscuity.

The music industry insists that they aren't educating kids but only reflecting the sexual values and commitments of mainstream America. They do, however, feel an obligation to educate kids about sexual responsibility. While this may sound noble, understand that this translates into teaching kids how to avoid messing up their lives by getting pregnant or catching AIDS.

Several groups promote the safe-sex message by distributing condoms at concerts. The hottest-selling item on U2's 1992 Achtung Baby tour was Achtung Baby Condoms. TLC sports condoms pinned to their clothes and over eyeglasses. A man known as The Tube dazzled thousands of teenagers during the summer of 1992's Lollapalooza tour (several bands on tour together) by snorting a condom through his nose and spitting it out of his mouth, only to do it again in reverse!

The rap song "Jimmy" by Boogie Down Productions is one example of a song that promotes the double-edged sword of sexual freedom and responsibility. Look at some of the lyrics to this song named for a slang term for penis: ". . . Too many people I see get dissed / Jimmy hats are now in style . . . So all you super hos wear your hat / 'Cause drippin' Jimmy is straight up wack . . . protect your Jimmy and keep it fresh."

The message is coming through loud and clear: Go ahead, kid. Anything goes. If it feels good, do it. Don't worry about anyone but yourself. Have a good time, but don't catch anything.

Sexual perversion

Some of the voices of popular music are taking the message of sexual promiscuity a step further by inviting kids into the world of various sexual practices and perversions. While several fringe performers have been peddling this kind of filth for a long time, more and more mainstream singers and bands are stretching the limits and dumping this garbage into the ears, hearts, and minds of our kids.

One of the first groups to launch an all-out assault with their arsenal of perversions was the Beastie Boys, a white rap trio from Brooklyn. Their 1986 album *Licensed to Ill* went to the top of the charts, thanks to the hit single "Fight for Your Right (To Party)." The group exercised its "rights" by indulging in all kinds of extreme party behavior, including sexual promiscuity and perversion. The video from the album included several spontaneous episodes of Beastie Boys behavior that made the movie *Animal House* look tame and tasteful. The album included the song "New Style," which boasted about having sex with twin sisters at one time. The song "Paul Revere" describes having sex with the sheriff's daughter by using a Wiffleball bat. Their live concerts brought their tasteless lyrics to life. A girl would be recruited from the audience to strip to her underwear, dance in a cage, and act like she wanted to have sex with all the guys in the audience even though stuck in the cage. Backstage passes would be distributed to girls in the audience. And a safe-sex rider in their contract ensured that there would be a variety of condoms available backstage after the show. The entire concert culminated with the on-stage erection of a twenty-foot hydraulic phallus.

Since the Beastie Boys' arrival in 1986, sexual perversion of this type has become so normal that it increasingly fails to draw opposition. In fact, it is becoming acceptable material for songs, videos, and concerts.

At the 1992 MTV Video Music Awards, the hottest band in America at the time, Red Hot Chili Peppers, took the stage to receive the award for the Most Innovative Video. Bassist Flea jumped on the lectern (while on national TV) and began to simulate masturbation while drummer Chad Smith stood in front of him pretending to perform oral sex. The crowd roared with approval. And in 1991, heavy-metal band Skid Row released a song called "Get The F___ Out," which was described as "nothing more, or less, than gratuitous groupie bashing, a cheap macho swipe at a woman who is used, then abused, just to satisfy the singing cocksman's lust and ego."[49] The lyrics include the line "So keep your mouth busy and wrap your lips / All around my attitude."

Rapper Kool G. Rap uses graphic terms to brag about his sexual abilities and preferences in the song "Talk like Sex." He leaves nothing to the imagination as he talks about sexual intercourse, anal sex, and oral sex so violent that the girl has to have her stomach pumped: "I'll leave you holdin' your swollen backside and rollin' / Fillin' all three holes just like bowlin'. . . chicks are on my d___ like a human shish kebab."

In his album *Dirty Mind,* Prince sang about oral sex in the context of an incestuous relationship with his sister in the song "Sister": "My sister never made love to anyone else but me / She's the reason for my sexuality / Show me where it's supposed to go / A blow job doesn't mean blow / Incest is everything it's said to be." Nirvana toyed with the same theme with the title of their 1992 album, *Incesticide.*

With the increased acceptance of homosexual, lesbian, and bisexual lifestyles, it is no surprise that these themes are becoming more common in popular music. Heavy-metal band Living Colour released the album *Stain,* which includes the song "Bi," a playful tribute to bisexuality that includes the chorus "Everybody loves you when you're bi."

Madonna, who has been outspoken about her willingness to "mother" her entourage of gay male dancers, speaks about her own sexual preferences. While she prefers "hetero sex" to sex with women, she has a lot of "sexual fantasies about women."[50] Her $49.95 best-selling book *Sex* is a photo collection of her sexual fantasies. Included are pictures of Madonna hitchhiking nude, pumping gas topless, and eating pizza naked. There are also photos of a naked Madonna groping rap stars Vanilla Ice and Big Daddy Kane. Other photos show her unclothed while French-kissing model Naomi Campbell and skinny-dipping with actress Isabella Rosselini. In another photo Madonna is tied to a chair by two tattooed lesbian skinheads. The book contains numerous other graphic depictions of bondage, lesbianism, and group sex.

When it comes to sexual perversion, the attitude is that anything goes. And our kids watch, listen, and learn.

Violence

On April 2, 1992, the Center for Media and Public Affairs reported that, on that day, there were an average of 12.5 violent scenes per hour on MTV.[51] A more extensive monitoring of 750 music videos from cable and broadcast television was conducted by the National Coalition on Television Violence during November 1991. That study found an average of 20 acts of violence per hour on broadcast TV and 29 instances of violence per hour on MTV![52] Another study showed that 57 percent of the videos on MTV contained violence.[53] No matter how you add it up, violence has made its way into the music of our children and teens.

Studies on the effects of television violence on children and teens can be applied to music videos. While there is no unanimous verification, these studies do suggest that "there is a causal connection between television violence and subsequent aggressive behavior. . . . Those who view an excessive amount of television violence tend to regard the world as mean and hostile."[54]

Much of the violence in today's music is found in heavy metal. Heavy metal's long history is full of examples of violent lyrics and images. Speed and thrash metal's angry and chaotic nature lends itself to expressions of violence. The names of bands like Impaler, Slayer, Napalm Death, Cadaver, Morbid Angel, Deicide, Overkill, Stormtroopers of Death, and Body Count give obvious clues to the lyrical and thematic content of their songs.

Heavy-metal band Guns n' Roses' video for their song "Don't Cry" tells a story that includes several episodes of violence, including a gun to the head, male-female fight, female-female fight, and murder by way of a car accident. The band Malevolent Creation, a heavy-metal band obsessed with violent themes, sings a nightmarish song called "Systematic Execution," which includes the lyrics: "Hot steel prods into your eyes / Executioner nods, optics spew / Tanks roll forward claiming lives / Focus of death, nothing new." Dismember's album *Pieces* includes the songs "I Wish You Hell" and "Soon to Be Dead." Not exactly easy listening. The album cover for *Fistful of Metal,* the 1992 release from Anthrax, shows a chain-wrapped and metal-spiked fist smashing a man's face into a disfigured and bloody mess.

Rap music is also known for its obsession with violent themes. The usual justification for these brutal lyrics is the hopelessness and anger resulting from the sense of being trapped in the ghetto with no way out. While some rappers openly speak of the futility of looking to violence as the answer (D Nice's "Few Dollars More"), many in rap's hard-core contingent see violence as a legitimate response that should be encouraged.

While much of the anger falls wherever it may, there are some specific targets that rappers are aiming at more frequently. One popular target is the police. Main Source likens killing cops to a game that must be played if one wants to survive. In his song "Just a Friendly Game of Baseball" he raps, "Instead of cops shooting me, I'm going out shooting them / And let 'em cough up blood like phlegm / It's grim, but dead is my antonym / And legally they can't take a fall / Yo, check it out, it's just a friendly game of baseball."

Rapper Ice-T fused rap with heavy metal when he began to tour with the heavy-metal band Body Count. Their song "Cop Killer" was by far the most controversial song of its type and was eventually pulled off their album in July of 1992. Ice-T explains that the song's lyrics, "I'm 'bout to bust some shots off / I'm 'bout to dust some cops off / Die, Die, Die, Pig, Die!" are more a response to unfair treatment by the police than a call to arms. While songs of this type can serve to shed light on the struggles of ghetto life, their call to violence is troubling.

Other rappers suggest violent responses to their white oppressors. Ice Cube's "Amerikkka's Most Wanted" encouraged black-on-white violence: "Word, yo, but who the f___ is heard / It's time you take a trip to the suburbs / Let 'em see a nigger invasion / Point blank, on a Caucasian / Cock the hammer and crack a smile."

Several major labels used wisdom when they declined to produce the album *Sleeping with the Enemy* by rapper Paris. He released the album independently, including the controversial song "Bush Killa," described as "a gangsta' rap fantasy about gunning down the President, among others."[55]

This very brief sampling doesn't even begin to touch the many examples, types, and targets of violence in popular music. Parents should be aware of and concerned about the rising tide of teen violence and the type of music that teaches that violence is a legitimate method of dealing with both justified and unjustified anger.

Sexual violence

Popular music has always been known for its ability to foster feelings of romance and describe young love. Tragically, more and more of the music that speaks about male-female relationships is using terms that have nothing to do with tender love or romance. By combining sexual promiscuity and perversion with violence, some of the music encourages behavior that reduces the value of a person to less than nothing.

Sexually violent lyrics and video portrayals are cropping up with increased frequency. Typically, it is men who are the violent aggressors with women on the receiving end of their disgusting and degrading behavior, including gang rape, sodomy, necrophilia, and sexual death fantasies.

Several years ago Fee Waybill, the lead singer of The Tubes, described his band's obsession with sexual violence:

> We have this number "Bondage" in the show. And a lot of people think it's too violent. I mean, it could be really violent. It's more violent than it looks like on stage. I mean, we've got bruises all over our bodies. . . . It's all good clean fun . . . the simulated kidnapping . . . the gun at the young girl's throat. . . . In the end I get killed. I chase her around and she ends up blowing my guts out . . . and I hang upside down on a tower and lay there, and then, just when you think I'm dead and gone, I grab her and tie her up and rip her clothes off. . . . But don't worry about that . . . it's only fun. . . . The kids want to see action.[56]

Rap music's fascination with sexual violence has been well-documented. The *Newsweek* article "Rap Rage" notes that "it is not just that romance has gone out of music—attitude has done the seemingly impossible and taken sex out of teenage culture, substituting brutal fantasies of penetration and destruction."[57]

One example of this brutality is The Geto Boys' song "Mind of a Lunatic," which graphically describes an angry Peeping Tom who violently rapes a woman, slits her throat, and then proceeds to have sex with her corpse. The album that included this song sold 150,000 copies within a week of its release. N.W.A.'s 1991 album *Efil4zaggin* championed gang rape, killing prostitutes, forced oral sex, and raping a woman with a broomstick. Ice-T's song "Shut Up, Be Happy" describes using a flashlight to have sex with a woman. The 2 Live Crew's *As Nasty As They Wanna Be* album was as nasty as an album could get as it described all sorts and variations of violent sex. One song, "Dirty Nursery Rhymes," included several rewritten X-rated versions of children's favorites. The verse "Jack and Jill went up the hill to have a little fun / Jack got mad, kicked Jill in the a__ 'cause she couldn't make him c___" is tame compared to the remainder of the album.

In an interview with Parent's Music Resource Center founder Tipper Gore, Dr. Joseph Stuessy, professor of music at the University of Texas at San Antonio, described the way that sexually violent music affects the behavior of children and teens:

> What if I were an impressionable fifteen-year-old boy today? My rock heroes have told me that sex on a date is expected and that it is a violent act. My penis is a knife, a gun, a rod of steel. Intercourse involves thrusting, plunging, screaming, and pain. My date is to be the object of my sexual cutting, slicing, and shooting. I must be very conscious of exerting my masculinity. I don't want my date, who for all I know, is "experienced," to think I'm a wimp! I will nail her to the bed and make her scream in pain! Boy, this sex stuff is great![58]

Many in our culture, including those who make the music, would dismiss Dr. Stuessy's link between sexual violence in music and actual teen behavior as paranoid and ill-informed conjecture. The evidence proves otherwise. Rapper Tone Loc's "Wild Thing," a boastful story of sexual conquests and acting tough, became the biggest-selling rap single of all time shortly after its release. The term *wild thing* soon became street slang for the good time associated with having sex. The song achieved further notoriety when a gang of six young Hispanic and black youths were arrested for raping a twenty-eight-year-old jogger in New York's Central Park. The teenagers, who were "just going wild-thing," were indicted on thirteen counts of rape, sodomy, sexual abuse, assault, and attempted murder. One reporter misquoted the description as "wilding," a term that caught on and is now used on the street to describe spontaneous and randomly aimed violence, robbery, and rape.[59]

If popular music continues to offer up a diet of sexually violent lyrics and videos, don't be surprised to see more and more young teenage boys innocently attempt to justify their sexually violent behavior by saying, "I thought that's the way I'm supposed to treat a lady."

Substance abuse

Most American adults would agree that something must be done about the problem of drug and alcohol abuse among teens. The shared concern over this problem has led to a concerted effort to educate children and teens about the dangers of drugs and alcohol. Young children are taught in school to "just say no." Media and sports heroes have used their platforms to encourage kids to stay away from drugs and alcohol through television ads, radio spots, and community programs. The government has invested millions of dollars in efforts to fight drugs, but kids continue to abuse drugs and alcohol at an alarming and rising rate. Part of the blame can be placed on the popular music industry because it continues to send out mixed messages on substance abuse.

Many performers in the industry have gone to great lengths to encourage kids to avoid drugs. Rap group De La Soul's song "Say No Go" is an anticrack anthem that includes a description of the results of cocaine use among expectant mothers. Donald D's antidrug song "F.B.I." (Free Base Institute) includes the lyrics "People of the world, there's a serious problem / And it's called crack. I'm tellin' you / Stay away from it. It makes you do crazy things."

But these efforts are too few and far between. Lifestyles, lyrics, videos, and comments by the performers continue to glorify drug and alcohol abuse. Sinéad O'Connor told *Rolling Stone* that "selling marijuana is one of the most respectable things anyone could do. I think everybody should smoke it. . . . It teaches you a lot about yourself. It forces you to feel."[60] Al Jourgensen, lead singer in the band Ministry, usually produces and mixes their albums while high on acid. He calls himself a "drug connoisseur" and describes the band's recording style this way: "Five-day sessions with strobe lights and psychedelic drugs."[61]

The heavy-metal music scene is well known for its tendency to preach the message of drug and alcohol abuse. In her book *Heavy Metal,* sociologist Deena Weinstein describes the crucial role that drugs and alcohol play in the subculture. She notes how many performers use the drugs and alcohol to overcome stage fright and relieve stress. With "life is a party" as the hedonistic theme of the lyrics, substance abuse by the performers is just another element in the message. Weinstein notes that bands who have cleaned up their acts and stopped using drugs, like Mötley Crüe and Aerosmith, downplay their sobriety in order not to compromise their hedonistic image. In heavy metal a life filled with excessive sex, drugs, and rock and roll is proof of one's charisma. Even better is dying from such a lifestyle.[62]

Rap music is also filled with lyrical, visual, and lifestyle references to substance abuse. Dr. Dre's 1993 album, *The Chronic,* is a perfect example of the popular music–pot connection. Named after a particularly potent strain of marijuana popular on the streets of Los Angeles, the album peaked at number two on the Billboard charts, stayed in the top ten for eight months, and went triple platinum (over 3 million copies sold), making it, at that time, the biggest selling hard-core rap album of all time.

The music charts lit up again in 1993 when Cypress Hill released their *Black Sunday* album, grabbing the top spot on the Billboard charts and selling a record-setting 260,000 copies in its first week. Featured songs include "Hits from the Bong," "Legalize It," and "I Wanna Get High."

John Scott, the producer of several rap artists, says that a number of them get high before going into recording sessions "because it helps ideas flow for music tracks, as well as for videos."[63]

Rap's continued relationship with marijuana influences even clothing style. House of Pain rapper Danny Boy is one of the original founders of Original Weed Wear, which produces embroidered hats and T-shirts sporting a marijuana leaf. Hats, shirts, and other clothing sporting the old logo for Phillies Blunt cigars indicate more than just a fashion trend. Several rappers are singing about the benefits of wrapping marijuana in the outside leaf of these cigars. This practice of removing the tobacco and replacing it with marijuana has given birth to the popularity of "Blunts" across the nation. One East Coast cigar distributor reports that two years ago he was ordering a thousand boxes of Blunts a month. Now he has increased his monthly orders one hundred times over.[64]

Numerous popular groups are on the marijuana bandwagon, openly supporting its use and legalization. Among them are Pearl Jam, the Spin Doctors, Faith No More, Brand Nubian, and Blind Melon.

Children and teens who want to abuse drugs and alcohol can find plenty of encouragement in today's music. Substance abuse is sung and talked about, lived and died. In the last five years, rockers who have died from their life of excess include Steve Clark (Def Leppard),

Brent Mydland (Grateful Dead), Hillel Slovak (Red Hot Chili Peppers), Johnny Thunders (New York Dolls), Will Shatter (Flipper), Andrew Wood (Mother Love Bone), and Stefanie Sargent (7 Year Bitch). Depending on who you talk to, they died as examples of either how to live the best life possible or how to die as the result of foolish self-indulgence.

The occult

On December 19, 1992, Glenn Danzig took the stage for a concert in New York City. *Rolling Stone* concert reviewer Mike Gitter described the concert's atmosphere this way:

> From the eerie, blood-red hue that engulfs the two 15-foot gargoyles flanking the Roseland stage to the Black Sabbath-on-steroids chords his band, Danzig, grinds out from the get-go, Glenn Danzig is a muscle-bound metalloid Dark Lord raising a leather-gauntleted fist at the heavens as if to challenge the gods themselves.[65]

Gitter describes how the concert included songs such as "Godless," "Snakes of Christ," "Am I Demon," and "Heart of the Devil." Many of the songs were from Danzig's new album *Danzig III—How The Gods Kill.*

This preoccupation with occult themes, particularly in heavy-metal music, might just be the most discussed and criticized aspect of today's popular music. Heavy-metal music has long been fascinated with the occult. Concerts, lyrics, and album covers are full of images pointing to satanic themes, symbols, and rituals. Those who take the time to listen to and understand the music of their children and teens will find it easy to discern these themes because of their blatant and obvious nature. Coven's album *Blessed Is the Black* contains satanic elements or lyrics that glorify the negative on every single song. Deicide's album *Legion* includes the songs "In Hell I Burn" and "Holy Deception." The album *Point of No Return* by Forbidden includes the song "One Foot in Hell." Iron Maiden, long known for their lyrical and visual obsession with the occult, includes the song "Children of the Damned" on their album *Number of the Beast.* Morgoth puts their beliefs to music on the song "Resurrection Absurd."

Bands that claim allegiance to Satan often sing descriptions of satanic rituals. Venom's song "Possessed" is one example: "Look at me, Satan's child / Born of evil, thus defiled / Brought to life through satanic birth." They go on to sing, "I drink the vomit of priests / Make love with the dying whore . . . / Satan, as my master, incarnate. / Hail!

Praise to my unholy host!" Their song "Sacrifice" describes the ritual of human sacrifice in graphic terms: " . . . Sacrifice to Lucifer, my master / Bring the chalice, raise the knife. . . . Plunge the dagger in her breast. . . . Demons rejoice. . . ."

Other songs appear to be satanic creeds put to music. Mercyful Fate's song "The Oath" is one example. "By the symbol of creation / I wear henceforth to be a faithful servant / Of his most persistent archangel, Prince Lucifer / Who the Creator designated as his regent / And the Lord of this world, Amen / I deny Jesus Christ, the Deceiver. . . ."

Trey Azagthoth, whose surname comes from the Sumerian god of Warhas, is the guitarist for the band Morbid Angel. He says that the band is into the occult and that he is a reincarnated demon. "[Satanism]'s actually something we take very seriously."[66]

There is no question that there are overt occult themes in heavy-metal music. But all too often, critics oversimplify what actually lies behind much of the music and, by doing so, focus their criticism on things that are not really there. As a result, critics argue with the musicians over the motivations behind the music rather than the effects that the music can have on kids.

There really is no way of knowing if a particular group or artist is actually a consciously practicing satanist unless they make that claim themselves. The inclusion of occult lyrics, symbols, and themes may often be used as a tool to sell albums. In addition, many of those who make use of these themes and symbols are adamant about the fact that they don't believe in or worship a personal being named Satan. Rather, they say that they use these symbols and themes not to denote rebellion against God but as an expression of youthful power and rebellion against authority. The authors of *Dancing in the Dark* suggest that the urge to live life free of limits and disentangled from responsibility is:

> sometimes expressed in extreme ways: goat heads, blood, horns, flames, and the like decorate certain album covers, and references to cultic rituals appear in the lyrics of some heavy-metal songs. This is not Satanism, as some of its critics contend; more likely it is an emphasis that grows out of the romantic desire to view Satan as the one who successfully escaped societal and cultural limitations.[67]

As parents, our criticism is often misdirected when it is aimed at the "satanic" practices or motivations of the music makers. They will usually deny these accusations. But what they cannot deny is the destructive results that can occur when kids turn on music that is full of these themes. It is difficult enough for an adult to know what lies behind the satanic themes. Teenagers who are open to new ideas and unable to call upon well-developed critical faculties will listen to this stuff and take it at face value. Those who are fed a steady diet can easily buy into it lock, stock, and barrel, becoming dabblers and practitioners of satanism themselves. Even music that contains occult themes for the sole purpose of generating sales can be an effective evangelistic tool in the hands of the devil. While the musicians' motivations may differ, the results are the same.

While only a minority of kids are drawn to and involved in overtly satanic heavy metal, there is a greater danger that lies in the covert occult themes present in the mainstream music heard on Top 40 radio and seen on MTV. These themes are best explained by Anton LaVey, the organizer of the Church of Satan and the author of the *Satanic Bible*:

> We feel a person should be free to indulge in all the so-called fetishes that they would desire, as long as they don't hurt anyone that doesn't deserve or wish to be hurt. This is a very selfish religion. We believe in greed, we believe in selfishness, we believe in all the lustful thoughts that motivate man, because this is man's natural feeling. This is based on what man naturally would do.[68]

LaVey's remarks betray what is at the core of satanism, that is, a redirecting of one's allegiance away from the almighty God to a focus on self. The nine satanic statements in *The Satanic Bible* include these: "Satan represents indulgence, instead of abstinence!" (#1) and "Satan represents all of the so-called sins, as they lead to physical, mental or emotional gratification." (#8)[69] The emphasis is on hedonism, materialism, fleshly desires, and worldliness. Thus, it might be more accurate to refer to music that contains these themes as "fleshly." But don't be fooled. An individual's fleshly nature is influenced and directed by the world and the devil, forces that lie outside of oneself. Music that educates and encourages our kids to indulge recklessly and selfishly in life's pleasures leads kids away from God. In this way, it serves to further the message of the kingdom of darkness and point kids away from the kingdom of light.

Political commentary and social concern

If you were watching or listening during the 1992 election campaign and the 1993 inaugural, you couldn't help but notice the full-scale marriage of popular music and politics. While certain elements of popular music have always been concerned with political and social activism, it is now more unusual for a band or singer *not* to make comments regarding some pressing political or social issue.

The appearances of Michael Jackson, L.L. Cool J, and other stars at the 1993 Presidential Inaugural Celebration and the star-studded first-ever MTV Inaugural Ball (with the newly elected president's brother Roger singing with En Vogue) were all part of the celebration of the popular music industry's continued involvement in politics and social issues. While opinions and views vary among singers and bands, there are several themes prevalent in today's music.

The Rock the Vote campaign of 1992 enlisted the help of artists, radio stations, MTV, record companies, and record outlets in an effort to register eighteen- to twenty-four-year-old voters. Rock the Vote volunteers were out in force during most of the summer's major tours, including Guns n' Roses, Metallica, U2, and the Lollapalooza music festival. Public service announcements featuring Aerosmith, Michael Jackson, Red Hot Chili Peppers, and Marky Mark were featured on MTV. When all was said and done, millions of new voters had been registered, and MTV could take credit for their major role in electing a new president.

Numerous music festivals have been staged over the last several years to raise money and awareness for different charity and relief efforts. Live Aid and Farm Aid raised money for the hungry and hurting. Other festivals raised money to go towards Amnesty International's efforts to free political prisoners and correct human-rights violations. The 1992 Concert for Life featured Queen, David Bowie, Def Leppard, Elton John, George Michael, and several others making appearances to raise money to fight AIDS.

Other members of the music industry have organized to form Rock for Choice, an effort to further the pro-abortion movement. Members of Rock for Choice include R.E.M., Nirvana, the Black Crowes, and Pearl Jam. The 1992 Lollapalooza festival was a multimedia sociopolitical event that played to more than half a million North American rock fans during its stop in several cities. Manning booths at this rock festival were activist organizations ranging from Rock the Vote and Hand Gun Control to the Cannabis Action Network. Also present were Coalition for the Homeless, Greenpeace, College Democrats, Lifebeat, and Refuse and Resist representatives. Subsequent Lollapalooza festivals have had more of the same.

Parents should be aware of the fact that most concerts, songs, albums, and interviews are outlets for musicians to preach their social and political agendas. Many of these efforts are admirable and worthy as they raise our children's awareness and offer them ways to get involved in helping those in need. Other efforts tend to be partisan and extreme in nature. Regardless, all of these messages shape our children's world and life views. It is important that parents take the time to discover what the messages are so that they can help their children consider the content and impact of these messages.

Rebellion

Rebellion is defined as "opposition to one in authority or dominance."[70] As adolescents move from childhood to adulthood, there is always a tendency to rebel, and rebellious music can become an outlet for some of the aggression they feel. Kids who are fatherless or who grow up neglected or abused at home, school, or even church have a legitimate reason to complain. They are naturally drawn to music that challenges anyone in authority. If you were to read the stories of those making the music, you would find that their music often serves as an outlet for the anger and frustration they feel as a result of growing up in a terrible situation themselves.

Much of the rebellion in today's music is directed toward parents. Some of the music encourages rebelliousness of this type by encouraging kids to do whatever they want. Other music is more direct. Twisted Sister's "We're Not Gonna Take It" is the classic antiparent song whose video depicts a rock-music-loving son throwing his father down a set of stairs and through a window. Def Leppard's 1992 hit "Let's Get Rocked" encourages kids to forget their parents and party instead. Michael Jackson's video of the song "Black or White" begins with child film star Macaulay Culkin playing a young boy whose father cramps his style by insisting that he turn his music down. Instead, he turns his strategically placed speakers all the way up, blasting his father through the roof and into another dimension.

Rebellion is also directed against the church and organized religion. Sinéad O'Connor's appearance on *Saturday Night Live* in October 1992 is an example of this type of defiance. After singing the song "War," she held up a photo of Pope John Paul II and slowly ripped it to pieces while encouraging the audience to "fight the real enemy."[71] This was not some spontaneous publicity stunt. Rather, it was rooted in O'Connor's deep disdain for the church. She once said that "the very tiny bit of religion which I experienced has induced in me this huge guilt complex—so imagine what it does to somebody who's had a lot? . . . I believed it all—that you're going to be punished and that you're going to hell. So [religion]'s very dangerous."[72]

When teachers and school are seen as a roadblock to adolescent freedom, they can become the targets of rebellion. One example is the band Jackyl's song "The Lumberjack," a lusty anthem to unbridled pleasure. The video concludes with one of the band's members sawing the schoolteacher's desk in half with a chain saw.

Singer Tori Amos is more direct regarding her rebellion against her upbringing in the home of a Methodist minister and her resulting disdain for God. Her popular song "God" includes the words "God, sometimes you just don't come through / Do you need a woman to look after you?" In her song "Icicle" she distances herself from the Bible, Communion, and other elements of Christianity.

Distrust of and dissatisfaction with the government lead to musical rebellion directed at Washington. Megadeath's 1992 video hit for the song "Symphony of Destruction" has a political meaning. According to the band's explanation, the song likens U.S. citizens to rats being pulled through the streets by the pied piper (the government). The band 7 Year Bitch gets more direct in their accusations with their song "No F_____ War." They sing "So Bush pull out / Like your father should have" as a direct verbal assault on the former president. Madonna described the former president as one who "doesn't give a s___ about family values. He's a bigoted, narrow-minded fascist."[73]

A child's obsession with blatantly rebellious music should serve to tip off parents to their teenager's pain and hurt. Usually teens who are obsessed with this type of music identify with it and, in doing so, find its unhealthy messages to be a therapeutic outlet for pent-up aggression. Observant parents and other adults can initiate relationships and begin to offer healing to teens who use the music to react against deep hurt. But there is always the danger that this same type of music can come between well-adjusted "normal" kids and their parents by saying that it is all right to dishonor and disobey those whom God has placed in authority over them.

Truth is relative

While I can't say that I ever heard the phrase "truth is relative" in the lyrics of a popular song, I have heard entire songs built on this assumption. By denying the existence of God's truth and a divinely established moral order, songwriters and artists elevate themselves to the position of truth maker. In their quest to understand right and wrong, they have decided on those parameters for themselves. And they encourage our kids to do the same. The result is the massive quantity of popular music that encourages free sexual expression, sexual violence, rebellion, anarchy, violence, materialism, selfishness, and a survival-of-the-fittest mentality.

Popular music tells your child that truth can only be found inside oneself. To look elsewhere, even to God, is to be untrue to yourself. There is no universal right and wrong. Rather, you must find what is true for you while I discover what is true for me. You must ultimately appeal to self to decide on matters of sexuality, obedience, lifestyle, etc.

In his insightful book, *The Death of Ethics in America,* Cal Thomas comments on teenagers who, oblivious to any transcendent God-made standard, see nothing at all wrong with having sex before marriage (a consistent theme in today's music): "This amorality is worse than immorality. With immorality there is a standard to which one can appeal to bring back the errant. With amorality no one acknowledges the existence of any standard at all."[74]

One of popular music's best and most recent examples of this truth-is-relative mentality is rap star Sir Mix-A-Lot, one of 1992's hottest acts. His big hit of the year was "Baby Got Back," a lusty video and lyrical testimony to his desire to have sex with girls who have large posteriors. The song finished number one on the 1992 Billboard single sales charts. *Entertainment Weekly* magazine, in its year-end issue, asked Sir Mix-A-Lot what he felt were the entertainment highs and lows of 1992. His highlight choice was Red Hot Chili Peppers' performance at the MTV Music Video Awards. Even though they thanked Satan and simulated masturbation and oral sex on national TV, Sir Mix-A-Lot said, "I thought they were awesome." While this may not surprise you, his lowlight will: "Madonna's book *Sex.* That's not art. I have to defend her right to do it, but I just thought it was embarrassing, tacky and unnecessary."[75] Do you detect a contradiction here? Sir Mix-A-Lot is mixed-up-a-lot and a perfect example of the moral schizophrenia within our culture and the music industry.

Hopelessness

The final theme in popular music is the sum result of all the forces we have discussed—hopelessness. Kids who have forgotten, denied, or never even recognized the existence of the living God feel lost *and without hope.*

Kids who swim in a sea of hopelessness identify with music that expresses these feelings. In the song "Welcome to the Jungle," Guns n' Roses singer Axl Rose tells his listeners: "You know where you are? / You're in the jungle baby / You're gonna die in the jungle." For kids who are shut off from family, abused, forsaken, unaccepted, and forgotten, these words mirror their feelings and experience.

Metallica's 1992 hit "Enter Sandman" is a disturbing and frightening mix of images that make life out to be a never-ending nightmare. The song's portrayal of a young boy saying his bedtime prayers only to be visited by all the bad dreams a kid could imagine suggests that faith in God is ridiculous and ultimately meaningless. The song's message is that, no matter what, the beasts under your bed are going to get you. For many kids, life is one continuous nightmare.

Alternative band Depeche Mode, known for their dirgelike anthems of hopelessness, used a more direct approach to address the futility of faith in their song "Blasphemous Rumors": "I think that God's got a sick sense of humor / And when I die I expect to find him laughing." Some kids believe that they are the butt of some cosmic joke.

The music of Nirvana seethes with an anger rooted in hopelessness. Late lead singer Kurt Cobain, angry and confused himself, recognized that part of the appeal of Nirvana's music is its anger. Still, he wondered why kids were listening to him. He said he found this frightening "because I'm just as confused as most people. I don't have the answers for anything."[76] Nirvana's producer, Butch Vig, said that "what the kids are attracted to in the music is that . . . [Cobain]'s pissed."[77]

Today's music is full of nihilism, a total rejection of tradition, morality, authority, and social order. Nihilism breeds and feeds on hopelessness; hopelessness breeds anger; anger leads to anarchy. It should come as no surprise that the cheerleaders in Nirvana's angry anthem "Smells Like Teen Spirit" sport the emblem for anarchy (a large *A* in a circle) on their uniforms. Cobain's hopelessness found its ultimate expression in his song "I Hate Myself and Want to Die." Though tragic, it came as no surprise to those of us who closely followed his short career that he died of a self-inflicted gunshot wound on April 8, 1994.

Youth workers Mike Yaconelli and Jim Burns wrote the following words in 1986 that, prophetic at the time, have begun to play themselves out in the world of popular music today:

> There may be a very disturbing trend emerging that will affect future generations of adolescents. So far, it's only a hunch. And we hope we're wrong. But the signs all point to an emerging generation of adolescents who could erupt in an-

ger. . . . Our fear is that the emerging generation of young people will be angry but have no specific targets, no agenda; it will simply be anger directed at anything and everything. It will be anarchy.[78]

Today it is becoming increasingly difficult to find music that teaches positive values, the dignity of people, a sense of transcendent moral order, and hope for tomorrow. Parents who seek to discover and then intelligently discuss the themes of popular music with their children can guide them into learning how to discern the good messages from the bad.

What Types of Popular Music Does Your Child Listen To?

In 1992, *Rolling Stone* magazine asked its readers to vote for their favorite album of all time and to defend their vote in a brief essay. Reader after reader responded with eye-opening comments, some of them baring their souls to show how important music is in their lives.

Cathy, a sixteen year old from California, wrote about her love for the Guns n' Roses song "Welcome to the Jungle":

I first heard "Welcome to the Jungle" at a friend's house. It was the first heavy-metal song I had ever heard. I had been an abused child all my life, and something about the music moved me. Feelings of hurt and anger that had been bottled up all those years took over. I started shaking and crying, and that night I made the decision that what they were doing to me was wrong and I wasn't going to let anyone use me as a punching bag ever again.

Cathy goes on to describe how she wound up in court and eventually moved in with her grandparents for a year: "During that time, Guns n' Roses, cigarettes and alcohol were all that kept me from committing suicide."[79]

Cathy's comments give us insight into the incredible role popular music plays during the years of adolescent development and confusion. One of the reasons kids are drawn to certain types of music and bands is that the music speaks to them, addressing their specific problems and circumstances.

One person who has devoted his life to helping parents understand their teens by helping them understand popular music is Al

Menconi, the director of Al Menconi Ministries. Menconi describes this purpose of music when he says, "The key to success in dealing with today's music is to see it as *a window to our child's soul* [italics mine]."[80] Menconi acknowledges that popular music's themes can be frightening and threatening to parents. But he has found that parents who take the time to look into the window and understand and act on what they see are able to bring communication, unity, and spiritual health back into their families.

Menconi goes on to describe how our children feel personally attacked when we as parents knock their music:

> The key to winning this battle lies in understanding how personal this music is; it goes right for our kids' hearts. Their music can reveal inner struggles and needs; it can reveal the spiritual and moral health of a child; it can reflect doubts and fears, and even spotlight the happy places in their lives. Knowing this to be true, we can use the music to our advantage. It can help us get to those deeper places in our children's spiritual lives where real ministry can take place.[81]

The American Medical Association, recognizing this same principle, has said, "Physicians should be aware of the role of music in the lives of adolescents and use music preferences as clues to the emotional and mental health of adolescents."[82]

It is not enough for parents to understand the power of music to mold and shape adolescent reality. It is not enough to understand the many teaching strategies and outlets that music uses. And it is not enough to have a working knowledge of the prominent themes in popular music. Parents must go a step further and understand the different types of popular music, the unique features of each genre, and the reasons why kids are drawn to certain bands and types of music. As veteran youth worker and youth culture expert Dean Burgman says, "Behind music that shocks there are often neglected social and personal issues needing to be explored."[83] Many teens form genre preferences and allegiances that define who they are in relationship to their family, peers, school, and the broader society.

Following is a brief overview of the basic genres in popular music. Because the proliferation, fluidity, and blending of genres makes it difficult to keep up with the rapidly changing world of popular music, I have attempted to simplify the genres in an effort to eliminate confusion. In some cases, I have taken the liberty to classify a music group that could fit into more than one genre. While this overview certainly is not exhaustive, it will provide the basic information needed to help you begin to discern what type of music your child is listening to so that you might gain insight into your kids and their concerns, problems, and needs.

Rock

This is the music that most of us grew up with. Rooted in the hard rock of the sixties, today's rock is heavily inspired by the sounds of classic rock and roll.

Musical purists appreciate rock because of its "live" sound. Usually there are none of the computer-programmed artificial sounds that are common in most other genres. All the sounds come from real people playing real instruments. The drums maintain a steady beat; the sounds of the lead guitar dominate the music.

While there are a few new groups playing rock and gaining a following (the Spin Doctors and the Black Crowes, to name two), most of the interest is directed to groups who were big in years gone by. Some of them, like The Rolling Stones, ZZ Top, and the Grateful Dead, are still playing. Others, like The Doors and Jimi Hendrix, are either disbanded or dead.

In summary: Besides the appeal to aspiring young musicians and those who just like its sound, why the continued taste for this music? Some have suggested that this music's tendency to speak for a disgruntled generation in the sixties continues almost thirty years later with a generation that is similarly skeptical about the government, family, and church. While rock is not the number-one choice of the majority of today's teens, its popularity is big among some of the more intelligent kids who are thinking on a deeper level about the pressing issues of the day.

Sample of Rock Singers and Groups:

Bryan Adams	Tom Petty
John Mellencamp	Don Henley
Grateful Dead	Van Morrison
Robert Plant	Pink Floyd
The Doors	ZZ Top
The Who	Peter Gabriel
YES	Robert Palmer
The Rolling Stones	Led Zeppelin
Black Crowes	Glenn Frey
Eric Clapton	Patty Smyth
Spin Doctors	Lenny Kravitz
Bruce Springsteen	Meatloaf

Pop/Dance

The musical tastes of most kids in middle to late grade school and into junior high begin to gravitate towards mainstream pop music. In past years, this age group has latched on to Michael Jackson (the self-proclaimed "King of Pop"), Madonna, New Kids on the Block, George Michael, and Amy Grant, to name a few. These and other recording stars sing the "hot hits" that get played over and over on Top 40 radio.

The pop/dance music of today is relatively uncomplicated in nature. A continued pulsating beat coupled with a simple melody that is repeated throughout the song makes the songs easy to dance to and learn. (This explains the popularity of these songs at junior high dances and among little girls who emulate the stars by singing and dancing to the songs at slumber parties and in their bedrooms.) The faster songs are catchy and danceable. Other pop/dance tunes are slow emotional ballads, stressing themes of romance and young love, providing background music for slow dancing and daydreaming about that special person.

Pop/dance music is typically electronic in nature. Drum sounds often come from programmed electronic drum machines, eliminating the need for a drummer. Elaborate keyboards and digital samplers are used to reproduce virtually any desired sound. At many concerts, band members "fake it" while a prerecorded sound track plays part or all of the accompaniment. At other times, the singers will lip-synch to prerecorded voice tracks while dancing at a feverish pace that leaves them breathless and unable to sing.

Young girls are especially susceptible to the messages of pop/dance. Stars like Madonna, Paula Abdul, Janet Jackson, and others provide girls with definitions of what a desirable, beautiful, and sexy woman is. Girls who are looking for love, companionship, and male affirmation are often easily tricked into buying and becoming the sexually explicit images peddled by these and other pop/dance stars. These same images teach young boys that girls are sexual objects. Both boys and girls hear few positive messages about the nature of commitment and long-term love, while they learn lots about lust and feelings-based romance.

George Michael's recent pop/dance hit video "Too Funky," the latest in his string of sexually explicit releases, opens with a beautiful model on the screen while a woman's voice asks, "Would you like me to seduce you?" In the video, Michael is a camera operator at a fashion show. A string of models parade their skimpy wares in endless procession as he sings about his desire to see them naked, feel their hands all over his body, and get inside of them. The song is a perfect example of a variety of pop/dance elements all rolled into one package.

In summary: Parents should carefully examine the pop/dance songs, videos, and artists that their children listen to. While this type of music is relatively tame and innocent compared to some other genres, this is no reason to give it *carte blanche* approval. While preteens and adolescents may initially be drawn to its sound, it is not long before pop's messages and images are learned. Discussing pop/dance music with your child provides opportunities to deal with the pressing adolescent issues of self-image, sexuality, dating, the nature of love, and peer relationships.

Sample of Pop/Dance Singers and Groups:

Madonna	Taylor Dayne
Michael Jackson	Michael Bolton
C & C Music Factory	Roxette
Mr. Mister	Amy Grant
Janet Jackson	Vanessa Williams
New Kids on the Block	Jody Watley
Mariah Carey	Sade
Whitney Houston	Shai
Wilson Phillips	Technotronic
Londonbeat	Boyz II Men
Michael W. Smith	Snap!
Color Me Badd	Tony! Toni! Toné!
Sophie B. Hawkins	Me-2-U
Right Said Fred	Jade
Prince	Inner Circle
Paula Abdul	Jodeci
En Vogue	Silk
George Michael	SWV (Sisters with Voices)
Bobby Brown	Mary J. Blige
Richard Marx	Tevin Campbell
Gloria Estefan	Ace of Base

Alternative/New Music

If ever there was a genre of popular music that was difficult to define and understand, alternative is it! By its very nature, alternative music, also known as new, progressive, or modern music, is always changing and stretching the proven success formulas of popular music. Anthony Kiedis, lead singer of alternative band Red Hot Chili Peppers, describes it this way:

Basically, kids got disenchanted with what they were being force-fed on radio, and they were looking for something more sincere to help them through the stage in their lives when they're searching for meaning and rebelling against the Establishment. Something more heartfelt, than, say, Def Leppard.[84]

While it is difficult to stereotype alternative music and even harder to predict what the genre holds up its sleeve for tomorrow, there are some general character traits of the music that are identifiable.

First, it is a very eclectic genre. The influences are many, and there are no specific rules. One of the most popular alternative bands of the last few years is the Red Hot Chili Peppers. They have their own distinctive sound that is a fusion of rap, funk, rock, punk, and heavy metal: five types of music that in their purest forms are very different. Somehow, the Chili Peppers have climbed the ladder of music success by combining them all.

Second, the lyrics tend to be introspective, abstract, and so poetic that they are difficult to follow and understand, even if you have the printed words in front of your eyes. The difficulty of interpreting the messages reveals the deep-seated confusion of singers and songwriters who find themselves wandering aimlessly in the search for life's meaning. Many of the band R.E.M.'s lyrics are cryptic in nature. Lead singer Michael Stipe once described the band's music as "a bunch of minor chords with some nonsense thrown on top."[85] When asked if it is important for people to understand what he is singing, Stipe replied, "No. I don't see any reason for it. I think music is way beyond rational thinking. It doesn't have to make any sense."[86]

Third, videos produced by alternative bands are typically on the leading edge of creativity. Kids find them exciting and fun to watch. Most of the videos are "concept videos" (as opposed to "concert videos" that portray the band either in concert or in the recording studio). Some of the videos tell a story that either explains or confuses the song's lyrics. Other videos employ a variety of new and unusual visual effects that offer a surrealistic quality that leaves the viewer even more confused about the song's meaning. Australian band INXS has become known for the unusual nature of their videos. In "Not Enough Time" viewers are treated to a nonstop parade of band members doing everything from walking to having sex while situated in leaping flames or underwater.

Fourth, the lyrics tend to ask lots of questions about life. This explains the music's appeal to kids as they search for answers to the normal questions of adolescence. The difficulty lies in the fact that very few answers are given, and when they are, they are usually not hopeful in nature. Depeche Mode's "Waiting for the Night" describes the night as the answer to all of the day's problems. But the tone of the song betrays the fact that the singer knows this exercise in futility must be endured every twenty-four hours.

Fifth, while sexual promiscuity and hopelessness are the dominant themes mentioned, many alternative bands employ lyrical, visual, and/or lifestyle references to violence, politics, and moral relativism.

Finally, while a wide variety of kids from different age groups, socioeconomic backgrounds, and life situations listen to alternative, the majority of kids who listen are mid- to late-adolescent social climbers. In other words, high school kids who are not outcasts love alternative music. It could be considered suburban "preppy" music because of its popularity among the studious, popular, and athletic kids.

While the alternative scene is a potpourri of musical styles, there are five subgenres evolving that deserve special mention.

Goth or mope rock is a strain that utilizes sulking guitars and synthesizers to make music sound like a funeral dirge. The downbeat music enhances a lyrical and visual message that is typically depressing. Goth is lyrically obsessed with the hopelessness that flows from unanswered questions. Its only hope is that there might be hope somewhere. The Cure's songs are dark and depressing pictures of futility. Lead singer Robert Smith's dark hair, clothes, and eye sockets contrast sharply with his lily-white face: "Knowing that everything's futile but still fighting, still raging against the dying of the light—that's what motivates me all the time."[87] Kids who are obsessed with goth bands like The Cure, Depeche Mode, Sisters of Mercy, The Mission, and Nick Cave and the Bad Seeds tend to dress like the bands, with jet-black hair and long dark clothes.

Alternative pop is lighter, happier, and very danceable. The guitar sound is distinctively chimelike, and there is less of a reliance on the electronic sound common in mainstream pop/dance. Themes tend to veer away from a hopeful adolescent romance and love to the type of love that never lasts more than a verse or two. Political and social concern themes are common. Popular alternative pop bands include

R.E.M., Teenage Fanclub, Chills, EMF, The Soup Dragons, and Jesus Jones.

Grunge is the newest and fastest-growing subtype of alternative. There are no artificial sounds here. Pounding bass, heavy drums, and splattering guitars combine with raspy and sometimes unintelligible vocals to create an angry and rebellious sound that has become popular among mainstream kids. The look combines long hair and untucked flannel shirts. While Nirvana best represents this subgenre, Pearl Jam, Soundgarden, and The Replacements can also be included. Kat Bjelland of Babes in Toyland says that grunge is "the attitude of we can do whatever we want, and if it sounds good to us, we'll just keep doing it."[88] That rebellious attitude permeates all of grunge as anger, hopelessness, chaos, and anarchy rule supreme.

Rave music, also known as **techno,** is typically computer generated, loud, thumping, fast, repetitive, and very danceable. Fans of this music will gather by the hundreds or thousands for all-night parties held in lofts, empty warehouses, the beach, or large fields. The music is the focus of these "raves" and is enhanced by elaborate and technical special effects. Raves have been described as being like "an atom with particles moving in it, making it move faster and hotter. When a group of people are all moving to that music, you feel that energy, and it's a blast."[89] Some of the more popular rave performers include Moby, Nexus 21, Psychotropic, Digital Bass, Grateful Techno, Aphex Twin, Orbital, and Vapour Space.

Riot-Grrrls is a new alternative phenomenon that currently is on the fringe of mainstream music. This movement is made up of a number of bands that hold several things in common. First, the bands are composed entirely of females. Second, they sing and scream openly about their radical feminism and their anger towards and hatred for men. Third, the lyrics and sound of their music is full of anger and profanity-filled rage. Bands like L7, Huggy Bear, Bikini Kill, Bratmobile, Heavens to Betsy, Gunk, Chicken Milk, Kreviss, and Siren deserve attention as the movement grows.

The musical hodgepodge known as alternative requires parental attention. This is the music that is most popular among the largest percentage of kids. While some may be tempted to write it off as "not as bad as rap or heavy metal," alternative is not as innocent as it seems. It speaks loudly on several issues, especially to kids who are introspective "thinkers." Parents should continue to listen to, evaluate, and discuss alternative music with their kids. Like all other types of music, it is "a window to your child's soul," giving you clues to the questions and concerns that your teen may indeed be dealing with.

Sample of Alternative Singers and Groups:

U2	Soundgarden
Depeche Mode	Alice in Chains
Sinéad O'Connor	Shakespear's Sister
Tracy Chapman	Blind Melon
The B-52's	Counting Crows
World Party	Beck
EMF	The Cranberries
Nine Inch Nails	Curve
10,000 Maniacs	Radiohead
My Bloody Valentine	Belly
Sisters of Mercy	Gin Blossoms
Nirvana	Kate Bush
Hüsker Dü	The Juliana Hatfield
Teenage Fanclub	Three
Matthew Sweet	Matthew Sweet
Pearl Jam	Screaming Trees
Temple of the Dog	Primus
Toad the Wet Sprocket	Possum Dixon
R.E.M.	Tori Amos
Annie Lennox	The Breeders
The Alarm	Smashing Pumpkins
Midnight Oil	Afghan Whigs
The Cure	Bjork
The Cult	Verve
Jesus Jones	Redd Kross
Red Hot Chili Peppers	The Lemonheads
Jesus & Mary Chain	Stone Temple Pilots
The Replacements	Dinosaur Jr.
Nick Cave and the Bad Seeds	Jesus Lizard
Sonic Youth	Tool
Chills	4 Non Blondes
The Smithereens	Concrete Blonde
The Soup Dragons	

Rap

The term *rap music* was first coined around 1976 as black disc jockeys in New York dance clubs began to play extended dance tracks by using two turntables and a sound mixer. By switching from one record to the other without stopping the music, they would get the crowd whipped up into an excited dance frenzy while using a microphone to insert their own personal commentary. As the popularity of this new urban dance craze grew, rap music was born. MCs (masters of ceremonies) developed and recited elaborate and lengthy rhymes.

DJs (disc jockeys) would back them up by playing and mixing dance records on the turntables.

In 1979, the Sugarhill Gang released the first big rap hit, "Rapper's Delight." From then on, rap grew as a distinctively black urban alternative to the white music so popular on the radio. It provided a musical background for the hip-hop culture of the inner city, a complex urban street culture that included break dancing and graffiti art.

In its early days, rap was exuberant and upbeat and became associated with parties and good times. By the early 1980s, it had begun to grow in popularity as it helped young African-Americans develop a sense of unity and identity.

In 1986 record producer Rick Rubin took a marketing gamble that forever changed the face of rap music and opened the doors of rap to a white audience. The gamble was the remake of Aerosmith's seventies hit "Walk This Way" by the rap group Run-D.M.C., which featured both groups on the song and video. The song was an MTV and radio hit. Shortly thereafter, the first all-white rap group, the Beastie Boys, exploded onto the music scene, selling four million copies of their first album. The album was a foretaste of mainstream rap's move towards a more explicit nature. More and more new rap was filled with explicit sexuality, violence, and rebellion.

Interest in rap continues to increase among white teenagers, especially rap that is defiantly black. While many have tried to explain the reason for this unusual phenomenon, one thing is clear: Rap music has found an audience that extends beyond the bounds of race and class. It is here to stay. Teenagers love rap. Rappers will tell you that they are singing about life: the sexually explicit and violent

While rappers claim that they are only reflecting the ugliness of life (which in many instances is true), they are also educating and directing impressionable young kids, both black and white, with those same ugly messages.

nature of life in the ghetto. Rappers see themselves as "Black America's CNN."[90] B-Real of the group Cypress Hill says, "We're journalists. I'll take an experience that involves one of us or a friend, and I'll explain what happened and why."[91] After a Los Angeles police officer pushed him onto a parked car, he wrote the song "Pigs." When rap music serves to address racism and other unresolved social issues, it can be a constructive force. Sadly, the constructive content often gets lost in the forest of rap's destructive messages.

Rappers also believe that they serve a prophetic role by communicating messages that show how those stuck in the ghetto can cope and survive. While some groups advocate positive routes to change (Arrested Development), many of the more popular groups promote and encourage violence and revenge against any and all oppressors. Regardless of the method they advocate, all serious rappers believe that the music will play a crucial role in bringing about social change.

The genre's diverse audience is getting the message. A recent study of seven hundred black teenagers from the East Coast and California, entitled *Reaching the Hip-Hop Generation,* reveals "that rappers are the only public figures still respected by black youth, the only potential role models left."[92] In addition, an entire generation of white teenagers are listening to rap and being exposed to black culture for the first time. The Recording Industry Association of America reports that 53 percent of rap CD's are sold to whites.[93]

Rap's power in popular culture is evident in its ability to influence conversation and attire. Rap has a complex vocabulary that is difficult to decipher. Some of the more common terms are *def* (good), *def jams* (good music), *dis* (disrespect), *skeezers* (women), *wack* (bad), the *wild thing* (sex), *forty* (a forty-ounce bottle of malt liquor), and *daddy mack* (pimp). It is not unusual to find white suburban kids communicating in the language of hip-hop. Parents who want to know more about the meanings behind rap's legion of terms should simply ask.

While those who wish to make a hip-hop fashion statement will find that styles change rather quickly, there are some recent hip-hop fashion trends that speak to the music's ability to influence kids from mainstream America. Kids are wearing what they see in the videos. Consider the recent surge in sales of sports attire. Fitted baseball caps, especially those sporting logos made popular by rap stars, are a must-have item for boys. NFL and NBA parkas and jackets by Starter found their way into youth culture through rap music. At the start of 1993, plaid shirts and jackets were preferred items. The baggy look with drooping pants was first modeled by rap singers. Pullover stocking caps known as "skullies" are back in style thanks to many rappers. One of the most unusual fashion statements was made popular by the young rap duo

Kris Kross when they appeared wearing their clothes backwards. The list of rap's influences on clothing and style goes on and on.

It would be unfair to say that all rap music is bad. Much of the music contains challenging messages that need to be heard. But how can a parent begin to discern the difference? While listening to your teen's music is the best way to learn, it is helpful to know that most rap can be divided into one of three specific subgenres, each with its own distinctive message and theme.

Party or **pop rap** is danceable music that sells well among white adolescents. Since it usually doesn't contain profanity or explicit violence, most parents believe that it is harmless, and much of it is. But much of party rap music is explicitly or implicitly sexual in nature. L.L. Cool J is one example of the attitude that exists among rappers. His name stands for "Ladies Love Cool James," certainly not the most humble name a man could adopt for himself. His song "Big Ole' Butt" describes his sexual attraction and escapades with three different girls who all have "big butts." Rappers Sir Mix-A-Lot ("Baby Got Back") and Wreckx-N-Effect ("Rump Shaker") had hits describing a similar fetish.

Many parents are surprised to discover that 1992's big rap duo Kris Kross aren't exactly squeaky-clean. Not yet teens themselves, Chris Kelly and Chris Smith had never rapped when they were "discovered" walking through an Atlanta mall. After a few months of coaching, they became the fastest-selling new artists in twenty years as a result of their hit song "Jump." Their schoolboy innocence and cute looks have led many parents to accept Kris Kross without any clue as to their worldview and the resulting message of their music. Of particular concern is the duo's rap names. They are known as Daddy Mack and Mack Daddy. In rap language *mack* means "to have sex." A *mack daddy* or *daddy mack* is a pimp. Armed with this knowledge, parents have a better idea what the boys are rapping about when they say, "My name is Daddy Mack baby / I'm totally krossed out / Catchin' all the ladies / This age I should be playin' with toys / But instead I put my head / Into makin' ya make noise."

Parents should examine the lyrics, videos, and themes of the party rap that is popular among preteens and adolescents. Rappers like TLC, Vanilla Ice, Tone Loc, Marky Mark, and Naughty by Nature (just to name a few) have all produced songs with sexually explicit lyrics and themes.

Alternative rap is the most positive and hope-filled subgenre of rap, suggesting constructive responses to racism and oppression.

Groups like De La Soul, A Tribe Called Quest, Jungle Brothers, and Queen Latifah have deliberately reacted against rap's aggressive and violent elements. P.M. Dawn sings positive messages of peace and hope in a way that might classify them as "rap hippies."

While alternative rap is relatively new, the group Arrested Development represents the potential positive effect that the continued growth of this type of music might have. The soul-searching and hope-filled lyrics in their song "Tennessee" read, "But Lord, I ask you / Be my Guiding Force and Truth. . . . Take me to another place / Take me to another land / Make me forget all that hurts me / Let me understand your plan."

While alternative rap is trying to move the genre in a positive direction, **gangsta'** or **hard-core rap** is moving to the opposite pole. This controversial rap's basic message is that life in the ghetto is terrible. The only answer is to survive and overcome in any way possible, including anti-Semitism, racism, police bashing, sexual violence, and anger. Sadly, this type of music is becoming so popular that fallen-from-fame artists like Hammer, New Kids on the Block, and Vanilla Ice are placing their hopes for a successful comeback on their newly adopted gangster images.

Critics accuse gangsta' rap of doing nothing to improve life in the ghetto. On the other hand, there are very few people who would say that it doesn't reflect the ugliness and hopelessness of living in poverty. *New Statesman & Society* magazine describes the music this way:

> Hard-core rap's psychology is survivalist, a fortress mentality that veers between delusions of invulnerability and a feeling of being under siege from all sides. What this soul on ice fears most is the thawing warmth of female desire. Gangster rap typically represents women as gold-digging, treacherous "bitches," or receptacles for male lust. . . . Some rap groups have found a way round this by deflecting their aggression towards its "proper" target: the "system."[94]

Rapper Ice Cube calls himself "the nigga you love to hate." He sends this taped message over the airwaves of his very own pirate radio station that expresses the core philosophy of gangsta':

> We will not be silenced. We will say what we want to say and do what we want to do without fear, and if you want to try and censor what we want to do, this means war, straight up. Hardcore will never die.[95]

It won't come as any kind of surprise that Ice Cube's songs are filled with images of death. "Black Korea" seems to encourage violence against Korean store owners. "Now I Gotta' Wet Cha" is about shooting people and even makes mention of killing the Rodney King jurors and cooking their hearts for dinner.

The catalog of hard-core gangsta' rap songs is thick and disturbing. For example, Willie D suggests that Rodney King should be murdered because of his appeal for an end to the L.A. riots in his song "F___ Rodney King." N.W.A. encourages violence against the police in their song "F___ the Police."

Sample of Rap Singers and Groups:

L.L. Cool J	Wreckx-N-Effect
Public Enemy	Biz Markie
Beastie Boys	Cypress Hill
Tone Loc	Digital Underground
The 2 Live Crew	EPMD
Young M.C.	Kool Moe Dee
Heavy D. & the Boyz	Mellow Man Ace
Ice Cube	Salt'N'Pepa
Vanilla Ice	Slick Rick
Queen Latifah	Sugarhill Gang
The Geto Boys	A Tribe Called Quest
Marky Mark	YoYo Honey
Arrested Development	Leaders of the New School
P.M. Dawn	Snoop Doggy Dogg
Jungle Brothers	Tupac Amaru Shakur
House of Pain	Boss
Sister Souljah	Digable Planets
Kris Kross	Onyx
Run-D.M.C.	Kool G. Rap
Fat Boys	CB4
3rd Bass	Father M.C.
Ice-T	Casual
N.W.A.	Guru
MC Lyte	Shabba Ranks
Hammer	Tha Alkaholiks
Big Daddy Kane	Dr. Dre
Sir Mix-A-Lot	Wu-Tang Clan
Naughty by Nature	Funkdoobiest
Oaktown's 3.5.7	Brand Nubian
Eazy-E	The Pharcyde
Another Bad Creation	Intelligent Hoodlum
Deee-Lite	Born Jamericans
M.C. Ren	KRS-1
De La Soul	Masta Ace Inc.
TLC	Hi-Five
MC Brains	Judgment Night
Das EFX	

Parents whose kids are listening to gangsta' and hard-core rap need to be aware that this is some of the most angry, violent, and sexually explicit music on the market. While it can serve to raise awareness of racial inequality and injustice in America, it serves the dual purpose of functioning as a call to arms and a manual for ghetto warfare.

In summary: Rap serves as the voice of poor black youth in urban culture. As such, it is a valuable cross-cultural window into a world that many of us have never experienced. It reaches all races. Suburban kids may grab onto its hard-core elements for some excitement and relief from boredom. While much of rap is nothing more than musical pornography and violence, we should not give in to the temptation to write off the entire genre. Parents need to exercise discernment and discretion, deciding which rap music belongs in the garbage and which can be used to generate Christlike compassion and understanding for individuals caught in the vicious cycle of poverty, fatherlessness, and hopelessness. Rap has the capacity to serve with equal strength as either a positive or a negative molder and shaper of teens.

Heavy metal

Of all the types of music popular among teenagers today, there is no genre that has been as enduring and distinct as heavy metal. It is difficult to pinpoint when and where heavy metal was born. Rock music historians can't agree whether to give credit to Led Zeppelin, Black Sabbath, or Steppenwolf. What they do agree on is that Steppenwolf's 1967 hit "Born to Be Wild" contained several elements of modern heavy metal along with the words *heavy metal thunder* in one verse of the song.

A look at heavy metal's bands, themes, fans, and unique features proves that heavy metal has endured because it serves a purpose. Many of the music's followers are outcasts who have found meaning and acceptance in the world of heavy metal. At the root of heavy metal's attraction is its obsession with power. The sound of power is echoed by the continued beating of elaborate drum sets, particularly the low *boom-boom* of the amplified bass drum. The loud thumping of the bass guitar can literally be felt in the chests of concertgoers. A screaming lead guitar competes with a screaming lead singer whose throat-wrenching vocals combine with the instruments to create a musical experience that I once heard described as "music to melt your face off."

Thematically, heavy-metal music addresses where kids are at developmentally. All teens go through periods of questioning and change.

Sadly, many endure a painful adolescence alone due to alienation from family, adult culture, and the mainstream peer group. It is this type of hurting teen who is especially drawn to heavy metal as they internalize the music's message.

Many heavy-metal musicians also grew up in difficult home situations where they felt "powerless." Kirk Hammett, the lead guitarist of the band Metallica, says:

> Some of us in the band grew up in family situations that weren't healthy. My dad was an alcoholic. And my parents split up. All the problems that come with that sort of thing made a mark on me. From the time I was 11 or 12 till I was, like, 16 or 17, it really made me angry—and one of the few escapes I had was music. And, for a lot of the same reasons, that's why I still play now.[96]

Heavy metal is music for outcasts—kids who have never found their place at home, at school, or in society. It speaks to the simmering discontent of its listeners, providing them with an identity that they can't find anywhere else. As a result, very few kids who are popular at school or who come from healthy homes become an active part of the heavy-metal subculture.

Like rap, heavy metal originally had a small, yet dedicated, homogeneous following. However, due to effective marketing by record companies, exposure on MTV, and the declining condition of childhood in America, an increasing number of kids find themselves attracted to the music's messages and themes. It is not surprising that twenty-one of MTV's 1993 Top 100 Videos featured heavy-metal bands.

Heavy metal attempts to give power to the powerless by suggesting one of two approaches to life.

APPROACH #1: Let loose and live a life of hedonistic excess. Sexual promiscuity, perversion, and substance abuse become the key elements in life. Aerosmith's endless parade of songs celebrating lusty sexual escapades are a good example of this party-hearty attitude. Their song "Love in an Elevator" recounts a hasty sexual encounter between floors. The video of their song "Rag Doll" leaves everyone sure of the fact that the video's main character, Steven Tyler, has slept with all the women in the neighborhood. Def Leppard's hit "Let's Get Rocked" encourages adolescent hedonism and rails against responsibility, obedience, and respect for authority. When heavy metal pursues this theme, kids are encouraged to live for today, lose themselves in physical pleasure, and forget about all the concerns of yesterday.

APPROACH #2: Totally rebel against a world that is hopeless. This kind of heavy metal encourages kids to feel power by running their own lives independent of any adult guidance. In this vein, heavy metal attempts to take whatever is seen as respectable, acceptable, and orderly in society and turn it upside down, replacing it with disorder, upheaval, and chaos. The music inevitably is filled with images of conflict, violence, satanism, dismemberment, death, and the grotesque. Dave Mustaine, the lead singer and guitarist of Megadeath, says that he thinks of his band as a group of "modern troubadours who are spreading joy and harmony by saying 's___, f___, p___, kill' and all the rest of it."[97] The band Anthrax, long known for their fatalistic and rebellious music, sings "Wasting your life / No future is bright / Dancing on your grave / Living like a slave" in their song "Efilnikufesin." (If you want to understand the angry flavor of the song, sound out the title backwards.)

Heavy-metal concerts function like church, where disenfranchised kids come to find comfort and solidarity in their pain and alienation. Together they party, celebrate, and share their anger at the system. As the music pounds, kids thrust clenched fists in the air, keeping time with the music. "Headbangers" thrash their heads up and down to the music's furious pace. Most concerts feature a "mosh pit" directly in front of the stage where kids "mosh," a chaotic and disorganized dance where participants frenetically stomp, flail, and bounce off of each other. Bands and concertgoers often drink beer, smoke marijuana, and "get wasted" as part of the concert ritual. The concert experience leaves kids with the feeling that no matter what happens, they have become one unified voice of power, along with the band, against society's oppressive and repressive norms.

The unwritten code of heavy-metal videos requires that the video contain some elements of the group singing in concert or at a studio. Heavy-metal expert Deena Weinstein describes the typical heavy-metal video this way:

> Visions of sexually provocative women, acts of revolt against figures of authority such as parents or teachers, and scenes of general disorder are usually intercut with the actual or simulated concert scenes. . . . Rebellion against the dominant culture is the visual kick to compensate for the lack of the sonic

power of the stereo system or of the live heavy metal performance.[98]

Whether they are attending a concert, at school, or just hanging out at the mall, kids who are into heavy-metal dress in an easily identifiable manner. This dress serves as a uniform for kids who have joined forces and finally found acceptance with other "metal heads." Their long hair, black T-shirts featuring band logos and tour information, and leather or denim jackets all combine to say, "We are different from everyone else, we love each other, and we are in this together."

As with other genres of popular music, heavy metal has spawned several subgenres, each with its own unique sound, themes, lifestyle, and following.

If heavy-metal music is described in relative terms, the most "innocent" subgenre is **pop metal** (also known as melodic metal, lite metal, glam metal, and party metal). The majority of MTV heavy-metal videos, heavy-metal Top 40 songs, and heavy-metal best-sellers are pop metal. The songs are more melodic with a tendency toward nice harmonies in the vocals, making the lyrics easier to hear and understand. Pop metal often strays from the conventional faster forms of heavy metal with an occasional slow ballad that, while slower and lower in volume, is still easily identified as part of the genre.

Pop metal's performers usually adopt a "prettier" look than the typical blue-collar working clothes of most heavy-metal bands, explaining their attraction to an audience that is younger and includes a lot of teenage girls. Lusty love and romance are at the heart of pop metal's themes. Sex is nothing more than a celebration of life to experience in every possible way and as often as possible. The lyrics also stress reckless involvement in anything else that is fun. Many of the bands reinforce their lyrical messages with videos and album covers that portray scantily clad women as "boy toys." This life-is-a-party mentality has been preached in recent years by bands like Mötley Crüe, Van Halen, Aerosmith, Skid Row, Def Leppard, Guns n' Roses, Poison, and Slaughter.

Aerosmith's recent song "Young Lust" includes a lyrical warning to parents: "You'd better keep your daughter inside / Or she's gonna get a dose of my pride. . . ." Lead singer Steven Tyler's comments about the song are representative of the pop-metal mentality: "I mean, what do you want to be telling your child? That lust is bad? Get outta here."[99]

Preteens and early adolescents who are discovering and experiencing sexual urges for the first time will find most pop-metal music exciting, entertaining, and educational. Parents should be aware of pop metal's tendency towards sexually explicit lyrics and ability to teach kids that love is nothing more or less than lust.

Black metal is the second subgenre and the type of heavy metal that has caused the most concern among parents, teachers, church leaders, and law-enforcement officials. Also known as death metal, hardcore, splatter metal, and Satan metal, it is preoccupied with occult and violent themes.

Music critic David Browne has accurately described the sounds and themes of black metal:

> The front man isn't singing, he's belching. The guitars and drums imitate the rapid heartbeat of someone looking up as the guillotine blade falls, and the songs are obsessed with decaying corpses, the nuclear immolation of the earth, blood-drenched massacres, and other everyday situations.[100]

The songs of the band Coven provide an example of lyrics with satanic themes. The song "Blessed Is the Black" tells listeners "Blessed are the wicked / Cursed are the weak." In "Burn the Cross" they attack Christianity with the lyrics "Your God is dead now and you die / Satan rules at last."

Black-metal concerts, album covers, videos, T-shirts, and other visual outlets reinforce these themes. The performers often dress in ghoulish costumes. Stage shows include skulls, pentagrams, blood, instruments of torture, red lights, smoke, and a variety of other satanic symbols and effects that combine to create a hellish atmosphere.

It is difficult to know for sure how many black-metal bands consciously practice satanism or witchcraft. Bands like Venom, Slayer, and Morbid Angel leave little question as to their allegiance to Satan. Yet most bands would deny any active participation in the occult. Instead they claim that they utilize satanic themes and symbols as a sign of youthful rebellion against authority and moral order, that the music serves more as an outlet for angry, displaced kids. Guitarist Trevor Peres of the band Obituary says, "Everybody has a lot of anger in them, so this music is a release. By the time you're done hearing an album, you can leave the house with a totally better outlook on life."[101]

One of the most disturbing interviews I've ever read sheds light on the inspiration behind some black metal. *Rolling Stone* columnist Mikal Gilmore interviewed Tom Araya, the vocalist and lyricist of the band Slayer. While the band's early songs were filled with references to Satan and hell, their emphasis has shifted to include themes of political oppression, warfare, and murder. One of their most chilling songs is "Dead Skin Mask," about mass murderer Ed Gein. The following excerpt from the interview describes the band's obsessions with such subjects.

> "And then I [Araya] came across another book about this guy named Albert Fish, who murdered these little boys and then ate their penises. He said he tried eating their testicles, but he found them too chewy." As he speaks, Araya's face gradually lights up until, by the time he gets to the part about chewy testicles, he is smiling delightedly. After a moment or two, he catches what he's doing and blushes. "You know," Araya says, "I can sit here and talk about mutilation with a smile on my face because of the things these people do, but I do know the difference between wrong and right. I mean, I can sit and think about murder, and sometimes I think it would be real easy to do. And then I write the stuff, and for me it works as kind of a release. I figure, I've thought about it, I know what it would feel like—and that's good enough for me."[102]

The key issue is how to discern those who believe their message from those who don't. If it is difficult for adults to tell the difference, how can we expect children and teens to differentiate? The bottom line is that we can't. Black metal, whether meant to be serious or a joke, often serves as a gateway to involvement in the occult. In that sense, it should never be viewed as just a funny joke.

Kids who listen to black metal are typically white males in their middle teens. They come from either blue-collar or broken/fragile home situations. Plagued by a lack of self-worth, black metal gives them a feeling of power that can overcome their problems, particularly if those "problems" are the parents and peers who make them miserable.

Wise parents who find that their kids are listening to black-metal music will do more than try to remove the music from their home. They will try to discover and address the deeper problems their children are having. While the music can open the door to the occult for our teens, black metal more often gives parents a window into the lost, hurting, alienated, and angry souls of those who listen.

Thrash metal is the last subgenre of heavy metal and is often referred to as metal core, speed metal, punk metal, power metal, and hard core. The entire thrash-metal package oozes rebellion, hopelessness, and chaos.

The loudest and fastest of the heavy-metal types, thrash metal is like a never-ending high-decibel car crash. There is no place for melody and harmony; the rhythms are hysterical and frenzied. Vocalists growl and snarl their way through the songs, their vocal chords sounding like they have swallowed boiling acid. The music is powerful, disorderly, and full of rage.

Thrash metal's themes reinforce the sound of the music. The lyrics bemoan the hopeless state of the world, society, and all of its institutions, focusing "on the bleak but concrete horrors of the real or possibly real world: the isolation and alienation of individuals, the corruption of those in power, and the horrors done by people to one another and the environment."[103] It preaches that anarchy, violence, retreat, and even death and suicide are legitimate responses to a world on the verge of collapse. It should come as no surprise that thrash metal appeals to white teenage boys whose problems and anger are deep-seated. Commiserating with others who feel similar pain is seen as one way of facing problems in a world that has no answers.

The performers are typically dressed in simple blue-collar type clothes. There are no elaborate costumes or stage sets. The look is sloppy. Jeans, T-shirts, denim jackets, and flannel shirts are thrash-metal staples. The clothing reflects the content of the music.

Metallica is the band that is credited with inventing thrash metal. At the outset, the band felt that their newly discovered beat plugged right into the frustration, instability, and suppressed emotions of angry teens. Their first album was originally going to be titled *Easter's Canceled; The Body's Been Found.* If you can get past the blasphemous nature of the title, you can hear its hopeless tone. The band then decided to change the title to *Metal Up Your A___*, with the album cover featuring a picture of a sword rising up out of a toilet. *Kill 'Em All* was the title that they finally settled on.

While it maintains a religious following among extremely unhappy and disturbed teens, more and more of the "kids next door" are listening to the hopeless sounds of thrash. MTV is giving more and more exposure to thrash bands, as evidenced by the inclusion of four Metallica videos in the 1992 Top 100 Videos list.

In summary: Heavy metal speaks to and for a generation of misdirected and confused kids shut off and unloved by family, friends, and the world around them. Understanding the message and meaning of heavy metal can help us understand and reach the many kids for whom heavy metal has served as teacher, family, and friend. Most of the kids who are heavy into heavy metal are simply looking for someone to love and understand them.

Sample of Heavy Metal Singers and Groups:

Pop Metal
Bon Jovi
Cinderella
Van Halen
David Lee Roth
Europe
Aerosmith
Skid Row
Winger
Lita Ford
KISS
Tesla
Billy Idol
Extreme
Firehouse
Damn Yankees
Mötley Crüe
Def Leppard
Guns n' Roses
Poison
Whitesnake
Warrant
Living Colour
Britny Fox
Great White
Ratt
Slaughter
Queensrÿche
Saigon Kick

Black Metal
W.A.S.P.
Impaler
Iron Maiden
Judas Priest
Black Sabbath
Ozzy Osbourne
Slayer
Blessed Death
Corpse
Celtic Frost

Napalm Death
Cadaver
Morbid Angel
Deicide
Lizzy Borden
Piledriver
Nuclear Death
Venom
King Diamond
Rotting Corpse
AC/DC
Danzig
Carcass
Entombed
Obituary
Malevolent Creation
Type O Negative

Thrash Metal
Motorhead
Anthrax
Overkill
Circle Jerks
Metal Church
Stormtroopers of Death
Prong
Metallica
Suicidal Tendencies
Megadeath
Crumbsuckers
Ramones
Agnostic Front
Ministry
Helmet
Rollins Band
Body Count
Revolting Cocks
Annihilator
Nuclear Assault
Vio-lence
Sacred Reich

▮ IT'S YOUR TURN

Music has power. Our extended look at the world of popular music has only scratched the surface of music's ability to mold and shape the values, attitudes, and behaviors of our children and teens.

The world of music changes constantly; new bands come and old bands go. While the task may seem overwhelming, parents can and must take the time to know what is happening on the popular music scene. While your children may or may not spend four to six hours a day listening to and watching music, they are living in a world where most teens do. Our kids are part of a youth culture that is defined and directed by the music and musicians they listen to. By knowing the world of music, you will be better equipped to know your teen, understand the world of teenagers, and lead your child into a healthy adulthood.

In short, your kids know music. The music industry knows your kids. Get to know your kids by getting to know their music.

MEDIA:
WHAT IS IT TEACHING
YOUR TEEN?

░░

**Unless you move to a mountaintop, you can't opt
out of today's media culture. Media no longer just
influence our culture. They are our culture.**

Rosalind Silver[1]

SOMETIME DURING THE midsixties, three little boys got in big
trouble. Their behavior around the house was increasingly out of
control. While they claimed it was all being done in fun, there were
times when their make-believe eye pokes, kicks, slaps, and pratfalls
led to anger, tears, and real fights. It wasn't long before their mother and
father discovered that the boys were only imitating antics they had
seen during their daily TV dose of *The Three Stooges*. My brothers and
I still maintain our innocence, but that didn't stop our parents from
removing Moe, Larry, and Curley from our TV diet for a few weeks.

It has been said that art imitates life. But there is a very real sense
in which life imitates art. The experience of my parents' three impressionable young boys is representative of all children, teens, and
adults. The fact is that whether we realize it or not, what we see, hear,
and experience in and through the media influences our values,
attitudes, and behaviors.

In the last chapter, we examined the role of popular music in
shaping and defining reality for children and teens. But the heavy
media involvement of our kids is not limited solely to the world of
popular music. Television, movies, advertisements, radio, and magazines serve as surrogate parents and educators. Like music, they
exercise a powerful ability to define reality. Neil Postman has said:

> Whether we are experiencing the world through the lens of
> speech or the printed word or the television camera, our media-
> metaphors classify the world for us, sequence it, frame it, en-
> large it, reduce it, color it, argue a case for what the world is like.[2]

This chapter examines the influential role that these other media outlets play in the lives of our children and teens. My goal is not to provide you with an exhaustive critique but to raise your awareness of several trends and issues that should be of concern to those who care about kids. While the media has the potential to serve as either a positive or negative force, this chapter focuses on some of the more negative matters related to today's television, movies, advertisements, radio, and magazines.

Is the TV On at Your House?

There's a house in my neighborhood that stands as a late-night monument to the place of television in American culture. Night after night, the eerie blue glow of the television provides the only visible illumination in the house. For many men, women, and children, TV has taken its place as an illuminator, clarifying and explaining life.

Television first captured the imagination of America at the 1939 World's Fair. Network service began in the late forties, and by the 1950s the medium was growing by leaps and bounds.

In his book *Redeeming Television,* Quentin Schultze calls television "one of the major educators of modern society."[3] As television communicates its lessons to a passive and usually uncritical audience, it becomes, as communications theorist George Comstock has said, "an unavoidable and unremitting factor in shaping what we are and what we will become."[4] We are all vulnerable to the messages of television. Among other things, television teaches us how to resolve problems, how to relate to others, how families work, what to wear, how to talk, how to walk, and how to love. Carole Lieberman, a Beverly Hills psychiatrist who frequently serves as a TV script consultant, says:

> Kids are especially vulnerable to these messages. The younger ones watch and frequently mimic the actions and sayings of their favorite characters, like current rage Bart Simpson. That's why millions of children all across America woke up one morning saying, "Don't have a cow, man."[5]

Like popular music, television's ability to define reality and guide children and teens through life has increased over time in proportion to the decreasing influence of the family, school, and church. Parental influences deteriorate when parents are absent from the home or oblivious to what their children and teens are watching. These children learn about life and the outside world from someone other than Mom or Dad. All too often, that someone is the electronic baby-sitter. As long as they have the ability to turn on the TV and operate the remote, children of all ages have unlimited access to television's good and bad, including information and programming that is often unsuitable for adults.

Television viewing facts and figures

The famous children's writer E. B. White once predicted that television "is going to be the test of the modern world. . . . We shall stand or fall by television."[6] If White was right, then television's pervasiveness in our culture and world should cause us to evaluate ourselves carefully to see if we are standing tall or teetering dangerously.

In 1946 there were 10,000 television sets in America; by 1950, 10.5 million sets; by 1960, 54 million sets.[7] The Nielsen Media Research organization reported that by 1989, 92 million households owned televisions and two-thirds of those households owned two or more sets and also VCRs.[8] One study reported that by the mideighties, there were an average of 3.4 television sets in each household where a young adolescent lived![9]

Not only are Americans faced with choosing which of their TVs to watch, but they are also given a smorgasbord of channel choices. The average American household now receives thirty-one different channels. Only 7 percent pick up fewer than seven channels.[10] Industry experts predict that it won't be long until the average home will have a choice of five hundred channels and a host of new TV technologies at its fingertips.

Living rooms, family rooms, and dens across America have become television's temples. Typically, the furniture is arranged so that every seat in the house affords an unobstructed view of the tube. And every day parents, children, and teens across America gather in the temple, together and alone, to view the electronic god. Studies have shown that "program content is not the principal factor in assembling an audience for television." . . . We just go and

Through the miracle of TV, our children can witness war, murder, rape, hate, prejudice, sexual promiscuity, and a host of other inappropriate behaviors before they are even allowed to cross the street alone!

turn it on "when no other activity is preferable, obligatory, or necessary."[11]

How much TV do we watch? The average household in America has the television on over seven hours a day.[12] Households with children have the set on for a total of fifty-eight hours and forty-three minutes during the average week.[13] The average American child aged two to five years watches over twenty-seven hours of TV per week.[14] This means that these young children, who are unable to distinguish fact from fantasy, will have spent roughly six thousand hours watching television before they begin formal schooling! One study conducted in the early eighties offered four and five year olds the choice of giving up television or giving up their fathers. One-third said they would give up Daddy.[15]

According to a survey conducted for the Corporation for Public Broadcasting, children aged six to seventeen years watch an average of 2.5 hours of TV on school days and 4.33 hours a day on the weekend.[16] More specifically, teenagers between the ages of twelve and seventeen watch an average of twenty-two hours a week.[17] Forty-seven percent of school-age children have a television set in their room.[18] After sleep and time spent in school, children and teens spend more time watching TV than any other out-of-school activity.[19] By the time the average American child graduates from high school, he or she will have watched about twenty-three thousand hours of television, as compared to the eleven thousand hours spent in the school classroom.[20]

It's not just children and teens who are spending countless hours in the temple. Three-quarters of college students have their own televisions in their dorm rooms. Half of them have a VCR, and half have cable.[21] The move into the adult years brings an increase in weekly viewing with the average American adult watching anywhere from twenty-seven to forty-two hours of TV a week depending on age and gender.[22] After time spent sleeping and at work, adults spend the greatest amount of their time in front of the TV.[23] It is not surprising that one-quarter of Americans over the age of eighteen say they wouldn't give up TV, even for a million dollars.[24]

We have become, as Quentin Schultze has suggested, a nation of "grazing videots."[25] Like cattle eating grass in a pasture, we sit comfortably in our chairs flicking the remote and satisfying our televisual hunger with hour upon hour of TV's oftentimes unhealthy fare.

What are we learning from television?

There are those in our culture who have had it with television.

Believing that the medium is inherently evil, they call us to lock our sets in the attic or throw them out. But we need to recognize that television can and does teach us and our children positive messages about life. TV can raise our awareness to problems in the world; it gives us insight into the pressing issues of our time; it opens us up to the wonders of the world by taking us to places we have never been; it makes us laugh. And it can stimulate spontaneous discussion on important issues when families view together.

But too often, we give television and all of its characters, messages, morals, and values, whether good or bad, unlimited and unchallenged access into our homes and lives. Columnist Richard Reeves makes a good point when he writes, "If TV is producing trash, guess what it considers its waste dumps. That's right: your living room, your brain and your soul."[26]

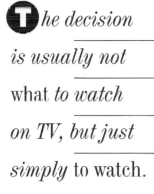

he decision is usually not what *to watch* on TV, but just *simply* to watch.

While television can and does educate viewers in positive and constructive ways, there are some alarming trends. Children and teens, as they move through the crucial developmental stages of childhood and adolescence, are especially susceptible to television's negative and destructive themes and messages. The remainder of this section offers an overview of several negative thematic emphases of television that kids see on a regular basis and that merit continued parental awareness and attention.

Violence. A few years ago, television viewers in parts of Pennsylvania were watching the broadcast of a live press conference at which a state official was making an announcement regarding some financial matters. To the horror of everyone watching, he pulled a loaded pistol from his jacket, made a few frantic remarks, inserted the gun into his mouth, and pulled the trigger. The TV audience had witnessed an actual suicide. Several stations across the state were chastised for their decision to run the uncut tape of the incident on newscasts later that day.

On an evening in early 1992, viewers watching the NBC network news were treated to another horrific piece of videotape. The tape showed a fatal meeting at a Florida cemetery where the burial of a teenage suicide victim had just concluded. The dead girl's father, divorced from her mother, arrived at the cemetery and angrily blamed his ex-wife for their daughter's death. The video showed the man pulling a gun and murdering the woman. The TV audience had witnessed an actual murder. The similar airing and re-airing of actual video violence served to make Rodney King and Reginald Denny household names.

Why is the American news media showing more and more acts of real-life violence? The answer is simple. The name of the game in television is to build an audience, and violence is an effective means to gain viewers. One Fox Network executive admitted that the highest rated segments of its *Reporters* series were the ones that featured lots of blood.[27]

In an effort to boost ratings and compete for greater audience share, network and cable broadcast outlets have provided viewers with a steady and graphic dose of televised violence. In February of 1992, the NBC series *I Witness Video* came on the air and showed a replay of murders that had been taped by amateur camera operators. *TV Guide* reported, "For the first time in history, a major network started programming death as entertainment."[28] Tabloid TV and reality shows like *A Current Affair, Unsolved Mysteries,* and *America's Most Wanted* pepper promotional spots featuring the violent and sensational content of upcoming episodes throughout the broadcast day. Talk shows regularly cover topics ranging from sexual violence to murderous love triangles. Phil Donahue said that he would go so far as to broadcast an execution.[29]

TV's violent trend has even served to make real-life criminals rich. One example was the well-publicized 1992 attempted-murder case of seventeen-year-old Amy Fisher, the "Long Island Lolita." Hollywood agents and TV producers scrambled to get the rights to her story. Tabloid-TV show *Hard Copy* reportedly offered $200,000 for those rights. Fisher's attorney offered exclusive rights to her story to anyone who would post her two-million-dollar bail. Several networks produced made-for-TV movies about the case. This type of movie is not unusual. Forty percent of the prime-time movies produced by the networks are "true" stories based on criminal acts and cases.[30] The Fisher incident has already generated at least ten million dollars in revenue from books, TV movies, and tabloid shows.[31] Other violent crimes that have paid in similar ways include the Menendez murders (tabloid TV, three books, two TV movies), the attack on figure skater Nancy Kerrigan (tabloid TV, six books, and three movies), and Lorena Bobbit slicing off her husband's penis (tabloid TV, movies, and John Bobbit's line of twenty-dollar *Love Hurts* T-shirts).

One of the most violent shows on television today happens to be targeted at and watched by teenagers. MTV's animated show *Beavis and Butt-Head* draws three times the normal MTV viewing audience. A preshow warning tells viewers that the characters are not real and that they are "dumb, crude, thoughtless, ugly, sexist, and self-destructive. But for some reason, the little wiener-heads make us laugh." These characters' violent and abusive adventures include cutting the head off a praying mantis with a chain saw, using frogs for batting practice, and setting fire to anything and everything they can get their hands on.

Both formal and informal studies show that TV violence has increased over the years. Sherwood Schwartz, the creator of *The Brady Bunch* and *Gilligan's Island,* conducted his own survey of prime-time programming, going back over thirty years. He found that in 1955, there were no violent crime shows on the air during prime-time viewing hours. In 1965, there were six hours of violent programs, including one in the 8 P.M. (EST) slot (a time when children and teens are usually watching). In 1975 there were twenty-one hours of violent shows with two broadcast at 8 P.M. And in 1985, violent programming had increased to twenty-seven hours with nine such shows at 8 P.M.[32]

Other studies measure the exact amounts, types, and distribution of television violence. One study conducted during the fall of 1991 found that nonchildren's cable programs averaged 9.2 violent acts per hour while the broadcast networks had 4 acts per hour. Children's cable programming averaged 17.3 violent acts per hour compared to 32 violent acts per hour on the broadcast networks.[33] The 1990 violence profile completed by the Annenberg School for Communication found that violence on Saturday morning cartoon shows aimed at children feature 26.4 or more violent acts per hour.[34]

While life can be violent and ugly at times, TV paints an unrealistic picture of what real violence is actually like. As a result, our kids can grow up with a false notion of reality. First, violence occurs far more frequently on TV than it does in the real world. The actual real-life violent-crime rate in America is only one-eighth of the violent-crime rate on TV.[35] And second, crime has long-term ramifications and consequences for both the victim and aggressor. Crime hurts and kills people; criminals get caught and go to jail. I have been amazed by some of the stories I have read recounting incidents of violent juvenile crime. Kids don't realize that there are consequences. One teenager was shocked to discover after getting shot that it actually bled and hurt!

What price, if any, do our kids pay for being on the receiving end of TV's hefty diet of violence?

First, television may lead our children and teens to become immune to the horrors of violence. "So, what," says the teen, in response to a mother's horrified reaction to a graphic TV scene. "I've seen all this and much worse before. That's nothing." Our kids risk losing a sense of the true value and dignity of persons when they become insensitive to personal violence as well as violent behavior in society.

Second, children and teens can come to accept violence as a way to solve problems. Playground and backyard conflicts are being settled in ways that would make Dirty Harry proud. Youth-violence expert Deborah Prothrow-Stith says television teaches us that "good guys use violence as a first resort. Any amount of killing is all right, so long as one's cause is just. Violence is a hero's way to solve problems."[36] Dr. Aletha Huston of the University of Kansas says, "We keep pumping children with the messages that violence is the way to solve their problems— and some of it takes hold."[37] As a result, thousands of kids walk the halls of America's high schools and junior highs fearing for their lives each day. Numerous schools across the nation are instituting programs to teach kids that there are options other than fists, knives, and guns in settling disputes.

Third, television violence serves to make kids more aggressive. In 1960, Dr. Leonard Eron studied 875 third-grade boys and girls and discovered there was a direct relationship between the violent TV programs they watched and their aggressiveness in school. He again examined the subjects when they were thirty years old. Those who had watched significant amounts of violent television were more likely to have been convicted of more serious crimes, to be more aggressive when drinking, and to inflict harsher punishment on their children. Concludes Eron, "What one learns about life from the television screen seems to be transmitted even to the next generation."[38]

And finally, kids might begin to imitate some of the more violent behaviors that they have seen on the small screen. In his study on television and violence, Dr. Brandon Centerwall found that following the introduction of television in the U.S., the annual white homicide rate increased by 93 percent from 1945 to 1974. While he doesn't blame TV as the sole factor behind the rise in violence, he concludes that "if, hypothetically, television technology had never been developed, there would today be 10,000 fewer homicides each year in the United States, 70,000 fewer rapes, and 700,000 fewer injurious assaults."[39]

Our children and teens imitate the world around them. Every week they turn on the TV and witness murders, rapes, assaults, gunplay, and a host of other violent activities. Heroes and villains solve problems and settle disputes with violence. What they don't see is the horror and pain of the aftermath. What they don't feel is the physical pain. It shouldn't come as a surprise that America has become the most violent of the industrialized nations with children and teens doing unto others what they have seen done thousands of times over on television.

Sex. Television audiences in 1952 learned that Lucille Ball was with child on the *I Love Lucy Show,* but the word *pregnant* was not allowed to be used. In 1961, Rob and Laura Petrie slept in twin beds separated by a nightstand on *The Dick Van Dyke Show.* TV censors banned Barbara Eden's belly button on the 1965 hit show *I Dream of Jeanie.* In 1978, the lead character in *James at 15* lost his virginity. Ted Danson's character Sam refused to get up from a table on a 1987 episode of *Cheers* because he had an erection. In 1992, *Civil Wars* star Muriel Hemingway appeared naked, with her arms strategically draped over her body. And in 1993, *NYPD Blue,* billed as network TV's first R-rated series, showed a policeman rolling around in bed with a woman, a drunken officer dropping his pants in anticipation of sex with a prostitute, and a policeman seen naked from the rear in the shower, all in it's first few weeks on the air. Yes, television has changed quite a bit over the last thirty years. Sex has gone from a dirty word to a regular event.

> **W**hen violence becomes familiar, it tends to lose its ugly edge and somehow becomes more acceptable as a normal part of everyday life.

Children and teens, struggling to understand and control their developing sexuality, used to rely on Mom and Dad for information about the birds and the bees. But now, if they want, Mom and Dad can allow television to explain the facts of life to their inquisitive children. Exposure to TV allows kids to see and hear numerous instances of sexually explicit, perverse, and violent programming during the crucial years of moral development. And judging from the rising rate of sexual activity among teenagers (and even children), they are following the lead of their TV heroes.

When researcher Barry Sapolsky analyzed one week of prime-time network television during 1989 to compare its sexual content to a week of programming in 1979, he found that sex is playing a bigger and bigger role during prime time. Young viewers are provided with frequent lessons on how to look sexy, act sexy, practice sex, and have sex. Every four minutes characters talk about sex or display sexual behavior—and in 1989, only one verbal reference to intercourse out of a total of ninety-one occurred between a married couple. Sapolsky writes:

> Premarital and extramarital sex is an accepted part of television comedy and drama; marriage is inconsequential. In an era when monogamy in marriage is promoted as an important means to avoid sexually transmitted diseases, sexual titillation abounds among the unmarried.[40]

Rarely does anyone in television's fantasy world ever pay the price of guilt, pregnancy, disease, or a broken relationship. Rather, the focus is always on the pleasurable aspect of freely indulging in promiscuous behavior. Sapolsky concludes:

> If an adolescent watches years of TV where people engage in flirtatious or explicit behavior, these thousands of images over the years will teach them that sex is pleasant—and without consequences.[41]

A 1987 study by Planned Parenthood found that there are a total of sixty-five thousand sexual references broadcast each year during the prime afternoon and evening hours.[42] Most of these references are outside the context of marriage and between all the "beautiful people." Ninety-four percent of the sexual encounters on afternoon soap operas (a favorite among many teenage girls and their mothers) occur between people who are not married to each other.[43] When taken together, what these statistics tell us is that *the average American television viewer now sees nearly fourteen thousand instances of sexual material every year.*[44]

The bottom line is that *sex sells*—it helps the networks and cable outlets to boost ratings and build an audience.[45]

It is not unusual for talk shows to feature an array of sexual oddities, violence, and behavior. By focusing on a few strange and isolated cases, they teach our kids that "this is the way normal people act." The Dallas Association for Decency listed the following as some of the topics discussed on *Donahue* between April and June of 1992: people marrying transsexuals; deviant sexual practices of religious zealots; seduction by a psychopath; deviant sexual abuse by doctors and ministers; I had a baby by my lover but my husband thinks it's his; men who have had sex with hundreds of women; prostitutes and pimps; husbands who slept with the baby-sitter; secretaries who have slept with their bosses; and the woman who slept with a Catholic bishop.[46] Other talk shows have featured married women having affairs, husbands who cheat on pregnant wives, sadomasochism, parents who encourage their kids to have sex at home, and masturbation.

One show even blessed a lesbian marriage. In October 1992, talk-show host Jenny Jones addressed these topics: my daughter slept with all of my husbands; my husband wants me to sleep with his friends; men who marry teenagers; and the Woody Allen Syndrome . . . men who have relationships with their stepdaughters.[47] Antipornography organization Morality in Media says that "the goal of talk show hosts in their blatant exploitation of human misery, human frailties, sexual voyeurs, and sexual dysfunctionals seems to be demystification, destigmatization, and desensitization."[48]

Sexual game shows like *Studs, Personals, Love Stories, Night Games,* and *Love Connection* are naturally attractive to young viewers who are interested in learning more about the romantic feelings and questions that accompany their sexual development. *Studs,* the popular show on the youth-oriented Fox Network, features two male and three female contestants. The two guys have already gone on blind dates with each of the three girls. The host reads a list of the guys' habits while the guys try to guess which girl said what. It is assumed that everybody has already had sex with everybody else, so it's not surprising that the comments are all of a sexual nature: "His hand shot up my skirt like a speeding bullet," "I held on tight and let the roar of his rocket surge through me," and "There's nothing cuter than a man who knows how to finger his puppet" are just three out of thousands of examples.

Children and teens who have access to HBO can tune in to the series *Real Sex.* One episode was described by TV critic Ken Tucker as including "a kinky granny, transvestite parties, and a Nobel laureate who teaches women how to masturbate (apparently men don't need lessons). Now that's entertainment."[49] An earlier episode featured a porn performer who allowed the studio audience to view her cervix with a flashlight through a gynecological instrument.

Voyeurvision is a show that, if its creators have their way, will soon be available across the country on pay-per-view. Presently on the air in New York City, the show stars Lynn Muscarella, a blonde housewife who sits on a brass bed barely clothed in lingerie while assuming suggestive poses. Viewers call the live show and pay five dollars per minute to describe their fantasies to Muscarella. While she looks into the camera and speaks seductively, many of the men who call masturbate.[50]

Granted, many kids may never discover or watch any of these adult-oriented shows. But some do. Most kids will settle in and watch those shows that were created specifically for the teen market. And if they do, they will hear and see the same basic "go ahead and do it" messages of adult TV.

What's Up, Dr. Ruth? appeared on the Lifetime Cable Network in 1989. Strategically placed during the Saturday noon hour, the program is aimed at the teen audience, with this advice to parents:

> You should keep your nose out of the teenager's sex life. The teenager has the right to have or not have sex, using personal judgement. I don't want [parents] to delve into the sex life of their adolescent. With education done at an early age, the child knows where the parent stands.[51]

Popular situation comedies like *Coach, Roseanne, The John Laroquette Show, Wings,* and *Seinfeld* are full of sexual suggestiveness and innuendo.[52] While these shows are targeted to the adult and young adult audience, they are also watched by children and teens. Sitcoms popular among teens have in the past few years featured numerous "coming of age" episodes. In 1991, teenager Becky asks her mom, Roseanne, for birth control and confesses that she has already been having sex. Brenda and Dylan sleep together on *Beverly Hills, 90210.* Dr. Doogie Howser, the adolescent brainiac, lost his virginity and entered into manhood. In 1992, he swam naked with one of his mother's friends. In most of these cases, sex practiced without bounds and consequences is assumed to be a normal part of life. And on one of the most popular shows among teens, *Married with Children,* family life is portrayed at the shallow level of hormones.

Where will it end? We can only guess. Television will surely stretch the bounds of decency even farther. In early 1993, the Fox Network reported on the developement of *Key West,* which has "strippers, hookers, and gay people. We'll have a quadriplegic buying a hooker to screw her husband on their anniversary while she watches and whispers in his ear. We'll be doing more than any other TV show," said executive producer David Beaird. And he said it would be done "with taste."[53]

TV's approach to sex education is working. Our kids (and those of us adults who watch) are learning that, when it comes to sex, anything goes and there are no consequences.

The family is a joke. The scene takes place every day in millions of homes across America. Dad comes home from work to the comforts of his castle. But life is different for Al Bundy, the TV father on the Fox Network's hit series *Married with Children.* On one early episode, Bundy walked in the door and muttered, "Ah, home sweet hell." Week after week, the show features grumbling and fighting family members who leave viewers with the impression that the normal home in America must be a living hell.

If you watch any amount of prime-time TV, you have no doubt run across numerous examples of antifamily sentiment. Dad is a weak-kneed bumbling idiot, possessing little wisdom or common sense. Often he's a lazy slob with little or no motivation, like cartoon father Homer Simpson. TV mothers used to be comforting, loving nurturers. But now they're more like ABC's Roseanne, who complains about housework, her job, or the kids. Children have become superbrats who lack respect for parents and anyone else in the adult world and sometimes wind up parenting their own fathers, like preadolescent Bart Simpson.

The real-life situation of many television viewers is that their families are either broken or failing to function properly. Those who grow up in dysfunctional situations know that it's not fun at all. Yet Matt Groening, creator of *The Simpsons*, believes that it's OK to make a joke out of family pain: "The Simpsons are definitely a dysfunctional family, but I think it's healthy to be able to laugh at them. That's part of the service we offer."[54] If they choose to follow the model of TV's moms and dads, our children and teens will grow up to pursue their own interests selfishly, at the expense of family life.

Television is teaching our children values that we may not want them to have.

Television has also declared open season on the institution of marriage. While marriage in America may be on shaky ground, TV usually misses the opportunity to provide positive models and encouraging messages that would facilitate stronger marriages. A young woman on the ABC miniseries *The Women of Brewster Place* says, "I don't have a husband." An older woman replies, "Well, I've had five, and you ain't missing much."[55] The great *Murphy Brown* controversy of 1992 was evidence of TV's willingness to legitimize parenting options that may be unavoidable in some situations but certainly are not the best. There is the attitude that it is all right for a woman to pursue a career, a baby, and whatever else she wants in life, with no need to have the added burden of a spouse. Nearly two out of three prime-time families in the fall of 1993 consisted of children and a single father or mother. When TV popularizes and legitimizes notions of home life and family roles that have never before been accepted as normal, our kids grow up to accept and act out these attitudes.

Television also separates kids from their parents physically and emotionally. When families who own multiple sets disagree on what to watch, each member goes his or her own way to watch in another room. Even if family members sit next to each other, they aren't focused on each other when all eyes and ears are focused on the television. And when TV teaches values that are opposite to what is being taught by the parents in the home, conflict can result.

While there are some signs of hope and change (CBS's *Christy*, if current trends persist, television will continue to contribute to the breakdown of the family by missing the opportunity that it has to shape and mold our children's view of the family in a positive and constructive direction. And future generations will suffer as a result.

No place for God. In 1982, 93 percent of Hollywood's most influential writers, producers, and executives reported that they had a religious upbringing. While 45 percent claimed present religious affiliation, 93 percent seldom or never attended services, and those that did appeared to attend nominally.[56] This may explain television's disdain for matters of religious faith.

A study of one hundred episodes of network TV revealed that 1,381 speaking characters out of 1,462 had no religion. Out of 155 total religious behaviors, 50 percent were clearly negative and 45 percent were personal prayers. The most common prayer was "Thank God!" followed by prayers hastily uttered to God as a last resort.[57]

When God's name is mentioned on TV, it is usually in the context of profanity. Researcher Randal Wright counted 158 profane references to deity and no other mention of God in one week of prime-time TV during 1992.[58]

The clergy are usually portrayed like the typical TV father: a bumbling moron. When a clergyman is depicted as compassionate and caring, the character's theology is so far removed from biblical orthodoxy that it is hardly recognizable. Consider the 1992 episode of *Beverly Hills, 90210* where one of the characters is deciding whether or not to protect her virginity. She consults her wishy-washy priest, who advises her to pursue whatever course *she* feels is right since God will never stop loving her.

Television is serving our children and teens as a sort of religious mentor. At a time when they are forming their spiritual values and beliefs, TV encourages them to forget organized religion and the God of the Bible to pursue whatever self-made religious beliefs make sense to them.

Meaning is found in materialism. In an article on the power of images, J. Francis Davis explores several of television's myths (stories

or ideas that explain the ⸺ of a people) and how
they shape our everyday li⸺

One myth cited by Davi⸺ life' consists of buying
possessions that cost lots ⸺ctional characters and
real-life stars live life with ⸺ses, expensive clothes,
and a host of other status s⸺

A second myth is that "⸺on and sex appeal, just
to name a few, are immin⸺ with the next consumer
purchase."[60] When we buy t⸺ir lives around the pursuit
of those things that we thin⸺ppy. We learn that things
are more important than p⸺

TV teaches little childre⸺ is a desirable lifestyle.
Teenagers act on that lesso⸺ to adults who, like most
of us, are on an endless p⸺od life. As media analyst
Todd Gitlin says:

> With few exceptions, prime time gives us people immersed in
> personal ambition. . . . Personal ambition and consumerism are
> the driving forces in their lives. The sumptuous and brightly lit
> settings of most series amount to advertisements for a consump-
> tion-centered version of the good life.[61]

Be a beauty, not a beast. Let's face it, ugly and
overweight people don't make it on TV unless
they are cast as ugly and overweight people.
Sadly, our definition of what is ugly and overweight has been defined by television. TV is
overloaded with the "beautiful people" who
don't look much like anything most of us see
when we look in the mirror. The women are
slim and trim. The men are slim and muscular.
And everyone is "good-looking." By setting narrow standards for beauty, TV fosters fear and
low self-esteem in children, teens, and adults
who become consumed with pursuit of the
beautiful image or who see that they don't have
a chance of even coming close.

There are two things that television characters rarely do: go to the bathroom and go to church!

Alcohol abuse. When it comes to the issue of alcohol, television
sends out a mixed bag of messages. When America finally realized
that there was an adolescent substance abuse crisis, television jumped
on the bandwagon to encourage kids to "just say no" through a
massive public service campaign. Producers and writers addressed

the issue directly on prime-time sitcoms and dramas that attracted teen audiences. This effort is proof of TV's recognition of its own ability to shape the values, attitudes, and behavior of young viewers.

But what about the mixed messages kids receive in shows that glamorize drinking as a sophisticated adult activity? What about shows that make drunkenness out to be something funny and without consequences? What about shows that portray teenage characters, smarter than their parents, sneaking around and drinking? The National Council on Alcoholism reports that the average child will see 75,000 incidents of alcohol consumption on TV before they reach the age of eighteen.[62] TV's educational power can cause viewers of these messages to accept such behavior as normal and appropriate.

Television in summary

In the last paragraph of the book *Watching America*, the authors speak of the incredible power of television in our culture:

> In the brief span of little more than a single generation, television has become the great American dream machine, the source of an alternate reality whose profound impact is widely assumed but little understood.[63]

As parents, we must understand the medium and messages of this educator of our children.

Going to the Movies

A 1984 study conducted by the Motion Picture Production Association found that 54 percent of the movie-going public were between the ages of twelve and twenty-four. The study also found that 51 percent of those between the ages of twelve and seventeen went to the movies at least once a month.[64] Teenagers, by virtue of the fact that they make up a significant segment of the theater-going population, are an attractive and profitable market segment of the movie-making industry. It is not surprising that 40 percent of the movie industry's annual profit comes from two months of summer releases, most of which are aimed at the teen market.[65]

PBS film critic Michael Medved has been watching movies for years, and his reviews cover the spectrum of Hollywood films. Adult moviegoers depend on his recommendations when deciding whether or not to attend a movie. He has concluded that parents better be careful not only about what they watch but about what they allow their movie-watching kids to see. Why? Because, as he says, Hollywood is no longer the place where dreams are made. Rather, "the dream factory has become the poison factory."[66]

If you have been to a movie lately, you understand Medved's analysis. While the technical brilliance, special effects, and acting are usually good, movie content leaves much to be desired. Without knowing it, our kids partake of the "poison" of morally and spiritually bankrupt films that harm their developing characters. Movie producers know that films that address a teen's search for identity, desire for intimacy, and quest for social acceptance will sell because they speak to the deep questions facing kids. As a result, the "poison factory" has an incredible ability to crank out values, attitudes, and behaviors that our teens readily absorb.

Movie viewing facts and figures

Do kids go to the movies? A 1986 study conducted by Teenage Research Unlimited found that 45.4 percent of twelve to fifteen year olds indicate that they rarely or never go to the movies; 39.4 percent of sixteen to seventeen year olds and 36.2 percent of eighteen to nineteen year olds never go to the movies. Surprised? Remember that the movie theater is not the only place to go and see a movie anymore. Most American households have a VCR. In 1991, the average household spent $160 renting and purchasing tapes.[67] The average teen watched twenty-six movies on the VCR in 1991.[68]

Access to cable TV and networks like Showtime and HBO also increases movie availability for teens who choose not to go to the theater. In 1991, teens watched an average of fifty-four movies on cable and regular TV.[69]

One survey of conservative Christian teens narrowed down the types of movies that they had seen over a six-month period. Thirty percent reported viewing a G-rated film; 71 percent PG-rated; 76 percent PG-13-rated; 68 percent R-rated; and 10 percent X-rated.[70]

> *Characters seldom acknowledge a belief in God or Jesus. When they do, it is ambiguous. It is especially strange that with all the major crises characters face in a week of TV, God is seldom seen as a source of hope, help, or direction.*

Many parents are happy when their kids choose to see a PG or PG-13 film. But don't assume that these ratings are a guarantee of a film's good quality or spotless content. Movie Morality Ministries has discovered that nearly one-quarter of all PG and PG-13 films include the "f-word"; 61 percent take the Lord's name in vain; 71 percent contain vulgar references to excretion, intercourse, or the genitals; 50 percent imply sexual intercourse while 13 percent show intercourse; 30 percent feature explicit nudity; 75 percent display moderate or severe violence; and 74 percent depict alcohol and/or other drug abuse.[71]

R-rated movie content is far more explicit. The R-rating signifies that a movie may contain a fair amount of explicit sex, violence, and/or profanity. In 1989, 67 percent of the movies rated by the Motion Picture Association of America received an R-rating.[72] While the R-rating should serve to restrict teens from attending, it actually attracts them. One Michigan State University study found that teenage girls see at least twenty-five R-rated movies a year. Teenage boys see at least seventeen.[73]

What are we learning from movies?

Movie themes fall into the same categories that we have already examined in our discussion of television. But there is one difference: Movies, by nature of the fact that they are never "censored," are able to carry out those themes in a more explicit and graphic manner. If our children and teens are seeing sex, violence, and rebellion on TV, they are seeing a more intense version of those same themes on the big screen.

In this section, I am going to highlight a few of the major themes in today's motion pictures. This section is in no way complete and exhaustive. Rather, it will provide you with a general sense of what our children and teens are seeing when they go to the movies, rent a tape, or watch one of the many movie channels available on cable.

Violence. In the film *Die Hard 2: Die Harder*, Bruce Willis uses an icicle to stab a man in the brain by way of the eye socket. In another scene, a man is sucked into a jet engine and unceremoniously discharged out the other end like ground meat. *Total Recall* features characters who explode violently when tossed outside of a protective covering on Mars. An elevator fight ends with a man falling to his death while hero Arnold Schwarzenegger holds onto the man's severed arms.

These and other films, all popular among teens, are part of Hollywood's growing fascination and glorification of bizarre and graphic

Does presence of violence in media cause children + teens + adults to be more vigilant + afraid of random violence

violent behavior. And, as the audience comes to expect bigger and better violence, the movie industry continues to make movies that are more violent and graphic than ever before. Michael Medved says that "the public has been dramatically desensitized by the overwhelming accumulation of violent images; it is far more difficult to frighten or disgust an audience than ever before."[74]

In the world of movies, violence is portrayed as a normal part of life, just like eating, drinking, and sleeping. And, absurd as it is, we pay to be amused by these violent images. The more violent and creative the death scene, the louder the applause from the audience.

Film critic Vincent Canby recently assumed the unenviable task of counting the number of deaths in several of Hollywood's most popular films of recent years. He counted 264 killings in *Die Hard 2: Die Harder,* 106 in *Rambo III,* 81 in *Robocop 2,* 74 in *Total Recall,* and 62 in *Rambo: First Blood Part II.*[75] In addition to killings, these films contain numerous other violent scenes in which people are left injured and maimed.

Parents need to be aware of the graphic nature of movie violence. Many of the movies marketed to children and teens contain a story line developed around violence with the plot being an afterthought.

Horror. The scene is familiar. A group of children or teens are gathered in a darkened theater or living room. Huddled together or sitting quietly on the edge of their seats, they nervously watch as Freddy Krueger or some other maniacal killer stalks his young victim. According to one recent survey, 89 percent of ten to thirteen year olds had seen at least one slasher film in the *Nightmare on Elm Street* or *Friday the 13th* series. Sixty-two percent had seen four of them![76]

"The popularity of horror films is indeed startling," write the authors of *Dancing in the Dark.* "In 1947, horror films were but .004 percent of the world's annual release; by 1967 the number had grown to 7.6 percent; and by 1987 one out of every six films made in America could be classified as a horror film."[77] One report says that "total viewership of horror, including home viewership, has increased roughly 300-fold."[78] This means that more and more of our children and teens are being exposed to the terror, torture, mutilation, and killing of slasher films.

Should parents be concerned? You bet! While these films appear to be so far-fetched that they could be construed as nothing but fantasy, kids may have difficulty separating the fantasy from reality. In addition, a steady diet of horror films yields the results of exposure to violence that we have already discussed.

It might not surprise you to know that in February 1992, an eleven year old in California accidently hung herself while reenacting a scene from Stephen King's *Pet Sematary* in the basement with her friends. Yes, our children are watching and learning.

Sex. If children and teens are looking for answers and direction regarding their developing sexuality, the world of movies and film is ready to help. Movies aimed at a younger audience appeal to this curiosity by including elements of sexual innuendo. They either portray adolescent sexuality in a manner that assumes that all teens are doing it or they encourage promiscuous behavior through humorous portrayals of the teen sexual appetite. Dramatic films made for older teen audiences depict numerous types of sexual promiscuity and perversion as a regular part of adult life. All of these messages combine to encourage kids to "go ahead and do it!"

A recent trend in Hollywood is to turn out films that stress two alarming subthemes of sexuality.

First, there seems to be a strange obsession with combining sexual pleasure and violence. Sex is now becoming synonymous with danger. *Fatal Attraction* was one of the first films in this new dating-death genre. Love and lust lead to death and abuse in *Basic Instinct* and *Love Crimes*. The 1993 film *Boxing Helena* took this theme to new extremes through its portrayal of a doctor so obsessed with a woman that he amputates her limbs and keeps her in a box until she falls in love with him.

Second, Hollywood is beginning to stretch the limits of acceptable sexual practice through films that appear to approve incestuous relationships. Mother-son intercourse is featured in the film *Sleepwalkers*. The film *Olivier, Olivier* traces the return of a young male prostitute to his home and his ensuing sexual relationship with his grown-up sister.

In the movies, sex simply is, and it sells. Our kids come away thinking that adolescent promiscuity is a normal part of life. And they risk buying the lie that the normal adolescent participates in what most of us know to be abnormal sexual practice and behavior.

Honor the dishonorable. Hollywood is feeding America a diet of new heroes. Somehow, filmgoers allow themselves to be manipulated by filmmakers into rooting and pulling for characters who believe or behave in ways that we once thought were wrong and dishonorable.

Michael Medved noted this trend in his analysis of the 1992 Oscar nominations:

Consider the anointed candidates for Best Actor: three of them played murderous psychotics; one of them played a homeless, delusional psychotic; and one of them played a good, old-fashioned, manic-depressive neurotic who is the product of a viciously dysfunctional family background. On the industry's glittering "night of nights," this collection of decidedly downbeat antiheroes is placed before the public as the representatives of the most noble and notable characterizations of which the acting craft is capable.[79]

Our children and teens must learn compassion for the poor and oppressed. What they don't need are lessons that lead them to pull for an underdog whose behavior warrants life in prison.

Religion as a crutch. Our children and teens need to know that there is an almighty God who cares deeply about them and who desires to guide and direct them through the maze of adolescence. Hollywood is teaching our kids about a God they have created in their own image and whose followers are fools, relying on the outdated "crutch" of religion. Michael Medved says that "in the ongoing war on traditional values, the assault on organized faith represents the front to which the entertainment industry has most clearly committed itself."[80]

Catholics, Jews, Christians, and the clergy are all fair game for moviemakers. Familiarity with stereotypical portrayals of these groups leads to acceptance of those stereotypes as reality. If you couple that with the basic underlying theme that most problems in movies are best solved by "self," kids are presented with humanistic enlightenment that far surpasses the perceived irrelevancy of the Christian faith. Sometimes it is the conspicuous absence of God, faith, and church in film that furthers this way of thinking.

Rather than mention specific films that promote a negative view of organized religion and Christianity in particular, I challenge you to view critically the next film you watch. Look for the obvious and not so obvious antireligious messages that flood the minds of your children and teens.

Who needs the family? In the blockbuster hits *Home Alone* and *Home Alone 2* viewers were treated to a series of slapstick gags that left them rolling in the aisles. This humorous film was a hit among children, teens, and adults. But beneath the laughter lay a frightening message: Parents are stupid and incompetent idiots who are lucky to have survived in life so long, while children are competent to survive on their own, even in the midst of life-threatening danger. The bottom line: Who needs parents?

Hollywood consistently attacks the traditional family as an outdated institution that serves to stifle personal growth, creativity, and advancement. In fact, members of traditional families are often portrayed as doomed to a life full of misery. The home is depicted as being stress producing rather than stress reducing.

Again, this theme is so prevalent that there is no need to document specific cases. Next time you watch a film, look and listen carefully for the hidden messages. How is marriage depicted? How are parents portrayed? Is family a problem creator or problem solver? Your careful attention will convince you that Hollywood is redefining the family for our children and teens.

Movies in summary:

The movie industry is a powerful element in the media package that influences the values, attitudes, and behaviors of our children. Christian film critic Ted Baehr tells of a fourteen-year-old daughter, at the top of her class in school, who saw the movie *Pretty Woman*. Full of questions about her own sexuality, she watched the story of a prostitute who finds the wealthy man of her dreams. Then she went and got drunk with a friend and proceeded to prostitute herself with two men at the same time. Her parents didn't find out until several weeks later. During that time, she had sneaked out of the house every night to prostitute herself to four or five men. The movie had defined reality for this poor girl, and she had pursued a similar ugly life.

Parents, movies fill the eyes and ears of our children and teens with the invitation to "come, follow, and experience life."

Advertising: What Does It Sell to Our Children?

James J. Smith, a child psychologist who spent six years helping advertisers research how to sell to children, says that his experience made him feel like he was "beginning to lose my soul." Smith learned that children want love and acceptance. And like adults, they are willing to spend their money to get it. The basic premise of advertising to kids involves "luring children" with a basic felt need and "cloaking the message." Smith cites a recent Oreo cookie ad as a perfect example. The ad, lasting thirty seconds, flashes thirty images of happy children playing while the product logo is shown only once. The intended result is to have children associate the cookie with love and happiness, therefore creating a desire for Oreo cookies.[81]

This basic approach to promoting products works. Our world is filled with constant pitches for this or that, and rarely do the pitches say much at all about the product. Rather, advertising deals less with proving a product's value and more with proving the inadequacy of the viewer's life without the product. We shouldn't be surprised at how our growing children and teens have become such easy targets for advertisers.

Advertising facts and figures

Advertising is a billion-dollar business. A large part of advertising's target audience is children and teens. Why? Kids have lots of money to spend! According to some estimates, four- to twelve-year-old children spend $9 billion of their own allowance, job, and savings money however they please. This same group influences purchases of more than $130 billion of goods, making them an effective path to adult dollars.[82] The teen market spends or influences the spending of $248.7 billion a year.[83]

Advertisements aimed at our children and teens come at them from many different directions. Television is the primary source of advertising exposure. Preschool children spend about five hours a week watching television commercials. This translates into over a thousand commercials a week.[84] Ads consume about 20 percent of television viewing time. This means that the average teen will see between three and four hours of commercials a week.[85]

You may be surprised to learn that advertising is present in movies without the distraction of commercial breaks. Have you ever noticed how many everyday products appear on kitchen tables, in bedrooms, and on billboards in the movies? Chances are that all of those products have been strategically placed as part of an advertising deal with the production company. Philip Morris reportedly paid $350,000 to have their Lark cigarettes placed in a recent James Bond film and $442,000 to feature Marlboros in *Superman II.*

Even the junior high and high school classroom is not immune from advertisements. Since 1989, Whittle Communications has been producing *Channel One*, a daily news show for the classroom. Schools that agree to carry *Channel One* receive two free VCRs, televisions for the classrooms, all the necessary wiring, and a satellite receiver. While there is no charge to the school for the service, schools must agree to show a certain number of shows to students. The system is paid for by two minutes of advertising during the daily twelve-minute news broadcast. As of early 1993, ten thousand schools were participating in the program, with a viewing audience of more than six million students. *Channel One* expected to be reaching 40 percent of America's teens by the fall of 1993.[86]

School hallways, cafeterias, and gymnasiums are being used by Market-Source Corporation to market products to teens. The company provides schools with sophisticated electronic billboards that include a calendar of school activities, backlighted color advertisements, and messages programmed by the school.[87]

What are the ads selling?

Advertisements sell more than products to our children and teens. They sell image. They sell satisfaction. They sell the teen dream of acceptance, popularity, love, and attention. And they also sell the following messages, loud and clear.

Sex. Sex sells more than television shows and movies. Sex sells products. Jacob Jacoby, a professor of business at New York University, says that the first aim of an ad is "to generate attention. How you do it does not matter."[88] Sex is used to grab attention and sell products on television, in magazines, in newspapers, and on billboards. It seems to be the attention grabber of choice for many youth-oriented products and ads directed at teens.

Fashion photographers shoot provocative pictures that show handsome and beautiful young models in a variety of suggestive poses. And, of course, they are wearing clothes or cologne that somehow imply that the photo fantasy could become reality if you just purchase and wear the product. Guess? jeans has taken this approach for years. Well-endowed models strike erotic poses and either expose large portions of their breasts or wear nothing but underwear in their ongoing series of magazine ads.

Calvin Klein uses a similar tactic to advertise their jeans. Interestingly, the pictures rarely show much of the jeans. One ad shows a couple from neck to knees. She is sitting on a vanity counter as they begin an embrace. His pants already unbuttoned and unzipped, there is no doubt as to what lies ahead as she begins to remove his belt. Another two-page ad features a muscular male torso from the neck to just above the knees. This faceless Adonis is photographed so that his midsection is right in the center of the picture. He is totally naked and in the shower, his crotch covered by a strategically placed corner of his jeans.

Calvin Klein's use of sex to sell carries over into their Obsession line of perfume and cologne. One ad shows a naked couple standing face-to-face on a swing. They appear to be lost in erotic ecstasy.

The Quiksilver denim company uses big-chested models to sell their clothing. One ad features a woman in a transparent fishnet bathing-suit top leaving nothing to the reader's imagination.

Bugle Boy sells their clothes with seductive and suggestive photos along with the phrase, "Few things will make you want to take them off."

Benetton raised some concern with a series of ads that neither mentioned nor showed their product. One two-page ad featured multicolored condoms against a white backdrop. Another depicts a nun and priest in the midst of a romantic kiss.

The Merry Go Round clothing-store chain ran an ad in early 1994 for SYN jeans for men that featured a scantily clad model in a form-fitting halter top assuming a seductive pose while standing in an elevator. The text reads: "Push my buttons. I'm looking for a man who can totally floor me, who won't stop till the top. YOU MUST LIVE in SYN."

One art critic has written, "Contemporary photographers use sexual innuendo to establish a psychological climate in which the use of certain products inflates the consumer's self-image."[89] It's no wonder that children and teens, in the midst of building their self-image during a relatively unstable period of life, would respond so favorably to ads that use sex to sell.

Beauty can be bought. All the sexual messages and images combine to define a standard of beauty that few people ever reach. You may wonder why your son or daughter is so consumed with spending time in front of the mirror. The answer is simple. They are trying to measure up to the images they've seen plastered on the TV, printed page, and billboards. They balance perilously between trying to measure up and the frustration of never measuring up. Girls have to look like Cindy Crawford, the Swedish Bikini Team, the Guess? Girl, and every woman who ever appeared on a makeup commercial to be acceptable to guys. Sadly, guys grow up believing that this is what a beautiful girl looks like. Guys spend their time trying to develop the muscles of Arnold Schwarzenegger and the look of handsome guys in ads who get attention from one or more beautiful girls.

Take the time to make your children aware of what the ads are really selling.

These images yield two results. First, they sell products. And second, they sell an image that 99.9 percent (or more) of the people in this world will never attain. And so kids and adults waste terrible amounts of time, energy, and money on pursuit of the dream, only to be let down over and over again.

Alcohol: Everybody's doing it. In June 1991, an ad for St. Ides Malt Liquor, featuring rap singer Ice Cube, appeared on national TV. He sang, "Why don't ya grab a six-pack and get your girl in the mood quicker and get your jimmy [penis] thicker with St. Ides Malt Liquor?" This ad was just one of a continuing series from the liquor industry that are targeted at underage drinkers.

The Center for Media and Values reports that beer ads do indeed target youth but remain acceptable because they don't show children or underage drinkers using their products. Rather, they show college students, barely legal themselves, living it up and enjoying life in a way that is only possible (they want you to think) if beer is involved. These ads appeal to kids because of the adolescent desire to be, feel, and act older than they really are. Of course, the beer companies deny it.[90]

In her assessment of the beer advertising environment, Teresa Riordan says that most beer advertising for college markets is based "on the rock-solid premise that university men have two overriding concerns: (1) getting drunk; and (2) getting laid. If you can't promise one . . . just promise more of the other."[91] As an example of this approach, Riordan cites Miller's recent spring-break ad campaign featuring a sixteen-page glossy magazine titled *Beachin' Times*. The theme of the ad is "babes" and how to "scam" them and "turn spring break into your own personal trout farm." An article on Miller's "Pro Beach Volleyball" program features the lead-in "Name something you can dink, bump, and poke. Hint—it's not a Babe."[92] Crass college humor like this has always had a ready and willing audience among high schoolers.

Our children and teens grow up believing that alcohol is fun, sexy, harmless, and desirable. Never do the advertisers mention that alcohol is related to a large percentage of suicides and sexual-abuse cases. Never do they show the terrible toll that alcohol takes in highway deaths. Nor do they show the years of sometimes endless pain that haunt the family of an alcoholic. No, alcohol is always shown as the key to personal, professional, and romantic fulfillment in life.

Researcher Jean Kilbourne has studied the alcohol-advertising industry for several years and has concluded that our children and teens (among others) are the target for several myths. Among those myths are:

- Drinking is a risk-free activity.
- You can't survive without drinking.
- Alcohol is a magic potion that can transform you.
- Sports and alcohol go together.[93]

Judging from the statistics on adolescent alcohol abuse and the many stories that I have personally come across, there is no doubt that the messages of alcohol ads are hitting home with our children and teens. Look out. They're after your kids!

Tobacco: start doing it. Children and teenagers constitute 90 percent of all new smokers. Once they're hooked, they're hooked. Does the tobacco industry market cigarettes to young people? While they would deny that they target the under-eighteen crowd, experts are convinced that cigarette companies are actively promoting nicotine addiction among youth.

In 1988, RJR Nabisco, Inc. launched an ad campaign featuring Joe Camel, a cartoon camel modeled after James Bond and Don Johnson's *Miami Vice* character. Several medical researchers from the University of Massachusetts set out to determine if Old Joe influenced children to smoke Camel cigarettes. Their findings are startling. First, they discovered that children are far more likely than adults to recognize the Old Joe character (97.7 percent to 72.2 percent). Second, their data indicated that in just three years Old Joe had an astounding influence on children's smoking behavior. The proportion of smokers under age eighteen who chose Camel rose from 0.5 percent to 32.8 percent! And finally, they estimate that the illegal sale of Camel cigarettes to children under eighteen rose from $6 million per year prior to the ad campaign to $476 million a year in 1991, accounting for one-quarter of all Camel sales.[94]

It is interesting to note that paid promotions for Camel appear in the Walt Disney movies *Who Framed Roger Rabbit?* and *Honey, I Shrunk the Kids,* an effective marketing technique for reaching kids. Like the alcohol companies, cigarette manufacturers depend on your kids for survival. They want your kids to believe that cigarette smoking is clean and safe. They want your kids to smoke. Take a good close look at the billboards next time you are out driving. Is there a message there for your kids?

Ads in summary:

The Griffin Bacal Advertising Agency specializes in creating ads for child and teen products. The company's president, Paul D. Kurnit, says that there are ten easy ways to make kids take notice:[95]

1. Know your niche—not all age groups are alike.
2. Position your product—kids should see how the product suits and serves their life.
3. Talk the talk—use the language of kids.
4. Pictures sell—kids are fashion and color aware.
5. Put it to music.

6. Move it along—fast-paced images.
7. Don't preach—kids will "get it." They want products that improve image and make them feel older.
8. Make it fun—use humor and poke fun at authority figures.
9. Groups are dynamic—teens are social beings that respond to a product that will invite them to join the crowd.
10. Be new, but familiar—you want kids to be talking about the ad in the school hall.

Note the above strategies carefully, since they are regularly employed to manipulate your kids. "Buy me!" is a call that our kids hear throughout the day. And because their age makes them especially susceptible to media's round-the-clock advertising, parents need to take the time to evaluate the messages their children are hearing and seeing.

Radio—Your Kids Hear More on It than Music

The radio is a media outlet used heavily by teens. Popular music and all of the themes and messages we have already discussed are transmitted over the airwaves around-the-clock. In addition, disc jockeys and other radio personalities fill the time between songs with comment and banter. While radio, like other media outlets, has the potential to be a positive and uplifting force in the life of a teen, a casual survey of the most listened-to stations and program formats indicates that radio has become increasingly negative as the moral landscape of America has changed.

In his study on teens and radio, Paul Gullifor says:

> Radio introduces themes that are ignored or downplayed by the dominant institutions such as the family. For example, many of the topics addressed on commercial radio are topics that are often omitted from family discussions.[96]

Radio speaks the language of kids. It has the powerful potential and ability to serve as a surrogate parent, providing teens with information and advice that they aren't receiving at home. Often that information is offensive, explicit, and inappropriate.

Radio facts and figures

Radio is cheap. For the initial cost of a set and maybe a few batteries every month, radio provides up-to-the-minute access to the world of popular culture. And you can turn it on while in the car, your room, or, through the miracle of the Walkman, anywhere you might be. Numerous studies and surveys indicate that children begin to listen to the radio at a young age. As they grow, listening time increases due to the increased importance of popular music in their lives. Ninety-four percent of all twelve to nineteen year olds listen to the radio.[97] According to one study, twelve to fourteen year olds listen to an average of five hours a day of radio during the typical school week.[98] That figure increases as kids pass through the high school years.

On the average, there are 4.5 radios in households with teenagers.[99] Sixty percent of all teens own a portable radio or cassette player (boom box), and 58 percent own a small personal stereo with headphones (Walkman). About 65 percent own their own nonportable home stereo.[100] Radio is certainly everywhere.

What are they hearing?

Nearly all adolescents listen to stations that feature popular music formats. But when they tune in, they hear more than music and advertisements.

Kids who get ready for school with the radio on are typically tuned in to one of the many "Morning Zoo" shows featured during the A.M. drive-time. The format features one or two personalities who solicit adolescent listeners and laughter through popular music, gross humor, and an emphasis on sex. Methods include song parodies, spontaneous live phone calls to unsuspecting persons, practical jokes, impersonations, etc.

Other morning shows feature "shock jocks," radio personalities who take indecency so far that one has to wonder why they don't get thrown off the air. The most famous of these shock jocks is Howard Stern, whose morning talk show is heard around the country by three million listeners every day in fourteen major markets. His show is so popular that it was number one in New York, Philadelphia, Boston, and Los Angeles at the end of 1993.

Currently under contract for about $2 million a year, Stern provides teen listeners with hour after hour of indecent fare. His shows have featured "The Lesbian Dating Game," a gay *Munsters* sketch, "Bestiality Dial-a-Date," and a *Family Feud* parody in which the hookers battled the call girls. In one *Honeymooners* parody, Ralph masturbates into a Tupperware bowl for the purpose of artificial insemination, but later eats the semen by accident when he mistakes it for custard.

For those who may still wonder why Stern has been labeled a shock jock, consider the following excerpts from his morning show:

> The closest I came to making love with a black woman was I masturbated to a picture of Aunt Jemima.

> First, I want to just strip and rape Mark and Brian [rival Los Angeles disc jockeys]. I want my two bitches laying there in the cold, naked. . . . I want them bleeding from the buttocks.

> [On Michelle Pfeiffer] I would not even need a vibrator. . . . Boy, her rump would be more black and blue than a Harlem cub scout.[101]

Stern also targets organized religion. One of his Christmas TV specials featured Stern giving birth in a manger.

Does all of this turn your stomach? Imagine what it does to the kids who listen to a diet of this garbage day after day!

Late-night radio can be just as bad. As of early 1993, the show *Love Phones* was being broadcast from New York City into several markets around the country. Several parents in Philadelphia told me the show had become the talk of the halls in area junior and senior highs. Once parents began to listen in on what their kids were hearing, the station moved the show from the 10 P.M.–12 A.M. slot to the 12 A.M.–2 A.M. slot. But the kids kept listening. Eventually, a small group of parents complained so loudly that the show was taken off the air in Philadelphia.

Were their complaints justified? Without a doubt. Callers ask for advice on everything from intercourse to oral sex to sex with animals. Sex "expert" and cohost Dr. Judy Kuriansky told one caller that there was really nothing wrong or strange about having sex with a cow. Another time she explained a technique for more fulfilling sex with a sheep. One teenage boy wanted to know if it was abnormal for his girlfriend to be sticking her finger in his anus during intercourse. A girl wondered why her boyfriend liked to taste his own ejaculate. The list goes on and on. The basic message of the *Love Phones* experts is "go ahead and do it however, whenever, and with whatever!" Children and teens who listen to caller questions may begin to wonder if they are the odd ones because their behavior differs.

There is some good news. There are those in the radio business who realize they have a responsibility for what goes out over the airwaves. In October of 1993, urban station KACE in Los Angeles decided to refrain from airing music that "glorifies drug usage, is sexually explicit, encourages violence, or denigrates women." Program director Rich Guzman explains, "Our offices are next door to the juvenile court, and every day we see kids come in shackled. We wanted to find a way for us, as a radio station, to affect their lives in a more positive way. . . . Instead of being part of the problem, we can try to be part of the solution."[102]

Radio in summary:

Radio's accessibility and ease of use mean that any child, no matter what age, can listen in if they know how to flick a switch and work a dial. While it may be easy to miss radio's messages because your kids listen in private, responsible parents will take the time to discover and address what their kids are hearing.

Magazines: More Answers to Life's Questions

Magazines are another segment of the media that is reaching out to the teenage population with suggestions, information, and answers to life's questions. Jane Pratt, the editor of the hit female teen magazine *Sassy*, says, "When you're feeling alone with a problem, a magazine talking about that problem can make you feel more connected."[103]

Magazine facts and figures

According to Teenage Research Unlimited, the typical teenager spends about 2.8 hours a week reading magazines. Boys spend more time reading magazines than girls, and older teens read more than younger teenagers.[104] A walk past the magazine rack in your local bookstore offers some clear insight into the types of magazines that kids are reading. Boys typically read magazines on sports, cars, hobbies, and music. Girls tend to read magazines that address issues related to beauty and relationships.

What are your teens reading?

A recent content analysis of the magazines most popular among adolescent girls shows that articles on fashion and clothing fill most pages. Other featured articles deal with beauty tips, entertainment, and health care. Advertising occupies 46 percent of the magazines' content. The researchers found that the magazines emphasize personal fulfillment and improvement through clothing style and beauty care. Articles that address relational aspects of an adolescent girl's life tend to focus on the opposite sex and sexual relationships.[105]

The history and content of the popular girl's magazine *Sassy* offers an eye-opening glimpse into what our kids learn from the glossy printed page. *Sassy* first appeared on the newsstand in 1988 with a paid circulation of 250,000. In just four years, this magazine is hitting its target audience of thirteen to eighteen year olds with a circulation of 715,000.

The first clue to *Sassy*'s content came with the prepublication promotional materials that were mailed to thousands of teens:

> Sassy is different, because after all, you're different. You're one of a kind. Right? You like to do things your own way and so do we. Your older sister or mother just wouldn't understand Sassy. . . . Sassy will help you with some of the really tough decisions you have to make, such as, "How and when it's time to say, 'No,' or 'Yes' to that special guy, and plenty of other things your mother forgot to tell you."[106]

During its early days, the magazine lived up to this advance billing with articles like "Good Manners for Good Mannered Sex," "Seductive Nights: Daring Designs That Will Make Any Night a Night to Remember," a "Condom Update," "Sex for Absolute Beginners," "Witchcraft Is a Religion," and a piece on two gay couples that promoted homosexuality as a normal lifestyle for teens. One 1988 editorial column read:

> Bad news guys. Ten states in the U.S. . . . have passed laws that state that any girl under 18 who wants an abortion must have one of the following: consent of one or both parents; the doctor who performs the abortion to notify her parents; or permission from a judge. What's worse, 24 more states are considering the same action. We think this stinks, how about you?[107]

Numerous complaints from parents and media watchdog groups led to a decision by the magazine to tone things down a bit. While there are fewer articles like those previously mentioned, *Sassy* and other teen magazines (including thousands of homemade zines, or underground periodicals, distributed at schools) continue to educate young girls by defining what makes a girl beautiful, sexy, independent, and desirable. In fact, the folks at *Sassy* began publishing *Dirt* in 1992 for fourteen- to twenty-year-old guys.

What about the Future?

As if our kids aren't already faced with media overload, the future of a technology known as virtual reality looms ever closer. Virtual reality is an interactive technology that creates an illusion of being immersed in an artificial world. Current technology requires the user to put on a computerized glove and a head-mounted display equipped with a screen for each eye. The user can choose the world he wants to enter and, in effect, get there through the equipment. The more advanced equipment will utilize a suit that will recreate every possible physical sensation on all parts of the body.

No doubt there are numerous ways that virtual reality could benefit people as an educational and training tool. But some have suggested other uses for virtual reality . . . like virtual sex. By slipping into the body suit and entering the world of virtual reality, a person could conceivably have sex with another person across the world through interfacing systems. Or as one expert on the technology has proposed, virtual reality can allow any sexual fantasy to come true, even sex with animals, fish, or some personally imagined and invented creature.

While virtual reality is still in its early developmental stages, it promises to be the biggest technological innovation since television. And someday it just might be found in every home on the block. Parents should closely follow this development as it will certainly impact the ways that our kids live, think, feel, play, and learn.

■ *IT'S YOUR TURN*

The media is everywhere around us, shaping our culture and guiding our children and teens. While it can serve as a productive force in society, media serves a destructive purpose far too often. Our children and teens, because of their age and stage in development, are easily fooled into believing what they hear and see.

As parents, we can begin to help our teens through the muddled maze of media's messages. Although watching and listening requires work, it pays off big dividends when we give our kids the opportunity to learn how to tell the difference between the media's truth and lies.

6 LEADING YOUR KIDS THROUGH THE MAZE OF MUSIC AND THE MEDIA

▮▮

Stop loving this evil world and all that it offers you, for when you love these . . . worldly things, these evil desires—the craze for sex, the ambition to buy everything that appeals to you, and the pride that comes from wealth and importance— these are not from God. They are from this evil world itself. And this world is fading away, and these evil, forbidden things will go with it, but whoever keeps doing the will of God will live forever.
I John 2:15-17, TLB

AFTER RECEIVING THE award for Best Male Rock Vocalist at the 1990 Grammys, rock musician Don Henley directed a few words to those who want to censor the messages of popular music: "A lot of people should look at the state of parenting and education instead of pointing fingers at rock & roll."[1]

Henley's words are worth thinking about. When kids buy into attitudes and values that are contrary to their parents', many parents are quick to lay the blame . . . somewhere else. But I believe that while media and music do affect children in powerful and many times negative ways, they should not become a scapegoat for all the ills of American adolescents. They didn't break down the door to get into our homes, cars, and schools in order to gain access to the hearts and minds of our kids. Rather, the door was left unlocked and wide open. They just walked right on in. And it is the family, church, and school who, by virtue of their silence and ignorance, are responsible for leaving the door wide open.

What then should parents do about the "pied piper" that plays such an important role in the lives of their children? This chapter provides an overview of the top five negative effects that music and media have on today's teens. As you learn to recognize the good and the harmful messages, you'll have the opportunity to evaluate the ways in which music and media have affected your family. Then we'll develop five parental guidelines for positive action in protecting the eyes and ears of your kids against the bombardment of media now . . . and in the future.

Five Negative Effects of Media and Music on Our Kids

If you watch TV, turn on the radio, rent a movie, subscribe to a magazine, or read the newspaper, you have opened yourself and your family up to the direct influence of today's media. And even if you have done none of the above, it is impossible to be untouched by the powerful influence of today's music and media—unless you are a hermit!

Here is a list of the five negative ways that music and media enter through unattended doors to leave their marks on our children and teens.

1. Media presents a false view of reality.

Music and the media often tell lies. When your kids don't have an opportunity to view the world through God's Word, they run the real risk of living those lies rather than learning the truth.

Parents who are committed to teaching their children biblical values find it difficult to reach out to their kids when they have been

WHAT MUSIC AND MEDIA SAY	WHAT GOD SAYS IN THE BIBLE
To be worthwhile, you must be beautiful.	I care about who you are more than what you look like.
Avoid pain at all costs.	Expect suffering and exercise perseverance.
Sex is recreation. There are no consequences. Everybody does it.	I give you the gift of sex for the purpose of procreation, intimacy, and expressing oneness in marriage.
Violence is an acceptable way to deal with problems.	Turn the other cheek. Love your enemy.
It's OK to use anyone you want— for any purpose you want.	Treat people with dignity. Love your neighbor. Sacrifice your own rights for the good of others.
Money buys happiness. Grab all the stuff you can.	Seek first the kingdom, and don't worry about things that moth and rust can destroy.

numbed to the truth. Media and music's messages stand in antithesis to what God says.

There is more to life than immediate personal gratification. Yet, we have a whole generation of kids who have bought the lies, are living for the moment, and are missing the truth.

2. Media provides heroes and role models not worth emulating.

When I was a little boy, I used to fall asleep visualizing my grown-up body in a Philadelphia Phillies' uniform. My heroes were the guys who had made it to the big leagues. I wanted to be just like Jim Bunning, Johnny Callison, or Richie Allen. Each spring, I would run onto the Little League field in pursuit of that dream with the number of one of my heroes displayed on my back. I'm not naive enough to think that all of my childhood heroes were the moral giants I once thought they were. But back then there was no reason to think that they weren't. All I really knew about them was what they looked like and how they played.

Today's heroes—and the knowledge that is made public about them—show that things have changed. A recent survey of junior high and high school students found that 36 percent choose actors as their top heroes. Musicians finished second with 19 percent, and comedians and athletes tied for third with 11 percent each.[2] The only qualification for being a hero or role model today is not what one stands for but one's celebrity status. And today's stars no longer let their abilities and accomplishments do the talking. Instead they believe their status should be a platform for expressing views on everything from religion to politics. Madonna, Rambo, Tom Cruise, Arnold Schwarzenegger, Bart Simpson, Arsenio Hall, and Eddie Murphy have all been listed in recent years as popular teen heroes. These people (or fictional characters) are rich and famous. They get to do exciting things in real life and in the movies. But if you listen to what they say, examine their lifestyles, and watch their movies, it isn't long before you realize that they lack a biblical sense of right and wrong. Their personal morality is just that, a "personal" morality.

We need to encourage and help our kids to examine their heroes according to a biblical standard. Otherwise, they run the risk of accepting the whole package and emulating traits and attitudes that are dangerous and wrong.

3. Media destroys our children's sense of who they are.

Adolescence is a time when our kids need to be encouraged and built up in their self-esteem. But by setting standards for beauty and status that are largely unattainable, the media can mentally and emotionally rip our kids apart.

A few years ago a junior high girl came to me in tears over her looks: "I'm too short. I don't like the color of my hair. And my face looks funny." When I asked her why she wasn't happy with the way she looked (she was a beautiful kid), she began to describe each feature that she would like to change and gave me an example of someone who had the particular characteristic she wanted to have. Sadly, each person she mentioned was one of the "beautiful people" she had seen on TV or in magazines. She wanted to become them because she hated herself. In later conversations I learned that she had been trying to build herself up by telling her friends that she had just signed a modeling contract. She also told me that she was thinking seriously about plastic surgery.

We are raising a generation of kids who believe that they are nothing without beauty, cars, certain clothes, and a host of other things. The media has used them to create a "consumption for the sake of consumption" youth culture. Never are they told by the media that if they have nothing else but a relationship with God through Christ, they will have everything.

4. Media teaches kids that life is boring.

"OK, I'm here now. Show me what you've got. I challenge you to entertain me!" The majority of today's kids are part of the MTV Generation. Through their constant passive immersion in the fast-moving world of media entertainment, they have forgotten how to actively listen and make their own fun. Compared to MTV, action movies, and Nintendo, real life is dull and boring.

While my informal surveys are not scientific by any means, I have seen a marked difference between children and teens who spend unlimited time in the media world and those who don't. For example, kids who watch a lot of television get bored when the set is turned off; they don't know what to do with their time. And the more they watch, the more they want to watch. It's almost like a drug addiction where constant use leads to increased tolerance. More of the drug is needed to get high, and withdrawal is painful.

Kids whose parents set limits on television viewing are better communicators. They develop the ability to make their own fun. Real life for them is anything but boring. When I asked several of these kids what they think of television, they said that they enjoy it. But when it's off, they don't even miss it. They realize that there are more important things to do with their lives.

If you or your children find it difficult to have fun alone or as a family, take note of how much television you've been watching. Sitting around with the tube on makes it difficult to get up and have fun. And years of sitting around with the tube on makes it difficult to remember how to get up and have fun.

5. Media causes "Christianity confusion."

In recent years, the Grammys, American Music Awards, and MTV Music Video Awards have offered a glimpse into popular music's curious interest in spiritual things. For some reason, a great many performers who receive awards take the time to include God or Jesus in their long list of thank-yous. It isn't unusual for deity to be mentioned first.

Christian kids are sometimes encouraged by the fact that secular music stars mention God and Jesus. "Did you hear Aerosmith thank 'sweet Jesus' after they got their award last night! They must be Christians!" Don't be fooled. Religious images, symbols, and chatter, whether in concerts or on album jackets, are becoming more and more a part of the music scene. But many of the artists who invoke the name of God or use religious symbols preach some of the most ungodly messages ever heard in popular music. Chances are that your kids could be confused by these messages that re-create God in the images of the musicians and lie about the true nature of the Christian faith.

When popular music addresses religious themes, it becomes a type of Sunday school or catechism class for our children and teens. We need to be conscious of the theological education music is giving our kids and to work on helping them distinguish what is good, true, and right from what is bad, false, and wrong.

Five Parental Guidelines for Dealing with Music and Media

What positive and productive steps can parents take to address the issues of music and media? I strongly suggest that we address the challenge of music and media in the same way that we are to face all difficult issues that life sends our way. The place to start is with God, the Creator of individuals, parents, children, and families. His Word, the Bible, provides direction, truth, hope, and strength in the midst of our confusion and questioning. In it we find useful guidelines on how to help ourselves and our children through the world of music and media. The remainder of this chapter offers practical and time-tested strategies from God's Word.

GUIDELINE #1: *Evaluate everything you hear and see.*

All of our beliefs are founded on some authority. Some choose to pass judgment based on their own personal preference. Others decide what they like and don't like based on what they were raised to believe. Others share the convictions of friends. But when it comes to evaluating what we see and hear, we must appeal to an authority that we can believe. I have attempted to base all my music and media judgments in this book on the criteria established by God in his Word. As Christians, we should use the Bible as our measuring stick for evaluating everything that we hear and see.

The difficulty lies in the fact that God never gives direct instruction on the types of media, styles of music, or particular bands. You can read the Bible from cover to cover and you will never find the words "Thou shalt not listen to Pearl Jam" or "In all your ways acknowledge him, and for goodness sake, trash your TV." But informed study of God's Word yields specific and helpful guidance on what to enjoy and what to avoid, and on how to tell the good from the bad and truth from lies.

Because I am limited here by space, I will highlight only two passages that shed light on how to evaluate music and media:

> Be imitators of God, therefore, as dearly loved children and live a life of love, just as Christ loved us and gave himself up for us as a fragrant offering and sacrifice to God.
>
> But among you there must not be even a hint of sexual immorality, or of any kind of impurity, or of greed, because these are improper for God's holy people. Nor should there be obscenity, foolish talk or coarse joking, which are out of place, but rather thanksgiving. For of this you can be sure: No immoral, impure or greedy person—such a man is an idolater—has any inheritance in the kingdom of Christ and of God. Let no one deceive you with empty words, for because of such things God's wrath comes on those who are disobedient. Therefore do not be partners with them.
>
> For you were once darkness, but now you are light in the Lord. Live as children of light (for the fruit of the light consists in all goodness, righteousness and truth) and find out what pleases the Lord. Have nothing to do with the fruitless deeds of darkness, but rather expose them. (Eph. 5:1-11, NIV)

Finally, brothers, whatever is true, whatever is noble, whatever is right, whatever is pure, whatever is lovely, whatever is admirable—if anything is excellent or praiseworthy—think about such things. (Phil. 4:8, NIV)

If these passages could be reduced to their simplest terms, they would say:

> Imitate God. Avoid those themes, messages, and behaviors that God says are wrong. They will harm and destroy you. Indulge in those themes, messages, and behaviors that God says are pure, true, lovely, and admirable. They will heal and preserve you.

Bad music and media can erode the faith of a child, teen, or adult just like pornography, adultery, or lack of fellowship can chip away at the well-established faith of an adult. God knew exactly what he was saying when he included these and other commandments in his written Word. By following these commands, we choose to protect ourselves from harm and open ourselves up to all the good things that God has in store for us.

In order to effectively evaluate everything you see and hear, you must know where God stands on the issues. This means that you must continue to study his Word and learn his will on a daily basis. This will provide you with a strong knowledge of right and wrong. Then, and only then, can you move on to evaluate the music and media that you and your children are exposed to every day.

Let me suggest a simple three-step plan for evaluating what you see and hear in the media. Learn it. Practice it. And pass it on to your kids.

STEP #1: Discover. Watch the show, movie, or video. Listen to the music. As you watch and listen, ask yourself these questions to help you discover the underlying philosophy and message of the piece:

- What does it say about God?
- What does it say about humanity?
- Is the one true God replaced by some other deity (self, money, etc.)?
- What does it say about happiness and where it comes from?
- Is it hopeful or hopeless?
- What does it say about the nature of sexuality?
- Are solutions offered to life's problems? If so, what are they?
- Who is the hero?
- Who is the villain?
- What character traits are promoted as positive? negative?
- How is beauty and personal worth established and defined?

- How is the family portrayed?
- What world and life view is behind what I am seeing and hearing?

STEP #2: Discern. Evaluate what you have discovered in Step #1 against the measuring stick of God's Word in order to ascertain whether or not the video, song, movie, show, etc. is in agreement or disagreement with God's never-changing truth. This will allow you to see what each media piece really is when it is scrutinized under the illumination of God's Word, instead of just evaluating it on the basis of personal taste or preference. With a little practice, this critical biblical thinking will help you determine whether the underlying philosophy and message is right or wrong.

STEP #3: Decide. If what is being taught is in agreement with biblical truth, then enjoy it! But if it contradicts what God has said is right, you need to ask yourself the following questions:

- *Should* I listen or watch?
- *Will* I listen or watch?

First, evaluate your reason for viewing. If you are watching to critique the media and gain further understanding of the world of your children and teens, then decide whether or not you can continue to watch carefully. Or are you watching for the sole purpose of entertainment? Only you know when you have crossed that line.

Second, evaluate what you're watching. If what you're watching is wrong or harmful or if you should redeem your time by doing something else, you need to choose. Will you change the channel or turn the set off? Or will you continue to waste your time and mind on meaningless garbage?

Most of us have never taken the time to watch and listen critically. Or perhaps the extent of our critique has been only to register disgust with the excessive violence, sex, and profanity that we see and hear. If this is true for you, you need to go a step further. There is much more in the media to be concerned about than gunfire, skin, and foul language. By taking the time to know God's Word and apply it through critical viewing, you will learn how to be a healthy media consumer, a skill that we desperately need to model and pass on to our children and teens.

GUIDELINE #2: Avoid extremes!

There is no possible way any of us can deny the potent power of music and media to manipulate our children and teens during adolescence. The lessons that they learn during the wonder years form the foundation for the way they will look at the world until the day they go to their graves. If we allow music and media an open door, our children will be impacted for the rest of their lives.

Faced with this real danger, many of us make the mistake of responding to the challenges that we have discussed by going to extremes. While reacting in these ways may be the easiest and most time-efficient responses, they do nothing to help our kids learn for themselves how to watch and listen with discernment. Here are two counterproductive extremes that you should avoid at all costs.

EXTREME #1: "Run for your life!" If you've ever watched the action-packed adventures of Indiana Jones or MacGyver, you know the heroes in these far-fetched tales always narrowly escape certain doom and death. The hero discovers a bomb that is ticking down with only seconds left. In one last desperate attempt to escape, the characters run like crazy and dive away just as the bomb explodes.

Teach your kids to listen and watch with discernment.

Many parents take the same approach to music and media. Once they discover what's actually out there, they grab their children and teens while screaming, "Run for your life!" Let's be honest. The world of music and media sometimes seems like a ticking bomb. If we hang around too long, we think it will blow up in our faces.

You may have been tempted to run into your teenager's room to smash their television and gather up their tape and CD collection for use as kindling. Some parents feel that the best way to deal with the threat is to simply eliminate it by separating their children from it: "There will be no rock music and no television in this house from this point on. You are not allowed to listen or watch anymore . . . and that's that!!" When the curious teen asks why, the typical response is "Because I said so!" Either no explanation is given or, if it is, it is done in a very dictatorial and angry way.

Is this approach healthy? I don't think so. *First, it equates the world of music and media to a ticking bomb.* But not all music and media is bad. Although there are certain messages and themes that must be dealt with, we shouldn't throw the baby out with the bath water. As Quentin Schultze has said, "Too many parents try to take the easy way toward holiness by naively and ignorantly rejecting culture."[3]

Second, this approach is totally unrealistic. There is no way that we can successfully separate our children and teens from the media's influence. All they have to do is walk out the door to play with a friend, pick up the phone, or go to school, and they'll interact with a peer group that has been living in a media-saturated world. Supreme Court Justice John Paul Stevens has a word for those who suggest that the answer is to separate ourselves: "To say that one may avoid further offense by turning off the radio when he hears indecent language is like saying that the remedy for an assault is to run away after the first blow."[4]

Third, by virtue of the fact that parents make all their teens' media decisions for them, their teens will miss out on the opportunity to learn how to make good judgments for themselves. Granted, there are times when parents must exercise their right to say no. But sometimes we forget that adolescence is the bridge from childhood to adulthood. We need to honor our teens' developing ability to think for themselves by walking them through the decision-making process. It is important for them to understand the whys behind our nos. If we want them to develop the ability to discover, discern, and decide on their own, we need to give them reasons, not just restrictions. In effect, we are teaching them to "defuse the bombs" that the media throws our way, therefore eliminating the need to run in fear. This is a valuable skill that they can pass on to others, including your grandchildren!

Fourth, I have seen this approach used enough times to know that it has the potential to destroy family unity and lead kids into rebellion. This is usually the case when parents whose teenagers have already established media tastes and music collections come on like gangbusters as a result of their newfound awareness. Older teens are insulted and angered. The apostle Paul speaks to this type of approach in Ephesians 6:4 when he says, "Do not exasperate your children" (NIV). While Paul is not encouraging parents to forsake their responsibility or undermining their authority, he is warning against inciting a state of perpetual resentment in our kids. Parents who suddenly change their approach and assume a dictatorial stance with their older children lack respect for their teens' ability to work through the issues with parental help, and they run the risk of losing the respect of their children. There are better ways.

Fifth, this "run for your life" approach is contrary to what God wants our children to become. When Jesus prayed for his followers, he said, "My prayer is not that you take them out of the world but that you protect them from the evil one" (John 17:15, NIV). The place for God's people, our children and teens included, is in the world, but not of it.

When our only approach is to tell our children to "run for your life," we are disobedient to God, we do a disservice to our children, and we fail to see the good potential in music and media.

EXTREME #2: "I didn't hear anything, did you?" My wife, Lisa, is good at hearing noises in our house during the middle of the night. Her first response is to sit up in bed and listen more closely. Because I tend to sleep through anything, she will nervously wake me up and say, "Walt, I just heard something. Go see what it was." Let me make a confession here. I usually don't want to get up. I'm tired. I want to keep sleeping. Even in those cases where there is a noise and I've heard it myself, I still don't want to get up! Why? I don't want to walk downstairs in the dark if there's someone down there waiting for me! It's easier to deny that I heard anything at all, avoid confrontation, roll over, and go back to sleep.

There are many parents who have slept through the many negative messages and themes thrown their way by music and media. The "noise" has been in their house for a long time. But one of the worst possible responses is to roll over, deny that they've heard anything, and go right back to sleep. They casually overlook the power of music and media to shape the values, attitudes, and behaviors of their children and teens. They don't say anything at all. Assuming that the best or easiest approach is to let nature take its course, they allow their kids to continue to listen to and watch anything and everything.

Is this a healthy approach? Certainly not, for several reasons. *First, children and teens see that parents don't really care about what they (the kids) listen to or watch.* This parental silence sends a loud message to the kids that they can partake of anything from media's diverse menu because it really doesn't matter.

Second, when parents become silent during the crucial years of adolescence, the door is opened even further for other voices to come in and answer the questions and concerns of teens. Music and media are happy to take on the job of socializing our kids and molding their life view. Without any counterguidance from parents, the media voice becomes even more effective.

Third, children run the risk of being rightly in the world and wrongly of the world. They are left unprotected from the evil one (see John 17:15). It is as if we send them to the front line of a military battle without weapons, armor, tactical knowledge, or camouflage. In fact, they stand there wearing a bright orange hunter's vest, giving an unspoken invitation to "go ahead and shoot me!"

And finally, failing to offer guidance and direction is an unrealistic, uncaring, and unloving approach to parenting. While Paul warns parents against exasperating their children, the second half of that instruction is to "instead, bring them up in the training and instruction of the Lord" (Eph. 6:4, NIV). If we love our children, we will be concerned about the voices of media that wander through our house. We will protect our children from those voices that seek to lead them away from the truth of God's Word, and at the same time, we will teach them how to protect themselves as they move through adolescence and into adulthood.

When our only approach is to roll over, turn our back, and say, "I didn't hear anything, did you?" we are disobedient to God, we do our children a disservice, and we fail to see the incredible negative power of music and media.

GUIDELINE #3: Examine yourself.

A positive approach to helping your children and teens face the world of music and media begins with you. *What are you doing personally to guide your children through the maze of media and music?* Following are a number of tasks that are crucial to your success in successfully addressing these issues.

Pray. The beauty of prayer is that we are able to talk to the all-knowing creator of the universe! When we find ourselves in situations where we don't have a clue what to do, we can pray. While we should be conversing with God all the time, it is reassuring to know that God wants us to openly share with him the longings of our hearts. When our children are immersed in a hostile media world and resistant to our efforts to guide them through it, we can pray.

- *Pray for yourself.*

Ask God to challenge and change your media consumption habits if they are not pleasing to him. Tell God that you need wisdom, courage, insight, and strength for the task of steering your children to make good media choices. As you begin to evaluate the world of music and media and teach your children to do the same, pray that you will be protected from the negative images and themes that you see and hear. Ask God to make it clear to you when you cross the fine line between critique and entertainment, so that you will know when to turn it off and find something else to do.

- *Pray for your teenager.*

Ask God to help them avoid confusion, develop wisdom to distinguish good from bad, and make appropriate decisions.

- *Pray for the people who control the media.*

The producers, directors, writers, singers, actors, and executives all need our constant prayers. Think about it for a moment. What would happen if God changed Madonna's heart and she began to use her talents in service to him? It seems ridiculous and impossible. But think about the apostle Paul and his experience on the Damascus road (see Acts 9). Stranger things have happened. If God is big enough to change the heart of the greatest persecutor of the church from a hater of God to a committed servant of God, he could do the same to Madonna—or anyone else, for that matter! Pray for them with passion and Christlike compassion.

Know where God stands and plant yourself in the same place. Build a foundation from which you can begin to discern right from wrong and truth from lies. Develop a growing knowledge of God's perspective. Take the time to study the Bible on a daily basis. Put your preconceived notions aside and ask him to make his Word live in your life. If you skip this step, all of your other efforts will be for nothing.

If we want to help our kids, we will evaluate our own listening and viewing habits.

Watch your step. Let me ask you a few difficult questions. How much time do you spend in front of the TV? What shows do you watch? Are there shows that you watch only if the kids are out of the room or in bed? And if so, why? Do you laugh at sitcom humor that is racist or sexual or that devalues people? Do you watch soap operas? Would it be difficult for you to turn off the TV and read a book or spend time with your family? What kind of music do you listen to? Do you avoid that "nasty" rock and roll only to spend time listening to country?

Each of us must be sure that we have evaluated and adjusted our own habits before we begin to deal with our kids. By consistently modeling responsible media behavior, we can become signposts pointing our kids in the right direction. Otherwise, we're phonies—and kids can sniff out phonies very quickly.

Familiarize yourself with what's out there. I am concerned about a disease that is infiltrating the church. I call it the egg-on-the-face syndrome. The symptoms are easy to spot. A group of Christians or an individual criticizes a film, television show, rock band, etc. as contributing to the moral decline of America and her children. They levy strong accusations against the "offender" and recruit others to get on the bandwagon. All too often, people who take this course act like they know what they are talking about, but they don't. Why? Because they react on the basis of information they heard second- or thirdhand. It isn't long before someone challenges their accusations, and they wind up with egg on their face because they have never seen, heard, or investigated the very thing that they are criticizing. They judge without knowing the facts.

If we are going to be responsible in our efforts to help our kids make good media choices, we had better prepare ourselves so that we know what we are talking about. We can't attack an album, show, or movie on the basis of what we've heard in an extended game of whisper-down-the-lane. We need to get the facts so that we can intelligently discuss those shows, films, and songs that concern us.

This approach has biblical precedent. When the apostle Paul approached the idolatrous people of Athens, he did so in an informed manner. The book of Acts recounts his experience: "Men of Athens! I see that in every way you are very religious. For as I walked around and looked carefully at your objects of worship, I even found an altar with this inscription: TO AN UNKNOWN GOD. Now what you worship as something unknown I am going to proclaim to you" (Acts 17:22-23, NIV). Paul didn't open his mouth until he knew what he was talking about; he had walked through the city with his eyes and ears open. He didn't rely on some book or seminar tape for his information; he went out and did his own research. This approach allowed him to be better informed, credible in the eyes of his audience, more convinced of his own message, and far more effective as a communicator of what was right and true.

People are more apt to listen to us when we have done our research. If we are misinformed loudmouths, they will laugh us off and never hear what we have to say. The account in Acts goes on to say that even though some of his listeners sneered in disagreement, many wanted to hear more. In fact, a few even believed and became followers (Acts 17:32-34).

Do you want to be credible in the eyes of your children and teens? Don't rely solely on the information in this book. This book has only scratched the surface. Continue to examine the world of music and media for yourself. Here are some suggestions to help you stay informed:

- Read the entertainment page in your daily newspaper. Look for information on music, shows, and films that interest your kids.
- Watch the shows your kids watch, and evaluate content, messages, and themes.
- Browse through your child's album collection. Read the lyrics on the sleeve. If the lyrics aren't printed, listen to the music. If you still can't understand what they are saying, ask your kids!

- Watch an hour of MTV each week. Check your TV listing for the day and time that the MTV Top 20 Countdown is aired. This will afford you a quick glimpse into the most popular music of that particular week.
- To keep up with popular music, browse through *Rolling Stone* or *Spin* magazines. *Entertainment Weekly* offers a weekly peek into the world of music, television, and movies and regularly prints a guide that offers an overview of movie content, plots, and themes. It even includes a rundown of objectionable content, including profanity, sex, violence, and story lines.
- Subscribe to *Media Update*, the magazine of Al Menconi Ministries. (See "Good Reading for Parents" at the end of this book.)

Exert consumer influence. The bottom line in the entertainment industry is money. That's why Dr. Richard Neill, a Fort Worth dentist, convinced advertisers to withdraw their dollars from the *Donahue Show. Tired of explicit content being aired at a time when children might be watching, Neill did his homework by taping dozens of shows and collecting transcripts. "I want to make sure everything is totally truthful. I want to be fair. There's no need to exaggerate. Truth is enough," says Neill.*[5] He then mailed his findings to advertisers. The truth was enough to convince many of them to remove their ads.

Letter writing and consumer influence works. But don't rely on preprinted petitions, opinion surveys, and postcards distributed by media watchdog organizations; sadly, many of those efforts are begun to raise funds for the watchdog group. A better approach is to write personal letters based on information you've gathered yourself. If you have seen or heard something that troubles you, register your complaint with advertisers, broadcast stations, and networks. And if you are impressed by the quality and content, register your approval with the same folks. A little encouragement can go a long way!

Find out why your child likes a particular show or type of music. Al Menconi has called music "a window to your child's soul." Responsible parents will work to understand their kids, recognize the signals, and discover and answer their child's questions.

Love your children. Studies show that today's kids are receiving smaller amounts of intimacy and attention from their parents. When intimacy and attention are absent from the home, kids will be more vulnerable to outside influences.

Media has an incredible ability to replace the family. When kids don't communicate with parents, they will sit and listen to the TV, radio, and Walkman. When kids don't feel respected by their parents, the media will accept them for who they are. When parents don't spend time with their kids, the TV is always there to keep them company. And when our kids don't feel like we are committed to them, the TV, in search of advertising dollars and ratings points, is there to let them know that they are important and needed.

Yes, the media has incredible power. It has the power to fill the void left by absent, detached parents and unloving homes. But this void can easily be filled by parents who express their love to their kids by giving them input, respect, time, and the sense that they are indeed valuable and important.

GUIDELINE #4: Be proactive with your kids.

When we begin to realize the powerful ability of music and media to shape our kids, our parental inclination is to do something fast to counter that influence. If you prefer quick-fixes like I do, you've probably been wondering when I was going to mention some hands-on approaches to use with your kids. Well, here they are. But don't make the mistake of skipping the guidelines I have already mentioned. If you don't follow those first three guidelines, you will be undermining and jeopardizing the effectiveness of the following strategies.

Listen and watch with them. God has given parents the treasured trust of children. As they grow older he calls us not so much to *guard* them as to *guide* them so they can function responsibly on their own in the big cruel world.

When student pilots first begin flying lessons, the instructor never begins the maiden voyage by saying, "Go ahead and take her up!" Rather, the student pilot sits and observes as the instructor demonstrates how to fly the airplane. Then, in subsequent lessons, the instructor hands over the controls little by little. Once the student has gained sufficient ability to take off, fly, and land, the instructor assumes the copilot's position and simply goes along for the ride. While I'm sure it requires great discipline on the part of the instructor to keep from grabbing the controls, the only way students learn is by flying the plane themselves. But during this step, the instructor is still there, offering suggestions and guidance, ready to take over in the case of an extreme emergency. Finally, when the instructor feels that the student pilot is ready, the instructor stays on the ground as the student goes solo. If the instruction has been presented effectively, the teacher has every reason in the world to feel confident in the student's abilities.

We can nurture our kids into making good music and media

choices through the same process. Sadly, many parents think that they are protecting their kids by making all the choices for them. But what will happen to them when they grow up and leave the house to fly solo without ever having had the opportunity to hold the controls on their own? Somewhere between parental modeling and the student solo must be a number of lessons.

Do your kids go to movies, watch TV, and listen to music? Then go, watch, and listen with them from time to time. Afterward, sit and talk about what everyone saw or heard. Take the time to walk them through the evaluation process of discovering, discerning, and deciding. Initially keep your hands on the controls to show your children how to evaluate everything they see and hear. Then gradually hand over the controls, and let your kids put into practice what you are teaching. Their abilities will be somewhat shaky initially, but don't grab the controls too soon. Most kids don't have the benefit of parents who care enough to take the time to watch and listen with them. You will be surprised at how much they will appreciate your involvement. And you will also be surprised at how well-equipped they will be to take off, cruise, and land by themselves as they leave you standing confidently on the ground!

Play "locate the lie." This game will make those long and boring television commercial breaks a little more exciting. It's simple: Whenever a commercial comes on, see who in the family can spot the lie first. Look for ways that the advertiser might be making the product look better than it is. Race to see who can be the first to figure out the hidden messages regarding what the soap, perfume, beer, soda, etc. being advertised will do for you. As you play the game, picture the advertiser sitting in a boat on top of your TV set. Imagine that he is dangling a fishing line with the commercial hooked as bait on the end. Then decide how he is trying to hook and catch you.

This little game will help your children learn the necessary skills to be discriminating media consumers who won't get hooked by silly lies and lures.

Don't argue and act like you have all the answers. I'm not going to pretend that the "flying lessons" will be smooth sailing for either parent or child. There will undoubtedly be times when you listen and watch together, only to disagree. In light of the fact that your growing teenagers have the ability to think on an adult level (as crude and undeveloped as that ability may be) and need to be treated as such, here are some suggestions on how to handle the turbulence:

- *Be sure that you listen hard.*

You might have to curb that parental inclination to assume that you know what your children are going to say. After all, you know that you're always right, so why waste time? But interrupting what your kids are saying tells them that you don't value their opinion, that you don't respect their ability to think, and that you don't want to hear what they have to say.

If we use this approach too often, our kids won't ever want to talk to us, and we close the door to good communication. Many kids cite this as the biggest problem with their parents. They tell me that their parents are always interrupting and never willing to listen to what they have to say. At the same time, these kids tell me that they would be more than happy to open up to their parents if they were sure that they would be respected and heard. Teens have taught me that there are times when I, as a parent, better be ready to listen hard and zip it!

- *Be sure you have the facts straight before defending your view.*

This requires you to listen to the information your teen is giving and to his or her perspective. There is no way to answer arguments that you haven't heard. And it requires that you examine the evidence for yourself before passing judgment. Our credibility with our kids will be on shaky ground if we keep winding up with egg on our face. There may be times that we say to our teens, "Hey, I really don't know. Let me listen to that with you so I better understand what it's all about."

- *Don't get angry.*

Our kids will use bad judgment from time to time. As parents, we need to demonstrate the same reconciling love that Christ has shown to us. We must be patient when they make bad music and media choices. By remaining calm, we open the door to effective communication even wider and compliment them by allowing them the opportunity to communicate with us on an adult level.

Eat together. A few years ago, when I asked a large group of high school and junior high students about the amount of time they spent with their parents, one student remarked that the only time he spent with his parents was at the dinner table. When I asked him how many nights a week they ate together, he said, "One or two." I then asked the entire group to tell me by a show of hands how often they ate with their families. The majority said their families ate only two or three meals together in an entire week!

Why do I mention table time as a suggestion for dealing with media and music? Because chances are that if you don't spend time together here, you don't spend much time at all together as a family. And if you aren't together, you can't communicate. We live in a busy day and age.

But if we want to fulfill our role as the primary molders of our children, we had better spend time communicating at the table.

Everyone in your family has to eat. If your children are still young, make it a priority to be together at the dinner table. Set a precedent early on so that the table is a place where the family gathers by habit to communicate. And if you find that you are already in the bad habit of not eating together, take whatever steps you must to break the habit. If you have a difficult time talking, ask your kids about the most important things in their lives. In case you haven't already figured it out, music is one. Ask for their opinion and then just sit back and listen. The door to communication will be opened.

Play with your kids. One of the best lessons I learned from my parents is that there is more to life than sitting around and doing nothing. My parents were available to us on those quiet evenings when it would have been easy to plop down in front of the tube. But they always had something fun to do. We would play board games or cards, wrestle or box with my dad, build models, work in the basement woodshop, etc. Sure we watched TV, listened to the radio, and played records. But those voices were tempered by the involvement of our parents in our lives. We even learned to enjoy listening to our parents; there was good communication taking place. Because I had such fun-loving parents most of the neighborhood kids wanted to spend time at my house.

Creating fun family times with your children and teens will help to counteract much of the negative media pressure.

The key to successfully implementing this approach is to start when your kids are young. They will grow up looking forward to those fun family evenings. And when they are fully grown, they will realize, as I did, how special and important those times really were. I don't think I can recount the plot of more than a handful of the TV shows I watched as a kid. What I do remember are the fun times I spent with fun-loving parents.

When the going gets rough, offer alternatives. One of my favorite television commercials is set in the family living room sometime during the fifties. Two young adolescent girls are sitting on the floor in front of the TV watching the *Ed Sullivan Show*. Their parents are sitting in overstuffed chairs behind them. Ed Sullivan appears on the screen as the two girls anxiously await the arrival of his next guest. As

Sullivan says, "And now, ladies and gentlemen, here's Elvis!" the girls begin to scream. Just then the TV goes dead. As the girls sigh in disappointment, their father, who unbeknownst to them has unplugged the set, comes around the corner and says, "Must be a power failure. Let's go to McDonald's!" In a flash, the girls are happy again as they forget about missing Elvis.

While life may not be that simple (and kids certainly aren't that stupid!), there is a positive lesson to be learned from that commercial: If we are going to take something away from our children, we can soften the blow by offering an attractive alternative. Be prepared with some good alternatives. A quick trip to do something special or some positive Christian music can all serve to fill the void that is left when parents exercise their right and responsibility to take away music and media that can be harmful. Don't just take it away; replace it with something better!

Have family devotions. Our children and teens need to know that our music and media guidelines are not based on our own personal preference and opinions. Rather, a higher authority—God—guides us through the confusing mix of choices that face children, teens, and parents.

When a family sets aside time each day to focus their thoughts on God, amazing things begin to happen. By reading and studying the Bible together, parents and their children will know which steps are right and which are wrong. The Bible is an anchor of unchanging truth that offers stability not only in a rocky media world but for all of life. (To get started, check out your local Christian bookstore for a current selection of family devotionals and other devotional tools.)

Develop media guidelines and learn to say no. One of the biggest problems facing children today is that many of them are growing up in families where their parents never say no. Our kids need us to help them learn how to function responsibly in the world. By providing them with clear-cut boundaries, we offer them the opportunity to make their own choices within the safety of limits while protecting them from the dangers of unrestricted freedom. One recent study showed that over 50 percent of six to seventeen year olds report that their parents have set rules regarding their television consumption.[6]

Good parents will exercise their God-given responsibility to protect their children from harm and provide for their well-being by establishing guidelines for their media consumption. If you have younger children, let me encourage you to discuss media and music standards with your spouse. If your children are older, you might want to include them in the standard-setting process.

How can you develop media guidelines for your family? Try the following seven suggestions:

- *Decide on how long the TV will be on in your house each day.*

A good start is to allow no more than one hour of television viewing per day by your children. Parents would benefit from setting and following similar standards themselves.

- *Be sure to spend time viewing together.*

This will give you the opportunity to talk with your child about what you have just watched.

- *Develop standards regarding the specific shows, themes, and program content that will and will not be part of the media menu in your house.*

I suggest that you require your children to get parental approval for each show or movie they watch, and each tape or CD that they purchase. Be sure that as your children grow you offer detailed and age-appropriate explanations for your decisions and standards. And be sure to practice what you preach. Don't adopt a double standard that allows you to turn on the garbage after the kids are in bed.

- *Eliminate your cable service.*

Or notify your local cable company and ask them to block out those channels and services that you don't want in your home.

- *Put the TV in a cabinet that closes or set it in a less-than-prominent place in your house.*

Don't arrange your furniture in a way that turns the room into a temple to the electronic god. You might even want to put the TV in the basement. I know one family that keeps their TV in a cold unfinished cellar. When they choose to watch a program they sit on a pair of old vinyl bench seats that they ripped out of a junked van.

- *Make use of your VCR to tape quality programs and to view rented tapes.*

This allows the family more control over program content.

- *Don't be afraid to lay down the law and say, "No, we will not watch that show, listen to that music, or go to that movie."*

Your job is to protect your children from harm, provide for their well-being, and guide them into responsible adulthood. Sometimes the parent-teen clashes on that road result in a logjam. Use your God-given gift of parental intuition and say no when you have to.

GUIDELINE #5: Have patience.

How easy it would be if adolescence were an overnight phenomenon that was here today and gone tomorrow! But the process of moving from childhood to adulthood takes time. Not only is the transition painful for teens but it can be grueling and frustrating for those parents who desperately want to see their kids make healthy choices on the road to adulthood. Some of our children and teens will resist our efforts to help them discover, discern, and decide on music and media. But don't give up. Your efforts will pay off even though there may be no immediate return. Your adolescents are in the process of testing the waters of your values. Your job is to close the wide-open access that media has had to your home and then to serve as a wise and discerning gatekeeper who lets in all that is good while keeping out all that is bad.

■ IT'S YOUR TURN

How has the world of the media affected your home? your attitudes, values, and behaviors? How have your kids been influenced in positive and negative ways by media's confusing mix of messages? Who are the heroes your children strive to emulate? Has the media chipped away at your children's concept of who they are as people created by God with value, dignity, and worth? Is life around your house boring when the TV is not on? Do you feel comfortable sitting together to just talk? Have the messages of popular music numbed your children to the truth about God as contained in his Word?

These are questions that we all must answer. And our answers will tell us to what degree we've opened the doors of our homes, allowing the powerful influence of media and music to walk right in.

Never underestimate the power of media and music to mold and shape your children. Take the time to understand the themes and messages. Be alert to the influence of media and music in your home. Be diligent in your efforts to guide and direct your kids. And, above all, heed the words of the apostle Paul: "Base your happiness on your hope in Christ. When trials come endure them patiently; steadfastly maintain the habit of prayer"(Rom. 12:12, Phillips).

Understanding the Pressures Your Teen Faces

7

BUT MY FRIENDS DO IT!

▮▮▮

Peer pressure is . . . having to be what other kids want you to be.

Ninth-grade student

WHEN I WAS a boy, our family traveled from Pennsylvania to Florida each summer for a month of vacation. When we weren't fishing, swimming, or visiting tourist attractions, my brothers and I would venture out on a "lizard safari." Although we knew chameleons were hiding in every bush and tree, at first we had a hard time spotting them. But it wasn't long before we learned that when the chameleons were hiding on the green leaves of a palmetto plant, we'd be looking for a green chameleon. Those same chameleons could sit on the trunk of a palm, turn brown, and be almost invisible. At other times, they would turn almost gray, camouflaging themselves from the "great hunters" while sunning on the stucco walls of the house. In an effort to protect itself from the danger of predators, a chameleon will change color to blend in with its environment.

When they become teens, our kids will be tempted, to one degree or another, to become like chameleons. Caught in the midst of change, confusion, challenge, media bombardment, family dysfunction, and a host of other stresses, they yearn for stability and normalcy. In an effort to protect themselves from feeling like they've been left alone to wander through adolescence, our teens will change colors and blend in with the surrounding environment—the peer group.

Negative peer pressure is frightening—perhaps even more so to those of us who remember facing it when we were teens. We don't want our kids to make the same mistakes and bad choices that we did. We want to protect them from the painful pull between doing what is easy and doing what is right. But peer pressure rears its ugly head when our children and teens begin to test and evaluate the values we have worked hard to instill. And it turns its head and snarls at us when the children we love compromise their learned commitment to right and wrong by going with the flow.

In this chapter we will examine peer pressure, the reasons it reaches its apex during the adolescent years, and how it works to mold and shape our children and teens. We'll discover some of the pressures today's kids face and look at the results of giving in to those pressures. And finally, we will discuss some specific strategies to help you counter the influence of negative peer pressure in the life of your teenager.

The Whats and Whys of Negative Peer Pressure

Adolescence is a time filled with pressures of all kinds. But the most common pressure facing our teens is the pressure to conform. In this section we will examine some of the whats and whys of peer pressure so that you will be better prepared to understand its effects on your children and teens.

Negative peer pressure is no respecter of age.

On the day before she started kindergarten, our daughter Caitlin asked me a startling question: "Daddy, when I go to school tomorrow, will people make fun of me?"

"Why would people make fun of you, Caitlin?" I asked.

"Well, what if they make fun of me because of what I look like or what I'm wearing?" she responded.

I wasn't sure why Caitlin had asked such a question at her young age. Lisa and I hadn't consciously done anything to instill prejudice or an obsession with clothes in Caitlin. That night I probed further in the hope that I might find what was at the root of her fear. As it turned out, she had overheard some children in her nursery school, several months earlier, making fun of one of the boys for the way he dressed and how his hair was cut. Consequently she feared that as she arrived in a new environment with unfamiliar faces, she might be singled out as one who didn't conform to the standards of the rest of the group. She was, at five years old, feeling the effects of peer pressure and expectations.

Peer pressure pays no attention to age. Anyone who has raised a child through elementary school knows that peer pressure exists there. Those children who don't fit in or conform to the majority's standards are excluded from playground activities and included when it is convenient for someone to use them as the butt of a joke.

One study of third through sixth graders examined the degree to which children are subjected to verbal and physical abuse by their peers. The study found that one in ten children appear to be severely abused by their peers.[1] Typically, these victims are the kids who are shoved aside because they fail to conform to the group's standards of dress, looks, economic status, or behavior.

Adults are victims and perpetrators in the peer-pressure game as well. Our clothing, houses, cars, and hairstyles usually reflect what is perceived to be acceptable in society at that point in time. Those who dress in outdated clothes are the targets of condescending stares and demeaning comments. Women are made to feel inferior if they don't get "their colors done" by those who suggest that femininity is brought to completeness by conforming to some humanly defined process and standard. Men often compete to earn more money or to buy better "toys." We become overly concerned with the appearance and content of our homes, going beyond just keeping them neat and clean to an obsession with having everything in order for fear that disorder might lead someone to think less of us.

Peer pressure is no respecter of age. Even young children are affected by it.

Peer pressure is a part of life for people of all ages.

Peer pressure reaches its greatest intensity during the adolescent years.

In the adolescent years, kids experience a natural shift in social focus from the family to the peer group. As part of their move toward self-sufficiency and independence, teenagers no longer see their family as the center of their social universe. They begin to disengage from the family while forming more and more meaningful relationships with same-sex and opposite-sex peers.

Some developmental experts have likened this transition to an orbiting satellite.[2] During the childhood years, thinking and behavior revolve around what a child has been taught by parents. The onset of adolescence brings with it a "desatellization" as the child spins out of the orbit of parental identity to define himself as a distinct person. Naturally, this quest to discover oneself, independent from parents, leads kids to look elsewhere for guidance and direction. Where do they find it? In the peer group.

This transition is often turbulent for parents, especially when kids take on thinking and behaviors drastically different from our own.

The sudden changes can leave parents feeling like they've failed. Some of the changes are troublesome and warrant parental concern, attention, and intervention (for example, when kids become sexually active, abuse drugs or alcohol, or participate in delinquent behavior, it shouldn't be laughed off as a part of normal adolescence). On the other hand, a change in clothing, hairstyle, or "look" shouldn't send us over the edge (for example, your son comes home with his ear pierced).

A walk through the halls of any junior or senior high school in the United States proves that peer influence is the strongest during these years. Look at their clothing; read the labels. Notice the athletic shoes they're wearing. Listen to the way they talk. Look at their hair. If you think that they look and sound alike, you are right. Most kids go out of their way to identify with some group of peers in their school. And if you are tempted to think that this is a phenomenon for this generation alone, take a walk through the halls of your high school yearbook!

As your children move through the post–high school and college years, the influence of the peer group gradually will decrease. They will become more secure in who they are, and a "resatellization" occurs. Amazingly, your children will begin to look more like you in terms of their values, attitudes, behaviors, and lifestyle even though they are well established in the groove of their own "orbit." While they will continue to experience peer pressure to one degree or another for the rest of their lives, young adult children already will have passed through the years when the pressure is turned up to its greatest intensity.

Parental absence makes the pressure stronger.

"It's great to be together as a family again!" a father said to his wife and sons at the end of a parent-teen weekend I had been leading. His words bothered me. Had they *not* been spending time together? Why? Had he been away on some extended business trip? Were the boys attending a boarding school? Had the parents separated in the midst of some marital difficulty? No, it wasn't any of these things. Rather, each family member, while living in the same house, had been so involved in their own activities that it took a weekend away from home for them to spend time together again!

While it is natural for parents and teens to spend less time together as the kids pass through adolescence, it is dangerous to assume that it is all right to avoid making time to spend as a family. Parents who choose to become overinvolved in work, recreation, and other outside activities are also making the choice to spend less time with the family. As a result, they open the door for their teens to spend more time living with and listening to the peer group.

Numerous studies all agree that kids spend far more time with their friends than with their parents. One survey found that teens spend four hours each day with friends, compared to one hour with both parents, forty minutes with their mother, fifteen minutes with other adults, and five minutes with their father.[3] Another researcher reported that teens spend an average of thirty-five seconds a day with their father!

It is normal for teens to spend more time with their peers than with their parents.

Developmental expert David Elkind encourages parents to spend more time with their teens. He cites the breakdown of the family as one of the main reasons for the crisis among adolescents in America. In his book *All Grown Up & No Place to Go,* Elkind says that what teens need is time to grow through the normal and confusing changes of adolescence. Yet, our society pushes them through adolescence, forcing them into a premature adulthood that they are unable to handle. The deteriorating family, including absent and uninvolved parents, is to blame. The result for our teens, says Elkind, is stress and its aftermath.[4] Much of that stress occurs when the powerful influence and expectations of the peer group are not balanced by loving, involved parents who spend time with their kids.

The majority of American teens answered True to the following statements in high percentages:

STATEMENT	PERCENTAGE OF TEENS THAT AGREED
My close friends understand me better than my parents do.	70 percent
I feel right now in my life I learn more from my close friends than I do from my parents.	70 percent
I'm more "myself" with my close friends than with my parents.	68 percent[5]

Although to some extent these are natural feelings for teens as they travel down the developmental road to adulthood, I believe these numbers would be significantly lower if parents and teens spent more time together. And more kids would be better equipped to handle the stresses and strains of negative peer pressure.

The worse their self-image, the harder they fall.

The commercial is fast and exciting. Handsome tennis star Andre Agassi moves back and forth across the court making shots that you and I could only dream of making. And then in an effort to sell viewers a high-tech 35mm camera, Agassi speaks what has become known as his personal motto: "Image is everything!"

"Image is everything." At those times when your teen's unusual values, dress, and behavior leave you angry, confused, and scratching your aging head, these three words bring meaning to why they do what they do.

Your kids will enter adolescence feeling unsure of themselves. They will wonder if they are OK, if they will have any friends. They might worry that they will never be accepted because of who they are, where they live, how they dress, or what they look like.

Today's teens want to feel like they belong. If they sense that they don't belong, they will begin to see themselves as abnormal.

Today's teens want to avoid the pain of being left out. If they made it a varsity sport, most kids would letter in the comparison game. The game is simple to play. First, you look at what everyone else is doing. Second, you look to see if you are doing it. And third, if you aren't like everyone else, you decide what you are going to do about it. Sadly, many kids will compromise their own identity to be accepted by their peers. Since peers become a reference point for attitudes and behavior during adolescence, kids will constantly be measuring themselves against that standard. Kids see what happens to the kid who doesn't fit in. They know that kid might have to eat alone, never get asked to a dance, or be made the butt of jokes, and they believe that anything is better than the pain of living like that. It all boils down to feeling good or bad about themselves.

Today's teens walk the fine line between conviction and compromise. In an effort to feel good about themselves, avoid pain, and be accepted, many kids face the struggle of being "forced" by peers to compromise their convictions in order to fit in. They want to be esteemed by others. As a result, they will often be too scared to stand up for what they believe. And when push comes to shove, acceptance by the crowd is more important in the decision-making process than personal convictions and values.

A few years ago I surveyed a group of Christian kids regarding the pressure to drink. Several of the high school students said that even though they believe that underage drinking is wrong, they felt they had to do it. For them, doing what was wrong was more acceptable than being left out.

Have you ever watched a flock of birds as they fly overhead? I don't know much about birds, but I do know they stick together. Sometimes I will stand and observe as they noisily move on to their destination. When the flock finally passes and the air is quiet again, there always is one bird lagging behind. My sensitive side takes over, and I want to yell, "Keep going! You're not far behind. You'll catch them." I feel bad that they've been left out. Kids who pass through adolescence, already unsure of themselves, can imagine no worse fate than being that last lonely bird. Because image is everything, some will do anything to catch up and settle in with the rest of the flock.

The nature of negative peer pressure has changed.

You probably can still recall what peer pressure felt like during your teen years. As a group of people invited you to "come on, do it!" you and they knew that what they were asking you to do was wrong. Today's peer pressure has changed.

First, many of those "bad" behaviors aren't seen as "bad" anymore. There is no longer the sense that if you do it (whatever "it" may be), you are doing something wrong. It follows that if everybody is doing it and there is nothing wrong with it, the pressure is more intense. A teen who refuses to do something universally accepted as wrong is somehow better off than a teen who refuses, on the basis of their values and convictions, to do something that the majority sees as normal and right. Today's moral relativism has actually intensified peer pressure.

A second change is that many of today's pressures are felt not as verbal invitation and temptations but as unspoken expectations. A seventeen year old explains it this way:

> When you hear "peer pressure" you think of people standing there going "C'mon, do it!" But it's not like that. You go to a party, and everyone's standing around drinking. And you feel left out because you're not. So you get a beer or whatever and you start feeling more relaxed: "OK, I'm fitting in." You start talking to people, and they start talking to you.[6]

Kids are aware of peer pressure.

Some adults believe that our children and teens are oblivious to the negative influence of their peers. But a poll conducted by *Teenage* magazine found that teens decide whether to drink, what to wear, and how to study based on peer pressure. Ninety percent of teens surveyed said they experienced peer pressure. Eighty percent said they gave in to peer pressure at least once a week, even if this meant doing something they knew was wrong. Sixty percent said they pressured others. Less than half said they try to stop peer pressure.[7]

When I asked a number of kids to complete the sentence, "My friends want me to . . ." the most common answer they gave was to "do and be what they want me to do and be." Our kids are aware of the incredible influence their friends consciously or unconsciously exercise on their daily lives.

The media throws fuel on the fire of negative peer pressure.

Some youth-culture watchers argue that peers have a greater influence on teens than the media does. But a close look at what kids pressure their peers to do offers evidence to the contrary. *It is the media that sets the peer pressure agenda and tells adolescents what to push on their peers.* Advertising tells them what kinds of jeans and sneakers to wear. The peer group, by encouraging kids to wear those jeans and sneakers, becomes the greatest sales force ever known to humankind! The "this is the nineties" attitude of today's media heroes saturates youth culture, rewriting values on sexuality, materialism, the value of people, and authority. Those in youth culture who don't buy into the latest attitude fads are seen by their peers as prudish and old-fashioned. The media has led our kids to believe that they can give them everything that they want and need: self-assurance, confidence, and a sense of security in who they are. Because of where they are in the developmental process, our kids buy into the lies. When the majority of the peer group has bought the lies, the pressure for the rest to conform is turned on full force. And once again the media finds it easy to have its way with our kids.

Christian kids are not immune to negative peer pressure.

In his enlightening book *Keeping Your Teen in Touch with God,* Dr. Bob Laurent examines the role that negative peer pressure plays in alienating adolescents from the church. After studying four hundred teens from Christian homes over a three-year period, he found that the peer group is their real world. Using statements designed to measure the influence of negative peer pressure, he asked for the response of Christian teens. Following are the results of his survey:

STATEMENT	CHRISTIAN TEENS' RESPONSE
I am more likely to act like a Christian when I'm with my Christian friends and to act like a non-Christian when I'm with my non-Christian friends.	Agree
I get upset when my non-Christian friends leave me out of their activities.	Agree
I'd rather be with my friends than with my family.	Agree
I try to keep up with the latest fads.	Strongly agree
My non-Christian friends' opinions are important to me.	Strongly agree
If I needed advice, I'd ask my friends before I asked my parents.	Agree
It bothers me when my non-Christian friends think I'm too religious.	Agree[8]

When their friends care little or nothing about religion, it becomes difficult for our Christian children to be enthusiastic about their own faith and consistent in the way they live it out.

In summary:
No matter what age we are, we can expect to face negative peer pressure from the day we are born to the day we die. Each of us will experience it in different ways and degrees, depending on our own life experience, peer group, and self-image. But at no time in the life cycle is negative peer pressure greater than during the confusing years our children spend between childhood and adulthood. Parents who realize the strong influence of peer pressure will be wise guides and guards of their kids.

Just What Are Our Kids Being Pressured to Do?

For the next few pages, I will walk you through five of the major "pressure points" that teenagers face each and every day. While this is not an exhaustive list, it will get you started on your quest to understand the nature and intensity of negative peer pressure. As you read through the list, keep in mind that peer pressure isn't unique to teens—it also enters the world of preteens and young children. And don't stop there. Do a little bit of self-evaluation to see if you, as an adult, are pressured in many of these same ways.

PRESSURE #1: To have the "perfect" body.

I love to watch people. Consequently, I don't mind spending time in airports and malls. I'll just find a seat, sit back, and watch the endless parade of characters. The sport gets especially exciting when I can observe people as they walk past a full-length mirror. Although some folks are too self-conscious to stop and gawk at their reflection, many nonchalantly sneak a peek at themselves. I've even seen some people turn around and come back for a second and third peek! It's hilarious! And I must admit, I'm guilty of the practice myself. Why do we do this? Are we afraid that if we go too long without looking in a mirror, we might forget what we look like? Is it because we are so taken by our stunning good looks that we just can't help ourselves? No, I think most of us are checking out those physical attributes that we believe are our shortcomings, hoping against hope that the next time we look in the mirror, things have changed. Let's face it: We are self-conscious and overly concerned with what we look like.

As bodies change and grow, our teens hope against hope that they will end up with the prototype physique and figure—like the beautiful people in the media. For a girl to be satisfied with her body, she must be shaped like Cindy Crawford. Guys need a chest, arms, and buttocks like the shirtless/faceless guys in the Levi's commercials. And, judging from the popularity of health clubs, workout videos, and fad diets, adults want their bodies to be perfect, too. The pressure is incredible. No matter what age you are, a perfect body draws attention and praise. Conversely, we have been taught to believe that an imperfect, out-of-proportion, or overweight body makes us less than desirable. Acceptance hinges on what we look like.

The pressure for the perfect body begins to reach its ugly peak during the junior high years. Self-conscious kids measure themselves against the standard and feel that they are growing too fast, too slow, too big, too short, too fat, or too skinny. They are concerned about their hair color and texture, their complexion, and the size of their breasts, noses, and muscles. David Elkind quotes fourteen-year-old George, a boy whose awareness of his physical self and the need for peer approval left him facing an intense dilemma. In a letter asking for help, he writes: "Help, I don't have any pubic hair that shows. The boys call me 'Baldy' and the girls want to know why, and it's so embarrassing. I'm fourteen. Shouldn't I have it by now?"[9] George knows that there is a standard, and he is painfully aware that he has fallen short. As a result, he has fallen victim to the embarrassing horror of being left out by his peers.

For those teens who don't measure up, the walk down the school hall can be lonely and frightening. Standing in front of the class to give an oral report can become an experience they dread for days. Taking a shower after gym class can be terribly embarrassing.

Teens feel incredible pressure to have a perfect body—to look like models or celebrities.

Other kids are haunted by the lie of the perfect body because of their own misconceptions about themselves. They can get to the point where they feel peer pressure that isn't even there simply because of how they see themselves. When I was in junior high, my posterior seemed to get a head start on all my other physical attributes. Numerous relatives commented that my rear end was a feature I had inherited from my grandmother. I laugh when I think about it now, but those remarks hung heavy on me whenever I would glance at my grandmother's backside. It hurt to know that I could only wear pants purchased in the Husky Boys department at Sears. I don't remember anyone at school ever commenting on the size of my buttocks. But I do remember walking down the hall thinking that, as I passed, every eye and every whisper was focused on what I thought was my jumbo backside.

Columnist Bob Greene discovered the intense pressure for the perfect body when he listened in on the Connections party line for teens:

> Out of curiosity I dialed into the junior version of Connections. I didn't say anything; I just wanted to see what kids had to say to one another. So I held the phone to my ear and listened. I'll tell you what I heard. It was like being dropped, invisible, into an adolescent netherworld where the boys and girls don't know you're there. A thousand interviews with kids fifteen and under couldn't elicit the information I gathered over two days and nights of listening silently and taking notes.

Greene says that after kids ask for first names, they want physical descriptions. Ninety percent of the girls seemed to say that they had long blonde hair, blue eyes, were five feet, five inches tall, and weighed in at 110 pounds. According to their self-descriptions, the guys seemed to stand six feet tall and weigh 170 pounds. They also had brown hair and liked to lift weights.[10]

The pressure to fit the mold has led many kids on a futile pursuit of the perfect body. More and more are taking drastic measures to get there. The prevalence of eating disorders among adolescent girls and women is due in large part to the cultural pressure on women to be thin. Those who suffer from anorexia nervosa are typically perfectionists who suffer from low self-esteem, irrationally believing that they are fat regardless of how thin they become. Those who suffer from bulimia seek to accomplish the same results by overeating and then purging themselves through forced vomiting. Eating disorders specialist Adel Eldahmy says that twelve to sixteen year olds suffer the most. More than a quarter of the girls in this age group resort to using laxatives, water-loss pills, and vomiting to lose weight.[11]

In contrast to girls, boys bulk up in the quest for the perfect body. More and more teenage boys are lifting weights and working out as they pursue this dream. Others combine hard work with the high-risk practice of taking steroids. It is estimated that over five hundred thousand adolescents nationwide are taking these synthetic male hormones in an effort to look better, run faster, and impress people.[12] Teens who use steroids report that they feel more confident and less shy in their personal relationships. By adding muscle they become more popular. Why? Because their peers see them as more attractive. The desire for the perfect body is so strong among most steroid users that they deny medically proven evidence that steroids are harmful. Some admit that the side effects of shrunken testicles, high blood pressure, liver malfunction, and psychological dependence are a small price to pay in exchange for adolescent popularity and acceptance.

If our society continues to equate personal value and worth with outward appearance, the pressure to have the perfect body will continue to be felt by all. Parents should be sensitive to the fact that this pressure peaks during the teen years.

PRESSURE #2: *To be dressed and groomed properly.*

Maybe you have a teenager or young child in your house who has said, "No way, Mom. I'd die if I had to wear that out of the house. People will laugh at me." Or maybe you've heard, "Come on, Dad. Please give me the money. I need those jeans. Everybody else is wearing them." Many of the teenagers I know are walking examples of an attitude—no, a *belief*—that clothes make the teen.

Kids become more clothes conscious at a younger and younger

age. Their concept of themselves hinges less and less on who they are on the inside and more and more on what they wear on the outside. Bruce Barol traced the development of the recently popular ripped-jean look among teenagers and found that "the most important determinant of a trend . . . is neither merchandisers nor the media. It's the vast, ineffable plasma of intra-teen peer pressure."[13]

Clothing is one of the main avenues teens will take on the drive to find their place as one of the group. If they want to be left out, they should just dress differently. If they want to be popular and accepted, they should dress the way that popular and accepted people dress. One study of high school students showed that those who wore out-of-style clothes were automatically classified as nerds who wore "ugly sweaters that look like their parents' choice, or hand-me-downs." Another commented, "They're in a different world. Like striped shirts that don't match."[14]

Help your children learn to discern between needs and wants.

The pressure to conform to the group in dress and grooming is the strongest type of peer pressure that adolescents report feeling.[15] This accounts for the fact that only 14 percent of teenagers "strongly agree" with the statement "I try to be different from my friends in the clothes I buy."[16] Rarely will you meet a teenager who is brave and daring enough to be the first person in the crowd to try something new.

Those of you who have access to Prodigy, the interactive computer network, can look into this adolescent obsession with clothes and grooming by logging on to one of the network's teen-fashion bulletin boards. Faceless guys use their computers to ask girls what kinds of clothes they like to see their men in. Faceless girls ask guys for their opinion on what's sexy. You'd be surprised at what you read!

The tragic murder of a seventeen year old in Philadelphia over her $450 gold earrings is one symptom of the pressure on kids to look good. Students who were interviewed after the murder complained about the pressure to keep in style and the resulting fear of traveling to school or work in public. Still, most of them said that they would stay on the cutting edge of clothing fashion and risk danger rather than risk losing acceptance and popularity.[17]

Responsible parents work to instill a sense of personal value and worth in their children that hinges on something other than how their hair is cut or what clothes they are wearing. They help their kids discern needs from wants; the health of our wallets and purses depends on it. But we cannot write off our children's concern with clothing and appearance. The pressure that they feel is very real and the price of peer rejection or being labeled a nerd is frightening.

PRESSURE #3: To be socially active.

We've all said it, and we've all heard it: "Aw, come on, Mom. It's not that bad. Everybody else is going. I'll be the only one left behind! That's not fair." As parents, we may have the best reasons in the world for saying no, but if our kids are the ones left behind, they will feel that we haven't been fair.

This pressure to conform in social activity is the second most intense pressure that teens feel from their peers.[18] One of the strongest instruments of adolescent pressure for generations is "everybody else is doing it." Kids pressure each other to do whatever the rest of the group is doing. It could be something as simple as a trip to the mall or movies, joining an afterschool sport or club, or taking a weekend trip.

While the tension increases as teens grow, parents will become aware of this pressure in two distinct stages. The first stage occurs on or near the onset of adolescence. As teens begin to move from dependence on parents to total independence, they will want to spread their wings and test them. Do you remember the first time you went out with your friends without parental supervision? Chances are that you were a young teen. Maybe someone's parents dropped you off at the mall or movies. You had your own wallet or purse, and you paid the cashier for your admission or purchase. You were doing it all yourself without the help of Mom and Dad, and you felt so big. For me, it was my first Saturday afternoon walk with the neighborhood "big" kids into a nearby town. The further I wandered from our house as we cut through yards and across a golf course, the more I felt like I had "arrived."

The second stage begins just about the time your kids and their friends get their driver's licenses. Armed with car keys and the ability to go wherever they want, whenever they want, some of your child's friends will put almost unbearable pressure on your teen to join in and "come along" on demand. If you are a parent who wisely exercises your God-given right and responsibility to set limits and say no, the pressure will become even more pronounced, at least for a while, for your teen.

The pressure to do what the rest of the crowd is doing can be intense. Teens do not want to be left behind, left out, or forgotten by the peer group that has become so important to them at this stage in their lives. Parents should recognize the power of this pressure and work to strike a balance between too much and too little freedom.

PRESSURE #4: *To drink and use drugs.*

When I surveyed a group of teens who were active in their church youth groups and professed faith in Christ, they told me that their greatest pressure was the pressure to drink and use drugs.

Are you surprised? I'm not. After all, today's teens are immersed in a youth culture that has been saturated with media and advertising messages telling them that alcohol does nothing but improve your life. They have grown up watching a generation of adults, sometimes even their own parents, model alcohol use as a way to relax and socialize. And as their drive for independence manifests itself in a desire to appear older than they are, they reason that smoking and drinking are surefire ways to look like an adult.

All adolescents encounter significant pressure to smoke and use alcohol. Even though there are fewer who identify feeling the pressure to use illicit drugs, the number is still significant. A 1987 *Weekly Reader* survey of 100,000 upper-elementary students found that kids in fourth to sixth grade are being pressured to use alcohol and marijuana. Thirty-six percent of fourth graders, 41 percent of fifth graders, and 51 percent of sixth graders reported experiencing peer pressure to drink beer, wine, or other types of liquor. Peer pressure to try marijuana was reported by 25 percent of fourth and fifth graders, and 34 percent of sixth graders.[19]

This pressure to drink intensifies as our kids grow older. Peer pressure to drink is so great among undergraduates that many colleges and universities are establishing "substance free" housing facilities. The University of Michigan has 1,200 students living in substance-free rooms. Each student promises not to drink, smoke, or use drugs while in their rooms or elsewhere in the dorms. The students who choose to live in these dorms say they have found relief from the intense peer pressure prevalent on so many college campuses today.[20]

While kids drink, smoke, and use drugs for many different reasons, peer pressure is a significant contributor to the alarming number of kids who choose to indulge. Nine out of ten teens experiment with alcohol; three out of five will experiment with an illicit drug. But ten out of ten will feel the pressure.

PRESSURE #5: *To have premarital sex.*

In 1987, popular singer George Michael climbed the pop charts with his song "I Want Your Sex." In it, he told kids that sex is "natural, chemical, logical, habitual, sensual, good, and fun." I'm a married man with four children. I have also spent time reading what God's Word has to say about sex. I'd have to agree with Michael on these points. But Michael takes the message further when he encourages free sexual expression outside of the bond of marriage. On this point I couldn't disagree with him more. Once sex before marriage becomes an accepted norm, the incidence of sexually transmitted diseases (STDs), teen pregnancies, and abortions increases dramatically among our youth. Unfortunately, our children and teens are part of a generation that has bought into this gospel according to George Michael and a host of other media heroes.

Chances are that your child, if they are a virgin, might wonder if they are one of the last few virgins on earth. While there are many kids who have held to their convictions and virginity, the majority are sexually active. Eight out of ten teenage boys and seven out of ten teenage girls will have sexual intercourse, many with numerous partners. That same majority, by virtue of the fact that they are a majority, pressures the minority to "get real, get normal, and get with the nineties" by getting sexually active. More and more braggers try to build themselves up in the eyes of their peers by describing real or imagined sexual conquests.

Changing bodies, exciting new sexual urges, and changing values all make our teens potential victims of sexual pressure. One study of a thousand teenagers found that 76 percent would go far enough sexually to feel experienced and not left out.[21]

Our kids are being lured and invited into sexual activity by many different and attractive voices. All too often the voice of their peers can't be resisted because resistance is a short, one-way street leading to the pain of rejection.

What Are the Results of Negative Peer Pressure?

The five pressures I have just described are very much a part of today's youth culture. Not all teens will come face-to-face with these five pressures in the same way. Some will struggle more with one pressure than another. Those who are more secure and confident (many times these are the ones who have seen biblical morality lived out at church and in a loving home) will find it easier to walk away. Other teens will give in willingly to any pressure that comes their way.

There are four results of negative peer pressure that can affect you and your children.

RESULT #1: Negative peer pressure can force our kids into moral dilemmas.

Several years ago I took thirty-five high school students on a white-water rafting trip. About halfway down the river, our guide instructed us to pull our rafts off to the side for a short break. He climbed out of his raft and went up a path that led to a huge boulder that jutted out into the river. He yelled down that anyone who chose to could follow him. He then proceeded to jump off the rock and fall thirty feet into the river. I sat there in amazement, wondering how anyone could have the courage to jump off anything so high. I knew that my fear of heights would keep me from doing anything so stupid.

In a flash, three-quarters of our group was up on the rock jumping. They would hit the water, swim out, and climb back up the rock for more. Then they started jumping in groups while holding hands. Soon I realized that I was one of only three people left sitting in the rafts. Then it started . . . *peer pressure.* My fellow rafters began to question my courage. "No thanks. I'm satisfied to watch," I yelled. Then one of the kids did the unthinkable. He questioned my masculinity! Soon all the kids were chanting my name and inviting me to join in. My good sense and experience told me to stay put in the raft. But I must admit, an insecurity welled up inside me. With my knees knocking like never before, I put on a false air of confidence (I was terrified!) and climbed out of my raft to their cheers. At that moment, it seemed easier to jump off a thirty-foot rock than to paddle down the river listening to remarks about my lack of courage or manliness.

On the media, sex before marriage is the norm. And your child is influenced greatly by the media.

From my vantage point on top of the rock, the water seemed so far away! But I jumped. I had a long time to think on the way down. I knew that if I had been going down that river alone, I would have paddled right past that rock. But there I was in midair, a well-adjusted self-confident adult leader. And I had jumped because of peer pressure.

My experience with peer pressure on the river was intense, but it doesn't even come close in its level of intensity and consequence to the dilemmas our kids face every day. When they are placed in situations where they need to decide, it is usually over a matter of right or wrong. Those who don't care give in without a thought. But those who know right from wrong become the rope in a massive tug-of-war.

Parents, be aware of the powerful pull of negative peer pressure. In your child's mind, moral dilemmas entail more than right or wrong. They are about acceptance or rejection by peers during a life stage when acceptance is more important than it ever was or ever will be again.

RESULT #2: Negative peer pressure can lead our kids into buying the lies.

The basic premise behind effective brainwashing is this: If a person hears and sees something over and over again, he or she will come to believe it, even if it's not true. Brainwashing is a tactic used to get people to buy lies.

Kids, by virtue of the fact that they spend so much time immersed in their peer culture, are brainwashed into accepting the values, attitudes, and behaviors that they hear and see over and over again each day. Their susceptibility to buying the lies is increased by the fact that they are by nature questioning many of the values that they have believed prior to reaching adolescence. Part of that process involves swimming in the waters of other value systems. This is nothing new or unique to this generation; we experienced the same thing when we were teens. But there is one difference: The values, attitudes, and behaviors are far more intense.

I've seen strong kids weakened. And when they believe the lies, it isn't long before they experience the ugly results of their actions. Some of us will bear the pain of watching our kids live through the guilt of premarital sex and the pain of sexually transmitted diseases. Others of us will walk our unmarried daughters through a teen pregnancy. Some of our children will follow the path of substance abuse and face legal trouble or addiction. Many of our daughters will buy the lies of physical beauty and become victims of anorexia or bulimia.

But there is hope. It's never too late for a child to turn and walk away from the lies. And wise and loving parents will help them.

RESULT #3: Negative peer pressure can destroy the very self-image our kids are trying to build.

"Peer pressure is hard not to give in to. My friends want me to be something that I'm not. I have to fit their mold or I won't be accepted." The great majority of teens would agree with this ninth grader that one of the greatest struggles related to peer pressure is that you must be untrue to yourself and become something you are not. One girl described it as having to "put on the mask" whenever she was with her friends.

By conforming to some peer-manufactured image that is different from what they really are, many teens commit self-image suicide. Living a lie makes them feel trapped and even more unfulfilled, making it successively harder to accept themselves. Some get in so deep that they find it almost impossible to get out.

One of the developmental tasks of adolescence is discovering who you are as an individual. When our kids suppress and deny their God-created individuality in an attempt to conform, they can't help but feel even worse about themselves. Survival means keeping the mask on while knowing the awful truth that you are living a lie.

RESULT #4: Negative peer pressure can place a strain on parent-teen relationships.

Parent-teen strain is inevitable. While God blesses some of us with kids who make parenting easy, most of us can expect to be faced with the normal relational stresses that come our way when dependent children begin to move into independent adulthood. The strain increases when parent and child don't let go of each other at the same rate. Negative peer pressure increases that strain even more.

Did your parents ever tell you, "I don't care what everybody else is doing! If they told you to jump off a bridge, would you do it?!" (I'm personally glad my mother never said, "If they told you to jump off a rock, would you do it?!") If you ever hear yourself using that line or one like it, you know that peer pressure has arrived. Although I've never heard a kid answer yes to that question, I have seen them make decisions that are no different than a yes. It defies logic, but, yes, they do "jump off the bridge" from time to time.

There will be times when our kids, in an effort to make their own decisions, assert their independence, and find acceptance in the peer group, will go against our wishes. Sometimes they'll tell us; sometimes we'll find out from someone else. We'll need to respond with discipline and correction. Other times we won't find out until years later, when our grown children are seated around the holiday table, confessing what they did as teens. At that point we'll probably just laugh, remembering what we did in our own teen years.

No matter how it plays out, you can be sure that there will be tension as you exercise your God-given right and responsibility to raise, direct, and discipline your children, and as they exercise their God-given gift of a new and developing ability to think and do things for themselves.

Parental Strategies for Dealing with Negative Peer Pressure

Our daughter Caitlin had been in kindergarten for six months when I heard the most amazing words come out of her mouth. As I stood near the cooler in the grocery store, looking for a bunch of flowers to take home to Lisa, a little voice over my shoulder said, "What the hell is that?"

I turned around in total shock and disbelief. Calmly, I said, "Caitlin, did you just ask me something?"

"Yes," she said. She pointed at a small potted cactus plant and repeated her question: "What the hell is that?"

Nothing had prepared me for this moment. The only reassurance I had was knowing that she couldn't possibly be aware of what she had just said. I knelt down next to her and said, "Well, Caitlin, first, that is a cactus. And second, where did you ever learn to talk like that?" Her answers revealed that she had learned her new vocabulary on the school bus. On the way home, we discussed the inappropriateness of her language.

When I got home, Lisa and I began to talk about how we were going to handle similar situations in the future. Caitlin had succumbed to a type of passive peer pressure. She had learned a behavior from her peers that was wrong and inappropriate just by being with them. On that day we began to realize that our own children, even at a young age, were facing peer pressure. We began to take steps to prepare ourselves for the effects of the negative peer pressure that our children would be facing during their childhood and teenage years.

The remainder of this chapter is an overview of some strategies that have been effectively used by parents as they guided their kids through the reality of negative adolescent peer pressure and into a healthy adulthood. As you read through these suggestions, I encourage you to put them into practice now, even if your children are young. Remember, peer pressure is no respecter of age. Even young children face the "big five" pressures that we examined earlier in this chapter. Therefore, we must begin to exercise a *preventive* influence early on so that our kids will be better equipped to handle the pressures when they come. And we must be prepared to exercise a *redemptive* influence so that we may help our children overcome the results of their bad choices.

STRATEGY #1: Realize that negative peer pressure is a spiritual battle that all of us will fight constantly.

Peer pressure is always there. It is a fact of life in a sinful and fallen world. We may know what is right and try with all our heart to do what is right, but still find ourselves giving in. The apostle Paul admitted his personal struggle with these sinful inclinations:

> My own behavior baffles me. For I find myself doing what I really loathe but not doing what I really want to do. . . . I often find that I have the will to do good, but not the power. . . . It is an agonising situation, and who on earth can set me free from the prison of this mortal body? (Romans 7:15, 18, 24, Phillips)

No doubt Paul would include in this struggle the moral dilemma between deciding to do what everyone else is doing and deciding to do what God says is right and true.

In Matthew 7:13-14, Jesus describes the spiritual struggle of choosing who or what we will follow in life. He calls us to make the right choice as we stand at a fork in the road. On one side sits a wide gate that opens onto a broad road. Those who look through the gate will see that the path beyond is wide and well-worn from the number of people who have gone down it. In fact, many can be seen walking that way. But this is the path that leads to death. On the other side is a narrow gate that opens onto a small trail. Maybe we see nobody going down that path, but Jesus commands his listeners to take this latter path. While very few travel it, he says it is the path that leads to life. While Jesus' words were intended to communicate truths about eternal life, eternal death, and discipleship, they also say something about the battle with negative peer pressure. In a sense, our kids find themselves standing at a similar fork in the road. Some of them stand there several times a day, facing the dilemma of choosing to walk the way of what is right or traveling in the same direction everyone else is going. It is the dilemma between standing alone as a follower of Christ and going with the flow.

While we need to recognize that our children will make many mistakes and poor choices, we must at the same time point them in the direction of Paul's answer to our tendency to give in to our sinful nature. Paul ends the description of his personal struggle with sin on a victorious note. "I thank God there is a way out through Jesus Christ our Lord" (Rom. 7:25, Phillips).

STRATEGY #2: Pray, pray, pray.

While it is a fact that children will be forced to face negative peer pressure, we cannot forget our source of hope and strength. God invites us to seek his help in the midst of our helplessness by praying regularly for ourselves and our children.

Ask God to give you wisdom and courage as you lead your children. Pray that he'll give you the right words to guide your children into making good decisions. Pray also for patience: The adolescent years can seem to drag on for a long time.

Pray for your children. Ask God to protect them as they live in the world of their peers. Ask God to guide them into making good decisions. Pray that they would make good friends who would be a healthy influence. Ask that your children would become a positive influence on their peers.

And finally, pray with your children as they face difficult situations. These prayers shouldn't be saved and stored up for times of crisis. Granted, we may need to crawl to God when things spin out of control. But our prayers with our children should start when they are young. They should grow up knowing that we depend on God and place our lives in his hands. By openly praying with your children, you will communicate to them that God does indeed care about their everyday affairs and that they should actively seek his will on all matters. And as they grow older, they will have the freedom to come and pray with you whenever they feel that need.

STRATEGY #3: Examine yourself.

The most effective teaching method is example. Our kids are incredibly observant and smart. We're only fooling ourselves if we think that we can say one thing and live another. Children learn from watching how we handle negative peer pressure in our own lives.

Let me ask you some rather pointed questions: Do you give in to peer pressure? Is your image of yourself healthy or dependent on what others think of you? Do you give in to the pressure to possess a certain type of body and work hard toward that end? Do you complain about your frustration with your imperfect body? How do you handle the pressure to stay in style? Do you emphasize outward appearance over inward condition? Do you worry about what people will think of your hair or clothes? Does your concern go beyond looking nice and neat to making an impression? When you are out socializing, do you have to have a drink in your hand to feel comfortable? Are you remaining faithful and obedient to God as you express your sexuality?

These are difficult questions that each of us must answer for ourselves. You are like all other adults in that you face peer pressure. But how are you responding? And what type of model are you presenting to your kids?

STRATEGY #4: Model the life of discipleship.

Our children need to learn that doing what is right is not always the easy choice. In fact, when Jesus called his disciples to "come and follow me," he was inviting them into a life that would be difficult. In the same breath, he told them to deny themselves and "take up your cross." On the surface, Jesus seems to be calling us to a very unattractive and undesirable life. But in reality, it is a call to the most attractive and desirable life a person could ever live.

We need to teach our kids by our words and example that following the crowd when the crowd is going in the wrong direction exacts a price. That price, according to Scripture, is lostness and the suffering of eternal death.

The flip side is that following in the footsteps of Christ also exacts a price. That price, according to Scripture, may be some suffering and alienation from others in this life. But that temporal suffering is minor when compared to the thrill of entering into the joy of the Lord as a reward for our faithfulness.

STRATEGY #5: Actively help your children build a God-centered self-image.

From the time our children are born, we need to teach them that their personal value and worth is rooted in who they are in God's eyes. God made them the way they are and loves them for who they are—not what they do, how they are shaped, or what they wear.

But it is not enough to tell them that God cares deeply for them in spite of what their friends think. Parents need to become the hands and feet of Jesus. If we knock our children down through our ignorance, absence, or cutting remarks, we will create in them a deeper desire and passion for peer group acceptance and approval.

Do you communicate to your son or daughter that their value and worth in your eyes do not hinge on their looks, clothes, or performance? Are your children certain of your love and commitment?

When your children reach the teenage years, your efforts to reaffirm their value in God's eyes may be met with disbelief or resistance. But don't stop telling them. They need to hear it now more than ever (even if they act like your words mean very little). In hindsight, they will thank you for the God-centered self-image that you worked hard to instill in them.

STRATEGY #6: Help them to learn by asking them good questions.

How will you handle it when your teenager gives in to negative peer pressure and makes a bad choice? Will you send him to his room and ground him for a month? Will you sit her down for a lengthy lecture about the mistakes she's made? There is nothing wrong with grounding, discipline, and communicating your reasons for those actions. But we do shortchange our kids when we handle their mistakes in a way that doesn't allow them to learn and think about the consequences of their actions.

Imagine that you are sitting up, waiting for your sixteen-year-old son to come home. After several hours of nervous pacing, you pull back the blinds to see the car in the driveway. There he is, slumped behind the wheel. You run outside in a panic to discover that he has passed out in a drunken stupor. What would *you* do? I know a family that had to handle such a predicament. The next day, while the young man was nursing a well-deserved headache, the father decided to do more than just lecture. He began to fire questions at his son in a loud voice. "Don't you know that you shouldn't be drinking? Don't you know that drinking is wrong? Don't you know that your mother and I are very angry right now?" Before the son had a chance to answer yes to each question, he was grounded and sent to his room. The problem wasn't that he didn't have a chance to answer the questions. Rather, his father's questions were bad questions because they could be answered with a simple yes, no, or grunt.

Good questions serve to open the floodgates of communication. They let your children know that you want to listen to what they have to say. Good questions force kids to think through their actions and the resulting consequences. Good questions give kids the opportunity to be treated like an adult rather than a child. And by forcing them to think through their actions, they help your teen to develop and form convictions.

This father could have asked these questions instead: "What happened? Why did it happen? Why was it important for you to get drunk? Do you think that you should be punished for what you did?"

My father used to ask good questions and then sit in silence until I answered. In hindsight, I realize he did a good job of forcing me to think and verbalize my thoughts. Three things happened as a result of his using this approach. *First, I learned to think through what I did and why.* It usually became very clear how stupid I had been. *Second, we always managed to talk about the real issues underlying my behavior.* The door was opened for us to discuss problems rather than symptoms. *And third, the process was more painful than any punishment he could have dished out.* Unfortunately, he didn't think the way I did. Punishment always followed our discussion!

STRATEGY #7: Give your kids the opportunity to make their own choices within clearly defined boundaries.

Parents who maintain total control over their growing teens risk finding themselves with an angry and rebellious adolescent on their hands. Many rebellious teens I've met have grown up in overly strict Christian homes. On the other hand, parents who release all control at once may get a positive reaction from their kids. After all, our kids want freedom. But they usually want that freedom in doses they can't yet handle. This approach is like putting our kids into a boat and pushing them out into the ocean without a rudder, sail, motor, paddle, or compass. They are left to the mercy of their environment.

Our children and teens need to learn how to live a disciplined life. They need to learn how to set guidelines and make responsible choices for themselves. It is advisable to allow them to develop these skills by using the "going out to play" model. When our children are little, we don't allow them to wander around outside by themselves. Mom or Dad take them by the hand and keep a careful watch on them while they play. When we are sure that they know not to wander out into the street, we might let them play in the backyard by themselves. Of course, Mom spends much of her time checking out the window or opening the door to yell, "Are you OK?" As our children continue to grow up, we begin to trust their judgment more and more. Soon they are able to cross the street without our assistance. They can walk to a neighbor's house or play in a friend's yard. Before long they take long bike rides into other neighborhoods. Even though we might worry about their safety, we trust their judgment because we have watched them make good choices on their own. We need to implement this "going out to play" model as we set and expand the boundaries of personal choice and responsibility. As our kids begin to earn our trust, we widen the boundaries further. My father constantly used to remind me that, in our house, "privileges come with responsibility." As much as those four words used to get on my nerves, his approach was totally right.

STRATEGY #8: Become a "peer" to your child.

Studies consistently show that kids who are being raised by parents who make a deliberate effort to be actively involved in their children's lives are kids who have an easier time handling negative peer pressure.

A study conducted to assess drug and alcohol use in relation to peer influence found that seventh and eighth graders who abuse drugs and alcohol spend more time with their friends than with their family. In addition, they communicate little with their parents. On the other hand, nonusing adolescents tend to spend more time with their family and less time with their peers.[22]

I am not suggesting that you become a teenager yourself. Don't try to dress and act the part. We've all been embarrassed for old people who try to act and dress younger than they really are. Rather, you should continue to function in your role as a parent and adult while working to become your teenager's friend. Discover your teen's unique interests and abilities. Make time to get involved in those activities with your child. Some fathers have purchased an old car to work on with their sons. Other parents make a point of setting aside time each week to ride a bike trail, play basketball, or attend sporting and cultural events with their children. While you might not enjoy the activity as much as your teen does, just being with them opens the door for communication and a stronger parent-child relationship built on respect and trust.

Here's one final suggestion on how to become a peer to your child: As your children grow older, begin to treat them in an age-appropriate manner. Don't talk down to them or treat them like little children. This is one of the biggest communication door slammers that teenagers despise. Make a conscious effort to talk to them in the same way that you would talk to any other adult. This will communicate to your child that you respect this emerging adult, thereby strengthening his or her trust and respect for you.

STRATEGY #9: *Get them involved in a positive peer group.*

This entire chapter has been devoted to an explanation of the power of negative peer pressure. The flip side is that positive peer pressure can be just as powerful in its ability to encourage our kids to make good, healthy, and moral choices.

The best positive peer groups I've ever seen are healthy church or parachurch youth groups. Kids in those groups learn to support each other as they work to live out their faith in school. Here are three steps that you and the other parents in your church and community can take in order to ensure that the youth group will become a positive place.

- *First, encourage your children's involvement in church activities and youth group, beginning when they are young.*

Be sure that they are actively building friendships with church peers. This will require you to be actively involved yourself.

- *Second, be sure that your church is committed to building a strong youth ministry.*

Your church budget should reflect that commitment, and your church building should be worn-out in an effort to live out that commitment. Your church should be committed to hiring a gifted youth leader whose goal is to build a group of loving adult lay leaders rather than start a one-person show or personality cult. And you yourself should put your money and your time where your mouth is. If good youth ministry is important to you, you will support the youth leader with financial, time, and prayer commitments.

- *Finally, pray and work with other parents and the youth-ministry team to make the youth group a place where all teens, not just the popular and athletic, will be accepted and loved for who they are.*

Our kids need a place to go where they can interact with their peers without the pressure to be or do something that they aren't.

STRATEGY #10: Open up your home to your children's friends.

No matter what they look like or how they act, all teenagers are yearning for adult love and acceptance. Kids who give in easily to peer pressure and go wrong are typically kids who lack the input, love, and acceptance of a significant adult in their lives. By opening up your home and making it a warm and inviting place for kids, you will ensure greater input into the life of your own teen while opening the door to other kids who desperately need it.

Get to know your child— his likes, dislikes, favorite activities.

How can you make your home warm and inviting? Convert your basement into a game room where kids can hang out. Turn a corner of the basement into a weight room where he and his friends can work out or socialize. Build a lighted basketball court in your driveway or backyard. Have your teen's friends over for dinner from time to time. Take a friend from a bad family situation along on the next family trip or outing. Be creative. Just be sure to make friends with your kids' friends by opening up your home to them.

STRATEGY #11: Work with other parents to establish "Parental Agreements."

Make an effort to get to know other parents in your neighborhood, church, and school. Go out of your way to establish relationships with the parents of your children's friends. Get to know them so that you will have the freedom to discuss their standards and expectations for their children. You might even want to start a parent network in your community for the purpose of setting agreed-upon standards for behavior, curfews, transportation, supervision of parties, and so on.

STRATEGY #12: Help your kids understand that, for better or for worse, friends influence friends.

Proverbs 13:20 says, "He who walks with the wise grows wise, but a companion of fools suffers harm" (NIV). Teach your children about the power of influences. Look for and discuss examples of this principle in the media and everyday life. Be vulnerable: Openly share stories of how you saw this truth acted out as you were growing up. Encourage them to spend time with Christian friends. Discourage their involvement with those who will drag them away from being true to God and themselves.

STRATEGY #13: Don't be afraid to draw the line and say no.

I have met many parents who are just plain scared of their kids. The fact that they are afraid to exercise their God-given authority over their children allows their kids to intimidate them even further. I also know parents who stand up and say no when they have to. Sure, their kids gripe and moan—they get angry. But even when these kids disagree with parental decisions, they respect their parents. Why? Because these parents are actively involved in their kids' lives. They love their kids, and their kids know it. For these kids, rebellion isn't even an option. So love your kids and express that love by saying no when they can't or won't say it for themselves.

■ IT'S YOUR TURN

In their book *Why Wait?* authors Josh McDowell and Dick Day challenge parents to be active in counteracting the powerful pull of negative peer pressure. Their words are appropriate as you consider what you will do to help your teens face the powerful influence of their peers:

Remember:
- If our kids can't talk to us, they will talk to their peers.
- If we don't spend time with them, they will spend more time with their peers.

- If they don't have intimacy at home, they will seek it among their peers.
- If they don't get hugs from Dad, they will get hugs from their peers.
- If we won't listen to them, their peers will.
- Teens respond to relationships. That is why they are so responsive to their peers.[23]

Think carefully through the time, love, and energy you spend with your kids. Have these words sparked any ideas about how to interact more positively with the children and teens in your home or world?

WHEN LOVE = SEX
IN TODAY'S WORLD

▪▪▪

I have the right to think for myself.
I have the right to decide whether to have sex
and who to have it with.
I have the right to use protection when I have sex.
I have the right to buy and use condoms.
I have the right to express myself.

from the "Teenager's Bill of Rights"[1]

APRIL 27, 1993, San Antonio, Texas (AP): Police are trying to verify reports by five teenage girls that they were dared to have unprotected sex with an HIV-infected male as part of a gang initiation. . . . Planned Parenthood of San Antonio said five fourteen- and fifteen-year-old girls who were tested for the AIDS virus told counselors they had sex with the HIV-infected male gang member to get into the gang. "If the test came up negative, then it was like they were brave enough to have unprotected sex and they were tough enough to fight the disease," said Planned Parenthood spokeswoman Jo Ann King-Sinnett. "They weren't really bragging. What they told us came out in the counseling session. The girls came off as being tough and unemotional."[2]

What would cause five young girls to take such a risk? In fact, what is causing the majority of our teenagers to risk destroying their physical, emotional, and spiritual well-being through promiscuous sexual behavior?

I can't say that I've ever met a parent who isn't concerned about the sexual well-being and behavior of their child. While parents may disagree among themselves about what constitutes appropriate and inappropriate teenage sexual activity, they all acknowledge that there are dangers involved. And our children are facing these dangers at a younger and younger age. Maybe we're behind the times if we talk about the *teenage* sexuality crisis. A more fitting label might be the *childhood* sexuality crisis.

Today's children and teens are facing a complex set of sexual messages and choices before their bodies are even equipped to reproduce themselves. I never dreamed that my daughter would arrive home from second grade on a warm spring day to announce that her friend was "having S-E-X" (yes, she tried to spare her parents some shock by spelling the three-letter word!). I was so taken back by her matter-of-fact announcement that I didn't know whether to laugh or cry. Lisa's jaw dropped to the floor. Since Lisa was shocked into silence, I was elected to do the talking. In my wildest imagination, I never believed that "the big talk" would be initiated by my daughter . . . let alone when she was in second grade! "What do you mean she's having S-E-X?" I asked.

"She told us on the playground, Dad. When she goes home from school, she goes next door to the neighbor's house. He's in third grade. They take off their clothes, get under the covers, and kiss and stuff."

Realizing that my daughter had a pretty advanced understanding for an eight year old, I seized the teachable moment and communicated that sex was a wonderful gift from God to be enjoyed by a man and woman after they get married. Poor Caitlin's face turned red as she looked at me with disbelief and disgust. Horrified by my comments, she angrily asked, "You mean you and Mommy do that?! That's disgusting!!"

Dealing with the sensitive issue of sexuality is not an easy thing for parents these days. But in the midst of all the sex education our kids are getting from their friends, the media, and their schools, parents cannot remain oblivious and silent. There is a message about sex and sexuality that needs to be communicated to kids. And I believe that our kids are ready and willing to listen. American teens are more concerned about sex than their peers around the world. A magazine poll of teens in fifty-nine countries found that 99 percent of the American teens surveyed cited sex as the most important issue facing today's youth.[3]

It's time for parents to open their eyes, learn the facts about the childhood sexuality crisis, and lead their kids into healthy and godly sexual behavior in the amoral nineties. This chapter offers an in-depth overview of the extent and scope of the sexuality crisis, the causes of our children's current sexual attitudes, and some practical strategies for reversing the tide of premarital sexual activity among our children and teens.

The Facts about Teens and Sex

Imagine ten chairs lined up side by side in your living room. In one chair sits your teenage child while the rest are filled with nine of his or her closest friends. Assuming that they will answer honestly, you ask everyone who has had sexual intercourse to stand up. How many do you think will stand?

If you live in the city of Philadelphia and those chairs are occupied by ten high school sophomores, two-thirds of them will stand.[4] "But that's in the city," you may say. "Only urban areas have problems like that!" Is that so?

Health Department officials in rural Maryland learned from a Johns Hopkins University survey that if those ten chairs are filled with eighth graders from the state's rural communities, six out of ten boys (61 percent) and five out of ten girls (47 percent) would have to stand.[5] "Well, those farmers' kids have nothing better to do. I know that most kids aren't that sexually active!" Think again. The latest statistics from the U.S. Center for Disease Control confirm the numbers that have come from numerous other

By the time they are seniors, 72 percent of teens will have had sex.

studies and surveys. The conclusion: *Our teenagers are sexually active.* Among the nation's ninth graders, 40 percent have had sex. At tenth grade, it's 48 percent. By eleventh grade, it's 57 percent. And by the time they are seniors, 72 percent of America's teens have had sexual intercourse.[6] Numerous other studies show that 86 percent of unmarried nineteen-year-old males and 75 percent of nineteen-year-old unmarried females will have had premarital sexual intercourse. In short, more of the kids in your living room will be standing than sitting.

Adding to these discouraging numbers is the age at which kids become sexually active. Most research shows that the average age for first-time intercourse is fifteen for girls and fourteen for boys. Sexually active high school boys report that they lost their virginity at an average age of 13.2 while sexually active girls report an average age of 14.6.[7] More and more children and teens are attempting to have intercourse at even younger ages. One doctor told me that he has treated girls as young as eight and nine years old for severe vaginal injuries resulting from sexual experimentation. Parents should be aware that most early attempts at having intercourse are often preceded by other sexual activity including fondling, petting, and oral sex.

Have you ever wondered where all this teen sexual activity is taking place? An extensive study on teen sexuality conducted by Robert Coles and Geoffrey Stokes found that more than half of the teens surveyed (54 percent) first had intercourse at their own or their partner's house! Another 15 percent were at a third party's house.[8] A more recent survey conducted by *Seventeen* magazine found that 78 percent of sexually active teens have sex at home, in their or their partner's bedroom.[9]

Researchers concerned about the spread of sexually transmitted diseases are focusing on the trend toward multiple sexual partners among teens. Nineteen percent of all ninth to twelfth graders report having four or more sex partners during their lifetime.[10] By the time they reach the twelfth grade, 28.6 percent report having had intercourse with four or more partners.[11] One can reasonably assume that the numbers for those having two and three partners are even higher.

Let's go back to those ten chairs in your living room. Assume now that the chairs are filled with teens who attend an evangelical church—Christian kids who come from decent homes where they have been taught that premarital sex is wrong. How many do you think will stand and indicate that they have had sexual intercourse? Assuming that they are all eighteen years old, 43 percent![12]

For the great majority of teens in the nineties, premarital sex has become a normal and accepted part of growing up. The comments of one seventeen-year-old girl sum up what many teens are feeling: "I just wanted to get it over with. I was sick and tired of hearing about it. I just wanted to say I had done it and no big deal."[13]

But teen sex *is* a big deal. Consider some of these very real consequences of premarital sexual behavior that are sweeping across the under-twenty population in epidemic proportions.

CONSEQUENCE #1: *Teen pregnancy*

More than one million teenage girls in the United States (one in ten under the age of twenty) become pregnant every year.[14] Most of these pregnancies will occur during the first three months after the adolescent becomes sexually active.[15] It is estimated that 40 percent of current fourteen-year-old girls will become pregnant at least once before they are twenty![16] Forty-eight percent of these pregnant teens will give birth (with the birthrate rising fastest among younger teens),[17] 11 percent will miscarry, and 41 percent will decide to take the baby's life through abortion.[18] Since the 1973 *Roe v. Wade* decision to legalize abortion, 26 percent of all abortions have been performed on teenagers.[19]

CONSEQUENCE #2: Sexually transmitted diseases

A host of sexually transmitted diseases are sweeping through the American population in epidemic proportions. The U.S. Center for Disease Control has estimated that thirty-three thousand people a day contract a sexually transmitted disease. That equals 12 million new cases a year![20] Of those, 2.5 million cases will occur in adolescents.[21] While it is difficult to determine actual numbers, a very conservative estimate is that one in five teenagers will contract a sexually transmitted disease.

Twenty years ago there were four types of STDs being spread through the teen population. Now there are over thirty. Here are some facts and figures on some of the more common STDs.

Chlamydia. Currently the most prevalent STD in the U.S., it infects approximately one in every thirteen sexually active women under the age of twenty-five.[22] Fifteen- to nineteen-year-old girls appear to have the highest infection rates of all age groups with 10 to 30 percent being infected.[23] Women with chlamydia experience vaginal itching, abdominal pain, nausea, and fever, while men will experience pain during urination and a discharge from the penis. Women who are pregnant may experience problems, including infections in the baby or the death of the fetus. Chlamydia can cause sterility in both men and women.

Gonorrhea. While the total number of gonorrhea cases among teens has decreased over the past several years, new strains developing among the teen population are resistant to penicillin. Most infected women show no symptoms while men may experience a discharge and a burning sensation during urination. Complications may include tubal pregnancy, sterility, arthritis, and blindness for the mother and eye infections in newborns.

Syphilis. The U.S. experienced a rising number of syphilis cases at the end of the 1980s, with rates reaching their highest levels since World War II. While it is more common in the adult population, the syphilis rate for teens aged fifteen to nineteen has jumped 67 percent since 1985.[24] The first stage of the disease begins with a painless sore on the genitals, fingers, lips, or breast. The second stage brings a rash, fever, and flulike symptoms. Long-term complications include brain damage, insanity, paralysis, heart disease, and death. Babies of untreated women may be born with damaged skin, bones, eyes, liver, and teeth.

Genital warts. The Center for Disease Control reports that genital warts may affect as many as 40 percent of all teenage girls.[25] Caused by the human papilloma virus, these small, often painless, itchy growths can be found on the vulva, vagina, cervix, anus, penis, and urethra. Other strains may grow in the throat. They are highly contagious and can spread and grow fast enough to block the vaginal opening. Doctors have discovered a possible link between genital warts and cervical cancer in women.

Herpes. More than twenty-five million Americans are infected with herpes.[26] The *herpes simplex* virus is relatively tame, producing cold sores on the lips. *Herpes genitalis,* however, makes its presence known through swollen, tender, and painful blisters that appear on the genitals. This form of herpes has no known cure and has been linked to cervical cancer. Infants infected during birth can suffer severe central nervous system damage and even death.

Pelvic inflammatory disease (PID). This infects two hundred thousand teenage girls every year.[27] Caused by the infections of several other STDs, PID results in inflammation and abscesses in the fallopian tubes, ovaries, and pelvis. One of the long-term consequences of PID is infertility.

AIDS. The surgeon general has described AIDS, the STD that has received the most attention in recent years, as "increasingly female, increasingly heterosexual, and increasingly young."[28] While no one knows how many teens are HIV positive, AIDS is now the sixth-leading cause of death among fifteen to twenty-four year olds.[29] Since the beginning of the AIDS epidemic, there have been just under six thousand diagnosed cases among children and teens.[30] In 1993 there were 214 percent more new AIDS cases reported in thirteen to nineteen year olds than in 1992.[31] But the fact that it may take as long as ten years between infection and the onset of symptoms means that many of the young adults who have AIDS today contracted the disease while they were teenagers. Many of today's teens are walking time bombs and they don't even know it.

One eighteen year old who was diagnosed with AIDS was told by her doctors that she had probably contracted the virus recently. They suggested that she contact anyone with whom she had had sex during the previous year. She says, "It was easy for me to list the guys I had slept with, but when I counted 24, I was like, gosh!"[32] Who knows where she got it or how many of the twenty-four guys she may have infected. The HIV virus that causes AIDS is spreading quickly among our children and teens.

CONSEQUENCE #3: *Guilt and heartache*

The epidemic of guilt and heartache nags at kids after they step beyond the bounds of God's guidelines for healthy sexual behavior.

Kids who choose to satisfy their sexual urges before marriage are often heard to say things like, "I have given myself away," "I feel empty and dirty inside and out," "I was wrong," "I wish I had never done it," and "I feel guilty." One young student who was serious about his faith came to me a few years ago to talk about the sexual temptations he was feeling. I gave him all the reasons I could for waiting until marriage. He tried to find all the reasons he could to justify having sex with his girlfriend. When he finally made up his mind, he chose premarital sex. After two or three months of acting like he was enjoying it, he came to me to admit his real feelings. "I am miserable. You were right. I feel like my search for physical intimacy has cut me off from the intimacy I had with God." He sounded like David after his sin with Bathsheba (see 2 Sam. 11–12). In Psalm 51, David cries out to God, begging God to restore the joy of salvation that he once knew, which was replaced by the guilt and heartache that resulted from his sexual sin. That same emptiness builds in kids today, whether they know where it comes from or not. Many would argue that the guilt kids feel is a false guilt resulting from preachy adults forcing antiquated, repressive, and Victorian ideas about sex down their throats. I don't believe it. The real source of their guilt and heartache is the chasm of spiritual alienation that grows between them and their Creator every time they abuse their sexuality by expressing natural sexual desires in unnatural and disobedient ways.

In an effort to fill the void that exists because of bad choices, some sexually active teens choose to sleep around with numerous other partners. With each experience comes a deeper sense of emptiness and heartache and a greater desire to move onto another sexual relationship, all in a never-ending quest to make things right.

When God created Adam and Eve, one of the most beautiful gifts he gave them was the gift of sexuality. From that time on, men and women have had the opportunity to experience the God-given joy of sexual intimacy and pleasure within the bonds of marriage. Sadly, many children and teens are abusing that valuable gift in ways that are harmful to themselves and others. How and why is this happening?

Why Are Today's Children and Teens More Sexually Active?

Mike and Cathy were high school sophomores when they met at Andrew's party. Andrew's parents were out of town for the weekend, and he decided to invite some friends over for a few hours of fun. Although Mike and Cathy had never met each other before, it wasn't long before they were dancing, talking, and sharing a few beers.

Before the night was over, they found an empty bedroom, closed the door, and had sex. These two teens, who hadn't known each other four hours before, shared themselves on the most intimate level humanly possible! And if their situation played itself out like thousands of others would that same night, they might never see each other again.

Mike and Cathy, along with the rest of our society's sexually active teens, made the decision to give themselves away for a variety of reasons. What follows are descriptions of eight of them, which when combined and taken together, have done a good job of convincing our kids to head for the bedroom.

REASON #1: Society says, "Do it!"

Sex is everywhere—we can't seem to get away from it. A recent editorial in *Spin* magazine describes sex this way:

> Sex is . . . an instinct—timeless, immortal, indiminishable, and apolitical. It is the most powerful force known in the universe. . . . It is also the very source of all human life, the reason we're here, hurling ourselves vainly against its infinite power.[33]

Sex has become a god, and it has changed the beliefs of the American people. As of 1987, 61 percent of the general population and 78 percent of all eighteen to twenty-nine year olds believed that there is nothing wrong with having sex before marriage.[34] Chances are those numbers have increased as attitudes have loosened up more over the last few years. *Seventeen* magazine's 1991 survey of fourteen to twenty-one year olds found that only 21 percent of girls and 15 percent of guys think that premarital sex is a "bad idea" for everyone.[35] Society has said, "Go ahead and do it," and our teens and even some parents are buying this lousy lie.

This "go ahead and do it" message is being shouted at our kids by a variety of different voices that are loud, consistent, and convincing. What are some of these voices? We've already discussed in chapters 4–6 how television, movies, advertising, and popular music reinforce the message that promiscuous behavior is as normal as riding a bike, going to school, or shopping at the mall, but what about the schools and Planned Parenthood?

Many school sex-education programs encourage sex by presenting so-called safe-sex messages instead of recommending abstinence. Other schools present abstinence as an option but confuse kids by teaching about contraception. Sex is rarely linked to marital commitment or taught from a biblical perspective. Rather, teens are encouraged to wait to have sex until they are "older, more mature, and responsible." *Intimacy* rather than *commitment* becomes the bottom line for "doing it." Tony Campolo is right on the mark when he says:

> With sex ed, we show them how to do it, then we warn them not to do it—but we tell them if they decide to do it, to be careful, because it could kill them, make them sick, or produce an unwanted baby. Talk about confusion![36]

Comprehensive sex education is one of the most popular approaches to sex education being used in our schools today. This approach is based on four foundational presuppositions about teens and sexuality. First, it is assumed that all teens will have sex. Second, since teens are going to be doing it, schools and educators need to teach them about it. The third premise is that when teachers discuss matters of sexuality, they should take a neutral stand on morality. While good sense and logic prove this an impossibility, this approach has been used to justify the absence of any biblical moralizing in the sex-ed classroom. And finally, since kids are going to be sexually active, comprehensive sex education teaches kids about contraception.

When our children and teens sit through comprehensive sex education courses, they learn the facts about reproduction, sexual development, obtaining and using birth control, sexual abuse, and abortion. In many cases, morality and parental authority are undermined. Kids are encouraged to make personal choices based on what they feel is right for them.

Comprehensive sex education was instituted in an effort to curb teen pregnancy. Has it worked? Not at all. Since 1970, teen pregnancy among fifteen to nineteen year olds has risen by 32 percent.[37] This should come as no surprise since studies have shown that teens who have received this type of sex education are more likely to engage in premarital sexual activity than those without instruction.[38] Much of the formalized sex education available to children and teens today not only says "go ahead and do it" but shows them how!

Another voice promoting the "do it" message comes from groups like Planned Parenthood. While I fully believe that these groups are sincere when they say they have the best interests of our children and teens in mind, I fully disagree with their message, approach, and services. In her excellent research report, *Has Sex Education Failed Our Teenagers?* Dinah Richard quotes Planned Parenthood's Faye Wattleton as she describes the organization's mission:

> The answer to teen pregnancies lies not in preaching the return
> to a morality of an earlier time but in making teens have access
> to sex education and contraceptives. . . . We are not going to be
> an organization promoting celibacy or chastity. Our concern is
> not to convey "shoulds" and "should nots," but to help young
> people make responsible decisions about their sexual relation-
> ships. . . . We've got to be more concerned about preventing
> teen pregnancies than we are about stopping sexual relation-
> ships.[39]

Several years ago a friend handed me a copy of a letter that had
been included in a fund-raising appeal from a well-known Christian
ministry. The letter had been written by a mother who was concerned
about a presentation by Planned Parenthood representatives in a
local ninth-grade biology class. Here are some excerpts from that
letter:

> They included in their presentation a detailed explanation of all
> methods of birth control and brought to class a plastic model of
> a vagina. This plastic model was used to show the students
> SEVERAL TIMES how to insert contraceptive sponges. . . . Con-
> doms were passed around and the Planned Parenthood coun-
> selor said to the class: "Now these cost about x amount in a store
> or pharmacy, but WE CAN PROVIDE these for you at little or no
> cost. Our days and hours of operation are such and such and our
> address is such and such." She then put her name and number
> on the board and assured the kids that any contact with them
> would be strictly confidential, especially as far as mom and dad
> are concerned. . . . Kids also told me about valentines Planned
> Parenthood gives to kids. I could hardly believe this, so obtained
> one myself. . . . The valentine has a big red heart on the front
> and says "love carefully." On the inside is a red condom. When
> I called the PP office about obtaining this valentine, the recep-
> tionist cheerfully told me that "oh, yes, these are very popular
> with kids because it's such a cute thing to give to their boyfriend
> or girlfriend." . . . The receptionist also told me that they are
> waiting to get some flavored condoms as well.[40]

I must be honest. When I finished reading this letter, I was skeptical. I thought that this was another sensationalistic fund-raising appeal that couldn't be true. I hopped in my car and drove to our local
Planned Parenthood office to politely ask some questions and get

more information. When I arrived, I was asked to remain in a waiting area until someone could see me. Scattered on tables around the room were baskets filled with three different types of condoms. The receptionist told me that they were free and pointed me to a stack of plain brown paper bags that I was invited to fill. The wall was loaded with free literature that encouraged safe sex, some in a very explicit manner. When the director was finally able to see me, I asked about the valentines. She told me that they didn't carry those things there, but that I should call the main office in Philadelphia. When I called, a friendly operator enthusiastically told me about an entire line of greeting cards and novelty items that were available. She encouraged me to come down and take a look. The letter had told only part of the story. Planned Parenthood was definitely sending teens the message to "do it."

If our kids don't get love and time from us, they'll seek it elsewhere.

The collective voice of culture is calling our kids to participate in premarital sexual behavior. Maybe we shouldn't be surprised that nearly a quarter of the boys and a sixth of the girls in a survey of seventeen hundred sixth to ninth graders said that it is acceptable for a man to force a woman to have sex with him if he spent money on her.[41] And maybe I shouldn't have been surprised when, while discussing sex with my third grader, she turned to me and said, "Dad, I know a lot more about sex than you think I know."

REASON #2: Kids are craving love.

I've never conducted any research studies on teens who are promiscuous. But I have made an effort to spend a little extra time with them in order to figure out why they are sexually active. While I have learned that there are multiple reasons for their behavior, one thing I hear repeated over and over again, particularly from the girls, is the phrase "I just want to be loved."

It's easy for us to give time and attention to our children when they are little. After all, they start out totally dependent on us for everything they need. But as they grow older and enter the awkward and independent years of adolescence, we sometimes falsely assume that they don't want or need our time, attention, and expressions of love. But if they don't get it from us, they will look for it somewhere else.

What does parental love and attention have to do with premarital sex? Research has shown that teens will often use sex as a means to express and satisfy emotional and interpersonal needs that have little or nothing to do with sex. Sexual intercourse becomes a coping mechanism to deal with the absence of love and affection at home.[42]

The weakening of the family unit in recent years has contributed to the sexuality crisis among children and teens. This growing obsession with sexual intimacy and longing for love can be seen in the changing content of girls' diaries. Social historian Joan Jacobs Brumberg has extensively studied the diaries of teenage girls that have been written over the last 150 years. (Can you imagine doing this for eight hours a day?) She found that girls used to write about their rich inner spiritual and intellectual lives. But in recent years, the pages have been overtaken by the quest for boys' attention and with beauty and grooming. She says that adolescent girls today are "overwhelmed with insidious feelings of unworthiness and low self-esteem as they obsess about boys and body."[43] I believe that it is a longing for parental love and the weakening of the family that have led many of our kids to feel bad about themselves, hop into bed at a young age in a search for intimacy, and keep on hopping into bed as the years go by. An alarming trend directly related to this adolescent hunger for love is the growing numbers of adolescent girls expressing the desire to get pregnant and have children, some as young as twelve years old. One explanation is that these kids see a baby as someone who will give them the unconditional love that they have been longing for.

REASON #3: *Permissive parents*

It doesn't take a parent long to realize that in a "do anything" environment, children will choose to do anything. The most sexually active teenagers are those who come from homes where parental rules and discipline are lacking or absent. In addition, these teens are considered to be at the greatest risk for pregnancy.[44]

Parents who allow their daughters to date at a young age are contributing to the sexuality crisis. One study found that 91 percent of the girls who are allowed to begin dating at twelve will have sex before graduating from high school. As the age of the first dating experience increases, the percentage having sex decreases in proportion. Fifty-six percent of those who date at age thirteen, 53 percent of those who date at age fourteen, 40 percent of those who date at age fifteen, and 20 percent of those who date at age sixteen will have intercourse before graduation day.[45] In addition, girls who had an early dating experience are more likely to go through the teen years having had older sexual partners, a greater number of sexual partners, and sexual intercourse on a more regular basis.[46]

A child who comes home to an empty house and is left unsupervised is more likely to participate in premarital sexual behavior. One California doctor reports that about 80 percent of his sexually active adolescent patients tell him that they have sex in their own homes during the afternoon while their parents are still at work. One seventeen year old says, "Nobody I know has ever had to have sex in a car. It's so much easier right at home. There's always plenty of opportunity."[47]

All of the evidence points to the fact that when parents exercise good judgment through providing clearly defined boundaries, supervision, and consistent discipline, their teens will be less likely to participate in irresponsible and inappropriate sexual behavior.[48]

One teenager has written:

> I think one of the most important reasons people become sexually active before marriage may be as simple as the word *parent*. Too many parents let their children rule the house. They do not give teenagers the guidance and discipline that they ask for. I think of the many times my parents said no to me. I think it is one of the best things they have ever done for me. I wish the world was filled with parents like mine![49]

Sadly, there are also an increasing number of parents who believe their kids are going to have sex no matter what they do or say, so in an effort to protect their kids from "harmful" or "dirty" sex, they encourage and allow them to have sex at home where it is "safe" and they have the necessary birth control.

REASON #4: Peer pressure

Teens overwhelmingly say that peer pressure is the reason that they give in and have sex. Who wants to be left out when it seems like everyone else is doing it?

One out of five guys who engaged in sexual activity on dates says that they have done so under pressure. Fifty percent of the girls said the same thing.[50] This pressure kids feel to have sex is increased by phrases used during the vulnerable heat of the moment when a couple is alone in the car or house: "Let me prove my love for you" or "If you loved me you would do this."

School hallways and lunchrooms are filled with discussions about even the most personal and intimate details of teens' sexual experiences. One girl says, "In high school, everyone assumes you've already done it. The emphasis moves from 'Are you doing it?' to

'How are you doing it?' "[51] A teenage boy reports, "You hear, 'Well, I got some last night'—it's kind of like a competition to see who got the most."[52]

REASON #5: Hormones

"See that girl over there?" my youth-worker friend said. "She's only twelve." The girl looked like she was twenty-two. As I looked around the room, I realized that dozens of young male adolescent eyes were filled with hormonally active wonder and awe as they stood staring at her. Could I blame them? After all, their emerging sexual identity was being put to the test.

When the beautiful God-given gift of sexual maturity begins to blossom, teens go through an exciting and confusing time. Many eleven, twelve, and thirteen year olds are physiologically capable of having intercourse. Some eleven- and twelve-year-old girls can bear children, and active sperm cells are present in some boys of the same age. Both experience strong sexual urges and desires that they are tempted to satisfy. Couple that with a society that says "Go ahead and do it," and you've got emotionally immature kids making some very unwise choices. Many kids allow themselves to be controlled by their sexual thoughts and desires instead of responsibly managing their sexuality.

REASON #6: Lack of information about sex

Some kids initiate premarital sex because they know all the facts about how to do it, but have had little or no parental guidance on what constitutes appropriate sexual behavior. Most teens want their parents to share sexual knowledge, opinions, beliefs, and attitudes with them. Yet only 15 percent say that their parents are a major source of this information.[53] Parents who take the time to teach their kids about sexuality and continue to talk about it guide their children into making good choices.

But the sad fact remains that most kids go elsewhere for their sexual know-how. When Christian teens were asked to rank their sources of sexual information, parents came in third, after friends and movies! School classes and television tied with parents.[54] Who knows how many kids become sexually active because they were never taught right and wrong regarding sexuality.

REASON #7: Feelings of invulnerability

There are those teens who get all the correct information and still choose to have sex. They know that guilt and heartache may follow.

They know that God does not desire that they ruin sex by having it before marriage. They know all about the dangers of STDs and pregnancy. But why do they go ahead and take the risk? Simply put, teens suffer from a strong sense of invulnerability that leads them to reason, Those things only happen to other people. They will never happen to me.

REASON #8: Feelings of vulnerability

Chuck, fifteen, is honest about why he is sexually active. "There isn't a week that goes by that someone in my neighborhood doesn't get shot. I sometimes wonder if I'll live to see my twentieth birthday." With violence and death becoming more and more a part of life for America's urban teens, some of them become preoccupied with two pursuits: survival and pleasure. They recklessly pursue pleasure during their teens years so that they don't die before experiencing all that life has to offer.

Take all these voices and reasons together and think about them for a minute. Imagine what it must be like to hear and feel all of these things while growing and developing through adolescence. Now you're getting a picture of why it's so easy for teens to become sexually active.

What Can You, As a Parent, Do about the Teen Sexuality Crisis?

The increased number of kids who choose to be sexually active is symptomatic of many factors that together have chipped away at any sense of sexual right and wrong that our kids might have, leading them to believe that premarital sexual activity is as normal as doing homework and getting a driver's license. Unfortunately, too many parents feel powerless in helping their children wait until marriage. They cave in and feel they have been successful if they can convince their kids to hold off a little longer. And when their teens do decide the time is right for them to have sex, these parents encourage them to do it safely. The tragic end of this approach is that it not only sacrifices right for wrong, but it contributes to the trail of teen pregnancies, sexually transmitted diseases, abortions, guilt, heartache, broken relationships, and shattered dreams. To put it bluntly, it promotes sin and its consequences!

The good news is that our children are capable of making healthy and proper sexual choices! The key ingredient that has been missing in this battle is parental involvement. We each have a significant and deliberate role to play to ensure that the tide turns in this sex-saturated society. Following are a number of steps you can begin to take now to lead your kids into experiencing the beauty and wonder of God's incredible gift of sexuality according to his purpose and plan.

STEP #1: Love your kids.

Before heading off to church one Sunday morning, I turned on the TV and flipped through the channels to see which television preachers were on the air. I came upon a show sponsored by a hunger-relief group. As the narrator spoke about the famine in a war-torn country, I watched a mother send her three young children out of their dilapidated shanty to look for food. The cameras followed them as they walked to a trash heap and began to pick through the rotting, fly-infested garbage in search of even a morsel of food. And then I watched in horror as they carried home small bits of trashy scraps that they would eat in an effort to satisfy their hunger pains.

Children in America are starving emotionally. When parents don't take the time to provide their kids with love, intimacy, and affection, they drive them out of the house in search of some morsel of "love" that might satisfy those desires. Sadly, many children and teens think that a few moments of "making love" between the sheets will gratify their hunger when, in effect, they have settled for a piece of rotting garbage that makes them feel better for only a few moments. Many continue to hunt and eat the garbage, which in the long run is even more unhealthy than not eating at all.

A family's strength determines much about its young members' sexual lives. Kids who come from committed families where there is an abundance of love are kids who aren't starving. The constant flow of intimacy and affection that is spread before them each day is like a daily feast. They leave the table satisfied rather than hungry. These kids are less likely to engage in premarital sex. They know that their mom and dad, even though they have problems, are stuck to each other like glue. They don't wake up wondering if today will be the day that their parents decide to get a divorce. They see the value of a strong marriage and sexual fidelity by their parents' modeling it— right in front of their eyes. And these children know beyond a shadow of a doubt that they are more important than a job, hobby, or social commitment. Secure in the knowledge of their parents' love, they are less inclined to look elsewhere.

Children who come from families where parents are absent or detached are far more likely to engage in premarital sex. One young girl who struggled for years to win the love and attention of her father entered into a relationship with a boy that immediately became intensely physical. After having intercourse with him on a regular basis, she confessed that she felt "cheap" and "used." The paradox can be heard in her words: "But I finally feel like I am being loved." She also realizes that saying no to her boyfriend would only lead her to experience more of the rejection that she hates so much. Her sad story is being lived out by more kids than you and I can imagine.

The results of one adolescent-parent study confirm what has been discovered through research, observation, and experience over and over again:

> Adolescents in a close family unit are the ones most likely to say "no" to drug use, premarital sexual activity, and other antisocial and alienating behaviors. They are also the ones most likely to adopt high moral standards.[55]

Loving your spouse and children does more than meet their basic needs. A stable and loving home fosters a climate of openness and honesty between parent and teen, making it possible to discuss teen sexual challenges and choices. In addition, it provides your children with a model for how to do the same when they have a family of their own.

STEP #2: Teach and discuss God's sexual standards.

A few years ago I led a Bible study on the topic of temptation with a group of high schoolers who didn't know much about the Bible. To bring the lesson to life I asked them to think about a time they had been tempted sexually. Then I told them that God's Word had something to say about sexual temptation. "You mean the Bible actually talks about sex?!" one high schooler blurted out in amazement. "It sure does," I said. "There's an entire book in the Old Testament that is a graphic celebration of the beauty of physical love between a man and woman." They couldn't believe it! "Where?" they asked. I directed them to the Song of Solomon and watched them flip frantically through their Bibles to find it. Needless to say, I don't think anyone heard anything else I said that entire evening. On the way out the door, one girl said, "This was great tonight. I learned that God doesn't think sex is dirty!"

For too long our children and teens have been subjected to sex education that is anything but correct. The messages of society teach them to express their sexuality freely. On the other extreme are churches and many parents who treat sex as a taboo subject, leading kids to believe that *sex* is a dirty word. Sadly, many kids (like those in the Bible-study group) are left not knowing the truth about sex.

The sex education that our kids so desperately need will lead them into understanding that God created sex to be marvelous, wonderful, and fulfilling when experienced within the bounds of his plan. Research has shown that teens want to learn about sexuality from their parents, "yet a survey of 1,400 parents revealed that less than 15 percent of mothers and 8 percent of fathers had ever talked to their children about sexual intercourse.[56] Here are some suggestions on how and what to teach your children about sexuality.

First, give your children truthful answers to their questions in an age-appropriate manner. Discuss reproduction using accurate and correct terminology. Even though you might feel uncomfortable with the types of questions young children are asking these days, you must give them answers. If you remain silent, you risk being the last to be heard. Studies show that the more parents talk to their children about sexuality, the less sexually active their kids are.

Second, take the time to understand and discuss God's design for sexuality. Spend time reading and studying God's Word, making note of passages dealing with sexuality that you can discuss with your kids. Be sure that they know that the Bible affirms sex as a beautiful gift from God for a man and woman to experience within the context of marriage. Sex is not dirty! God invented sex and gives it to married couples as a way to enjoy themselves, show their love for one another, and have children.

Third, teach your children that God's guidelines for sex don't result from some divine desire to take all the fun out of life. Rather, they are given to make our sexual lives as fulfilling, safe, and enjoyable as possible. God has reasons for condemning fornication, adultery, and homosexuality, and those reasons flow from his perfect love. Teach them that living a pure life is pleasing to God.

Finally, remember that the most effective teaching tool of all is modeling. Provide your children with an example of living out God's sexual will. If you are married, remain faithful to your spouse and work at building a strong marriage. If you are a single parent, don't give in to sexual temptation. Kids need to see that it is possible to live a life that is faithful to God's sexual plan.

God's Word is full of passages that will help you in your efforts to teach your children:

- Genesis 1:27-28
- Genesis 2:18-25

- 2 Samuel 13:1-20
- Proverbs 5
- 1 Corinthians 6:9–7:9
- 1 Thessalonians 4:1-8

Use these and others to get yourself started in talking about sexuality with your children and teens.

Christian scholar Carl Henry offers some straightforward and convincing words to parents about teaching God's sexual standards to their children during these sexually liberated nineties:

> The Creator of life entrusted humans with responsible intercourse within monogamous marriage, both for procreation and pleasure. The cure for an unzipped and depanted generation is a dose of regenerative religion and biblical morality, a new generation that focuses on the greatness of God and on the primacy of His will rather than on the size of the human penis.[57]

STEP #3: Teach your children about the many good reasons for waiting.

Paul's words in 1 Corinthians 6:18, "Flee from sexual immorality," conjure in my mind images of a person running out of and away from a burning building. These are timely words for children and teens in the nineties. Too many are staying in the inferno as the building burns to the ground. But we must do more than tell them to *run*. We must tell them *why*. Kids should avoid premarital sex not because we said so but because there are several good reasons.

There are physical reasons for waiting. Teens who choose to have sex risk doing great harm to their physical bodies. There are millions of teenagers in America who, thinking they were invulnerable and somehow immune, wound up with one or more sexually transmitted diseases. Millions of others have gotten pregnant. Still others have had abortions. Kids need to know that safe sex is a lie. Using a condom isn't the answer to all of their fears: They have a 20 percent failure rate against diseases when used by teens, and they don't prevent pregnancy. And considering the fact that a sperm is five hundred times larger than the AIDS virus, condoms aren't anywhere near reliable at preventing AIDS.

A young college student had a chance to ponder the physical consequences of premarital sex after getting pulled over by the police late one Saturday night. In the car with him was a young girl he had met earlier at a party. They had gone to a local motel, had sex, and were on their way to another party. When the policeman came to the car, he asked the young man for his driver's license. While he was handing the officer his license, the girl opened the car door and ran off into the woods. When the student told the officer her name, he had it run through the computer and discovered that she was wanted on prostitution charges and was a known AIDS carrier. When he reported this to the student, the young man fell to his knees and wept. He realized that a few minutes of sexual pleasure might have cost him his life.

There are emotional reasons for waiting. Teens who are sexually active often feel used. While this may sound crude, one promiscuous girl admitted she felt like a urinal on a men's-room wall. An endless parade of guys, caring nothing at all about her, chose to relieve themselves in her. We shouldn't be surprised at the emptiness that follows a premarital sexual encounter or the ending of a long-term relationship. God created intercourse to serve as a total expression of the lifelong love commitment between a man and a woman. Take away the lifelong part, the commitment, or the love, and sex becomes empty and cheap.

There are relational reasons for waiting. For six months Jean told me about her new boyfriend. "Jeff's wonderful. We do so many fun things together. I really do love him. But he keeps pressuring me to have sex. I told him I want to wait until I'm married." I told Jean that she should break off the relationship immediately. Rather than take my advice, she continued on and eventually had sex with Jeff. As is the case in most adolescent relationships where kids have sex, intercourse became "the main course" for each of their dates. No longer did they do those fun things that Jean had loved so much. "We don't communicate anymore," said Jean. "All he ever wants to do is get physical." When premarital sex starts, strong relationships end, even though the couples may continue to date and spend time together.

Premarital sex also affects all of a person's future relationships, including their marriage. Every sexual relationship and partner that follows will be compared to previous partners. This comparison game can continue to haunt and follow a person right into the marriage bed.

There are future reasons for waiting. Kids who have sex are putting their hopes, dreams, and plans for the future in jeopardy. None of them plan an unwanted pregnancy, birth, or disease. These aren't things that kids experience and magically forget. These things are life changers!

Premarital sex impacts the future in many ways. Girls who are sexually active prior to marriage face a higher risk of divorce and marital disruption than girls who are virgin brides.[58] Those who become teenage parents are more likely to drop out of school, live in poverty, and forfeit all of their future plans.

And most importantly, there are spiritual reasons for waiting. Premarital sex is sinful. Our children need to learn that while God is pro-sex, he is anti-sin. Making the choice to enter into a premarital physical union with another person is also a choice to drive a wedge into the spiritual union one has with God.

STEP #4: Help them to grow spiritually.

Studies show that teenagers who attend church regularly and who value religion in their lives are less permissive in their sexual attitudes and less experienced sexually.[59] It makes sense that kids who are truly committed to Christ will be committed to living out a biblical approach to sexuality.

Get your kids involved in a church youth group where they will be encouraged by leaders who teach practical ways to face sexual pressure. They will benefit from being surrounded by friends who share the same standards for sexuality, dating, and marriage.

The most effective way for you to instill a desire for spiritual growth and church involvement in your children is to model those things yourself. Make spiritual growth a personal priority, and you will pass it on to your kids.

STEP #5: Help them to establish dating dos and don'ts.

Teenage dating can be either safe or risky. Dating remains safe when there are predetermined rules to follow and obey. But if a couple heads out on a date and makes up the rules as they go along, chances are that the date may go in whatever direction their hormones take it.

Wise parents will openly discuss and establish dating standards with their teens that will lead to dating practices that honor God by ensuring sexual purity. Establishing these guidelines ahead of time will help your teen know and understand clearly defined boundaries for what is and is not appropriate—before the hormones kick in. By having standards, kids can be prepared to make quick decisions when needed.

Here are some suggested dating dos and don'ts for you to decide upon with your teen:

- Since marriage is the result of dating, date committed Christians only.
- Allow your parents to meet and get to know your date before going out for the first time.
- Plan your dates ahead of time. Decide when you will leave, where you will go, what you will do, and when you will be home. Share those plans with your parents before you leave.
- Pray together before and after your date.
- Don't get stuck alone in the car with nothing better to do.
- Agree to be home by a predetermined curfew time.
- Talking alone after a date is fine as long as it is not in the car, but in the girl's living room (with her parents home) or some other place where it will be difficult to be tempted.
- Establish an agreement to call home and ask to be picked up if your date begins to exert sexual pressure.
- Decide when it is and is not appropriate to hold hands or give a kiss.

You may be thinking that dating standards are a ridiculously archaic idea that your kids will laugh at. But think again. Josh McDowell asked teenagers to commit their thoughts about dating standards to paper. Here's what a few of them wrote:

- Sexual desires are practically impossible to harness once let loose. It is important to stop the process before it begins.
- You must determine where you want to end . . . before you begin.
- Set your standards now, not when you're deep into a relationship. Set them according to what is right in the eyes of God.
- Draw a line that you will not cross over. Define those areas you think are restricted to marriage. Consider these areas off limits.
- Don't test your limits. Don't play games with sexuality. Don't experiment to find out how far you can go without sinning. Set limits and stick to them.
- Don't put yourself in a position to be tempted.
- Write down on paper exactly what your moral standards are and then find a reliable person to keep you accountable. A parent is an excellent person to help you. They love you and you can be certain that once you share your struggle, they will be watching over you.[60]

Working with your teen to set dating standards ahead of time won't be an easy task. And once they're set, there will be moments where it is difficult to keep them. Although controlling our God-given sexual drive is not easy, this difficulty is no reason not to set standards. In fact, this difficulty is one of the best reasons for taking the time and making the effort to discuss and establish dating dos and don'ts with your teen.

STEP #6: Help your school develop or choose a good sex education curriculum.

Battles rage in communities all over America regarding the type of sex education children and teens are receiving in school. The best way to have a say in what your kids are being taught is to study and evaluate the curriculum being used and make recommendations based on what you discover.

Establish dating dos and don'ts with your teen before he or she goes out. Agree together on the standards.

The Family Research Council suggests that parents use six criteria in evaluating sex-education courses.

Role of parents. Does the program encourage parental participation? Is the program open to parental input and review?

Abstinence. Does the program clearly and unequivocally encourage children and teens to abstain from sexual activity before marriage?

Contraception. Does the program send mixed messages to teens by including encouragement and instruction on contraceptive use?

Abortion. Does the program present abortion as a solution to teenage sexual activity and pregnancy?

Linking sex to marriage. Does the program follow God's design and encourage kids to wait until marriage? Or does the program encourage them to wait until they are "older" or "more mature"?

Homosexuality. Does the program correctly identify homosexuality as sinful behavior rather than an alternate lifestyle?[61]

If you are interested in conducting an in-depth evaluation of your school's sex-education curriculum, I suggest that you secure a copy of the book *Healthy Sex Education in Your Schools* (see "Good Reading for Parents" at the end of this book).

■ IT'S YOUR TURN

A recent letter to Ann Landers from a teenage girl sheds light on the way that children and teens in the nineties are thinking about sex:

> Dear Ann Landers,
> I am a fifteen-year-old girl from a good family. My parents are well-known in this city. I have two terrific brothers. Ann, please excuse my language, but I just had the hell scared out of me. My boyfriend and I had sex without any protection, and I was three weeks late. I was absolutely sure I was pregnant and didn't know what to do or who to talk to. No way could I go to my parents. We never talked about things like that. I was sure my mother would die of shock and my father would kill me. I decided to confide in my best friend. She yelled at me at first, but then she gave me some advice—go to a clinic and get tested to find out for sure if I was pregnant. The next day, an hour before we were to head for the clinic, I discovered I wasn't pregnant. Please tell your teenage readers that if they don't use contraceptives, they are just plain crazy. From now on I'm going to insist on a condom. If my boyfriend doesn't agree, he can find himself another girl. I feel so lucky that I didn't get caught. I want to help others stay out of trouble. P.S.: Don't suggest abstinence. It's almost impossible once you've crossed that line. Relieved and Lucky in PA[62]

If this sad letter proves anything, it's this: *Our children and teens need parents who will help them understand God's wonderful plan for their sexual fulfillment.* What are you doing to accomplish that goal?

Don't give up. Helping your teen to maintain his or her sexual purity is very possible. More and more kids are openly discussing the emptiness of promiscuity, the benefits of virginity, and their decision to wait until marriage. Already, over five hundred thousand teens across America have stood in front of their parents and peers to recite the following pledge to wait until marriage for sex as part of the True Love Waits program: "Believing that true love waits, we reaffirm our commitment to God, ourselves, our families, those we date, our future mates, and our future children to be sexually pure until the day we enter a covenant marriage relationship." In order to do so, our kids want and need our help.

LIVING IN A
MATERIAL WORLD

■■■

He Who Dies with the Most Toys Wins

American bumper sticker

vs.

■■■

What good is it for a man to gain the whole world, yet forfeit his soul?

Mark 8:36, NIV

"THIS JUST ISN'T fair!" Doug said in disbelief as he read an article on 1991 sports salaries in the newspaper I was sharing with him and a group of his high school friends. We all looked up from the sections we were reading as Doug read the astounding figures in black-and-white: Quarterback Joe Montana made $12,461 for each pass he completed. Boxer Buster Douglas fought two fights, making $1.3 million for beating Mike Tyson and $24.1 million for losing to Evander Holyfield. Gerry Cooney lasted five minutes in the boxing ring with George Foreman . . . and made $2.5 million! Basketball star Ralph Sampson made $18,349 for each point he scored during the NBA season.[1] The list went on and on.

I sat back and listened as the guys talked about how unfair and unjust it all was. I had to agree. It didn't seem fair that someone could demand and receive so much for playing a game.

The discussion took a not-too-surprising turn when each of the guys confessed that the salaries would be just and fair if they themselves were one of those sports stars. They would trash all of their other career hopes and dreams if they could cash in on fame, celebrity, and the big money. Each one said they would give it all up in a minute to be "successful."

I have spent a lot of time thinking about that conversation. Each of those guys would tell you that his most important goal in life was to follow in the footsteps of Jesus Christ. But that day they shared a tempting dream that betrayed a different commitment and desire.

And I have to be honest: I've questioned my own priorities. I might climb into the boxing ring with Evander Holyfield for a million dollars. Sure, I'd use some of the money to pay for the resulting hospital and medical expenses. But there would be plenty left over to use however I pleased. And I probably wouldn't give it all away. There are some things that would be awfully tempting if my wallet was ever that thick.

The world of sports and sports salaries mirror a commitment that runs deep and wide through the American spirit. Success, winning, and getting ahead have all been defined in material terms. This way of thinking has a profound effect on the way we choose to live each and every day. It determines how we make and spend our money. It dictates how we spend our time, where we go to college, and the type of career track that we pursue. And to a large degree, it determines how we approach parenting and the few short years that we have with our children. In his continuing research on American values, George Barna has found that "materialism, despite the bad rap it has received from the press and from the Christian community, continues to rule the minds and hearts of Americans."[2]

Webster's Dictionary defines *materialism* as "the doctrine that the only or the highest values or objectives lie in material well-being" and "a preoccupation with or stress upon material rather than intellectual or spiritual things."[3] In this chapter we will examine the powerful pull of materialism in American culture (and on our own lives, if we're honest) and the specific ways this world and life view affects the values, attitudes, and behaviors of our children and teens. We'll also discuss parental pressure and how it tends to be linked with material pressure on our kids. Much of our unhealthy pushing and encouragement is rooted in our desire to see our children succeed in the world.

This may be the most difficult chapter for you to read. Personally it is the most indicting for me to write. Not all of us have had to deal personally with suicide, depression, substance abuse, and many of the other problems addressed elsewhere in this book. But if you are a living and breathing human being who lives in America, you've had to deal with materialism. As you read, keep an open mind. Look for ways that materialism has affected you, your children, and your family. Be honest with yourself as you look to discover the ways that you might be pressuring your children. Ask God to lead you to reconsider and change any attitudes or lifestyle choices that are unhealthy or wrong.

What Teens Believe about Materialism

When it comes to materialism, our children have learned their lessons well. They carry on a legacy that has been handed down to them from generation to generation. How have these lessons influenced their thinking and behavior? This section examines five core attitudes that children and teens have about money and things. While children don't articulate them in so many words, their actions speak for them. As you read through each of these attitudes, don't just focus on how they manifest themselves in your kids. Think about your personal world as well. Are you like me—guilty of living out these same attitudes yourself from time to time?

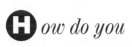

How do you define success?

ATTITUDE #1: Things bring happiness.

Our children learn early that things bring happiness. As teens, they believe that their self-worth and satisfaction in life are rooted in what they have, how they look, what they wear, where they go to school, and what they drive. Self-definition hinges on possessions. It is not who they are as unique individuals created in the image of God that makes kids feel good about themselves. Rather, I Am What I Have becomes the life motto of many children and teens. This attitude, already learned from an adult culture that lives the same way, becomes entrenched in their world and life view as it is reinforced by a materialistic peer group.

A few years ago I had the opportunity to hear a group of teenage girls describe this way of thinking about life. It was 5 A.M., and we were heading out in a car caravan for one day of skiing in the Pocono Mountains. My station wagon was loaded with kids, including five sophomore girls who sat in the two rear seats. It was a Friday, the first day of their four-day holiday weekend. As we pulled out of the church parking lot, one of the girls asked if I would turn on the rear dome light and leave it on. I told her that having the light on would make it difficult for me to see in the predawn darkness. "Please leave it on," she begged. "We have to study!" I was curious. Why would a group of girls have to ruin a great start to a four-day weekend by hitting the books? "Do you have a test on Tuesday morning?" I asked. "No," they responded. "Are you behind in your work?" "No, we just want to get ahead." When we arrived at the ski slopes, all of us took off for the lifts so that we could get in a full day of skiing . . . or so I thought.

These five girls stayed in the lodge studying! By the end of the day, they had only gone down the slopes a handful of times.

On the way home, I asked them about their strange behavior. What followed was a discussion about their life goals. My conversation with them and several with other teenagers since have yielded insight into how these kids were thinking:

> I have to study hard so that I get good grades in school. I have to get good grades so that I can be in the honors classes and keep up my class rank. Colleges look at that, you know. If I can get into the *right* college (not just any college), then I will be able to graduate and go to the *right* graduate school. This will lead to the *right* job where I will be able to make lots of money. Then I will be able to get all the things I want, retire early, and enjoy life.

The underlying motive for this approach to high school academics was their desire to achieve so that they might find happiness in the material rewards of their efforts.

USC demographer Richard Easterlin has tracked the values of high school seniors and college freshmen for two decades. He has told marketers that this generation will be as materialistic a crowd as they could ever hope for. Today's kids equate happiness with the acquisition of more and more consumer goods, especially luxury items. They express a desire for at least two cars, clothes in the latest style, vacation houses, and recreational vehicles.[4] They are spinning the wheel of fortune and hoping for the big money. For many, this track appears to be the only path to happiness and meaning in life.

ATTITUDE #2: Money buys things.

In 1991, 74 percent of American college freshmen declared that an important goal in life was to become "very well-off financially." That's nearly double the 39 percent who felt that way in 1970.[5] A survey of the incoming class at Harvard in 1989 discovered the same attitude. Their three highest goals in life were: money, power, and reputation, in that order. They believe that lots of money leads to financial security and the assurance that happiness can be bought.

The business and retail communities are so sure of America's commitment to spend money in pursuit of happiness that they spend plenty of their own money each year to discover how to get you to spend yours! Advertisements, packaging, and displays are all carefully crafted to trigger the desire to buy and facilitate a sale. One writer's description of a Philadelphia-area mall makes it out to be a den of temptation for teens:

> Come see all the beautiful and exciting merchandise we have for you. Touch it, feel it, smell it, pick it up, try it on, need it, want it, pay for it with cash or without cash, now or later. It will make you happy, intelligent, accepted, loved, pretty, younger, older. . . . There is nothing haphazard here. No clocks, except those for sale, and few windows—the timeless, weatherless environment favored by casinos. There are no doors on the stores—the one thing nicer than an open door is no door at all. There are no signs on the shop windows—lest shopper's eyes be diverted from the merchandise. The colors of the mall are off-white, quiet and restrained—so the merchandise can shine. The entrance and passageways of the mall are tiled, but store interiors are carpeted—people tend to walk faster on hard surfaces, slower on soft ones. The music is carefully engineered to encourage shopping—slow music boosts sales—and smells of chocolate, pizza and bread are wafted into the air chemically to stimulate the appetite. . . . [This is] a place where people follow the path of most insistence.[6]

Is money spent on marketing to children and teens well spent? You'd better believe it. The spending power of America's children and teens is incredible. As the years pass and materialism takes root in their lives, their spending power increases as well. Consider the following facts.

Children between four and twelve control an estimated $14.4 billion. Their income has increased 82 percent from 1989 to 1992.[7] In addition to having their own money to spend however they like, four to twelve year olds influence the purchases of more than $130 billion in goods![8]

There has also been a significant increase in teen spending power over the last few years. In 1983 people aged thirteen to nineteen spent $40 billion.[9] Believe it or not, the average teen actually had about $200 a month discretionary money![10] By 1991 teens were spending $95 billion[11] and influencing the expenditure of $250 billion.[12] And if that's not enough to shock you, a study conducted by the University of Michigan on teen earning and spending in the Minneapolis metropolitan area found that the average weekly amount received from jobs and parents was $205![13] That is more money than the average family has left over to spend any way they want in two or three months!

Where do teens get all this money? The two main sources are jobs and allowances. Teenage Research Unlimited tracked teen allowances in 1990 and found that the average thirteen- to fifteen-year-old boy received $15.25 a week while sixteen to nineteen year olds received $27.20. The average thirteen- to fifteen-year-old girl received an allowance of $16.90, and sixteen to nineteen year olds pocketed $28.80.[14]

As of 1992, five million kids between the ages of twelve and seventeen were working, many more than twenty hours a week. In his *Newsweek* article on working teens, Steven Waldman describes them this way:

> The prevalence of youth employment has transformed what it means to be a teenager. Kids who take jobs by choice, not necessity, have worked themselves into what one scholar called "premature affluence"—the ability to finance consumer binges even as their parents are cutting back.[15]

The true measure of materialism among teenagers is their spending patterns. Do they buy the lies sold to them by marketing experts and spend, spend, spend? Or do they work to save their money for college and other expenses? The evidence consistently shows that teenagers use their money to buy things.

Waldman continues:

> They buy clothing with all the well-heeled restraint of Imelda Marcos. Many have cars, which they use to go on lavish dates. Despite the recession, only 10 percent of high-school seniors surveyed last year said they were saving most of their earnings for college, and just 6 percent said they used most of it to help pay family living expenses.[16]

Teen boys spend their money on food, clothing, entertainment, tapes/CDs, and grooming, in that order. Girls go for clothing, food, entertainment, cosmetics, and tapes/CDs.[17]

One interesting new trend is a shifting emphasis from quantity of purchases to quality of purchases. Demographer George Barna feels that, having failed to achieve satisfaction through possessing more, we are seeking it through possessing the best.[18] This would explain the number of bigger and better purchases being made by teens. In

1968, only 7 percent of driving-age teens owned their own car. Now 35 percent of them do.[19] Today half of all teens own their own TV, and 28 percent own a phone.[20]

As I have examined all the lists of how teens spend their money, there is one gaping hole. Nowhere is any mention made of how much our children and teens are spending to meet the needs of others. Instead, their money is being spent on a selfish pursuit of happiness. Little or no money is spent on charities, missions, or the work of the local church. Should we be surprised? Probably not. The example that we have passed on to our children in this area is weak. A recent Independent Sector/Gallup Survey found that the more people make, the stingier they are. Those with household incomes of $100,000 or more contributed 2.9 percent of their income to charity while households earning under ten thousand dollars gave 5.5 percent.[21] We can assume that if our children make as much as they hope to (which is more and more), they will be willing to give away less and less.

When money and material possessions become the driving passion of a person's life, that person is prone to go to any length to get what he or she wants. Our newspapers are filled with stories of individuals who have lied, cheated, and stolen to get what they wanted. Is it possible that our kids, if consumed by the same desires, could meet the same end? A survey conducted by the Pinnacle Group (a consortium of public-relation firms) found that high school students are far more likely than businesspeople to exploit a situation for personal gain:

- Seventy-one percent of the students admitted that they would inflate and falsify business expenses as compared to 15 percent of the businesspeople.
- Fifty-nine percent of the students answered "definitely yes" or "maybe" when asked if they would be willing to make $10 million illegally, even if it meant six months' probation.
- Two times as many students as businesspeople said they would cheat to pass a certification test, lie to get ahead in their business, and exaggerate to claim more insurance.[22]

When our children and teens start to believe that things bring happiness and that money is the pathway to things, don't be surprised if they take some morally bankrupt detours on their way to making and getting money!

ATTITUDE #3: Get the edge.

Several years ago I was playing volleyball with a group of high school students. While waiting for my turn to get into the game, I was talking with a number of kids who were sitting off to the side. One young man who had been playing ran off the court for a substitution and came over to join us. As he leaned over to sit down, his sunglasses dropped out of his shirt pocket and onto the grass in front of me. I picked them up to hand them back to him and noticed that they were a very nice pair of sunglasses. I told him that I had been looking to buy a new pair myself and asked if I could try his on. He reached out his hand to take them back and said, "No. You don't want to try these on. I don't think you could afford them." I was surprised by his comment and allowed my defensive instincts to take over. "What do you mean, I couldn't afford them?" I asked. "Well," he answered condescendingly, "you're just a youth minister and these cost over $100 a pair." He was right—I couldn't afford them! He proceeded to rub salt into my wounds by saying, "I have three more pairs at home." I sensed a certain arrogance on his part as his tucked the glasses back in his pocket.

I came away from that incident feeling like I had been dragged into a race by this kid—the same materialistic race that our kids find themselves in each day. The winner is the one with the biggest, best, and most, and the loser keeps trying to catch up. Many of today's teens are caught in the vicious cycle of trying to keep up, outdo, and get ahead of each other.

This desire to get the edge on one's peers is especially evident when prom night rolls around. When I was in high school, it cost an outrageous seventy-five dollars for a guy to take a girl to the prom (far too much, I reasoned, to spend on someone you were sure you wouldn't marry). How things have changed. I have talked to guys who have spent over a thousand dollars on prom night. Some girls pay well over two hundred dollars for a dress they will probably wear only once. The difference between now and then is not so much inflation as the desire to outdo one another.

Where does all this prom money go? Besides the normal expenses of the evening, there are several other items kids are spending their money on. When I was in seminary, I worked in the hotel business. It was not unusual for a mother or father to come in a week or two before the prom to reserve a room for their child and their date. After-prom parties and cruises inflate the bill even further. In an effort to ride and arrive in style, many guys will rent limousines for the evening. One father I know rented a limo for his son and told the driver to go wherever his son asked. They stayed out all night, putting over four hundred miles on the odometer. I don't have any idea of the total cost for the car. What I do know is that the young man handed a two-hundred-dollar tip to the driver before sending him on his way! And if a limo isn't stylish enough, I know of one young man who arranged to have his date picked up and delivered in a helicopter.

The desire to gain the competitive edge is even more visible in our children's attire. Their obsession with having the latest and best clothing and footwear is unbelievable. Their wants and desires have become "needs," and they would rather crawl in a hole than be seen wearing something that is out of style. When I was a boy, I hated clothes shopping. Now little boys drag their mothers to the mall with a knowledge of what kinds of clothes are in and out of style.

In an article describing this clothing obsession, Ron Harris writes:

> What is important, youngsters say, are name brands. . . . They wear the names like badges of honor. Show up for school without them, students say, and they may be ridiculed, scorned, and sometimes even ostracized by their classmates. "When people look at you and you're not wearing something that has a name brand, they'll comment on it," said Aime Lorenzo, an 11th grader at Beach High School in Miami. "People will tease you and talk about you and say that you got on no-name shoes or say you shop at Kmart," said Darion Sawyer, 10, of Tench Tillman Elementary School in Baltimore. Children have developed derisive nicknames for non-name brands—"bobos, no-names and fish heads." . . . Teasing and arguments over clothes, particularly at the elementary level, result in fights and disruptions. On the high school level, counselors report that more and more students are working, often so they can keep up their wardrobes.[23]

Our kids are plunged into a materialistic rat race every day by the media and their peers. You, as parents, can help them find the balance.

Most of today's teens know that what you wear on your feet is an important determinant of status. As of last year, Reebok offered 175 different models of athletic shoes in 450 colors. Nike bested them with 300 models in more than 900 styles and colors! While most kids are begging Mom and Dad for a pair in the seventy-five to one-hundred-twenty-five-dollar price range, kids who really want to get the edge will go for one of the two-hundred-dollar-plus styles. In some cases, kids are acting like the value of a pair of sneakers exceeds the value of an individual's life. *Sports Illustrated* even ran a cover story on kids who kill for sneakers entitled, "Your Sneakers Or Your Life."[24]

Keeping up with and getting ahead of the Joneses is nothing new. But when that competition begins to cost more than a few dollars and cents, that is an indicator that the intensity of the race is building. Our children and teens are running hard in this race to get the edge. If they keep going the way they are, they will be sure to set some new records!

ATTITUDE #4: So what's wrong with being self-centered?

One sunny Labor Day, I had the opportunity to go boating with a group of high schoolers in the clear blue waters off the coast of Miami. Six of us enjoyed the beautiful weather while swimming and waterskiing off the back end of a pretty impressive boat that belonged to Dave's father. When it was Dave's turn to ski, I went to the back of the boat to throw him the skis while he dove into the water. When he came up out of the water, he leaned back and let out a comfortable sigh. "Ahhhh," he said. "I wonder what the poor people are doing today."

Dave had verbalized an attitude common among today's teenagers. They have become so consumed with meeting their own needs that they forget about or don't even care for those less fortunate than themselves. Their actions, particularly their unwillingness to help others, reveal the fact that they are satisfied with being self-centered.

When it comes to integrating their Christian faith into the material and financial part of their lives, even Christian kids—like the rest of us—are having difficulty. Kenneth Kantzer has said that "the most serious problem facing the church today is materialism—materialism not as a philosophical theory, but as a way of life."[25]

Tom Sine feels that adults are selling young people the wrong dream:

> We all seem to be trying to live the American Dream with a little Jesus overlay. We talk about the lordship of Jesus, but our career comes first. Our house in the 'burbs comes first. Then, with whatever we have left, we try to follow Jesus.[26]

More and more of today's teens, even many (possibly most) who profess faith in Christ, see nothing wrong with this type of lifestyle, in spite of the fact that Jesus called his followers to be totally committed to him, as opposed to being preoccupied with their own material needs.

In his research on how religion influences one's view of material things, Princeton University sociology professor Robert Wuthnow has found that these attitudes are a part of the fabric of adult culture. He writes:

> Much of the American middle class seems to have forgotten even the most basic claims that religion used to make on the material world. Asked if their religious beliefs had influenced their choice of a career, most of the people I have interviewed in recent years—Christians and non-Christians alike—said no. Asked if they thought of their work as a calling, most said no. Asked if they understood the concept of stewardship, most said no. Asked how religion did influence their work lives or thoughts about money, most said the two were completely separate.[27]

Perhaps we shouldn't be surprised by the selfish reflection we see of ourselves in the mirror of today's youth culture. Our kids have been exposed to the disease of self-centeredness. And like those of us who are adults, our kids run the risk of living with the disease so long that they forget that they even have it.

ATTITUDE #5: I'll never have enough.

Has material-ism become your or your teenager's way of life?

My brothers and I used to fight over the Sears Christmas catalog. Each of us would spend hours paging through the toy section in the back, dreaming about the toys and games we wanted for Christmas. By the time December rolled around, the pages of that catalog were dog-eared from use. On Christmas Eve we would go to bed wondering if Santa would bring us all of the items that we had circled and marked with our names or initials.

Do you remember the times you spent dreaming about one or two items you wanted so badly? And how if you got them, your life would be complete and you would never want another toy or game again?

Then there was the excitement of Christmas morning. Even

though you didn't receive all you asked for, you were excited about the things under the tree. But how did you feel two or three days later? If your experience was like mine, your satisfaction was only temporary. The novelty had worn off, and the toys you had longed for were not so great anymore. Perhaps they had broken. (Or maybe your father was still fumbling around in an effort to put them together.) I call this "the old lie of a consumer-oriented Christmas." What we thought would bring satisfaction doesn't. Instead we're left wanting more.

Those who believe that things bring happiness will never find the lasting happiness they are looking for. They keep grasping for more, but the pit of material desire is bottomless. When Americans were asked if they had achieved the American dream, 5 percent of the respondents who earn less than fifteen thousand dollars a year said yes. Six percent of the respondents who make more than fifty thousand dollars a year answered yes.[28] Do you know what that says to me? No matter how much you make, you will always want to have more.

Many have predicted that this generation of children and teens can expect downward mobility. They have been allowed to grow up with such a high standard of living that there will be nowhere for them to go but down. The sad result will be that those kids who expect to find meaning and purpose in accumulating more money and things will be faced with meaninglessness and purposelessness. Their sense of self-worth will be destroyed. The worst possible result of never having enough could be an increased number of young adults who suffer from depression and/or choose to cope with their "failure" through alcoholism and suicide.

Where does this frenzy of materialism lead? In *Time* magazine, reporter Otto Friedrich interviewed one of the rich Donald Trump's close confidants. Friedrich writes:

> Trump is a brilliant deal maker with almost no sense of his own emotions or his own identity, this man says. He is a kind of black hole in space, which cannot be filled no matter what Trump does. Looking toward the future, this associate foresees Trump building bigger and bigger projects in his attempts to fill the hole, but finally ending, like Howard Hughes, a multibillionaire living all alone in one room.[29]

If we love our children, we will do all that we can to point them away from this materialistic road that leads to nowhere.

The Hows and Whats of Materialism

Before we look at some practical ideas and responses to materialism, we must ask ourselves two questions. First, do we know *how* kids get pointed to a materialistic lifestyle? And second, do we know *what* the proper God-given attitude is that we should have toward money and material things?

The hows of materialism

The answer to the how question is fairly simple. Do you remember the last few words of Harry Chapin's famous song "Cat's in the Cradle"? When he sang, "He'd grown up just like me. / My boy was just like me," he was bearing witness to a biblical truth that has been supported for thousands of years through research, observation, and experience. Kids become like their parents. They learn what they have seen lived out in the home.

A recent article in *Psychology Today* describes the values and life-styles of America's "twentysomethings," those recent college graduates who are looking to find their place in the adult world:

> Their first priority is themselves. They steer away from "altruistic careers" such as nursing, social work, and teaching; instead they choose professions that offer more opportunity for personal reward and advancement, such as investment banking. . . . They are materialistic. They want money, power, and status.

The article cites the main reason for these twentysomethings' attitudes and behaviors as "parents. The twentysomethings mostly raised themselves. Not only did 40% come from broken homes, but both their parents went to work and chose to define themselves through it."[30]

When it comes to the economics of lifestyle choices, the fact that your kids learn from your example could be good news or bad news. Remember, even well-intentioned Christian parents can pass on materialistic attitudes to their children.

The whats of materialism

The answer to the what question is equally clear: *Our job as parents is to help our children and teens redefine their idea of success by equipping them to understand and live out God's definition of success.* Of course, this requires that we understand and live out his definition ourselves.

Unfortunately, God never chose to include a clear one-sentence definition of *success* in his Word. But even though we can't point our kids to a specific chapter and verse where God says, "Success is . . . ," the entire Bible, from cover to cover, defines *success* as faithful devotion to God and obedience to his commands. That's quite different from the definition fed to us by the unwritten dictionary of contemporary American culture.

God cares deeply about our attitudes toward money and wealth. Did you know that more is said in the New Testament about money and wealth than about heaven and hell combined? Five times more is said about money than about prayer. And sixteen out of Christ's thirty-eight parables deal with money!

Look at a few of the words Jesus spoke about money and material things:

> Do not store up for yourselves treasures on earth, where moth and rust destroy, and where thieves break in and steal. But store up for yourselves treasures in heaven, where moth and rust do not destroy, and where thieves do not break in and steal. For where your treasure is, there your heart will be also. (Matt. 6:19-21, NIV)

> No one can serve two masters. Either he will hate the one and love the other, or he will be devoted to the one and despise the other. You cannot serve both God and Money. (Matt. 6:24, NIV)

> Therefore I tell you, do not worry about your life, what you will eat or drink; or about your body, what you will wear. . . . But seek first his kingdom and his righteousness, and all these things will be given to you as well. (Matt. 6:25, 33, NIV)

God also spoke about money and material things through the apostle Paul:

> People who want to get rich fall into temptation and a trap and into many foolish and harmful desires that plunge men into ruin and destruction. For the love of money is a root of all kinds of evil. Some people, eager for money, have wandered from the faith and pierced themselves with many griefs. (1 Tim. 6:9-10, NIV)

Throughout the pages of the Bible, God makes it clear that money in and of itself is not evil. Rather, it is the love of money and material things that clouds our view and leads us down the wrong road in the pursuit of success. This is exactly what happened to the rich young man in Mark 10:17-22 who sought out Jesus for the answer to the gaping hole he felt in his life. He comes to Jesus and asks what he must do to receive eternal life. Jesus tells him that he must give up his earthly treasures because they stand in the way of his finding treasure in heaven. The man left his encounter with Jesus sad because he was unwilling to stop worshiping the god of his wealth. Then Jesus turned and said to his disciples, "How hard it is for the rich to enter the kingdom of God!" (verse 23, NIV).

C. S. Lewis knew the dangers of wealth when he warned, "Prosperity knits a man to the world. He feels that he is finding his place in it, while really it is finding its place in him."[31]

In 1928 a group of the world's most successful financiers met at the Edgewater Beach Hotel in Chicago. It is said that, collectively, these seven tycoons controlled more money than there was in the United States Treasury. For years newspapers and magazines had been printing their success stories and holding them up as role models to young people across the nation. But do you know what happened to each of these successful men within twenty-five years?

- The president of the largest independent steel company, Charles Schwab, lived on borrowed money the last five years of his life and died broke.
- The greatest wheat speculator, Arthur Cutten, died abroad, bankrupt.
- The president of the New York Stock Exchange, Richard Whitney, served a term in Sing Sing Prison.
- The member of the president's cabinet, Albert Fall, was pardoned from prison so that he could die at home.
- The greatest bear in Wall Street, Jesse Livermore, committed suicide.
- The president of the Bank of International Settlements, Leon Fraser, committed suicide.
- The head of the world's greatest monopoly, Ivar Drueger, committed suicide.

Our children need to know that God's definition of *success* stands in marked contrast to the definition that the world would have us believe. Two different definitions of *success*. Two different paths to take in life. Two different outcomes. We must teach our children that the real measure of their success in life is how much they'd be worth if they had absolutely nothing.

Practical Steps You Can Take to Counter Materialism

What are some practical steps you can take to help your teen develop healthy attitudes toward money and wealth?

STEP #1: Lead and teach by example.

During a recent Christmas shopping rush, my wife had the opportunity to observe a mother and her junior high daughter as they waited in the checkout line. The mother was waiting to purchase a pair of jeans for herself. The daughter was registering her discontent with her mother's decision to buy off-brand jeans. "Mom, you know you only like to wear the expensive jeans with the Guess? label on the back. Why are you buying these?" The mother turned to her daughter and proceeded to explain her intentions to remove the label off a pair of her worn-out Guess? jeans so that she could sew it on the back of the pair she was purchasing! What kind of message was that daughter getting from her mother's example? Sure, she was saving a few dollars by being creative. But the real message was this: I, your mother, must wear jeans with a designer label.

What messages are you sending to your children through the example of your words and actions? What lifestyle lessons are you teaching them?

Here are some questions to ponder as you examine yourself. Take the time to answer them seriously. Discuss your answers with your spouse. You might even want to ask your children for their impression of what you are teaching.

- What do you want to pass on to your children? Money and material items or godly character traits?
- How much does your lifestyle reflect and conform to the values of American society?
- If you are a goal-oriented person, what are your goals for five, ten, and fifteen years from now? Are they primarily economic or material in nature?
- If your children were to write out a definition of *success* based on how you define it through your lifestyle, what would they write?
- Are you always looking to get the competitive edge or keep up with the Joneses? Are you jealous when someone you know acquires something that you don't have yourself?
- Do you wish for things that you don't have, believing that their acquisition would make your life better?
- Do you refer to your wants as needs?

- When will you know that you've made it?
- Someone once said to me, "You tell me who or what you spend your time daydreaming about, and I'll tell you who or what your god is." Who or what do you daydream about?
- Do you possess your possessions, or do they possess you?
- Do you focus on what you don't have rather than being joyful about those things that you do have?
- Are you a cheerful, generous, and joyful giver?
- Does your faith and security rest in God or in your things?

One of the most important lessons to teach our children is that God owns everything that we have and are. As a result, every spending or lifestyle decision is a spiritual decision. Do your spending and lifestyle decisions reflect that commitment?

I grew up in a home where, while we weren't poor, we had quite a bit less than any of our neighbors. My parents tell me that as a young boy I was puzzled by the fact that we were the only family on the street that didn't have a maid. Sure, there were lots of things I wanted to have while I was growing up, and I was disappointed when I didn't get them. But my parents passed on something far more valuable—their example. They taught us the difference between needs and wants. They taught us that everything is God's and should be used according to his rules of stewardship. They modeled thrifty living and generous giving. And they taught me that living hand-to-mouth isn't such a bad way to live when the hand belongs to God.

STEP #2: Don't push and pressure your kids.

There is absolutely nothing wrong with expecting kids to do their best . . . as long as it is *their* best and not some *socially defined* best that is pushed on them.

Let's face it. We live in an age of designer kids. Parents are often afraid of having an average kid. We buy into programs that will help our kids get ahead of the rest of the pack. We enroll preschoolers in reading classes or purchase Hooked on Phonics to get them reading before they even know how to play and have fun. Barbara Katz, writing in *Parents* magazine, says:

> Professional parents are downright driven to cultivate their children's abilities and college bound resumes—superparents raising superkids. Armed with expert advice, they view parenting less as an instinctive process than a quantifiable set of dos

and don'ts which, if applied properly, can transform any child into a runner by three, a reader by four, a writer by five.[32]

If you know anything at all about gardening, then you understand the idea behind a greenhouse. Seeds planted in the highly controlled greenhouse environment are grown much faster than those outside. Sadly, many parents have taken the same approach to parenting and resorted to "hothousing" their children. Children are placed in a high-pressure, highly controlled environment to nurture maximum performance and achievement. The process continues through the teen years as kids struggle to balance their studies, a full schedule of extracurricular school activities, part-time jobs, and music lessons. Some kids are so busy that they have resorted to carrying cellular phones or wearing beepers so that parents and friends can track them down in the midst of their busy schedules.

The primary goal of all this madness is usually admission to the *right* college. Not just any school will do. It must be a school whose diploma will continue to ensure maintaining an edge on the job-market competition. The *Chicago Tribune* reported on the many "war" stories that have begun to circulate among college admissions officers. What people will do to get themselves or their kids into the right college is unbelievable. One father was so embarrassed by his daughter's rejection by an Ivy League school that he resigned his country-club membership rather than face his friends! Then there was the high school senior who solicited the signatures of thirty-five hundred close friends, relatives, and complete strangers for his petition of appeal to the prestigious university that had turned him down for admission.[33]

Unfortunately, the end result of this parental pressure and pushiness is not what was always intended. Kids stress out. Haunted by the sense that they will never measure up, they begin to feel like failures. They start to believe that their parents' love for them depends on their performance (sometimes kids read the signals correctly). As the stress builds, the parent-child relationship weakens and often breaks as a result of rebellion. Forcing children to bear an unrealistic burden can also lead to the worst possible end: depression and/or suicide.

One summer, as I sat around the campfire with a dozen or so high school students I had known for years, the kids began to share openly about their struggles at home. One of them was a fifteen year old who had never really opened up with any of us about anything but always seemed to have it together. She was a smart kid who ranked number one in her class. Her parents both had multiple advanced degrees. I had assumed that her previous silence was due to the fact that she was thinking. But then, as the fire crackled, years of emotional heartache poured out as she shared her frustration with feeling like she would never be able to measure up to the academic and vocational expectations her parents had placed on her over the course of her life. We were amazed at her openness, yet saddened by the reason for it. The stress of parental pressure and pushiness had become too much for her to handle.

Developmental expert Cliff Schimmels offers parents some of the best advice I've ever heard:

> The one prayer I pray most frequently as a parent and a teacher is that the Lord will give me the wisdom to know how much to expect of my children. If I expect too little of them, they may waste their creative gifts. If I expect too much of them, I may destroy them with an unrealistic burden.[34]

STEP #3: Give them your time.

I recently read about a busy woman who was struggling to balance the demands of working outside the home while being a wife and mother. One night her nine-year-old son approached her as she typed diligently on her word processor in the corner of the family room. "Mommy," the little boy said, "if you had a dog, and you really loved this dog, and you worked real hard to earn the money to buy him the fanciest dog house and the best dog food, don't you think it would be better if once in a while you played with that dog?"[35] *Ouch!*

We live in an age of designer kids.

America's love affair with materialism sends us frantically up the ladder of success in pursuit of a better standard of living. Sadly, each step to a new rung requires that parents spend more and more time out of the home making the money necessary to keep up that standard of living. Moms and dads pursue careers that require long hours and busy travel schedules. The greatest price of this busyness is that more time away from the home means less time spent with the children. Millions of preschoolers and infants spend their days with someone other than Mom and Dad. Over ten million school-age children come home to an empty house each day. And when Mom and Dad do arrive home, they are often too tired to put forth any effort to spend meaningful time with their children.

Parents, when you aren't spending time with your children, three things happen.

First, someone else raises your children for you. That "someone else" could be anyone from a baby-sitter to a day-care worker to a schoolteacher to the television. One of the risks of living in a materialistic society is that these surrogate parents can instill false values in your children.

Second, your children will learn from your busy lifestyle. They will look at how you live out your commitments to career, family, and church and learn that it is more important to achieve, work, and expand social circles than it is to be at home. And what they learn gets passed on to the next generation. If you find it difficult to be at home with your family, your children will find it even harder to spend time with your grandchildren. If you place a premium on job and career, they will grow up to do the same.

Third, your children may suffer in ways you never imagined. When we are not available to help them through the difficult years of adolescence, we open the door for our children's involvement in a vast array of dangerous behaviors and problems. Medstat Systems, a Michigan healthcare information firm, surveyed large corporations and found that 36 percent of the children of executives undergo outpatient treatment for psychiatric or drug-abuse problems every year compared to the 15 percent of the children of nonexecutives in the same companies.[36] The major difference between the executives and nonexecutives was the amount of time they spent on the job. It's hard to be there for the family or even notice the kids when you're working twelve to fifteen hours a day.

When we choose to have children, we make another choice commonly forgotten in these materialistic days: We choose to become parents. Parenting takes time. Don't allow yourself to fall into the trap of believing that "quality time" is more important than "quantity time." Quality time always has a way of fitting a parent's schedule while disregarding the need of the child. We must learn to say no to other demands that are not as important as our children. When we don't spend time with our kids, they will begin to interpret our actions as rejection. It isn't long before rejection becomes resentment, and resentment turns into hostility, which in turn leads to rebellion.

There is an old Navajo saying: "A man can't get rich if he takes proper care of his family." If we were to add some more time-tested wisdom to that saying it would continue on: "but a man who spends time with his family can pass on a legacy of what it means to love God and his family more than his things."

STEP #4: Give your kids the best life, not the good life.

When I was in elementary school, my parents allowed me to spend a week at a Christian camp. But for my parents, camp was much more than a way to get me out of the house. They knew that I would learn skills there that would help me grow up into a healthy, spiritually mature adult.

I seriously wonder about parents' motivation for sending their kids off to another type of summer camp that I read about a few years ago. It's the Money Management Camp in Palm Beach, Florida. For $550 a week, twelve to fifteen year olds learn how to read the *Wall Street Journal*, follow the stock market, and invest in stocks, bonds, and mutual funds.[37]

Many well-intentioned parents work hard to give their kids the "good life." Believing love means giving them all the things they never had themselves, parents shower their kids with cars, money, special classes, trips, and activities. Yet these same parents wonder why their kids never seem to be happy and satisfied: "Why do they want so much more? Why aren't they happy with what they already have?" The answer is fairly simple. Teaching kids to pursue the good life turns them into materialistic monsters who get caught up in the lie of the "things bring happiness" mentality.

The negative results of being handed the good life can be seen in the values, attitudes, and behaviors of today's teens and young adults. Their values are very shallow and self-serving. *What's in it for me?* they wonder. They have little or no motivation to do things for themselves. They have learned that all you have to do is sit back and everything will be handed to you. As a result, they never learn how to take responsibility for themselves or develop healthy work habits. They grow up with no clue as to what the real, dog-eat-dog world is like.

Dr. Bruce Baldwin has done extensive research on the effects of giving our kids an overabundance of money and things. Out of his research evolved the concept of Cornucopia Kids. They are children who have been raised in good homes with interested, involved, and well-intentioned parents. However, their parents have given them so much that it is difficult for them to develop into healthy self-sufficient adults. Baldwin defines a Cornucopia Kid as "a child who develops an expectation, based on years of experience in the home, that the good life will always be available for the asking and without the need to develop personal accountability or achievement motivation."[38] Baldwin says that you may be giving your children too much if you find yourself having to hound them into keeping commitments or taking responsibility for the consequences of their actions.

More and more, the nasty effects of giving the good life are being seen in even our youngest children. Pediatrician Ralph Minear was puzzled by the physical and emotional symptoms of stress that he and his colleagues were seeing in children as young as preschool age. He has diagnosed the malady as Affluenza or Rich Kids Syndrome because the children have been given too much of something— "whether it's pressure to perform, freedom, money, food, protection, or parental sacrifice."[39] These are children whose parents want them to have all the benefits of the good life. Consequently, they push them to be perfect children, cramming them with more cultural, educational, and material opportunities than they can handle. And its victims aren't just those from wealthy homes. The disease is as common in middle-class and poor families as in those with lots of money. Included are nausea, headaches, eating disorders, anxiety, depression, and high blood pressure . . . all because they've been given too much of the good life!

What are the options for those of us who realize that it is dangerous to give our kids the good life? The good news is that there is something better. In fact, it's the "best life." Our lives and actions should communicate to our kids that the best life is found in living by God's values and according to his standards of success. The best life consists of directing all that we have, do, and are towards loving God. And then, because of our love for him, we should love those around us rather than treating them as competition or the means to material ends. John Wesley had these priorities in mind when he gave this timely and timeless advice: "Work as hard as you can, to make all the money you can, to save as much as you can in order to give away all that you can."

STEP #5: Let your kids be themselves.

I have attended more than my share of high school wrestling matches. Initially, my attention was focused on the wrestlers as they competed on the mat. Then I started watching the parents as they nervously paced the floor or sat on the edge of their seats while their boys wrestled. There was one father who was especially animated. During the course of his son's match, he would make his way around the gym several times, stopping to yell instructions or chomp away at his fingernails. He would alternate between yells of joy and protest, depending on how his boy was faring on the mat. Those of us who followed the team knew that this man lived and died by his son's wrestling career. On one occasion I overheard him say, "I know I get excited when Drew is wrestling. But I feel like it's me out there on that mat, and I have to win!"

While there is nothing wrong with taking a healthy interest in our children's lives, it is dangerous to live vicariously through them. When our own insecurities lead us to push them to become all we weren't or to accumulate all we never had, we force them to become something they are not. If you grew up in a situation like that yourself, you know firsthand about the incredible weight this approach puts on a child's shoulders. That's one reason why Drew grew up to hate wrestling and his father's unreasonable pressure. We would do well to remember that our children are not status symbols like a car or a house.

Think about each of your children and ask yourself these questions:

- What are my child's unique abilities and interests?
- How does my child use spare time?
- How is my child different from the rest of the family?
- What career does my child wish to pursue?
- Am I pushing my child to be or do something that they were never meant to be or do because of my own insecurities?
- Am I encouraging my child's abilities and interests?

God has blessed each of our children with unique gifts, abilities, and interests that they are to use in service to him. Let's point our kids in his direction rather than our own.

■ IT'S YOUR TURN

Have you ever wondered how they catch all the monkeys that you and I see on our trips to the local zoo? The traps they use in Africa are rather unique. A coin, button, or some other shiny metallic object is placed in a long-necked glass jar that is then attached to a tree. As the monkeys swing through the trees, the reflection of the sun on the shining object catches their eye. Reaching into the jar poses no problem at all for the curious monkeys. But when they try to pull their closed fists out of the narrow openings, they can't do it. To gain freedom, all the monkeys need to do is let go of the worthless object. Instead, the monkeys sit by the jar holding onto the object until their captors come to take them away. "Stupid monkeys," you say. I know. But are they that much different from you and me?

My wife and I know that the shiny objects of materialism are awfully attractive. There are many times when we find ourselves trapped when we hold on and don't let go. We have learned firsthand how easy it is to lose our freedom at the hands of misplaced values and priorities. Our personal experience and study of God's Word has led us to make some serious decisions regarding what we want to teach our children. I encourage you to do the same. Let me share those decisions with you in the form of three questions and their answers:

QUESTION	ANSWER
What is success?	True success in life is faithfulness to God and obedience to his commandments, whether you are worth ten cents or ten million dollars.
What do you and I want our children to become?	Our desire for our children should be the same as our heavenly Father's desire for them: that they become like Christ in all things.
What must you and I do to make this happen?	We must know the truth as it is contained in God's Word, talk about it, model it, experience it, and prayerfully trust God to change our children's hearts and minds.

C. S. Lewis once said, "If I find in myself a desire which no experience in this world can satisfy, the most probable explanation is that I was made for another world."[40] Are you pointing your children to that other world?

Understanding Substance Abuse and Teenage Depression

10 HOLDING YOUR OWN AGAINST ALCOHOL AND DRUGS

::

One pressure young people face that inherently makes my job and our hopes for the future that much more difficult to guarantee, is the pressure to drink alcohol, or abuse other substances.

Surgeon General Antonia C. Novello[1]

IT WAS ONE of those childhood images that cements itself in your mind forever. I was nine when I attended a neighborhood annual Memorial Day picnic. The peanut scramble for the children was over, and the adults were gathering to play their games. Dozens of wives and children watched as several fathers positioned themselves at the starting line for their annual forty-yard dash. The only difference between their race and the sprints at the local high school track meets was that these men were to complete their run while chugging a sixteen-ounce can of beer.

On "go" the fathers took off for the finish line with their heads tilted back, beer cans to their lips. It was strange for me to see my friends' fathers "let down their hair" as they dashed across the yard with beer running down their necks and onto their chests. Their wives and children laughed and applauded louder than they would the rest of the day, leaving me with the impression that everyone thought this was the best part of the gathering. To my nine-year-old eyes, drinking looked like a lot of fun.

But as I grew up, my parents' sound advice and several other experiences taught me that substance abuse was anything but fun. When I was in high school, I worked as a volunteer at a psychiatric hospital. On one occasion I helped chaperon an educational trip to a local greenhouse for several adolescent patients. I watched as one of the residents, a fifteen year old named Tom, approached an elderly woman who tended plants at the greenhouse. He politely asked her, "Excuse me, ma'am. Where do you keep your marijuana plants?" Tom wasn't joking around or being disrespectful. His question came from a brain that had been severely damaged by a self-administered overdose of the drug PCP (also known as angel dust). He had allowed substance abuse to visit his life, and while he looked and sounded normal, it had taken its toll.

On another occasion a group of teenage guys that I knew were out on one of their regular weekend drinking binges. As they drove from house to house in search of another party, Rich stuck his head out of the car window to vomit. When the other guys in the car, all drunk themselves, pulled him back into the car, he was dead. His head had struck a telephone pole. He had allowed substance abuse to visit his life, and it had done damage that could never be corrected. But in just a matter of weeks, the shock of his death had worn off, and the guys were back to getting drunk again. I wondered if any would wind up following in Rich's footsteps.

If you are concerned about teen substance abuse in the nineties, your concerns are well-founded. Since my initial exposure to drug and alcohol problems during my high school years, I have met hundreds of teenagers who have struggled personally with recreational and addictive substance-abuse behavior. Every day over five hundred American children between the ages of ten and fourteen begin using illegal drugs. Over a thousand start using alcohol.[2]

But substance abuse is not a problem limited to the teenage population. Teenagers have grown up in a world filled with attractive substance-use messages. Others have experienced the harsh reality and ugliness of the costly toll of substance abuse. When the laughter and fun of our neighborhood picnic ended, a few of my old friends went home to houses that were filled with the pain and nastiness of alcoholism. Some kids today are too scared to turn out the lights or close their eyes at night for fear of what might happen when their father comes home drunk.

In this chapter we will examine the problem of teenage substance abuse and these parental questions: Are kids really using drugs and alcohol? If so, why? What substances are today's teens using and abusing? How can I tell if my teen is using drugs or alcohol? What can I do to prevent my child from becoming a substance abuser? And finally, what should I do if I discover that my teenager has a problem?

Facts and Figures: What Are Teens Using and How Much?

Sometime during the 1980s, America woke up. Athletes, politicians, the media, educators, community leaders, and parents pulled together to attack the growing social problem of teen substance abuse. America had been in denial, doubting that teen substance abuse was as widespread or intense as some had suggested. But an honest assessment of the situation led to a concerted effort to stem the tide of this epidemic problem. Schools instituted antidrug and alcohol assemblies. The media ran antidrug public-service announcements featuring celebrities and sports heroes. Mothers Against Drunk Drivers, Students Against Drunk Drivers, and other grassroots organizations began chapters in communities and schools all across the country. Parents banded together with community leaders to run substance-free after-prom parties so that kids would stay sober and off the road. The combination of all these efforts led to a slight drop in teen drug and alcohol abuse, welcome relief after years of skyrocketing statistics.

But don't be fooled by the numbers. Teen substance abuse continues to grow at rising rates. Perhaps this is due to the growing spirit of complacency among adults due to the small decline in the problem over the last few years. We adults have somehow come to the conclusion that we don't need to work as hard at fighting the problem since we assume it isn't as bad as it once was. As a result, substance abuse remains a major problem among children and teens in the nineties.

In this section we will examine the current statistics and facts on teen substance abuse in an effort to come to an understanding of who is abusing substances, what they are abusing, and how much.

Alcohol

Americans love to drink. The U.S. Commerce Department reports that the average American drinks 22.4 gallons of beer, 1.85 gallons of wine, and 2 gallons of hard liquor each year.[3] This love affair with alcohol is shared by the teen population. Alcohol is by far the number one drug used and abused by teenagers today. Drinking has become a normal adolescent activity and serves as a rite of passage for kids as they move from childhood into adulthood. While they and their parents may view drugs as dangerous, stupid, and addictive, it appears that they see alcohol as safe, normal, and acceptable.

Teen-drinking facts and figures. While most students take their first drink between the ages of twelve and thirteen, the trend over the last few years has been toward earlier and earlier use.[4] Thirty percent of all students reported taking their first drink between the ages of nine and twelve while 5 percent took it at age eight or younger.[5]

The trend toward initial alcohol use at earlier ages can be seen in several statistics relating to alcohol use among elementary school students. Twenty-six percent of all fourth graders say they've drunk alcoholic beverages.[6] Of the fourth, fifth, and sixth graders surveyed, fewer than half consider alcohol a drug.[7] Only 21 percent consider wine coolers a drug.[8] By the time kids reach the sixth grade, 40 percent have tasted wine coolers.[9] The Search Institute found that the church is not even immune to alcohol use among elementary-age children. Their survey of church-connected fifth and sixth graders found that 25 percent report alcohol use "during the last year."[10]

Those who haven't gotten a head start at drinking during the elementary years are sure to catch up during their junior high and high school years. Developmental psychologist Stephen Small says of today's teens, "The use of alcohol appears to be normative. By the upper grades, everybody's doing it."[11] Of the 20.7 million students in seventh to twelfth grade nationwide, 68 percent have drunk alcohol at least once, and 51 percent (10.6 million) have had at least one drink within the past year. Of those who drink, eight million drink weekly.[12]

At least 5.4 million students have binged at least once. A *binge* is defined as drinking five or more drinks in a row. Three million students had binged during the month prior to the survey of seventh to twelfth graders with the number of binges ranging from one to twenty per month. Almost half a million students binge every week with an average consumption of fifteen drinks weekly.[13]

By the time they reach their senior year in high school, nine out of ten teens will have experimented with alcohol, and 39 percent will get drunk (or binge) at least once every two weeks.[14] It should come as no surprise that 3.3 million thirteen to seventeen year olds in America have serious alcohol problems.[15]

What teens are drinking. The Department of Health and Human Services surveyed teens who drink to discover what they are drinking and how much. They found that students drink alcoholic beverages from one or more of four popular categories and types.

Over nine million students have drunk beer. When teen beer consumption is averaged out over the entire teen drinking population (10.6 million), the average teen drinker consumes 3.5 beers weekly. While students drink less than 2 percent of the sixty-two billion bottles and cans of beer consumed annually in the U.S., the fact still remains that these seventh- to twelfth-grade minors illegally consume over a billion beers each year. Included in these totals are malt liquors, which contain up to twice as much alcohol (8 percent) as beer (between 4 and 4.8 percent). Drinking malt liquor is becoming more and more popular among teens of all races because it is cheap, powerful, and fast-acting. It is also highly addictive.

Why do kids say they like to drink beer? Teens who choose beer as their favorite alcoholic beverage say they do so because it tastes good, is easy to get, is cheap, and doesn't get them drunk as fast as other alcoholic beverages. Also, beer is always plentiful at teen drinking parties.

Another popular drink among teens is the wine cooler. Nearly nine million seventh to twelfth graders have drunk wine coolers, and 42.1 percent of students who drink say that it is their favorite drink. According to estimated sales figures, 88.8 million gallons of wine coolers were sold in the U.S. in 1988, with high school and junior high students accounting for the consumption of 35 percent of that total. The average teen drinker in America consumes 1.6 wine coolers a week. Wine coolers are popular among teens because they taste good, are fruity, do not have a strong taste of alcohol, and don't seem to contain much alcohol. Another reason for the popularity of wine coolers among younger students is their confusing packaging. It is difficult to distinguish them from mineral waters and sodas that are very similar in color, labeling, and bottle shape. While most wine coolers have an alcohol content ranging from 4 to 5 percent, the controversial Cisco fruit-flavored fortified wine has a 20 percent alcohol content. More than a third of all students didn't know that Cisco contains alcohol.

Drinking is seen by many teens and their parents as normal and acceptable.

Wine is consumed by 6.2 million seventh to twelfth graders. The average teen drinker in America drinks 1.4 glasses of wine a week.

And finally, 7.2 million students have drunk hard liquor, with the average teen drinker drinking 3.5 drinks each week.[16]

When all is said and done, American teens are really putting it away!

Other alcohol facts. There are other aspects related to teen drinking that parents should be aware of. *First, teenagers find it easy to get alcohol.* While many teens can get their alcohol out of the family liquor cabinet, from a friend, or at a party, almost two-thirds, or 6.9 million of the students who drink, buy their own alcoholic beverages![17] Despite the fact that all states have minimum-age laws, students as young as twelve and thirteen say they have purchased alcoholic beverages in a store. Some are able to make the purchases by using fake identification. Others buy from stores known to sell to minors. Many teens say that they buy alcohol at stores who have young clerks. If they want it, any teen in America can get it.

Second, drinking and driving remains the number one killer of adolescents.[18] While most students would say that it is wrong to drink and drive, roughly half will at least once during their teenage years accept a ride from someone who has been drinking. In 1990, 25 percent of sixteen- to nineteen-year-old drivers of passenger vehicles who were fatally injured in crashes had high blood alcohol concentrations (.10 percent and higher). An additional 10 percent had lower, but still positive, blood alcohol concentrations.[19]

Third, many parents actually encourage their children to drink. Not only do parents encourage drinking through their own behavior, some even provide alcohol in their own homes. They assume that their children will drink anyway, so why not give them the alcohol and the place to do it safely?

Fourth, teen alcohol use plays a role in promiscuous and criminal behavior. According to a report released by the surgeon general in 1992, 55 percent of the perpetrators and 53 percent of the victims of sexual assault were under the influence of alcohol at the time. Forty percent of boys and 18 percent of girls think it is all right to force sex if the girl is drunk.[20] And almost one-third of the young people who commit serious crimes have consumed alcohol just prior to committing those crimes.[21]

Finally, alcohol is the leading "gateway" drug. There is a definite link between alcohol use and the tendency to move on from alcohol to heavier types of drugs. Sixty-one percent of all drug abusers report that alcohol was the first drug they ever used. In addition, those who use alcohol are six times more likely to use other drugs than those who don't.[22]

Tobacco

America's addictive behavior is also evident in our dependence on tobacco. Fifty-seven million Americans are hooked on cigarettes, and twelve million use smokeless tobacco.[23] The high price paid by smokers extends beyond the price of a pack of cigarettes. Those who smoke one pack a day add an average of 18 percent to their medical bills and cut their life expectancy by six years.[24] According to the surgeon general's office, 434,000 Americans die of smoking-related illnesses each year.[25] When all is said and done, smoking costs the U.S. $439 billion a year in medical expenses and lost workdays.[26]

It would seem that the grim reality of the effects of smoking would serve as a danger sign to our children and teens, leading them to say no to tobacco use. But judging from the statistics relating to tobacco use among teens, kids riding on the highway from childhood to adulthood are driving right past the danger signs and into an unhealthy adulthood.

Teen tobacco facts and figures. Each year the tobacco industry spends $3.6 billion dollars advertising cigarettes.[27] Billboards, magazines, and even race cars are used to encourage children, teens, and adults to partake of the "benefits" of smoking. Everyone knows that when it comes to tobacco addiction, if you can hook 'em young, you'll have 'em forever.

Many elementary-age children let their curiosity get the best of them, and they enter the grown-up world of adults and older teens by trying to smoke. My father was aware of the temptation to smoke that I would feel while growing up because of his own experience as a young boy. Consequently, when I was in elementary school, he told me on several occasions that when I wanted to try smoking, all I had to do was come and tell him. He also let me know that my initial puffs would be on several of the biggest cigars he could buy, all smoked in succession. He knew that my curiosity would be satisfied quickly if I had a near-death experience that included coughing, choking, and vomiting! Needless to say, I never became a smoker.

K*ids want to be adults, and they think smoking makes them look older.*

But smoking addiction begins for many people before they reach their adolescent years. One percent of all eleven year olds smoke regularly. That number jumps to 5 percent by the time kids are twelve and thirteen.[28] Nineteen percent of all high school seniors report that they initiated cigarette use by the sixth grade.[29] What most parents don't realize is that early tobacco use isn't just limited to cigarettes. Twenty-five percent of all smokeless tobacco users (snuff and chewing tobacco) began using it between the ages of five and eight! An additional 25 percent began to "chew" between the ages of nine and twelve.[30] This means that one-half of all smokeless tobacco users got their start before they reached their teenage years.

As children grow older, smoking increases. In fact, "cigarettes have consistently comprised the class of substance most frequently used on a daily basis by high school students."[31] Three million American teenagers under the age of eighteen are smoking 947 million packs of cigarettes a year.[32] A 1991 survey conducted by the Center for

Disease Control found that three-quarters of all teens had smoked cigarettes at least once, and 28 percent had smoked in the thirty days preceding the survey.[33] By the time they reach their senior year in high school, 19 percent of all teenagers are smoking on a daily basis.[34]

The number of teens using smokeless tobacco increased eightfold during the fifteen years prior to 1993.[35] The Center for Disease Control reports that one in five high school boys used snuff or chew during 1991 with a total of half a million using it weekly.[36] Teenagers are responsible for consuming twenty-six million containers of smokeless tobacco each year.[37]

No matter what they say, the tobacco industry is targeting your children. Their economic survival depends on it. They know that six thousand children and teens must begin smoking each day if they are to maintain their current sales levels.[38] Current tobacco-use trends among teens indicate that the industry's efforts are successful and that if they carry along the same track, 90 percent of American smokers will continue to become regular smokers before they reach the age of twenty-one.[39]

Teenagers want desperately to be adults. Smoking is a quick, yet dangerous, path that many are taking in an effort to "grow up" and appear older than they are.

And finally, studies indicate that if your children are smokers, they are many times more likely than teen nonsmokers to use a variety of other drugs. According to the National Institute of Drug Abuse, smokers between the ages of twelve and seventeen are twenty-three times more likely to use marijuana, twelve times more likely to use heroin, fifty-one times more likely to use cocaine, and fifty-seven times more likely to use crack.[40]

Drugs

Despite the improvements in recent years . . . it is still true that this nation's high school students and other young adults show a level of involvement with illicit drugs which is greater than can be found in any other industrialized nation in the world.[41]

America has a drug-abuse problem that is touching too many of our children and teens. Six out of ten teenagers will have used illicit drugs at least once before finishing high school.[42] In 1990, 33 percent of America's high school seniors reported using illicit drugs during the last year.[43] Some of these students had their first exposure to drugs at an early age. The Search Institute estimates that between one in five and one in three eighth graders have tried an illicit drug.[44]

Statistics for the entire U.S. population show that 80 percent of all American adults have used an illicit drug by the time they reach their late twenties.[45]

It is sad to note that many parents are in the dark when it comes to teens and drugs. Not only are they unaware of the types of drugs that kids are using but they often don't know when their kids are using. Researchers at the Emory University School of Medicine surveyed a group of high school seniors and their parents to see how aware or unaware parents really are. The teens were asked whether they had used various drugs in the past month, and parents were asked if their children had used drugs during that time. In every single case, the parents' estimates were way off the mark. Sixty-seven percent of the teens said that they had used alcohol during the past thirty days. Only 35 percent of the parents said they thought their teens had used alcohol. Three percent of the parents thought that their children had used marijuana when, in fact, the actual number was 28 percent. Eight percent of the students had used stimulants while only one percent of the parents thought so. None of the parents thought their children had used cocaine or inhalants while 6 percent of the students had used cocaine and 2 percent used inhalants.[46]

Parents must be aware of the fact that many teens are experimenting with illicit drugs and some become regular users. What types of drugs, specifically, are teenagers using in the nineties? For the next several pages, we will examine the facts and unique features of some of the most common drugs that kids are using. Take the time to become familiar with each of these drugs. Although my descriptions are by no means exhaustive, they will serve to raise your awareness so that you can recognize both the appeal and danger of each and discuss them intelligently with your children.

Depressants. Teens who want to relax or reduce their level of anxiety will often turn to depressants. While these drugs sedate and slow down the activity of the central nervous system, many teens will use stronger and more toxic doses in order to enter into a state of euphoria and excitement before the sedating power of the drug takes effect. These drugs initially elevate a person's mood.

Approximately 8 percent of America's high school seniors report having used some sort of depressant.[47] Alcohol and tranquilizers are the most commonly used and abused depressants. Other popular depressants include barbiturates and Quaaludes, a commercial drug that was removed from the market in the early 1980s due to widespread abuse, but continues to be manufactured and sold illegally.

Depressants are highly addictive, and long-term users develop physical and psychological dependence on these drugs. In addition, those who abuse depressants on a regular basis build a physical tolerance, requiring greater and greater dosages in order to feel the desired effects of the drug.

The physical side effects of depressant addiction can include convulsions, drowsiness, confusion, cirrhosis of the liver, sexual impotence, paranoia, irritability, mood swings, violence, coma, and death.

There are several trade and slang names for the different types of depressants, most of which are ingested orally in the form of tablets and capsules (although some forms are injected): methaqualone, phenobarbital, Nembutal, Seconal, Amnytal, Luminal, Valium, Librium, Equanil, Serax, Tranxene, Dalmane, ludes, soaps, quacks, blue devils, yellow jackets, blue heavens, downers, barbs, red devils, purple hearts, rainbows, double trouble, Christmas trees, goofballs, and blockbusters.

Hallucinogens. Ten percent of America's high school seniors report using a hallucinogen sometime in their life.[48] Hallucinogens act on the central nervous system, producing mood changes and perceptual changes, including a loss of contact with reality. Teenagers report using them because they give "insightful experiences," feelings of exhilaration, and a sense of being powerful.

Chronic users of hallucinogens can become psychologically dependent on the drugs, craving the altered mental state produced by their use. There is no proof that any sort of physical dependence develops.

There are several types of hallucinogens popular among teens today. The first is LSD (lysergic acid diethylamide), a drug thought to be unpopular after the sixties, but now making an incredible comeback among teens, particularly those from affluent suburban communities. LSD is relatively cheap. A hit that lasts from ten to twelve hours can be purchased for two to five dollars on the street. Kids who use LSD will ingest it orally, lick it off paper, place it in their eyes with an eyedropper, sniff it, or inject it. What they can expect in the short term is an exhilarating trip through a hallucinatory fantasy world. While there are some who claim that LSD is relatively harmless, it is extremely dangerous. One doctor says, "Taking acid is equivalent to playing Russian roulette with chemicals."[49] Users can suffer from panic attacks, nightmares, and psychosis. Another common adverse reaction is the flashback, a reexperiencing of the effects of the drug sometimes weeks and months after taking it (this has been known to occur among 25 percent of LSD users). "Bad trips" can lead to violence and self-destructive behavior. LSD is also known as acid, sugar cubes, trips, windowpane, blotter, big D, the beast, blue cheer, California sunshine, the hawk, the ghost, and sacrament.

Another popular hallucinogen is PCP (phencyclidine). It was first developed in 1959 as an anesthetic agent to dissociate or detach patients from all bodily sensations so that no pain was felt during surgery. Because of its negative side effects, its use on humans was discontinued, and it was used solely in veterinary medicine. PCP users usually smoke the white crystalline powder in tobacco or marijuana cigarettes and may also snort, eat, or inject it. Initially, this dangerous drug produces colorful hallucinations and an out-of-body experience. While under PCP's influence, users can experience blurred vision, slurred speech, muscle rigidity, seizures, bizarre behavior, violent behavior towards self or others, coma, and even death. The full range of PCP's long-term effects is not known; however, some users experience long-term psychosis. This psychologically addictive drug is also known as angel dust, horse tranquilizer, crystal, super-weed, rocket fuel, peace pill, Shermans, and hog.

Although not as popular as LSD and PCP, other hallucinogens that teens are using include psilocybin (a brown mushroom) and mescaline, a substance found in the peyote cactus, which has been widely used by Indian tribes as part of their religious rituals.

Narcotics. These drugs depress the central nervous system and, at the same time, relieve pain. Most of the narcotics that are being abused illegally today were legally used by the medical profession as painkillers until they were discovered to be highly addictive.

Narcotic users like the drugs because of the initial euphoric high and the feelings of relief and relaxation. The user feels an almost immediate surge of pleasure that yields to a gratifying high. Users become very docile and dreamy when under the influence. This would explain their reported use by one in twelve high school seniors as many teens seek relief from the anxiety they feel as they pass through adolescence.[50]

There are many short- and long-term negative effects related to narcotic abuse. Drowsiness, nausea, vomiting, and death due to central respiratory system depression can occur during usage. The symptoms of heavy long-term use are severe psychological and physical dependence, high tolerance and the accompanying need for bigger and bigger doses, constipation, loss of appetite, and death from overdose. Since many narcotics are taken by injection, users run the risk of contracting AIDS, hepatitis, and other communicable diseases that might be spread through the use of a dirty needle. Those who try to get off the narcotic habit find it extremely painful and difficult to withdraw. Narcotics are so addictive that even short-term use can result in enough dependence to cause severe withdrawal symptoms.

There are several types of narcotics, most of which are derivatives of opium. Opium is made by air drying the juice that has been extracted from the unripened seed pods of the oriental poppy plant. The juice dries into a brownish gum that is formed into cakes or bricks. After being ground into powder, opium is either smoked or eaten. It is also known as O, op, black pills, black stuff, tar, gum, and hop. Other opium derivatives include paregoric, Dover's powder, and parepectolin. The chemical substance in opium that causes its effects is morphine, which is injected or sniffed by those who abuse it.

The most well-known derivative of opium is heroin, a narcotic gleaned from morphine. Developed in 1898 by the Bayer Company in Germany, heroin was found to be a more effective pain reliever than morphine. Pure heroin is a white crystalline powder that is sniffed, smoked, or injected. It is usually liquified from powder, cooked, and injected ("shot-up" or "mainlined"). At the present time, there are four hundred thousand to seven hundred thousand Americans who are addicted to the deadly drug.[51] Heroin is also known as H, horse, junk, smack, scag, stuff, harley, harry, brown sugar, mud, hairy, joy powder, and thing.

Some teens will abuse prescription narcotics found in the family medicine cabinet. These include anything containing codeine, Darvon, Percocet, Demerol, and Percodan.

Designer drugs. Relatively new, these drugs are manufactured by "street chemists" who alter the molecular structure of illegal drugs, thereby making them "legal." Designer drugs are sometimes several hundred times stronger than the drugs they imitate. As a result, it is not uncommon for designer-drug users to overdose.

Injected, inhaled, or ingested orally, these drugs mimic the effects of other drugs. Feelings of strength, confidence, and euphoria are often accompanied by hallucinations. The side effects include tremors, impaired speech, paralysis, drooling, and permanent brain damage.

The most popular of all designer drugs is ecstasy, which has been promoted to teenagers as a way to warm, loving relaxation. The drug is finding widespread acceptance by teenagers who attend rave parties, all-night celebrations where party-goers dance to one-hundred-thirty-plus-beats-a-minute electronic music, computer-generated videos, and laser light shows. One twenty-two year old says, "Raves are like an atom with particles moving in it, making it move faster and hotter. When a group of people are all moving to that music, you feel that energy and it's a blast."[52] After paying a twenty-dollar admission fee, the "blast" can be induced and intensified by paying another twenty dollars for a dose of ecstasy.

Designer drugs come in powder, capsule, and tablet form and are known by the names ecstasy, X, Adam, essence, China white, and Eve. They are sometimes called by their chemical names MPTP, MPPP, PEPAP, XTC, MDMA, STP, PMA, DOB, DOM, PCE, TCP, and MDA.

Inhalants. Several years ago I was speaking at a junior high retreat when the camp's kitchen crew discovered that an entire case of canned whipped cream was faulty. Every can was out of gas. After further investigation, my theory proved correct. A group of boys had raided the kitchen and sucked the nitrous oxide propellant out of the cans in an effort to get high.

Inhalants are easy to obtain, inexpensive, and popular especially among thirteen to fifteen year olds, who have difficulty obtaining alcohol and other illegal drugs. Like other central nervous system depressants, inhalants are used for the initial high and euphoria they give. Eighteen percent of the high school seniors surveyed report having used inhalants at least once.[53] Researcher Lloyd Johnston says that they are "the most widely used class of drug among eighth-graders."[54] Kids will sniff them directly from the source, from a paper bag, or from rags that have been saturated with the substance.

The most popular of these "garbage drugs" are Scotchgard, non-stick cooking spray, gasoline, turpentine, nail-polish remover, butane, Freon, typewriter correction fluid, room deodorizers, brake fluid, glues, hair spray, and aerosol propellants. Some teens have even started to get high from bromochlorodifluoromethane (BCF), the propellant used in gas-based fire extinguishers. Others are using butane-lighter refills, squirting the butane down their throats.

Inhalant abuse kills brain cells, damages the liver, kidneys, lungs, and bone marrow, and can cause cardiac arrest. Death can result from heart attack, choking on vomit, losing consciousness while a plastic bag is over the head, or losing consciousness in a dangerous place (falling or drowning).

While use is difficult to detect, you can discern signs of teen inhalant abuse by looking for teary, glazed, or red eyes; facial rash; chemicals on their breath; erratic behavior; slurred speech; and a decrease in school performance.

Teens refer to these garbage drugs as laughing gas, whippets, poppers, snappers, bullet, locker room, bolt, rush, climax, gunk, and buzz bombs.

Steroids. Five hundred thousand adolescents currently use anabolic steroids (synthetic growth hormones) in an effort to improve their speed, strength, athletic performance, physique, and popularity.[55] The great majority are boys. Over half the teens who use steroids start before the age of sixteen. In one study, 7 percent said that they started by age ten.[56]

Teens who use steroids find that the habit is costly. A typical one-month supply costs anywhere from eighty to a hundred dollars. Some teens are so naive that they might even pay up to three hundred dollars a month in their quest for the desired results.

The high cost of steroids extends beyond a teenager's wallet. The physical effects of anabolic steroid use include severe acne, premature balding, jaundice, breast enlargement, shrinking testicles, stunted growth, liver disease, heart disease, cancer, kidney disease, sterility, and blood pressure problems. Also common are sudden bursts of anger and violent behavior.

Sadly, most kids ignore the nasty side effects of steroid use because of their preoccupation with looking better. Ninety-three percent of adolescent steroid users said they believe they made a good decision by starting to use steroids. Eighty-seven percent would make the same decision today "without hesitation." More than 80 percent of the users said steroids had made them bigger and stronger and that "the improvements I achieved by using steroids made me more popular."[57]

Cocaine. By age twenty-seven, 40 percent of all Americans have tried cocaine, the most addictive drug currently known to humankind. As early as their senior year in high school, 9 percent have done so.[58] Cocaine has become very popular as a white-collar drug that is used socially and extensively among middle- and upper-class adults. One addict I talked to assured me that I would be surprised by the number of parents using cocaine in the neighborhood we lived in.

Cocaine, a central nervous system stimulant, is a white powder that comes from the leaves of the South American coca plant. Relatively inexpensive at seventy to a hundred dollars for a gram, cocaine is usually inhaled through the nose. Frequent use can lead to ulcerated and collapsed nostrils. Cocaine is also injected under the skin or into veins, increasing the risk of becoming infected with a communicable disease transmitted through dirty needles. A more dangerous method is known as freebasing in which volatile solvents are used to prepare the drug for smoking. Death or severe injury (as in the case of comedian Richard Pryor) can occur when the mixture explodes.

Used in low doses, cocaine produces a short-lived sensation of euphoria with feelings of increased energy and alertness. Larger doses intensify the high but can lead to bizarre and violent behavior. Coming down from the high can slide the user into a depression. Physical effects include accelerated heartbeat, faster breathing, sweating, rise in body temperature, tremors, nausea, chest pain, convulsions, and impotence. Death from overdose is not unusual. Those who become addicted begin to center their lives on obtaining the drug and getting high. The drug becomes central to their thoughts, emotions, and activities.

Cocaine is also called coke, snow, flake, white, blow, nose candy, big C, snowbirds, lady, star dust, happy dust, and toot, and taking the drug is often referred to as doing a line.

Crack. Roughly one in every thirty high school seniors and 5.1 percent of those under the age of twenty-seven have tried the highly addictive and inexpensive smokeable form of cocaine known as crack.[59] For five to ten dollars, a teenager can buy a product that is four to ten times stronger than cocaine. The effects of crack's potent high are felt within ten seconds and last for five to twenty minutes. Users describe the initial feeling of euphoria as similar to having sex. The craving for another high can cause psychological addiction in a matter of days. Coming down from the high has been described as a crushing depression.

Some kids take drugs to become more popular or to escape from stress.

The process of converting cocaine to crack is so easy and simple it is performed in kitchens all over the U.S. by mixing cocaine, water, and baking soda. The finished product looks like small lumps or shavings of soap that have the texture of porcelain, and it is usually packaged in small vials.

The physical and psychological side effects of crack are virtually the same as those of cocaine.

Crack is also known as rock, readyrock, french fries, and teeth.

Stimulants. Drugs that stimulate the central nervous system and increase the activity of the brain or spinal cord are known as stimulants. The 18 percent rate of usage among high school seniors can be explained by the drug's production of greater energy, increased alertness, and feelings of euphoria. Kids under tremendous pressure to perform are especially attracted to stimulant abuse.[60] Kids are also attracted to the feelings of self-confidence, competence, and power that come from using the drug. The downside is that as the drug wears off depression and drowsiness occur.

The class of stimulants known as amphetamines produces effects that resemble those of the naturally occurring substance adrenaline. Amphetamines were initially used during World War II when high doses were given to soldiers and pilots in an effort to combat battle fatigue and to increase alertness. Today many truck drivers and students use them in order to stay awake for long periods of time. Amphetamines appear most commonly as capsules and tablets.

Methamphetamine is an amphetamine derivative that is a more potent central nervous system stimulant. It is usually used in a powder or crystal form and is illicitly manufactured.

When it is taken in low doses, breathing, heart rate, and blood pressure all increase. Higher doses are accompanied by a dry mouth, fever, sweating, dizziness, and irregular heartbeat. Stimulant users build a tolerance to the euphoric effects of the drugs and need more and more in order to achieve the desired level of feeling good. Psychological dependence on stimulants leads to long-term addiction and can sometimes end in brain damage or death.

A run is an extended period of stimulant use that lasts from three to five days. During the first day, the user feels euphoric, self-confident, and extremely sociable. The second day brings an inability to concentrate and severe mood swings. Visions, paranoia, and violent, aggressive behavior are not unusual. Towards the end of the run, the user finds it increasingly difficult to cope with the world and will sink into an exhausted and lengthy sleep.

Common terms used by kids to refer to the many different kinds of stimulants include speed, crystal, meth, bennies, dexies, uppers, pep pills, diet pills, hearts, footballs, cranks, splash, black beauties, copilots, bumble bees, and mother's little helpers.

Ice. This new smokeable form of methamphetamine deserves special and separate mention due to its rising popularity among young adults and upper- and middle-class teenagers in the United States. Ice is high in purity and similar in size and appearance to quartz or rock salt. As addictive as crack and cocaine, ice is so pure that all of its stimulant properties are intensified. Users feel an immediate and powerful euphoria, followed by a long-lasting high of eight to twenty-four hours. An ice high makes one feel bright, awake, happy, and good about oneself. During initial use, ice facilitates the ability to function so effectively that more can be accomplished in less time. In addition, users report an increase in sexual pleasure and performance.

Ice was invented in 1893 and was used extensively in Japan during World War II. The Japanese fed it to war-weary soldiers and munitions workers in an attempt to increase output and win the war. In the United States, ice has become very popular among young corporate executives who are working long, hard hours in an effort to climb the ladder of success. One former user says,

> A lot of people who do ice are in high-demanding jobs. In society today so much is expected of you. Ice makes you feel more productive, makes you do things you want to accomplish. That's why people do ice. It makes you an achiever. It's the American way.[61]

It's no wonder so many achievement-oriented high school and college students are using ice as they work to balance the demands of school and busy activity schedules.

Ice has been reported to cause nausea, vomiting, rapid respiratory and heart rates, increased body temperature, and comas at high dosage levels. Overdoses are common as it is difficult to control the amount of potent smoke that is inhaled. Long-term side effects include aggressive behavior, hallucinations, paranoia, and fatal kidney failure.

Parents should be aware of the fact that ice has surpassed cocaine as the number one drug problem in Hawaii and is spreading like wildfire across the U.S. Some have suggested that the nineties might just be the dawn of America's new "Ice Age."

Cannabis (marijuana). The cannabis plant, or hemp, is the source of marijuana, hashish, and THC (tetrahydrocannabinol), its biologically active ingredient. Forty-one percent of today's high school seniors say that they have used marijuana.[62] As one of the "gateway" drugs that leads to further and harder drug use, marijuana is popular among younger teens. A Search Institute survey found that one in five eighth graders reports using marijuana.[63]

The least potent and most commonly used form of cannabis is the dried leaves, buds, and stems of the plant. Hash, a more potent form of THC, is made from the plant's resin and is pressed into small cakes or bricks. The most potent form of THC is hashish oil, a condensed and distilled liquid resin that is often added to a joint (marijuana cigarette) and smoked. While marijuana's potency varies from climate to climate and ounce to ounce, today's crop is two to ten times more potent than the marijuana of ten years ago.

Sold by the ounce or "lid" (slightly less than an ounce), users smoke marijuana in a joint or pipe. A bong or rush tube is used to send the smoke to the lungs more efficiently. A small clothespin-like roach clip is used to hold a joint and allows the user to smoke it right down to the end. Some users bake marijuana into brownies, but less THC is absorbed when it is eaten.

Teens smoke marijuana for a euphoric high that often leads to fits of laughter and talking more than usual. Other short-term effects include increased heart and respiratory rate, reddening of the eyes, and sleepiness. Used in very high doses, marijuana may have effects that are similar to those of hallucinogens.

Continued use can lead to respiratory problems, lung cancer, loss of energy, confused thinking, slow reactions, impaired memory, and apathy. Some frequent users lack initiative and don't seem to care about the future. They find it difficult to stay motivated, thinking things will take care of themselves. This is often referred to as amotivational syndrome. Regular use builds up tolerance to the drug, requiring increased dosages in order to achieve the desired high. Physical and psychological dependence may result.

Teens will often refer to marijuana as pot, grass, weed, reefer, dope, Mary Jane, Thai sticks, Acapulco gold, herb, joint, smoke, buds, bag, dime, sinsemilla, and refer to the effects of the drug as getting high, getting wasted, getting stoned, and getting loaded.

Why Are Kids Using Drugs and Alcohol?

Not long ago I visited a young man at a local rehabilitation hospital. He was recovering from a severe spinal cord injury that had left him a paraplegic and was sharing a room with several other spinal cord injury victims. Each one had been involved in an accident that had left him either partially or fully paralyzed. As I looked around the room, I was struck by the collections of photographs that hung on their bulletin boards. Many of the pictures were of these young men before their horrible accidents. They were all standing. My friend told me that alcohol was a factor in two of the accidents and that in both of those cases, the two men lying in those beds were teenagers. I couldn't help but shake my head and wonder under my breath, *Why did these kids make such a stupid choice?*

A woman who works with teenagers recently wrote a letter to the editor of *Time* magazine to share her answer:

Your article on alcohol abuse by America's youth discusses a problem I encounter daily as an English instructor in a community college. To me, the most frightening thing is that even though young people seem to know about all the dangers inherent in drinking, they simply ignore them. They turn in their freshman themes about the negative effects of alcohol—and go out into the hall to discuss their weekend keg parties. Perhaps their confusion is a result of the mixed messages they receive from parents who drink, from the law that seems to treat under-age drinking as a rite of passage and from TV's reminding them that people who drink have more fun.[64]

This woman's perceptions are right. There are many different reasons kids get involved with alcohol and drugs.

REASON #1: Curiosity and experimentation

I have never met a teenager who has used drugs and alcohol with the intent of getting hooked. The fact is, most kids, especially those who are younger, have their first experience with drugs and alcohol without understanding that there are dangers involved. Those who are aware of the dangers somehow think that they are immune—the it-will-never-happen-to-me syndrome.

All of us can remember feeling the urge to try new things while growing up. Many children will satisfy their curiosity about the un-known world of tobacco, alcohol, and drugs by trying them to find out just what smoking, drinking, and doing drugs are like. It is not unusual for adolescent curiosity to lead to a first puff on a cigarette or an initial sip from a can of beer.

This was the case for the group of sixth-grade boys and girls that I once found huddled around a single cigarette they were sharing in the woods during a church youth retreat. My adult presence scared them. They assured me that there was only one cigarette and this was the first time they had ever tried it. Judging from the fact that from my vantage point behind a tree I had just observed eight inexperi-enced kids nervously struggle to light and smoke one cigarette, I had to believe them. I knew these kids well enough to know that this was nothing more than an attempt to satisfy their adolescent curiosity.

REASON #2: Peer pressure

When asked why they drank, the teens taking part in a recent Roper survey cited peers as their number one reason. Seventy per-cent said they drink because their schoolmates and friends drink.[65] My informal surveys of high school students indicate that the pres-sure to drink alcohol is the greatest pressure that churched kids feel from their peers.

In a desire to fit in and be accepted and loved, children and teens who feel insecure and unloved at home give in to the pressure. Smoking, drinking, and using drugs become less of a price to pay than alienation from the crowd.

REASON #3: It's fun

When asked why she drinks, Mary Ellen speaks for many teens: "It's fun, and besides, life is boring. I drink because there's nothing else to do." Today's teens are bored. Many of them find drugs and alcohol to be an exciting form of recreation that is cheap, easy, and fun to do with a group of friends. While sports requires a significant personal investment of time, energy, and personal discipline, a chemical high is much easier to achieve.

One recent report shows that of the 10.6 million seventh- to twelfth-grade students who drink, 25 percent do it because they are bored.[66] Twenty-five percent say they do it to get high.[67] Rap singer B-Real of the group Cypress Hill says, "We gotta find some weed; otherwise we ain't gonna have any fun."[68] Other teens say that "undergrounders" are the thing to do on boring weekends. Undergrounders are wild parties that are held between midnight and sunrise at secret locations. They feature high-volume music and all the beer and cheap wine you can drink. They are advertised by word of mouth and sponsored by young businessmen who are looking to make a quick buck off of teens looking for fun.

We live in a society that places high value on having fun and feeling good. Substance abuse among teens is often initiated in an effort to alleviate boredom and satisfy their thirst for fun.

REASON #4: To look grown-up

When teens realize they aren't children anymore, they don't want to look like children. Sometimes they will make an extra effort to look older than they really are. Teenagers think that a beer in their hand or a cigarette in their mouth will make them look older.

A girl named Stacey says that drinking "is a rite of passage," a ritual associated with changing one's status from child to adult. Adam says that guys do it because they want to look and be "macho."[69] Drinking to appear grown-up was the third-highest reason listed by teens in the Roper survey of why teens drink.[70]

REASON #5: Availability

Children and teens find drugs and alcohol easy to get. Data from the National Crime Victimization Survey showed that in the first half of 1989, two out of three students aged twelve to nineteen reported the availability of drugs at their school. There was very little differ-ence discovered between students residing in cities, suburbs, or rural areas.[71]

In spite of the fact that it is illegal in all states for minors to purchase alcohol, other teens find alcohol easily accessible in stores. As one student says, "Sometimes they don't even ask your age. I could go out right now and buy some."[72]

But the most unbelievable source of alcohol for many teenagers is their parents. Some younger teens take their first drink from the family liquor closet when left unsupervised at home. One study reports that young teens who come home to an empty house are twice as likely as those supervised by adults to use cigarettes, marijuana, and alcohol.[73] Other kids report that their parents allowed them to sip alcohol or even drink a full glass during holiday celebrations as early as the elementary school years. And I know of several cases where parents of teens actually supply the alcohol and the location for parties in the hope that this will keep their kids from drinking and driving. In fact, 35 percent of the seventh to twelfth graders who drink say that their parents tolerate their drinking under certain conditions.[74] When Mom and Dad put their stamp of approval on drinking, how can a teen believe any other voices that might say teen drinking is dangerous and wrong?

REASON #6: Advertising

Ads are especially effective as smoking and drinking recruiters. The Department of Health and Human Services survey found that 39 percent of all teens named something they like about ads for alco-holic beverages. While their likes vary widely, most teens say they like the ads because they spotlight attractive people and make drinking look like it's lots of fun. Some specific responses included:

- They are very convincing. They make it look very glamorous.
- They look exciting and fun. The message is: It's all right to drink, not that it is bad.
- Some of them are funny, and some have sexy women.
- They make you look like you're cool and accepted.
- Girls in the ad are skinny, and I want to be like that.
- The slogan "The Right Beer Now" makes you think "Is now a good time to drink?"[75]

As Surgeon General Antonia Novello has said, "Alcohol advertis-ing goes beyond describing the specific qualities of the beverage. It creates a glamorous, pleasurable image that may mislead youth about alcohol and the possible consequences of its use."[76]

Because of where they are developmentally, teens are fair game for advertising messages that suggest drinking and smoking lead to maturity, sophistication, beauty, fun, and acceptance.

REASON #7: *Family problems*

Numerous studies have shown a relationship between the family environment and the use of drugs and alcohol among adolescents. But anyone who has ever spent any significant amount of time with kids doesn't need scientific studies to prove the link. Kids who come from homes where there is divorce, separation, an absent parent, discord, marital conflict, poor communication, abuse, and alcoholism are more likely to abuse drugs and alcohol. Conversely, kids who come from homes characterized by love, nurturing, affection, involvement, and marital harmony are less likely to abuse drugs and alcohol.

I know a young man who has already passed through his adolescent years but continues to struggle with a drug and alcohol problem that began in his early teens. As a young teen, his committed Christian parents seemed to be preoccupied with two things: their restaurant business and keeping him in line. Consequently, they spent a lot of time running the business and little time with their son. Their communication with him was limited to enforcing their legalistic set of rules dictatorially. His reaction to this loveless home was to rebel against what he saw his parents holding nearest and dearest to their hearts: their faith and their business. His avenue of rebellion was drugs and alcohol.

Teen substance abusers often get involved with drugs and alcohol as a result of the pain and misery of family problems.

REASON #8: *Escape*

The life of the normal teenager is filled with all kinds of stresses. Drugs and alcohol often become coping mechanisms for teens who have no other way to grow constructively through adolescence. Of the teens who drink, the largest amount (41 percent) say they drink when they are upset because it makes them feel better.[77]

Some kids get high or drunk to escape from the problems of the world. They worry about AIDS, pollution, violence, and war. The high brings temporary relief in a world that they feel is destined to self-destruct.

Others try to escape from the many pressures to succeed and

achieve that are placed on them by parents, teachers, and peers. One MIT student reasons, "I work hard during the week and play hard on weekends. Although work is necessary in college, without partying your work has no payoff."

Kids who suffer from low self-esteem and poor self-images find alcohol and drugs to be an escape from the torment of what they see in the mirror. One study found that girls who see themselves as unattractive are four times more likely to use cocaine, marijuana, hallucinogens, or amphetamines than those who believe they are average looking or attractive. Underweight girls who ranked themselves as unattractive were six to ten times more likely to use drugs.[78]

K ids who have loving, committed parents are less likely to abuse drugs and alcohol.

Seemingly unsolvable personal problems often lead to a desire to escape from feelings of hopelessness through alcohol and drugs. The trauma of divorce, illness, moving, death, or a breakup can be overwhelming to a teenager.

In spite of the fact that alcohol and drugs deliver a high and escape that lasts only temporarily and is often followed by an even deeper depression, most kids feel that even if the high is only short-lived, it is better than suffering all the time.

REASON #9: Addiction

Teens who abuse drugs and alcohol on a regular basis risk becoming one of the 3.3 million adolescents in America who have serious problems with addiction.

In their book *Adolescents, Alcohol and Drugs,* Judith Jaynes and Cheryl Rugg describe the stages of drug and alcohol addiction among teens.

Stage 1 is known as Experimentation, the time when the teen's occasional use leads to mood changes that are generally positive and enjoyable with few or no side effects. The change is reliable, predictable, and enjoyable. They feel the same sensation each time they use the drug. Not all adolescents stay in the experimentation stage. Some, their curiosity satisfied, quit. Others move on to stage 2.

Stage 2 is known as Social Use. Adolescents remain in control of how much they use, when they use, and the effects of use. The use is moderate and for the purpose of fitting in. Kids in this stage will limit alcohol and drug use to weekend parties and social gatherings.

Stage 3 is known as Misuse. The focus shifts from socializing to a personal desire to get high. The euphoric effect becomes more important than having a good time with friends. Use becomes more frequent and is not limited to weekends and parties.

Stage 4 is known as Abuse. When an adolescent enters this stage, there is a preoccupation with being high. It is during this stage that parents, friends, and family members begin to see the obvious and ugly effects of substance abuse in the life of the adolescent. Many kids in this stage will steal to support their daily habit. The goal of the teen is to stay high since a letdown leads to depression and aggressive behavior.

Stage 5 is know as Chemical Dependency. When teens are depending on drugs and alcohol to feel normal, they have entered this stage. No longer does the teen find alcohol and drugs to be fun. The sense of euphoria is gone. Getting and taking drugs becomes a matter of survival. If daily, twenty-four-hour use is interrupted, the adolescent feels powerless to function physically or mentally.[79]

Drug and alcohol addiction is the ugly end to what begins as experimentation. Drugs and alcohol become the objects of worship in a life of physical and psychological dependency.

Signs and Symptoms of Teen Alcohol and Drug Abuse

How do you know if your teen needs help? Following are several charts listing major signs and symptoms of teen substance abuse. Parents must not assume that their children are somehow immune to the pressures that lead to experimentation and addiction to drugs and alcohol. Instead, they must be aware of the signs so that they will know what to look for. Ignorance can be a parent's worst enemy!

If you see a few of these signs present in your teen, he or she might simply be struggling with the normal changes of adolescence. But a combination of several of these signs warrants your immediate attention. Talk with your teen and take action before addiction occurs. The presence of any of the obvious signs and symptoms is an indicator that your teen has a serious substance abuse problem that requires immediate intervention and professional help.

Behavioral Signs of Teen Substance Abuse
- An increase in erratic and drastic mood swings for no obvious reason
- Hostility and rebellion towards those in authority (parents, teachers, church, etc.)
- Stealing and shoplifting

- Unexplained increase in spending
- Little regard for personal safety and an increase in risky behavior (driving fast, etc.)
- Traffic tickets
- Vandalism
- Signs of depression (see chapter 11)
- Change in eating habits
- Promiscuous sexual behavior
- Withdrawal from family and a dramatic increase in time spent alone at home
- Disorientation as to time
- Memory lapse
- Cutting class at school
- Truancy and tardiness
- Decline in grades
- Involvement in fights at school
- Inability to concentrate
- Lack of motivation
- Verbal abusiveness
- Lack of communication with family
- Secretive behavior and telling family members to "stay out of my business"
- Panic, paranoia, suspiciousness
- Hallucinations or loss of touch with reality
- Change in activities
- Dropping out of sports programs
- Inability to hold down an afterschool job
- Staying out all night
- An increase in mysterious phone calls
- Preoccupation with heavy-metal music or other music promoting party and substance abuse themes

Social Signs of Teen Substance Abuse
- Change in circle of friends
- Suddenly becoming more popular
- Suddenly becoming a loner and separates self from others

Physiological Signs of Teen Substance Abuse
- Disheveled appearance
- Lack of concern for personal hygiene
- Alcohol on breath
- Smell of smoke on clothing

- Constant smell of mints or onion rings on breath (to cover up alcohol/marijuana use)
- Dilated pupils
- Bloodshot eyes
- Staggered speech
- Lethargy
- Long periods without sleep
- Long periods of sleep
- Sickly appearance
- Dramatic weight loss or weight gain

Obvious Signs of Teen Substance Abuse
- Discovering drug paraphernalia (pipes, rolling papers, vials, lighters, burners, mirrors, razor blades, scales, matches, small plastic bags, pills)
- Spending time with kids who are known to use drugs and alcohol
- Disappearance of money or alcohol from the house
- Intoxication
- Expressed concerns about their own substance abuse problem
- Burn marks on clothing or furniture
- Needle marks
- Arrest for drug- or alcohol-related incidents

What Can Parents Do to Help Their Kids Hold Out against Drugs and Alcohol?

Lee Dogoloff, the executive director of the American Council for Drug Education, has issued this statement to parents:

> Every child in this country between the ages of 12 and 14 will be called upon to make a decision about drugs and alcohol. The only option is what decision they will make. Parents who do nothing to help kids make that decision, who merely hope for the best, who blithely assume Not My Kid now and forever, are abandoning their children at the edge of a whirlpool.[80]

The following suggestions for preventing and dealing with teenage substance abuse in your home might sound ridiculous because of their commonsense nature. But by making the effort to implement these strategies in your home, you will be taking steps to lead your child away from the whirlpool.

SUGGESTION #1: *Take a look in the mirror.*

When it comes to drugs and alcohol, what kind of lifestyle are you modeling for your kids? Parents who drink raise kids who drink. Alcoholics often raise alcoholics. Those who rely on prescription and over-the-counter drugs for relief from every little ailment raise kids who learn to do the same.

So ask yourself the following questions:

- Do you find yourself needing a drink in order to wind down at the end of the day?
- Do you feel you must have a drink in your hand in order to socialize at parties and with friends?
- Do you medicate yourself or your children at the first sign of fever, tension, or the smallest pain?
- Does your family have a history of alcoholism?
- Is your medicine cabinet full of remedies?

I was raised in a home where total abstinence was practiced. While my parents didn't believe that taking a drink put someone on a fast one-way trip to hell, they did believe that drunkenness was wrong. Lisa and I have chosen to practice abstinence in our home. With the number of alcohol and drug problems that we have experienced with family, friends, and the teens we've worked with over the years, it's been an easy choice that makes good sense to us. While some might argue that we should be modeling responsible drinking, I'm convinced that we are.

SUGGESTION #2: *Establish standards and rules.*

While discipline without love usually leads to rebellion, discipline with love is one of the greatest gifts that we can give to our children. Contrary to what some people may think, alcohol and drug use is relatively low among adolescents whose parents have set strict rules about chemical use. These rules are most effective when parents monitor their child's behavior and enforce those rules with rewards and punishments.

A study by the Search Institute found that the factor that most distinguished chemical users from nonusers was the response to the question, "How upset would your parents be if you came home from a party and your parents found out you had been drinking?"[81] For those who indicated that their parents would be very upset, chemical abuse was limited. For those with parents who didn't care, chemical abuse was much more pronounced.

Take a stand and set some boundaries. Tell your children what behaviors are and are not acceptable. Tell them why you won't allow them to drink, smoke, or use drugs. Spell out the punishment for breaking the rules. And if the rules are broken, carry through.

There are times when your kids will be out with their friends and forced to make a snap decision on whether or not to participate in drinking or using drugs. The decision will be a whole lot easier for them to make if they already know your rules and expectations. It is at these times that kids really appreciate the rules that you have set for them. To be able to say, "No, I can't drink because if I do my parents will flip" or, "No, if I drink I'll lose my license for a year" is a perfect avenue for your children to take out of a pressure-filled situation.

SUGGESTION #3: *Encourage involvement with a peer group that doesn't support drug and alcohol use.*

Substance abuse is strongly related to what one's friends do. The Search Institute has concluded that "parents can undermine the negative influence of friends both by steering children away from certain associations and toward other relationships where the influence is known to be more positive."[82]

So get to know your teenager's friends. Unite with other parents in your community to ensure that social events for young people are substance free. And take the steps mentioned in previous chapters to build a strong positive peer group at your church. Healthy youth groups exercise a tremendous amount of positive influence on children and teens.

SUGGESTION #4: *Don't be an enabler.*

Don't make it easy for your children to drink and use drugs. Parents who give their kids lots of money and freedom risk letting them step beyond their abilities to make the best choices that they can. Kids who are given free use of the car, unlimited gas, and unsupervised use of the house are at greater risk for getting into trouble with drugs and alcohol.

Don't give your teen alcohol or allow parties in your home that provide alcohol. It will not help them to drink more responsibly just because you are there and able to monitor intake.

And finally, don't give them any excuse to drink. Build their self-concept by loving them for who they are. Let them know that they are important to you by giving them your time. Build a strong home and make your family life a priority.

SUGGESTION #5: *Teach your kids about drugs.*

Almost half of America's teenagers get their information about drugs and alcohol from unreliable sources. More than four million learn from their friends, whose information may or may not be accurate. In addition, more than five million say that they "just picked up" what they know.[83]

Drug education should start when we tell our preschool children not to accept candy, gifts, or pills from strangers. As they grow older, we should take the time to educate our children on the different types of drugs that they might encounter along with the dangers and effects of each. Don't overstate the danger by saying that everyone who drinks beer will die or other generalized nonsense. Rather, tell them about the potential short- and long-term harmful effects of each drug in a truthful and realistic manner.

Tell your children the truth about drugs and alcohol—no more, no less.

Another way to teach your children is by seizing the teachable moment as they encounter drug and alcohol use and abuse in the media. Teach them to discern the true and false messages on TV shows. Help them pick apart the ridiculous nature of alcohol and cigarette ads.

And finally, teach them that it is against the law for minors to buy or drink alcoholic beverages.

SUGGESTION #6: *Teach a biblical theology of substance abuse.*

Our bottom-line desire for our Christian children and teens is that they will be obedient to God's will. We must help them come to an understanding of what it means to live the life of discipleship in regard to alcohol and drug attitudes and behaviors.

First, we must teach them that God has given them the responsibility to obey the laws of the government. Take the time to read and study Romans 13:1-3, 6-7 with your kids.

Second, study together what Scripture has to say about drunkenness in passages such as Proverbs 23:20-21; 1 Corinthians 5:11; Galatians 5:19-21; Ephesians 5:18; and 1 Thessalonians 5:5-8.

And finally, discuss the spiritual nature of the problems that lead kids to drink. Study the Bible together to look for God's answers to those problems.

My Child **Is** Abusing Drugs and Alcohol—What Do I Do?

If your child is abusing drugs and alcohol, intervene!

Rather than burden you with several pages of intervention guidelines to follow, let me give you four briefly stated steps to remember if you discover that your child has a substance abuse problem.

- *First, don't panic.* Losing your cool, composure, or head will only make the situation worse. Stay calm.
- *Second, don't feel guilty.* Your first priority is to eliminate the nasty influence of substance abuse on your child. Wallowing around in guilt can paralyze you and keep you from taking the action that you need to take. Remember, your children have the freedom to make their own choices. For whatever reason, they have made the choice to abuse drugs and/or alcohol. However, as you begin the long process of recovery, remain open to evaluating your role in the problem, and be ready to make changes in those areas where you may have contributed to your child's addiction.
- *Third, love your children.* Now, more than ever, your kids need to know that you are going to stand by them and love them unconditionally, in spite of their bad choices.
- *Fourth, get help immediately.* Go to your pastor or a trusted counselor for a referral to a competent treatment program that takes into account the spiritual dimension of the addiction problem. Look for a hospital or counseling center that sees God as part of the solution, not as part of the problem.

■ *IT'S YOUR TURN*

Over the past few years I have asked several former teen drug addicts and abusers to commit their stories to writing. Their stories are gut-wrenching. They include long lists of the types of substances they abused and how often. On the average, they began use during the junior high years and were alcoholics or addicts by the time they reached high school. When asked why they turned to drugs and alcohol, they consistently mention their struggle with the difficult years of adolescence and parents who were detached or absent. Another common thread to many of their stories is that most come from upper- and middle-class homes where parents were oblivious to their kids' spiritual, emotional, and developmental needs.

I asked each of these young adults to look back over their own experience to see if there is any advice that they would like to share with parents raising children and teens in the drug-and-alcohol-filled nineties. One young woman who had been heavily into alcohol, amphetamine, barbiturate, marijuana, and LSD use shared these words:

> Do I have any advice to offer to parents? I certainly do! The Lord Jesus Christ needs to be at the center of every husband and wife relationship. I know that you are not immune to facing difficulty and problems when you have him in your heart, but I do know that he supplies the answers and strength to get through them. Provide a solid foundation in your home with Jesus Christ as the foundation. Kids need home to be a refuge from the pressures they face in school.
>
> Know that some rebellion is a part of growing up. Your kids won't always agree with you or live up to your standards of conduct. They will disappoint you. But love your children unconditionally through the adolescent years and be there for them. Admit your mistakes to them and model for your children how to learn from those mistakes.
>
> Finally, stress the importance of knowing Jesus Christ personally. Pray for your kids and ask God to guide you and give you the wisdom to handle each problem. . . . I wish my parents had done all these things for me.

What about you? Do you take an active role in your children and teens' lives? Do you model godly values and behaviors? Do you pray for them continually? If you do, you are more likely to have substance-free children and teens who move into healthy adulthood. If you don't, now is the time to begin.

GUARDING YOUR TEEN'S EMOTIONS

Why are you downcast, O my soul?
Why so disturbed within me?

Psalm 42:5, NIV

"I NEVER THOUGHT this kind of thing would happen here." These words are repeated again and again in quiet communities all over the United States as people learn that one of their local teens has decided that dying is easier than living.

They were spoken in suburban Philadelphia on November 18, 1983 after seventeen-year-old Dan Ferdock and sixteen-year-old Marc Landis handcuffed themselves together and jumped off a two-hundred-foot ledge into a quarry. Plagued by self-hatred and confusion, the boys had gone to the quarry with sleeping bags, cigarettes, LSD, and a tape recorder. The two tapes that the boys recorded that night were filled with messages to parents and friends. "For any of you younger adults in the audience, I'd rough out your lives if I was you," said Dan. "This is definitely not something I'd recommend for young children."[1] The second tape contains the eerie sound of the two boys taking a few steps backwards while one says, "Ready?" The handcuffs jingle as they run past the tape recorder and over the edge. After ten minutes of silence, the tape reaches its end and the recorder shuts off with a loud click. People wondered how this type of thing could happen in their community. Two months later, Marc's girlfriend, Michelle, took her own life with a self-inflicted gunshot through her heart, and people wondered again.

The same words were spoken on November 1, 1984 in Leominster, Massachusetts, after two fifteen year olds were found shot to death in one of the girls' bedrooms. Melissa Poirier and Melody Maillet left notes. Melissa wrote to her family:

> I love you all very much! I really do! I know this is going to hurt you all very much but I'm sorry. It's not any of your faults.

Believe me! You were all very kind to me even though sometimes we didn't get along. I know it was for the best. I can't handle this sucky world any longer.[2]

The two said they were going to be with four recently deceased teenage friends, two who had died accidentally and two who had killed themselves.

And then there were the heavily publicized Bergenfield, New Jersey, suicides on March 11, 1987. The whole country wondered what would lead four teenagers to drive into an abandoned garage, shut the door, and deliberately die from carbon monoxide fumes in less than an hour. When Cheryl Burress, seventeen, her sister Lisa, sixteen, and friends Thomas Olton, eighteen, and Thomas Rizzo, nineteen, took their own lives, the nation began to ask, Why is this happening to our kids? The people of Bergenfield wondered again when, exactly one week later, another couple attempted suicide by carbon monoxide poisoning in the very same garage.

Teen Suicide Facts and Figures

The National Youth Suicide Prevention Center in Washington, D.C., says that every hour of every day 228 teenagers in the United States will attempt to take their own lives. That's two million teenagers a year![3] Official statistics say that over six thousand teens a year kill themselves, but Mitch Anthony, executive director of the National Suicide Help Center in Rochester, Minnesota, estimates the actual number of teen deaths to be somewhere around twenty thousand since many suicides are reported as accidents in an effort to protect a family's reputation or secure insurance settlements.[4] Anthony says:

I know of a woman whose son hung himself. Even as he hung by the rope, the police officer asked her if she wanted him to report it as an accident. I have interviewed funeral directors who have confirmed that many so-called accidents were really suicides.[5]

The growing number and intensity of problems associated with passing through the teenage years have contributed to this crisis. The Center for Disease Control reports that suicide rates among Americans age fifteen to nineteen have quadrupled in four decades, from 2.7 per one hundred thousand in 1950 to 11.3 in 1988.[6] Suicide is now the second leading cause of death among teens in this age group.[7]

The teen suicide crisis has led researchers and the government to examine the problem closely. Many studies and surveys have shown that suicidal thoughts and considerations are far more prevalent than anyone ever knew. One sociological study found that among those surveyed who were age thirteen and under, 32.2 percent reported considering suicide one or more times during the twelve months prior to the survey. The percentages for older teens were as follows: fourteen year olds, 39.7 percent; fifteen year olds, 38.3 percent; sixteen year olds, 40.3 percent; seventeen year olds, 38.6 percent; and for those eighteen and older, 38.2 percent.[8] A recent Gallup survey found that 85 percent of the teen respondents believe that "thinking about suicide is endemic in their culture."[9]

Teenage girls make five to eight times as many suicide attempts as teenage boys.[10] When all is said and done, 18 percent of all adolescent girls will attempt to take their own life.[11] Girls typically choose more nonviolent methods such as pills, carbon monoxide poisoning, etc.

While 10 percent of all teenage boys will attempt suicide,[12] their success rate is four times greater than that of girls.[13] The reason for this difference is that males typically choose the more violent means of guns and hanging. The highest rate of teen suicides in America is among white males, four times the national average.

There are those who would argue against using the word *epidemic* to describe the current suicide situation among our teenagers. But the statistics and hard facts tell another story. Suicide has become like a disease among the teen population, and as with any other communicable disease, those who know someone who has it are at risk to contract it themselves. Suicide "clustering" is a new phenomenon which suggests that those who have friends or family members who have committed suicide may catch the inclination to follow and do the same. Officials at one Pennsylvania high school canceled final examinations and the graduation ceremony after they learned of a possible suicide pact among the friends of a student who had shot and killed himself at home over Christmas. Some of these students were talking about making the graduation "a memorable graduation" that nobody would ever forget.[14] These clusters of suicides typically take place in middle- and upper-middle-class neighborhoods with a transient population. The lives of these kids are filled with numerous stresses, including high levels of divorce among their parents, two-career families, pressure

Teen suicide is an epidemic in our country.

to perform, and the absence of an extended family. In addition to these pressures, their situation is often complicated further by frequent family moves or best friends moving out of town.

But don't be fooled. Suicide doesn't play favorites. Teens of every age, from every socioeconomic group, geographic area, and type of family situation have become statistics. George Gallup has concluded that one-fifth of our teenagers should be considered to be at high risk for suicide. And he says, "The entire teen population should be viewed as at least potentially at risk, given the normal stresses of adolescence and the added pressure of modern-day society."[15]

Teen Depression Facts and Figures

No discussion of teen suicide would be complete without a look at teen depression. Of course, there have always been teens who say they are depressed. When I was in high school, it was not unusual to hear one of my peers say, "Oh, I'm so depressed," in response to any number of unhappy situations. Sometimes it was a breakup with a boyfriend or girlfriend. At other times it was a rejection by that potential "special someone." A bad grade, failure to make the team, or a college admission rejection letter could be upsetting. But somehow, through the support and encouragement of family and friends, most teens were able to bounce back pretty quickly.

But times have changed. The increased intensity of peer, media, and family pressures has made the teenage years more difficult. The constant barrage of confusing messages and expectations can be too much of a burden for some teens to handle during the normal adolescent developmental shake-up, especially when parents are absent or ignorant of what is going on in their teenager's life. It is estimated that 10 percent of all children in this country suffer from some form of depression before they reach the age of twelve.[16] As many as 20 percent of all school-age children suffer from some form of depression.[17] Our children and teens are at risk for being more than down in the dumps. Teen depression has reached epidemic proportions.

While not always the case, most suicides are preceded by a period of depression. The American College of Emergency Physicians has found that the diagnosis of depression represents a major risk factor in the completion of teen suicide.[18] With that in mind, it is important that we take some time to look at, define, and understand the problem of teen depression.

Depression has been called the common cold of emotional problems. The American Psychiatric Association says that in any six-month period, 9.4 million Americans suffer from depression.[19] Depression is more than the normal feelings of discouragement or feeling blue that we all experience from time to time. A depressed person is one who can't snap out of it and move on with life. Feeling blue becomes like a black cloud hanging over their lives and affecting their performance in school, social, and interpersonal relationships. A teen is diagnosed with clinical depression when normal functioning is interrupted and professional counseling and help is needed. Between 3 and 5 percent of the teen population is diagnosed with clinical depression every year.[20]

Up until the early 1960s, researchers and other professionals didn't believe that depression occurred in children and teens. One reason for this is that teens don't react to depression the way that adults do. Their depression is often masked by behaviors that appear to be normal for someone going through the teenage years (moodiness, anger, withdrawal, etc.).

Common Signs and Symptoms of Adolescent Depression
- Persistent sadness
- Fluctuation between silent apathy and excited talkativeness
- An inability to concentrate
- A major change in eating and/or sleeping patterns
- Withdrawal from friends and family
- Complaining about headaches and stomachaches
- Severe weight gain or loss
- Decreasing grades and an unwillingness to work in school
- Truancy
- Rapid mood swings
- Lack of interest in regular activities (sports, church, music lessons, youth group, etc.)
- Pessimism about the future
- Expressions of helplessness, worthlessness, hopelessness
- Aggressive and rebellious behavior
- Preoccupation with death or suicide

Adolescent depression also manifests itself in the eating disorders anorexia nervosa and bulimia. Almost unheard of twenty years ago, these potentially deadly anxiety-related emotional sicknesses are becoming more and more common among preadolescent and teenage girls.

The overwhelming nature of the same stresses that cause teen depression and suicide are usually evident in the textbook cases of anorexia and bulimia. Those who suffer are typically middle- to upper-class girls who are driven to get ahead and achieve in everything that they do. Their parents are also achievement oriented and often place lofty and unfair expectations on their children. Many times the parents put up a facade of marital unity even though their marriage is on shaky ground. The mothers of anorexics and bulimics are typically demanding and perfectionistic, while fathers are busy with work and out of touch with family needs and concerns.

Anorexia nervosa actually means "nervous loss of appetite." Consumed by the irrational fear of being fat or overweight, the aim of the anorexic is to lose weight. Society's pressure to be thin and beautiful causes even the thinnest girls to look in the mirror and see themselves as fat. Edie, a slender twelve year old with anorexia, says, "I think my thighs are fat because when I move them, the skin shakes. When I sit down, they're real wide. They spread out." "People always tell me I'm not fat, but I don't believe them," says eleven-year-old Alice. "I'd like to be thinner, like, eighty pounds. I weigh 105 now." Hospitalized for anorexia, she looks forward to getting out and joining an aerobics class so she can lose weight.[21] If anorexia continues to progress to its ugly end, both of these girls will waste away to nothing and eventually die.

Signs and Symptoms of Anorexia
- Emaciation
- Loss of 25 percent of body weight
- No physical cause for weight loss (illness, etc.)
- Voluntary starvation
- Excessive exercise
- Depression
- Constant fearful talk about being overweight and too fat
- Dry skin
- Cessation of menstrual period
- Perfectionism

The goal of the bulimic is to eat large amounts of food without gaining weight. Bulimics consume food during binges that last anywhere from fifteen minutes to eight hours, eating between 1200 and 11,500 calories per binge. For fear of gaining weight, the bulimic then purges the food by vomiting or use of laxatives, enemas, or diuretics. Like the starving of anorexics, the binge eating of bulimics is often a response to loneliness, anger, pressure, or depression.

Signs and Symptoms of Bulimia
- Secretive binge eating
- Fasting
- Self-induced vomiting
- Laxative use
- Chewing but not swallowing food
- Irregular menstrual period
- Intestinal discomfort
- Fluctuating weight
- Tooth decay
- Irregular heartbeat
- Fainting spells

The potentially deadly nature of anorexia and bulimia classifies them as a form of slow suicide. Like suicide and depression, eating disorders are reaching epidemic proportions as more than one million teenage girls suffer from one or both of these tragic disorders.[22]

The Causes of Teen Suicide

The most-asked question after any crisis experience is "Why? . . . Why did this happen?" This is certainly true of teen suicide. But teen suicide doesn't just happen. There is always a reason. Teenagers who commit suicide don't do it because they are fully intent on dying. Rather, it is the result of an emotional tug-of-war between life and death that is going on in their mind. In an effort to escape the reality of a painful existence, many teens choose death not because they want to die but because they want to get away from life. On the tape-recorded message that he left to the world before jumping into the quarry, Marc Landis said, "C'mon heart, stop . . . stop keeping my physical body alive. That's all I wanna know, that I'm not alive. . . . I just don't like life, man. I'm goin' nowhere."[23] Melissa Poirier's note said, "I know it's gonna hurt. But after death I know there is a better life." Her friend Melody wrote, "Good-bye cruel world."

Teens who commit suicide don't want to die. But they see no other way out of living.

What then, specifically, is it that makes the ugliness of death more attractive than life? What are the factors that make life so painful? Typically, there is no one cause for teen suicide. But teen suicide is always the result of a three-step process: *"a previous history of problems* compounded by *problems associated with adolescence* and finally, *a precipitating event* (death, breakup, etc.) triggers the suicide."[24]

What follows are eight of the most common factors in teen suicide and depression. Read through them carefully so that you will be able to develop a sensitivity to the special needs and circumstances of your children and their friends.

Developmental factors

The turmoil of adolescence is sometimes too much for kids to handle. The collective "normal" changes that we have discussed in previous chapters can be especially difficult for teenagers who experience these changes in what is perceived as an "abnormal" manner. Life can get ugly if you are the biggest, shortest, fattest, or youngest looking of your peers.

The Search Institute looked at the worries of eight thousand preteens and early adolescents. Fifty-three percent of these ten to fourteen year olds said they worried about their looks. Forty-eight percent said they worried about popularity.[25] Our kids walk on self-image eggshells as they gingerly tiptoe through the barrage of changes they face during adolescence.

Because of the very nature of the adolescent period, teenagers are more vulnerable to stress than any other age group. Things that would never bother an adult can be devastating to a teenager. When something as simple as a pimple on the end of their nose becomes a major stress producer, one wonders what might happen when they face problems of a more severe nature!

The adolescent years are a time of change, pressure, crises, and a tendency for impulsive overreaction. Teens experience great emotional anxiety as the world of self seems to change before their eyes. Growing through this period of questioning and uncertainty makes life hard enough. Add to that the remaining factors that we will discuss, and you will begin to see why so many kids can't deal with the pressure.

Family factors

It used to be that home was the most stress-free environment for children and teens. But the many changes taking place in the American family have transformed the home from a stress reducer to a stress producer. Three thousand children a day see their parents' marriage end in divorce. Most of those kids will think that the breakup was their fault. Sixty percent of children born in the nineties will miss out on the stability of a two-parent home since they'll spend at least part of their childhood living with only one parent. Children growing up with both parents are robbed of precious time with Mom and Dad because of jobs and other outside-the-home commitments. The recent Gallup poll on teen suicide found that among those who had attempted suicide or come close to attempting suicide, the number one reason for considering this drastic action is "family problems" or "problems at home."[26]

Situational family factors that are beyond anyone's control also contribute to adolescent stress, depression, and suicide. For example, many teens who attempt suicide have lost a parent to death before reaching the age of twelve or had a parent become chronically ill during the child's early teen years. But there are family factors that are preventable. Nearly three-quarters of all suicide attempters come from unstable family situations characterized by divorce, separation, talk of divorce, fatherlessness, substance abuse, isolation, or lack of support.[27]

While observers might understand why a child from a terrible home situation would try to take their own life, family, friends, and neighbors of suicidal upper and middle-class kids from seemingly healthy homes are frequently left looking for answers. There are three additional family factors that are often present in these "healthy" situations.

First is a lack of time spent with one or more parents and the resulting feeling of abandonment. Kids interpret lack of time and intimacy as rejection. Most of the teenagers who attempt suicide claim they can remember no adult to whom they ever felt close. Young males usually point to the lack of an effective father figure in the home. In many of these cases, the father has been physically present but emotionally absent and unwilling to provide spiritual direction.

A second factor is unrealistic parental expectations. Faced with parental pressure to keep up the grades, stay involved in activities, earn money, and get ready for the right college is too much for some kids to handle. A recent "Who's Who Among American High School Students" survey of high achievers, many of whom have grown up in pushy homes, found that 30 percent had considered committing suicide while 4 percent had made an actual attempt. These high achievers claimed to have tried suicide because they felt worthless (86 percent), felt the pressure to succeed (71 percent), and were afraid to fail (65 percent).[28] The pressure to excel can be extremely destructive. Placing unrealistic goals and expectations on kids can literally kill them.

A third factor is a family history of depression and suicide. While there is no proven genetic link or biological predisposition to suicide that is passed from one generation to the next, family environment and the examples of others can play an important role in a child's decisions about their own future. Kids learn from their parents. If Mom and Dad model how to effectively handle stress in healthy ways, then chances are their children will learn those lessons well. But if Mom and Dad are paralyzed by stress and have attempted suicide themselves, kids may learn that taking one's own life is an acceptable way of coping. This truth became real to me when a depressed young woman phoned me for some counseling. Only in her twenties, she shared that her marriage was on the same destructive track that had been taken by her parents. When Marsha was a teenager, her mother chose suicide as a solution to her marital difficulty. This young woman told me, "My marriage is so bad that I have thought about coping in the exact same way my mother did."

If a difficult, unstable, or broken family situation is a major factor in teen suicide, then the exact opposite should also be true. Parents need to learn that kids will feel better about themselves and exhibit healthier reactions to stress when they are loved, nurtured, and cared for in a healthy home situation.

Societal factors

We live in a rapidly changing world. It has been said that all the knowledge that humankind has accumulated since the beginning of time is only half of what we will know in twenty or thirty years. This rapid accumulation of knowledge has been paralleled by changing morals, values, and lifestyles. Adults can only imagine what it must be like to grow up in today's world. Kids are finding it difficult to cope.

One of the societal causes of depression and suicide is the push to grow up faster. David Elkind talks about "the hurried child syndrome" and how kids who are pushed into premature adulthood are on a quick road to self-destruction. What they need is time to grow up and be children. What they get are the pressures of the adult world that many adults have difficulty handling. John Baucom says:

> We are all going so fast, our whole society . . . and the children in it have not had an opportunity to hang on, or to stay up, or to catch up. So what do they do? They do a lot of things, and some

of them we are reading about in the newspapers and hearing discussed on television. One of them is suicide.[29]

When kids are forced to be something other than kids, it can kill them.

A second societal factor is world and life view confusion. A Christ-centered world and life view offers meaning, purpose, and direction for the here and now, along with the joyful expectation of eternal salvation. But the nineties have become a time for laughing at such an "outdated" way of thinking. A tragic result of our vast and rapid accumulation of knowledge has been our willingness to think of ourselves more highly than we ought. When man sees himself as the measure of all things, God is no longer necessary. The lifestyle of adult role models has combined with our teenagers' music and media to send a strong message: "You don't need God."

The biblical world and life view has been replaced with the hopelessness of nihilism. Dostoyevsky wrote, "If God does not exist, everything is permitted. The most meaningful reality is individual freedom, its supreme expression suicide."[30] If our children grow up learning that life is futile, empty, and leading nowhere, it makes sense that dying could become more attractive than living. Conversely, it should come as no surprise that teens who attend church are less likely to consider or commit suicide.

The final societal factor is the devaluing of human life. Our children are growing up in a society where abortion has been legalized and normalized. Our teenagers know that other teens are killing their peers over a pair of sneakers. And they've all read about suicide doctor Jack Kevorkian's willingness to help people take their own lives. To many, these issues are facts of life rather than matters of right or wrong. Two interesting polls show how American attitudes toward life are influencing our attitudes toward death. The first poll, conducted by the Harvard School of Public Health, found that 64 percent of those questioned favor physician-aided suicide and 52

When God does not exist, moral standards become subjective, meaning is lost, and hopelessness reigns supreme. Increasingly, that is the state of today's youth culture.

percent would choose that option for themselves.[31] In addition, a 1991 Gallup poll found that 33 percent of Americans believe that a person has a moral right to end his life if under a "heavy burden." Alarmingly, 23 percent of those polled who identify themselves as being born again say it's OK.[32]

Society contributes to teen depression and suicide by telling kids that they must be more than they are, that there is no hope, that everything is meaningless, and that they are ultimately worth nothing.

"Lessness" factors

The first time I met Julie was one week after her second suicide attempt. I couldn't believe that this beautiful and gifted young college student would have any reason to want to end her own life. I asked her to tell me her story, and in the two hours that followed, she described her life by using several words that I hear from suicidal adolescents over and over again. These words make up what I call the "lessness" factors.

Julie was haunted by feelings of *uselessness*. She was the oldest of three children, and her two younger siblings had excelled in academics and athletics. Julie struggled with both. She might have been able to handle the struggle better if her father hadn't put her down by comparing her "inferior" efforts to those of her brother and sister. "He's always putting me down by telling me how I don't measure up. I feel useless," she said. As her father's words chipped away at her over the course of her high school years, Julie began to lose the little bit of confidence that she had in herself.

Like other teens who are suicidal, Julie suffered from extreme *loneliness*. One study of college students found that loneliness (cited by 67 percent of the respondents) was a major cause of suicidal behavior.[33] Julie's overwhelming sense of being alone had led her to pursue a promiscuous lifestyle in the hope that a chain of sexual relationships would fill the void. She told me that the exact opposite occurred as her loneliness increased with each new sexual partner.

It wasn't long before her efforts to eliminate her loneliness led to feelings of *worthlessness*. She had been treated like a piece of dirt for so long that she actually started to believe she was one. She wasn't much different from the young teenage girl whose father constantly reminded her, "You aren't worth the price of the paper your birth certificate is printed on." The Gallup survey on teen suicide found that "feeling worthless" was a reason given by 18 percent of those who had attempted or considered suicide.[34]

Julie was also experiencing feelings of *helplessness*. "It got to the point where I knew that there was nothing that I could do to make my situation better," she told me. The picture she painted of her helplessness reminded me of a scene from an Indiana Jones adventure movie. She described a life that was like hanging by one finger from the end of a rope over a deep ravine. She felt she could do nothing to help herself out of the situation.

Purposelessness was the next step in Julie's spiral into suicide. "Why am I here?" was a question that she answered by saying, "For absolutely no reason at all!" She saw no meaning for her existence.

Julie confessed that she finally came to the decision to kill herself because she could see her entire life funneled into one big bundle of *hopelessness*. This is the greatest predictor of a person committing the act of suicide. When they see no possible way out of the confusion, misery, and disappointment of life, death doesn't necessarily look good, but it looks much better than living. While Julie couldn't imagine how things could get any worse, she was convinced that they wouldn't get any better. This is one of the main differences between how adults and children handle stress and depression. Kids have greater difficulty dealing with the pain of living.

Julie's story is a perfect example of how feelings of "lessness" can build during the difficult period of adolescence. In her case, as in thousands of others, the loss of meaning, purpose, and love led to a loss of hope and almost to a loss of life.

The revenge factor

The tapes found after the deaths of Marc Landis and Dan Ferdock included numerous good-byes to friends and family members. Marc's messages to his parents were filled with hate and rebellion. It was as if one reason he was ending his life was to get back at them for how he felt they had made his life miserable.[35]

Many adolescents take their own lives in an effort to hurt or get even with someone who has hurt them. Rebellion against parents, the breakup of a romantic relationship, and divorce are common reasons for teens to choose suicide as a method of revenge.

After returning home from a vacation trip, we learned that a teenager in our neighborhood had committed suicide while we were away. Three facts of the story caught my attention. First, the young man had left a hateful note blaming his father for his miserable life. Second, he chose to kill himself by using his father's gun. And finally, he shot himself in his father's bedroom. This young man was so angry at his father that he chose to seek revenge in a way that he hoped would make the rest of his father's life more miserable than his own.

The publicity factor

The shocking nature of teen suicide means that a teen's self-inflicted death will usually be reported in the paper and become the talk of the school and neighborhood for several days.

Several studies have been conducted to discover whether or not there is a link between TV movies and news reports about teen suicide and actual suicide attempts in communities where those movies and reports have been aired. Several of these studies have concluded that suicide attempts among adolescents increase during the period immediately after the free publicity afforded by the media. Calls from distraught teenagers flooded radio stations across the country in the days following rock star Kurt Cobain's suicide as the kids shared the suicidal feelings they were having themselves.

Kids who have been driven to despair as a result of being shut off and left alone by family and friends long for love and attention. When someone in their school commits suicide, they see the student population focus all of their thoughts and discussions on that person during the days that follow. To them, they see that, even though the person is dead and gone, he or she is having a moment in the sun.

Knowing full well that the publicity surrounding a completed suicide could open the door for many more attempts, school counselors usually mobilize to encourage those who might pursue such a course to rethink their plans. This is why so many schools work to avoid glorifying the deceased by not scheduling memorial services or assemblies in the school.

It is wise for parents and educators to recognize the potential for a ripple effect following the death of a teenager by suicide. Andy Warhol once said that everyone is famous for at least fifteen minutes during their life. Many kids see the "fame" bestowed upon a suicide victim and choose to find their personal fifteen minutes of fame after their heart stops beating.

The substance abuse factor

Drugs and alcohol are a coping mechanism teens choose to deal with depression and stress. It is not unusual for alcohol and other drugs to intensify depression, irrational thoughts, and feelings of hopelessness. According to *The Fifth Special Report to the U.S. Congress on Alcohol and Health* (1983), as many as 80 percent of the people who attempt suicide have been drinking at the time.[36] Alcohol is a depressant and the most common drug used by suicide attempters, followed by marijuana and stimulants. There is strong evidence suggesting that the increased rate of substance abuse among teens over the last two decades is related to the dramatic increase in teen suicide.[37]

Although no one is really sure of the extent to which alcohol and drugs contribute to suicidal behavior, we do know that adolescents under the influence are more apt to act on impulse. Toxology reports found that drugs and alcohol were factors in each of the three suicide stories mentioned at the beginning of this chapter. Teens who abuse drugs and alcohol are at greater risk.

The sexual abuse factor

A grown-up victim of sexual abuse writes:

> I was very lonely, very starved for affection and love. There was a lot of sexual abuse from my uncle which left me feeling that I just wasn't good enough to be loved, and I deserved that type of treatment. . . . Looking back, I know I didn't feel much acceptance—just very hurt and lost. . . . I had never thought I was depressed as a child, but now I know I was.[38]

This story is shared by one out of four girls and one out of eight boys who are sexually abused by the time they are eighteen.[39] Eighty percent of them will have been abused between the ages of six and ten.[40] The probable effects of childhood sexual abuse include high rates of anxiety, depression, substance abuse, and self-destructiveness.[41] Sexual abuse combines many of the previously mentioned suicide factors into one big volatile bundle. It is no wonder that so many victims choose death over a very painful existence. Twenty-five percent of teenage girls surveyed who attempted suicide reported being sexually abused. That number is 900 percent higher than their nonsuicidal peers![42]

Our kids long for love and attention, and they'll do whatever it takes to get it.

In summary:

Parents, keep a watchful eye open. The presence of one or more of these factors in a teenager's life increases the risk for depression and suicidal tendencies or behavior. Stay alert so that you can offer positive, hope-filled responses and support to your teen as they grow through the difficult years of adolescence.

Warning Signs and Cries for Help

One of the most memorable moments of the 1992 Summer Olympics occurred when Britain's Derek Redmond was sprinting around the track in the four-hundred-meter run. As Redmond sped around the backstretch, his right hamstring tore. How did you and I know he was hurt? He showed us. He stopped running, limped a few steps, and fell to the ground. His face contorted in response to the physical pain he was feeling. He grabbed his leg and rolled around on the ground. Those who were in close proximity heard him scream out in agony. We knew he was hurt because he told us not in words but through his actions. His physical pain was obvious to anyone who was watching.

Teenagers who attempt suicide give signs. About 80 percent of those who take their life communicate their intention to someone prior to the act.[43] While they may not always communicate their pain and intentions with verbal clarity, the signs are there. But they may never be heard unless we know what to watch for.

In this section we will examine five categories of signs and cries that teens give before committing suicide. Carefully read through the descriptions of these signs, realizing that they will usually appear in some combination before a teenager reaches the end of their rope.

Emotional cries

Teenagers, by nature, can be moody. But not all of their moody behavior should be written off as just a part of the adolescent stage. There are several unusual and extreme emotional cries for help that can clue us in to our teenagers' struggles with hopelessness, depression, and suicidal feelings.

The first emotional cry can be heard in **the classical signs of depression** that we discussed earlier. If these symptoms continue for two or more weeks, then it is time to seek help.

Withdrawal from normal activities is a second emotional cry. When a teenager suddenly separates themseves from friends, family, objects, and activities that are normally a large part of their life, trouble may be brewing. Depressed and suicidal teens may want to spend more time than usual alone or in their room.

The calm before the storm occurs when a teen's spirits improve suddenly and dramatically after a period of deep and extended depression. Psychologists say that this is a very dangerous time since the teen's "peace" may actually exist because the decision has been made to take their life. They are excited because they feel like they have finally found the solution to their problems and the pain will soon be over. Parents should be very cautious when a teen who has a history of depression appears to be dramatically and suddenly improved.

Physical cries

Sometimes an observant eye is all it takes to tell that a teen is depressed or suicidal. Here are some physical cries that you can hear by being aware of your teen's physical demeanor and day-to-day habits.

Physical complaints are sometimes heard from teens who experience depression and suicidal thoughts. Stomachaches, headaches, and constant fatigue are a common occurrence among teens who are finding adolescence and the pressures of their life too much to handle.

K *now the signs of when your teen needs help.*

A neglect of physical appearance, characterized by sloppiness and poor personal hygiene, could be a way of saying, Why should I bother? Nobody cares about me anyway. Teens who feel worthless sometimes begin to look worthless.

A change in normal eating and sleeping habits is also a sign of trouble. Suicidal teens will sometimes sleep more, eat less, and even develop one of the eating disorders already mentioned.

Finally, **body language that shows an inability to concentrate** can be a sign that a child is preoccupied with depression and problems. Slouching, staring off into space, and constant daydreaming may occur when the pain of what is going on inside drowns out an awareness of what might be happening in the same room.

Behavioral cries

Teens who struggle with depression and suicide sometimes decide to become involved in some strange and frightening new behaviors.

Accident proneness can become a conscious or unconscious attention-getting device for teens who desperately want someone to notice them. Teens who feel shut off from others find the attention they receive after an accident to be a form of immediate reinforcement. These cries for attention can also be cries for help.

Acting out or other melodramatic behavior is another common attention getter. I remember one girl who always acted like the world was coming to an end. When she felt that her friends were starting to ignore her, she would quickly step on stage and respond like a terrible actress to some new crisis that she had thought up. It didn't take long for her friends to catch on to her act. As her fantasy world came crashing down, she would move on to a new circle of friends that would respond in the way she wanted. Sadly, this was a cry to be noticed, loved, and cared for by a girl whose father had emotionally rejected her, leaving her depressed and feeling worthless.

A preoccupation with violence and unusually aggressive behavior are clear signs that something is wrong. Some suicidal teens will fight, yell, break things, and throw objects during increasingly frequent fits of rage. Some will be mesmerized by movie and television violence, renting and viewing violent films. Others will purchase or attempt to build weapons.

Self-destructive behavior and involvement in dangerous activities are signs that a teen may have little or no regard for their personal safety or life. Many suicidal teens will live life on the edge by driving fast, playing dangerous games with weapons, or playing chicken with their cars and bikes. Any sort of high-risk activity of this type merits attention.

Promiscuous sexual behavior is often an attempt to sedate strong feelings of failure and depression. Kids who see themselves as worthless, unloved, and rejected will look for acceptance and love through sexual intimacy.

Drug and alcohol abuse has already been discussed as a factor contributing to suicide. While their abuse appears to contribute to suicide by aggravating and exaggerating depressed feelings and suicidal tendencies, their use can also point to the presence of depression and suicidal feelings.

Sudden rebellious and disrespectful behavior towards parents, teachers, and other authorities may indicate that a teen has decided to take their fate into their own hands rather than listen to the wisdom and advice of those they may have respected at one time.

A drop in grades and increased truancy are not uncommon when a teen is preoccupied with so many problems that they find it impossible or undesirable to care about schoolwork.

Teens who are thinking about killing themselves will sometimes become **preoccupied with death.** They may write poetry or stories focusing on death or other morbid themes. Their musical tastes may change and lean toward an interest in mope rock or heavy metal, two genres of popular music that glamorize occult themes, hopelessness, and death. Their preoccupation with death may even lead them to dye their hair and dress in black.

Preparing for death is a clear sign that a teen has decided to commit suicide. Many teens who have made the decision will begin to give away valued personal items to close friends or family members. They will say good-bye and take care of other personal business. And they will acquire the means by which they intend to kill themselves (rope, gun, pills, etc.).

It seems strange that this last behavioral cry has to be mentioned, but the fact that many parents don't hear this loudest of all screams warrants its inclusion. **A suicide attempt** should not be brushed off lightly. As Dr. Walter Byrd of the Minirth-Meier Clinic says:

> Any suicide attempt should be taken seriously . . . whether the attempt was a determined effort to end one's life or rather an act carried out in desperation to provoke the involvement of others in a help-giving model.[44]

Situational cries

Researchers and counseling professionals have noted that there are numerous unpleasant life changes that affect teenagers more deeply than any other group of people because of the difficult developmental stage at which teens find themselves. These events might precipitate feelings of failure, loneliness, depression, and suicide. One study found that, among those who attempted suicide, nearly 76 percent reported having recently experienced one or more of these changes.[45]

A teenager might commit suicide after losing friends and social status following a family move from one community to another. Other situations include a romantic breakup, death of a friend or loved one, divorce, or academic failure. Parents should be especially sensitive to the emotional needs of their teenagers during these times of personal crisis. Sometimes we falsely assume that they will be able to adapt to change as well as we can.

Verbal cries

Parents who listen to their children might be alerted to suicidal intent by the words they hear from their children. A child who says things like "I won't be a problem for you much longer," "Nothing really matters anymore," "It's no use," "I won't see you again," or "I'd be better off dead" is saying that they may have already decided their fate.

Some people have speculated that people who talk about suicide won't ever commit suicide. Don't believe it. It's only a myth. Most suicidal acts are preceded by some warning or cry. All of those cries and warnings should be taken seriously.

When Derek Redmond fell to the track in pain during the 1992 Summer Olympics, an amazing thing happened. As he stood up and began to hobble around the track in an effort to finish the race, his father came out of the stands, rushed past security guards, came to his son's side, and embraced him. With his son's head buried in his shoulder and the crowd cheering, Jim Redmond led his son around the track and to the finish line. It was learned later that when Jim Redmond came to his son's side, he told him, "We're going to finish this together."[46]

When our children and teens cry out in pain during the difficult years of adolescence, we must listen, drop everything, rush to their sides, help them up, support them, and tell them that we will work with them to get through the difficult race that lies ahead . . . *together.*

In the next two sections we'll look at the preventive measures and redemptive measures that loving parents can provide in order to help their children deal with the stress of adolescence, depression, and suicide.

Preventive Measures

From the day our children are born, we should take a positive and intentional approach to raising emotionally healthy children so that the problems we have discussed in this chapter may be prevented. What follows are a number of preventive measures and approaches that, if consciously instituted in your home, will reduce the risk of depression and suicide by providing your children with the strong foundation of a loving home and open lines of communication.

PREVENTIVE MEASURE #1: Do your best to create a stable family.

Teens who consider suicide talk about feeling alone, hopeless, and rejected. While these feelings will be experienced at some time by most teens as they pass through adolescence, many who suffer from depression and suicidal feelings identify feeling alone, hopeless, and rejected *at home.* They are more vulnerable to having these feelings if they have been abused, have parents with alcohol or drug problems, or have a home life characterized by arguing, discord, disruptions, separation, fatherlessness, or divorce. Nearly three-quarters of teen suicide attempters report family problems.[47]

Fathers, God has given you the gift of your wife and children. Mothers, God has given you the gift of your husband and children. Your marital vows and commitment should be taken seriously. In a day and age when Americans are committed to being uncommitted, you must be sure that your marriage is in order. I have often heard couples who are in crumbling marriages say that they are "staying together for the sake of the kids." While I think that this is important, I would challenge you to go one step further. Don't just endure a difficult situation for the sake of the kids. Rather, pray through your difficult situation and seek outside help with the intent of strengthening, restoring, and maintaining your commitment to each other. Your children are smart enough to know when you are just hanging on until they grow up and leave home. They will appreciate the positive model of a mom and dad who are intent on allowing God to empower them as they build and strengthen a marriage that lasts.

T he best prevention against suicide and depression is a loving, stable home.

If you or another member of your family is guilty of abusive behavior, alcohol abuse, drug abuse, or violence, seek help immediately. If your family finds it easy to argue and difficult to communicate, go to your pastor or a qualified Christian counselor for help in improving communication skills in your home.

God created the family as the basic unit of society. It is the unit into which our children are born, and in which they find their identity and are socialized and nurtured. God intended the family to be a place where each of us can find unconditional love, mutual caring, intimacy—a place where we can be ourselves without fearing rejection. When the family fails to function in this way, God's order is disrupted and people suffer. It is no coincidence that while the family in America has been falling apart, the rate of teen depression and suicide has been rising.

PREVENTIVE MEASURE #2: Lead your children to spiritual maturity.

The family has also been created by God to serve as a place of spiritual nurture. One of the awesome tasks of parenting is the job of serving as signposts. Parents are to point their children, by precept and example, to the God of the universe.

In chapter 2 we discussed how children grow and develop physically, emotionally, intellectually, socially, and spiritually. If their child's physical health is in danger, 99.9 percent of the parents I meet will take them to the doctor. Likewise, they are concerned and will help their children if they are emotionally down or depressed. In an effort to help their children realize their full intellectual potential, they make them go to school and do their homework. And, realizing the powerful influence of peers, they desperately want their children to choose good friends. But when it comes to the spiritual dimension of a child's life, often times little or no effort is made to provide spiritual nurture and direction for children who so desperately need it.

In his ongoing studies of teen suicide, Dr. Stephen Stack of Auburn University has found that suicide rates are significantly higher among individuals who do not attend formal worship services than among those that do. Stack believes, and rightly so, that religion reduces suicidal potential by giving people a sense of hope in the midst of difficult and trying circumstances.[48] Other researchers concur.[49]

There is nothing that can replace the hope that comes from a personal relationship with God through Jesus Christ as a stabilizing influence in the life of a teenager. One of your God-given tasks as a parent is to lead and disciple your children into Christian maturity. This means that you, as a parent, must be growing in your faith and modeling the life of discipleship. As you live out a life characterized by faith in God, you will become a stable rock and point of reference for your kids as they travel the rocky road of adolescence. When parents work, with God's help, to genuinely live out a life centered on faith in God, their children will learn by example to live out that same faith.

PREVENTIVE MEASURE #3: Model and teach a biblical theology of pain and suffering.

We live in a feeling-oriented society where we grow up learning to avoid pain and pursue pleasure. Because we don't like to suffer, we tend to look for easy and quick solutions to our problems. Children and teens who commit suicide often do so because they have concluded that the quickest way to solve their problems is to end their life. From the time our children are young, we must be making a conscious effort to steer them away from these conclusions by teaching and modeling three simple truths about life in this world.

First, pain and suffering are a part of life. All of us will experience our share of physical and emotional pain. There is no escaping it.

Second, while pain and suffering are temporary, suicide is permanent. Kids need to know that suicide is a permanent end to temporary problems and that there are a hundred other ways to deal with those problems. Several teens who had actually attempted suicide shared these words with George Gallup:

- Suicide is *not* the answer. . . . Things are better after a while.
- It's not worth dying.
- Time heals everything.
- Taking my life solves nothing. . . . Making some mistakes is definitely not the end of the world.
- It's a long-term solution to a short-term problem.
- Suicide is not the answer to anything. Life has its ups and downs, and you need to deal with them and move on.[50]

Finally, God is our source of strength in times of difficulty. On several occasions Jesus told his followers that they could expect pain and persecution. The Psalms are full of the moans and laments of human suffering and emotional misery. But all of God's Word points to the fact that God does not leave us alone in times of trouble. In the midst of intense personal pain the psalmist would write these words:

> Even though I walk through the valley of the shadow of death, I will fear no evil, for you are with me; your rod and your staff, they comfort me. (Ps. 23:4, NIV)

> God is our refuge and strength, an ever-present help in trouble. (Ps. 46:1, NIV)

> The LORD will keep you from all harm—he will watch over your life. (Ps. 121:7, NIV)

Our parental example should teach our children how to handle the difficulties that life sends our way. As we model the Christian way to handle pain and suffering, our children will grow up learning that they must place full reliance and dependence on God, even when they can't see the light at the end of the tunnel.

PREVENTIVE MEASURE #4: Spend time with your kids.

One of the greatest gifts that we can give our children is our time. Time together fosters an openness on their part and unclogs the lines of parent-teen communication.

Our children need our time and undivided attention even when no crisis exists. In fact, this is one of the best preventive strategies. If we only give them our attention and time when they are depressed or after they make an attempt on their life, we might actually reinforce the behavior and encourage more of the same. Our kids need our time *all* the time!

I recently attended a program on teen suicide that was sponsored by a local high school that had experienced three student suicides in a matter of two short months. Seated in the center of the room were a number of "suicide survivors," relatives of young people who had taken their own lives. At the end of the presentation one of these survivors, the mother of a young man who had killed himself, raised her hand and addressed the crowd. Her words to everyone: "Just be there for your kids."

PREVENTIVE MEASURE #5: Love them for who they are.

Bob Bennet's moving "A Song about Baseball" is a first-person account of a young boy's struggle to play the national pastime and play it well. In it, Bennet paints a picture that many of us who played Little League remember well:

> *Three and two, life and death*
> *I was swinging with eyes closed holding my breath*
> *I was dying on my way back to the bench*
> *But none of it mattered after the game*
> *When my father would find me and call out my name*
> *A soft drink, a snow cone, a candy bar*
> *A limousine ride in the family car*
> *He loved me . . . no matter how I played.*

Too many of our children and teens grow up thinking that the love of parents is merit based rather than unconditional. Praise and attention come only when the report card is up to snuff or when the child measures up in some other way. This is too much stress for any human being to handle—no wonder these kids rebel. And some find the pressure so great that it is easier to end their own life rather than live.

Let your children be themselves. Encourage them to do their best. Let them know that there is nothing that they can say or do that will make you love them less. Love them, no matter how they "play."

PREVENTIVE MEASURE #6: Develop a network of significant adults.

Teenagers need someone other than their parents whom they can go to and find a listening ear, encouragement, and wise advice.

Encourage your children to develop friendships with Christian neighbors, pastors, church members, and youth leaders who will love them and invest time in their lives. If your child clams up and won't talk to you, ask him to talk to one of these other adults he knows and trusts.

PREVENTIVE MEASURE #7: Attend a church that models Christlike love.

Many churches don't believe that real Christians are real people with real problems. While I've never seen a church where it is a written requirement, many churches are places where people feel they must be perfect. If they make mention of their problems, they sense that they would lose their spiritual standing in the eyes of other members.

One high school freshman I know was struggling with many of the problems that today's teenagers are facing. He was finding it hard to talk to his parents and had given in to some of the pressures thrown at him by his peers. When the church leaders and youth pastor discovered the problem, they issued an ultimatum: "Change or stop coming to church." How tragic! This church was doing a better job of modeling pharisaical judgment than Christlike love.

The *Gallup Survey on Teenage Suicide* found that most teens feel strongly that the church should be in the business of supporting them as they pass through adolescence:

> More than eight in ten (84 percent) favor the church offering drop-in groups for teens, counseling services (83 percent) and activities or courses designed to make teenagers feel better about themselves (82 percent). Sadly, the latter is mentioned by very few teens as currently offered by their church.[51]

Your teens need a church that is characterized by Christlike love, healing, openness, and compassion. If you are not attending a church like this, take steps to lead it to this point or find a church where this is already happening.

PREVENTIVE MEASURE #8: Encourage involvement in a positive peer group.

Several years ago a high school junior who went to school with several kids from our church took his life. I secured a copy of an anonymously written open letter that was distributed to students. The letter contained these words:

Most of you are still dealing with the shocking news of losing one of your classmates to the tragedy of suicide. Many probably wondered why their friend took such drastic measures and with that comes the gnawing guilt as you search for clues—cries of help overlooked, opportunities missed.

There is something about this tragedy that cries for some sort of justice. There is a challenge here. It clearly calls us to reach out to let others know we're there for them and to do it NOW!!

Easy enough to do with our good buddies and our family—what about those who aren't in those categories? Just people you haven't gotten to know too well or may appear a bit weird by your standards?

Somehow the poking fun and the sneers and the noticeable differences have a way of disintegrating—when it's too late.

Whether you're a Punker or a Doper, a Prep or a Head, Black or White doesn't matter—when it's too late.

Whether they "have everything going for them" or are loners, the pressures of fitting in were too great—and it's too late.

What it's not too late for is CARING. Appreciate all who cross your path.

This young man, who had few friends, had been shut off and ignored. This pressure, added to others he was experiencing, led him to take his own life.

Our teens need a place where they can fit in with their peers, where there is no pressure to wear a mask. The best place for teens to be themselves is in the positive peer atmosphere of a Christ-centered church youth group. Raise your children in the church so that they will want to be a part of the youth group. Be sure that your church is actively committed with time, money, and other resources to providing a healthy youth-group situation where your teens can be themselves, be accepted, open up, talk, be heard, and find sound biblical guidance.

PREVENTIVE MEASURE #9: Develop friendships with your teen's friends.

You can become a significant adult in the life of another parent's teen. Take the time to get to know your children's friends and work to foster an atmosphere of trust and openness with them. This will make it easier for them to come to you for guidance and advice when they are having problems. And your friendship with them will make it easier for them to come to you to tell you about the problems or trouble your teen is having. Good relationships with your children's friends will open the lines of communication in ways that you could never imagine.

PREVENTIVE MEASURE #10: Pray for your children.

The story is told of a young child who was acting up during the Sunday morning worship service. His parents were doing their best to maintain some sense of order in the pew but were losing the battle. The father finally picked up the little boy and walked sternly down the aisle toward the back of the sanctuary. Just before they reached the door, the little fellow screamed out to the congregation, "Pray for me!"

Our little ones will face numerous difficult situations, pressures, and choices on their way to becoming "big ones." They are crying out for parents who will be actively involved in their lives while placing them securely in the hands of the almighty God. Pray for your children from the day they are born. Ask God to protect them from harm, guide them into making good decisions, and provide for their well-being. Ask God to open your ears and eyes to the needs of your little ones. Pray that they would grow up to experience the joy of the Lord rather than the depression and suicidal feelings that so many teens are facing today.

Redemptive Measures

What should parents do at the moment of crisis when they realize that their child is suffering from depression or suicidal feelings? While it is understandably difficult to maintain one's composure during such a situation, there are six initial steps that can be taken to head off disaster so that the crisis can be redeemed, leading the child back to spiritual, emotional, and physical health.

STEP #1: Know the signs.

Remember, 80 percent of those committing suicide signal their intentions through clear verbal clues or behavioral changes. By knowing and understanding the cries and clues mentioned earlier in this chapter and by building a growing relationship with your teen, you will be more aware of problems and sensitive to any changes that would signal problems.

STEP #2: Take threats seriously.

Any verbal or behavioral threats should be taken seriously until proven otherwise. Suicide is so ugly that most of us choose to live in denial, thinking that the person making the threat isn't serious or is only trying to get attention. Don't turn your head and look the other way. Instead, take whatever action is appropriate and necessary—immediately.

STEP #3: If you suspect, ask!

Are you suspicious about your teen's behavior? Have the signs pointed to the fact that your child may be suicidal? Then ask him or her. Talking about suicide in a straightforward manner does not plant the thought in a teen's mind nor does it serve as a suggestion to go do it.

Have a heart-to-heart with your child. Ask, "Are you thinking about suicide?" This can be the first step to getting your teenager on the road to recovery and restoration. Suicidal teenagers are usually not fully intent on dying. Rather, they are waiting for someone to step forward and lead them out of their depression. In effect, they are looking for a savior. Inviting them to talk about their feelings by asking good questions opens the door for them to see life as an increasingly attractive option.

STEP #4: Listen and encourage.

Encourage the suicidal teen to express feelings openly by listening intently to what he or she is saying. Don't act shocked or give in to the temptation to nervously respond by using clichés. Don't say, "Oh, come on. Things aren't that bad. You really don't mean it. Everything will be OK. You're just overreacting." Be quiet and listen hard.

When you do speak, don't react judgmentally. Rather, be open and direct in a very loving manner. Let them know that you are there as a supporter, not a judge.

And finally, don't swear yourself to secrecy regarding their intent. The fact that they have spoken openly to you gives you the responsibility to take the steps necessary to prevent destructive action on their part.

STEP #5: Do something!

Take action. If the person has secured the means by which to take their own life, remove it. Do they have a gun? Ask for it. Do they have a rope? Take it away. Do they plan on using their car? Get their keys.

Don't leave them alone. Keep them with you at all times or get someone else to watch them while you go to get help.

Secure some professional help. There are many good Christian counselors who have training and experience in helping suicidal teens. Be sure to find someone who comes highly recommended. Most suicidal teens are more than willing to talk to someone who can help them ease the pain of living. If your own child is the suicidal person, a good counselor will involve the rest of your family in the counseling process. Decide to be open and vulnerable as that process unfolds. Listen willingly and intently for any behaviors or patterns you have adopted that may have contributed to the crisis. Take the counselor's advice to heart without being defensive. Remember, your child's life is far more important than your reputation.

And finally, make a deal with the suicidal person. Ask them to promise to call you, anytime, day or night, if they begin to feel suicidal. This will open the door for you to intervene if suicidal feelings increase again. If the suicidal person is your own child, encourage them to call you at work or get you out of bed. Let them know that you are so committed that you are willing to drop everything for their sake at a moment's notice.

STEP #6: Offer hope.

A suicidal person is a person who has lost all hope. The only true source of hope in this world is Jesus Christ. Minister to your child without preaching. Point them to the source of the peace that passes all understanding.

■ IT'S YOUR TURN

After delivering a presentation on the growing epidemic of suicide and depression among teens, I was approached in the parking lot by a father who had heard me speak. "I listened with interest as you described the causes and symptoms of teen suicide and depression," he said. "I want you to know that you were describing my situation twenty years ago."

After listening to the man's story, I asked him if he had ever considered sharing it with other parents. One year later, he sent me his story in the hope that others might understand the desperate need to spend time loving and nurturing their children through the confusing and difficult years of adolescence. While his situation was unique and the events took place years ago, the same family dynamics of absence of one kind or another can be found in more American homes than you can imagine. With his permission, I share his story. I hope that you find it eye-opening and helpful.

Kids who attempt suicide don't have to come from violent and abusive homes. Rigid and uncaring homes will do, even

Christian homes where little time is spent showing kids affection and giving them guidance. This is what happened to me.

My parents were devout Christians who dedicated their lives to advancing the kingdom of God. As foreign missionaries, they worked zealously to promote the gospel. My parents loved me and my brothers and sisters, but their ministry limited their time with us as we were growing up.

For the first few years of our lives we lived with our parents like any other family. Then, when we were ready for school, mission policy dictated that we go away to mission boarding schools. Home visits came on holidays, term breaks, or furloughs.

For the first six years of school, I attended mission boarding schools and received a good educational foundation with personal attention. The house parents and teachers were responsible for a dozen or more kids from several families. But I deeply missed my parents.

At first I had my older brother to turn to, but even that changed. When I was nine, following a furlough, my brother stayed in the U.S. while I returned with my parents to Africa. With my brother gone, I felt I had no one to turn to when bullied by other children.

In seventh grade, I moved to the U.S. to attend public schools. A group of a dozen missionary kids lived together on a small farm in Indiana set up for this purpose. The house parents were good Christian people who bore a heavy load of responsibility. After managing the farm, there was little time left to deal with our feelings, friendships, dating, college and career planning, and spiritual growth. In the middle of all this, there were times when my parents would return, and we would live as a family.

Despite Christianity being central to life on the farm, I felt increasingly distanced from the faith. My unchurched friends seemed to be kinder, more loving, and open than the people I knew at church. Before I finished high school, I completely rebelled against the faith that my parents were working so hard to establish through their missionary efforts. Through the process of thinking for myself, I came to believe that only the physical world was real and that the spiritual world was just a delusion.

High school life went on and, like other teens, I had frequent bouts of self-doubt. I became depressed and felt a growing sense of alienation from my family, friends, and self. Not being very athletic or socially at ease, I sought to excel in academics. My hard work paid off, and I did well in school.

Senior year arrived, and I had to decide on future plans. I accepted a generous academic scholarship to Ohio Wesleyan University. Once there, I felt I had made a mistake and decided to transfer to Stanford University, a highly competitive school on the cutting edge of intellectualism and scholarship. My scholarly intentions were soon lost in my desire to pursue a life of worldliness and self-gratification. I forced myself to start smoking, with the explicit intent of using marijuana or whatever might be necessary to gain acceptance in this community. It wasn't long before I started sleeping around.

Unsettled, I changed majors from math to philosophy, and eventually to comparative religion. I was no longer attending church. None of this met my spiritual longings but, rather, alienated me further from myself, my family, and God.

The major crisis of my life began in the middle of my junior year and continued for a year and a half. Eastern religions were influencing my thinking, and I began to smoke pot as a route to enlightenment. While isolated in an empty student residence, I had an experience using pot that almost killed me (it may have been laced with something more potent, a common practice at that time).

I fell into a major depression that lasted eighteen months. I felt like a totally inadequate failure. I could no longer handle my class work, dropped out of Stanford, and landed briefly in a psychiatric hospital outside San Jose.

After leaving the hospital, I went to live with my sister in Texas. My parents were still in Africa. While there I held a series of manual labor jobs between stays in a state psychiatric institution. Late one evening, while walking home along the railroad tracks from the meat-packing plant where I was working, I was overcome with an overwhelming sense of lost opportunity and failure to accomplish anything of significance. The next day, I went to the graveyard of a country church and attempted to take my own life by slashing my wrists. I would have died had some stranger not called the police after he noticed me lying unconscious in a ditch by the side of the road. Following my hospitalization and recovery, I spent more time in a state psychiatric hospital.

The next few months were filled with a confusing mix of experiences. I spent two unhappy terms in a trade school and moved to Wisconsin where I couldn't even hold down a job as a dishwasher and busboy. I attended meetings at churches, various cults, and even a witches' coven. In an effort to understand their message and meaning for the future, I carefully read the eschatological books of the Bible. Time and space took on strange elastic properties even though I was no longer using drugs. At the end of my resources, I landed back in a psychiatric institution.

When my parents' mission board learned of some of these events, they asked my parents to return from Africa to work at the home office in suburban Chicago. My parents did so and set up a home for us for three years. They showed constant love and concern for me and never gave up hope. Their example changed my attitude toward the faith. I had a renewed interest in the Bible and what Christ had done for me. I began attending a vital evangelical church and worked at a series of menial jobs. I was accepted back as a student at Ohio Wesleyan University and completed school, earning a degree in mathematics.

Since then, I have been living a full and healthy life. I married a Christian woman who has been a constant and stable influence in my life. My work in computer programming led to further schooling and a master's degree in computer science. I have held steady jobs as a computer programmer, software engineer, and consultant. My wife and I have a teenager daughter, and as a family, we are actively involved in the ministries of a large evangelical church in Chicago.

I hope my story is helpful to well-intentioned, but overly busy parents. Bringing young people to believe in the hope that we have in Christ requires that those who know and love him get to know and love those children they have received from him. Even when kids stray far from the faith, they can be brought back with the demonstration of unconditional Christian love. This is where the mission of the church impacts generations to come. *And it all starts at home.*

How are you doing in getting to know your kids? In what areas do you need to show them unconditional, committed love?

Understanding and Encouraging Your Teen Spiritually

12

POINTING YOUR TEEN TO CHRIST

> We proclaim him, admonishing and teaching everyone with all wisdom, so that we may present everyone perfect in Christ. To this end I labor, struggling with all his energy, which so powerfully works in me.
>
> *Colossians 1:28-29*, NIV

"SO WHAT ARE you hoping for . . . a boy or a girl?" is the question asked of expectant parents when the news gets out that a baby is on the way. Even though they may secretly harbor a desire for one over the other, most parents are too diplomatic to betray their preference. Instead, the standard answer is, "I don't care if we have a boy or girl . . . just as long as our baby is *healthy!*"

That parental desire continues long after we cradle our children in our arms for the first time. I've held each of my children and wondered what it will be like for them to grow up in today's world. Will they make good choices as they pass through the earthquake of adolescence? What kinds of pressures will they face in school and among their friends? Will they buy into any of the messages pounded into them by popular music and media? Will they be a part of the minority who say no to premarital sex, substance abuse, depression, and the host of other problems that have woven themselves into the fabric of today's youth culture? Will they be healthy?

Throughout this book I have challenged you to close and eliminate the cultural-generational gap in your home. I have attempted to lead you into an understanding of the normal changes that children face when they pass through adolescence. In addition to learning what is normal, your eyes have been opened to the changing world of nineties youth culture and how it is powerfully molding our kids. My goal has been to provide you with knowledge that will equip you to be a more understanding and effective parent. It is my hope that you will make use of this knowledge so that when your children are grown you will be able to look back over the years and say, "I was successful in helping my children face their teenage years and weather the storms and pressures of adolescence. They have made good choices, our family is close, and they have remained healthy."

As we come to the end of our examination of youth culture, I want to reemphasize the underlying theme of this book and the most important aspect of our children's lives: their spiritual health. You see, it's not enough to feel that we have been successful parents if our children have avoided the ravages of substance abuse or remained chaste during their teen years. I believe with my whole heart that the most successful parents in the world are the parents who determine that the spiritual well-being of their children is top priority. When asked, "What are you hoping your little boy or girl will become?" they answer, "I don't care . . . just as long as they are *spiritually healthy!*"

The process of leading our children through adolescence and into spiritual health and maturity requires hard work. But if you are a parent who is ready to face this God-given task and make the spiritual health of your children your top parenting priority, then this chapter is for you. In coming to an understanding of how to lead our children and teens to spiritual health, we must answer two foundational questions: What is spiritual health? And how can I lead my kids to hear the still small voice of God when all the voices of youth culture are screaming in their ears?

Just What Is Spiritual Health?

I grew up in a suburban Philadelphia neighborhood filled with boys. Our after-school hours and summer days were spent in search of adventure. Our greatest thrill was to indulge our boyish exuberance by engaging in what seemed like risky escapades, chosen because they stretched the limits our parents had set for us. One of the places we liked to go was the apple orchard. This promised land was reached by a short bike ride over some backyards and through a small section of woods. When we were younger, we would stand back and watch the big boys scale the eight-foot metal fence, run through the orchard, disappear over a hill, and then come back with a big red apple in their hand. Eating the apple was only part of the reward. The real prize was making it back without the orchard keeper unloading a round of rock salt from his gun into your rear end. While none of us had actually seen the orchard keeper or heard his gun fire, we nervously cheered and feared for the guys all the same. We would watch in awe as these heroes would come back over the fence and sit, proudly feasting on their apples. This ritual served as a neighborhood rite of passage to separate the men from the boys.

When I was finally old enough to face my fear of going over the fence, I was confronted with a major dilemma: Would I disobey my parents and step beyond the limits they had set for me, or would I follow the crowd into the orchard? While I can't remember my mom and dad ever telling me not to go into the orchard, I was smart enough to know that if I was ever caught, facing my dad would be much worse than running into the orchard keeper. As I look back on that day when I became a man, I can clearly remember three distinct feelings.

The first was of safety and security as I stood outside the fence. I was where I was supposed to be and right where I belonged.

The second feeling was one of being torn in two as I paused to straddle the top of the fence, trying to decide whether or not to continue on my journey. One leg hung on the side where the rest of me belonged while the other dangled in danger.

The third feeling came as I finally went over the fence and into the orchard. Strangely, it was nothing like the sense of freedom I had expected. Instead, it was an almost paralyzing sense of being where I didn't belong. Even though I gave in to the pressure and ran for an

Spiritual health is all-important to the future lives and happiness of our children and teens.

apple, I wanted nothing more than to be out of there. And quite honestly, I didn't care if I ever went back in again.

The spiritual development and health of our children and teens is much like my experience at that apple orchard. My children and your children are spiritual beings who will grow up to fit in one of three basic categories that coincide with my experience of going over the fence.

The first category includes those who give in to the voices of the world that invite them to climb all the way over the fence. Shaped by society and its institutions, they find it easier to be where everyone else is—even though they don't belong there. They grow to be adults whose personal sense of right and wrong hinges on what everybody else is doing. Before long they get used to being in the orchard and eventually call it home. They have no interest in or place for God in their lives. Their worldliness causes them to be spiritually unhealthy.

The second category of people is filled with leg-dangling fence-sitters. Unwilling to commit themselves to either side of the fence, they straddle the top and wind up living on both sides. When it is most convenient and easy to be in the orchard, they jump in. When it is to their advantage to be outside the fence, they stay there. Their habit of making decisions based on what is easiest or most convenient at any given moment leads them to live a life characterized by a commitment to be uncommitted. They know that they belong in a relationship with God. They know right from wrong. They talk about God, carry their Bible, pray out loud, and go to church. But their faith makes little difference in how they live their life day to day. Their fence-sitting wishy-washy attitude causes them to forfeit their spiritual health.

The last group of people are those who have come to an understanding of where they belong. Even though it isn't always easy, they go against the flow of the crowd and stay outside the fence. They are in a vital and growing relationship with the living God. Their commitment to him is characterized by a faith that is deep and real. While they are often tempted to climb the fence and do make mistakes, their desire to love and serve the Lord remains through their struggle. No one has forced them to stay outside the orchard. They have experienced the freedom of faith and obedience, and as a result, they don't ever want to leave. They will grow up to be spiritually healthy adults.

Take a minute and think ahead a few years. Imagine your children as young adults standing near that apple orchard. Where do you want them to be? Inside the fence, on the fence, or outside the fence? What do you want to see when you look into their eyes? Someone who has turned their back on God? Someone who only talks about God? Or someone who is sold out to God? My greatest desire as a father is to see my children standing outside the fence not because I've said so but because they know that is where they belong. I long for them to be spiritually healthy!

Jesus defined spiritual health and the spiritually healthy person during his discussion with a lawyer. He framed his definition in the form of a commandment: "Love the Lord your God with all your heart and with all your soul and with all your mind and with all your strength." And then he continued, "Love your neighbor as yourself" (Mark 12:30-31, NIV).

According to Jesus, living a life of spiritual health outside the fence is living a life of commitment. The first commitment involves focusing all that you have, are, and ever will be on loving God. The second calls us to serve God by loving others in the same way that Jesus has loved us.

Let me encourage you to make the spiritual health of your children your goal by making it your prayer. The next time you sit at the table with your family, quietly look at each of your children. Think about God's desire to see them love him with all of their being. Silently pray for each one and watch what happens when, over time, God's will for the spiritual health of your children becomes part of your will as you parent them through the adolescent years and into adulthood. I have often prayed:

> God, please grow Bethany (Caitlin/Josh/Nathaniel) to love you with all of her heart, mind, soul, and strength. Give her the compassion and sensitivity to love others as herself. Give her the strength to say yes to you and no to going over the fence.

I am convinced that is the most important, valuable, and necessary prayer we could ever pray for our children.

I trust that reading this book has served not only to increase your knowledge and understanding of the world that your kids are growing up in, but to raise your level of concern. After all, a lot of teenage values, attitudes, and behaviors that we have examined are horrifying. But the kids who stand the best chance to resist buying into those dangerous messages are the kids whose parents are committed to leading them to spiritual health and maturity on God's terms.

Leading Your Kids to Spiritual Health

If you are convinced of the need to lead your children and teens to spiritual health, you may wonder, *OK, I understand the goal and what it looks like. But how can I point my kids to Christ and nurture their spiritual health in a world that sends a different message and calls our kids to "come and follow me"?*

In an effort to get an answer to that question for myself, I've asked numerous parents who have raised spiritually healthy children to pass on the secrets of their success. And I've listened to a lot of good advice, which I will pass on to you after making one thing very clear: Even if parents do everything *right*, there is no guarantee that their children will grow up to be spiritually healthy.

I know one family who shared devotions and wonderful times together while the kids were growing up. They were a strong Christian family, and all three of the kids had chosen to follow Jesus when they were young. Two continued on that path right into adulthood. But one son left his parents in pain and confusion as he retreated from his faith and disappeared into the orchard. Devastated, the father said to me, "I never thought this type of thing could happen in a Christian home. I feel very helpless."

I don't know why God allows these things to happen. What I do know is that in the overwhelming majority of cases, parents who take the time to raise and nurture their children in the Christian faith will see their kids grow into spiritual health and maturity. But I also know that we can't force our children to love, honor, and obey God. They are human beings created by God with the ability to make their own choices. For many families, consistent spiritual nurturing didn't bear fruit in the children's lives until long after they entered adulthood. We can never presume to know God's perfect timing. There will be situations where we just don't know how he is acting out his will. Sometimes God takes us through the desert of watching our kids go wrong as part of his plan to parent us and lead us to depend on him, our heavenly Father, all the more.

Throughout the rest of this last chapter, as we examine four key elements necessary to raising spiritually healthy children and teens, ponder the ways in which you can improve as a parent.

Where I am as a parent.

I never realized how difficult it would be for my son Joshua to make the transition from his infant car seat to the "big-boy seat." Even before we were out of the driveway we would hear the click of his seat belt coming unbuckled. It seemed like he was unbuckling his seat belt every five minutes. "Josh, get your seat belt on!" became our family battle cry during even our shortest drives.

One day Josh and I were coming back from a trip to the mall. We were a few blocks from home when I noticed a white car coming at us from the left as we passed through an intersection. The car was traveling so fast that I knew it was going to run the stop sign. In an effort to avoid a collision, I stomped on the brakes and skidded to a halt. Without hesitating even a second, Josh looked out his window at the other car as it continued down the street, raised and shook his fist, and yelled, "You idiot!" I wondered, *Where in the world did he ever learn to talk like that?!* I knew he had been spending a lot of time in the car with his mother . . . and then it hit me. He was responding to the other driver in a manner that he had learned . . . from *me!* All right. I'll admit it. I tend to regress a little when I'm out driving. My son was only following the behavior modeled for him by his dear old dad.

Do you want your children and teens to grow up to be strong in their faith and able to handle all that our world is throwing at them? Then ask yourself, What kind of example am I giving to them? Where you are as parent plays a more significant role in determining what your children will become than any other single factor. Where are you standing at the apple orchard? Outside the fence, on the fence, or inside the fence? You've got to be where you want your kids to be because they will follow your example and wind up right where you are. Better yet, you've got to be where you *belong* so that your kids will learn that that's where they belong, too.

In Deuteronomy 6, Moses shares God's plan for who was to teach God's truths to succeeding generations and how they were to be taught:

> These commandments that I give you today are to be upon your hearts. Impress them on your children. Talk about them when you sit at home and when you walk along the road, when you lie down and when you get up. Tie them as symbols on your hands and bind them on your foreheads. Write them on the doorframes of your houses and on your gates. (Deuteronomy 6:6-9, NIV)

Are you modeling strong Christian faith, church attendance, and loving family values to your child?

God's *who* are parents who have his commandments written on their hearts and gladly love God with their whole being. God, in his perfect wisdom and plan, has chosen to do his work through the family. He began with a family in Genesis and continues to use the family as the primary arena for bringing people to himself. God's *how* for imparting these truths to our children is by a diligent commitment to teach and model wholehearted and single-minded devotion to God twenty-four hours a day. When his truths become the central overriding interest and purpose in our lives, teaching them to our children will happen almost unconsciously.

It is no mistake that our children grow up to look, act, think, and be like us. While similarities in physical appearance are inherited through the genes, our attitudes, values, and behaviors are passed from generation to generation by example. God made it this way.

This is especially true when it comes to faith development and spiritual health.

After working with teenagers for several years, I heard someone say that in families where neither parent attends church regularly, only 6 percent of the children will grow up to be faithful to Christ. If only Mom attends regularly, 15 percent remain faithful. If only Dad is consistent in his attendance, only 55 percent remain faithful. But in those families where both parents are regular in church attendance, 72 percent of their children will remain faithful. My experience with teens and their families validates these figures. Granted, there is more to spiritual health and vitality than church attendance. But those numbers speak volumes about the importance of parental example.

How do you measure up in this first element necessary to pointing kids to Christ in the nineties? Here are some specific questions you can use to evaluate your own spiritual health and vitality:

- When my children look at me, are they learning what it means to love God with all their heart, soul, mind, and strength?
- Do they see me trusting in God for guidance and wisdom as I plan the future, run my business, manage my home, etc.?
- Do they see me turning to God when anxious, troubled, or ill?
- Do they see me living out my commitment to Christ by spending time reading and studying the Bible?
- Do they know that prayer is an important part of my life?
- Are they learning what it means to carry the cross and live a life of Christian discipleship?
- Do they see that God is central to my thoughts and actions constantly or just on Sunday mornings?
- Do they see me care for family, neighbors, friends, and the "lepers and outcasts" of the world?
- Are they learning to be compassionate and Christ-centered rather than insensitive and self-centered?
- Are they learning not to talk behind people's backs?
- Are they learning that God is the source of all they are and have, including the gift of salvation?

We all have wishes, dreams, hopes, and desires for what our children will become. When you dream about the spiritual future of your children, don't forget that they will probably be where you are now.

What I know as a parent.

If we are to live out our God-given calling to model and teach the Christian faith to our kids in a relevant manner, we need to understand the cultural forces shaping the head and heart commitments of our kids. Only then can we teach them the value of using God's Word to navigate through the adolescent years and into adulthood.

Josh made me feel old the other day when he discovered that I didn't have Rollerblades or a SuperSoaker when I was a boy. I know that my age automatically categorizes me in his young mind as old and out of touch. But I don't have to be out in the dark when it comes to understanding his world. I can keep listening, looking, and learning.

The coming years will bring more change as youth culture continues to snowball away from your experience of growing up. This means that you will have to be more intentional about keeping up. I trust that reading this book will be only the beginning of your quest for youth culture knowledge. Continue on in the task you've begun because you need to know!

How I approach parenting.

I despise the job of painting. There's nothing that I hate more to do around the house than spend my days on a ladder with a brush in my hand. I'll do it when it needs to be done, but my endless grumbling and clock-watching betray my disdain for the job.

Children watch what you do more than they listen to what you say.

I know a mother and father who view raising their children the same way. At first glance they appear to be wonderful parents. They are not physically abusive towards their kids, and they give them a lot of things. But they really aren't enjoying the opportunity they've been given to raise their kids. One day I was standing with the father as our children were playing together. He was complaining about how much it costs to raise children, keep them clothed, help them with homework, run them from here to there, and anything else that required time or sacrifice. He looked at me and said, "You know, I can't wait until those bozos grow up. Then, me and my wife are going to start having some fun. Bahamas, here we come!" I know him well enough to know that he wasn't joking. I felt bad for his kids, but I felt worse for him. His approach to parenting is terrible, and my guess is that it won't be long before his children figure out what he really thinks about being their dad.

Parents who hope to raise spiritually healthy kids in these challenging nineties must take a different approach to parenting. Instead of wishing the days, months, and years away, we should ask God to help us make the most of the time that we have with our kids so that we can do as much as possible to point them in the right direction.

Here are five elements that must be a part of your approach to parenting as you travel through the few short years you have with your children.

Your approach to parenting should be biblical. When scuba divers are down deep, it is easy for them to become confused and disoriented. Since water diffuses light, divers often find themselves surrounded by illumination, making it difficult to discern which way is up. Feeling weightless and without a sense of gravity contributes to this confusion. The only way to distinguish up from down is to watch the direction in which your air bubbles travel. Divers who lose their sense of direction risk drowning if they trust their inner senses more than their bubbles. They are taught early on that no matter how they feel, no matter what they think, their bubbles are always right.

I know a mother who is confused and disoriented. She desires to be the best mother in the world. Consequently, her shelves are filled with parenting manuals and books that she has read from cover to cover. She has attended the many parenting seminars offered in her local schools and community. She even makes a point of going to other mothers to ask for guidance and advice. No doubt she has learned a lot. But she is the first to admit that she has been left confused by exposing herself to dozens of different parenting philosophies and techniques. She needs to learn that no matter how she feels, no matter what she thinks, no matter what subjective advice any book or parenting expert gives, the Bible describes things accurately and clearly. Like the scuba diver's bubbles, the Bible is always right!

From the moment they are born, our children need parents who tune themselves in to the most reliable source of parenting information and instruction. God has given us the Bible to guide us through these difficult and confusing days. Your approach to parenting should be informed and guided by God's Word. Study the Bible with diligence on a regular basis. Discover how it speaks to the molders and shapers of contemporary youth culture. Uncover the character traits and attitudes that God calls us to exhibit in our families and other interpersonal relationships.

Your approach to parenting should be realistic. One of my most vivid baseball memories occurred on Father's Day in 1964. That was the day that my hero, Philadelphia Phillies pitcher Jim Bunning, pitched a perfect game. Twenty-seven times, the New York Mets came to the plate. No one made it to first base. Bunning was absolutely perfect and didn't allow any runs, hits, walks, or errors.

That day wouldn't be so special if perfect games were commonplace. But they're rare. There are times when years pass before another major league pitcher throws a perfect game. Only a handful of pitchers have ever had the experience of pitching nine perfect innings. There are hundreds of others who have never accomplished the feat, but that doesn't make them bad pitchers.

Why is it that so many of us feel like failures when we or our children make a mistake? My guess is that we are disappointed because we expect ourselves and our children to be perfect—a very unrealistic expectation. But our gnawing sense of imperfection should not keep us from being good parents.

Realistic parents pave the way for family closeness and build their children's self-esteem by parenting with grace. They aren't paralyzed by feelings of fear and inadequacy when they make mistakes. They know that since the beginning of time, God has used imperfect people to carry out his plan, and he will use them as they raise their children in spite of their imperfections.

Your approach to parenting should be preventive. A working couple who had just had their first baby came to visit us before deciding whether or not they wanted Lisa to baby-sit their new arrival during the day. As we were getting to know each other, they asked to take a tour of the house. As we walked from room to room and around the outside of the house, they looked for safety hazards. The safety inspection was not complete until they had gotten answers to all of their questions. "Will you put covers in the unused electrical outlets? Do you keep a gate at the top of the steps? Are the basement doors left open or shut? Does your dog like children?" I must admit that their endless stream of questions was starting to get on my nerves. But they wanted to be sure that we would take steps to protect their child from physical harm.

All of us share that couple's concern for our children's physical well-being. We tell our kids to stay out of the street, to look both ways, and to keep away from hot stuff. Parents who expect to lead their kids through adolescence and into spiritual health should also take preventive measures.

Our children should be equipped to face life and all of its challenges. They need us to pass on the valuable information we have learned about life. We need to speak openly about the results of substance abuse, premarital sex, peer pressure, and materialism.

Another preventive measure is teaching our kids decision-making skills. There will come a time when they are out in the world without Mom or Dad at their side, and they will be called upon to make some crucial choices. How will they know how to choose wisely if we haven't taken the time to tell them?

And they need parents who will teach them the relevance of the truths of God's Word and how it applies to all of life. A working knowledge of God's transcendent standards of right and wrong is the best dose of preventive medicine.

Your approach to parenting should be redemptive. How will you respond to your children when they make a mistake or do something wrong? What will you say if your daughter turns her back on all that you taught her and winds up pregnant? What will you say if your son gets suspended from school for fighting? What will you do if you find drug paraphernalia in your teen's room? Most teens make bad choices, and the determining factor in whether or not a bad choice turns into a situation that gets better or worse will depend on your response.

Let me suggest that your goal should be to redeem these situations by turning a mistake into an opportunity for your teen to become a better person. I once heard John White say that his rule for parenting through and redeeming difficult situations is this: "As Christ is to me, so must I be to my children." Don't write your teen off as hopeless or boot him out of the family. Rather, treat him as you think Jesus would treat you if you were the offending party.

I wondered how Mike would handle it when his sixteen-year-old daughter Kate told him she was pregnant. They were a Christian family, but over the last couple of years there had been some growing tension between Kate and her dad. But to be honest, her pregnancy was quite unexpected and shocking to me. How would her father, a church leader, react? Kate sat alone with her parents at the kitchen table on the night she gave them the news. They later told me they were shocked and disappointed that Kate had slept with her boyfriend. I asked Kate what her father said when she dropped the bombshell. "He stood up, walked around the table, put his arms around me, and said, 'Kate, I love you. What you did was wrong. But I want you to know that your mother and I will not stop loving you. We will stand behind you and we'll love this baby together.'" She continued, "I never felt closer to my parents in my life. I love them so much!" A broken relationship was on the road to being redeemed.

Your approach to parenting should be prayerful. As I write these words, it's 11:50 A.M. on the National Day of Prayer in the U.S. In just a few minutes, millions of people will pause for a moment to ask God to heal our land. But wouldn't we be making better use of our time, as some people may reason, if we were doing rather than praying? David Bryant, director of Concerts of Prayer International and a leader in the prayer movement in the U.S., says, "The primary reason there is an acceleration of prayer [is that] we are becoming more and more of the conviction that we don't have the answers any longer."[1]

Parents, we need to pray for answers—answers to the questions that we have about raising our children and answers to our children's adolescent questions and their deep spiritual longing for him. You see, our children grow in the wisdom and nurture of the Lord in spite of us, not because of us. Sure, they learn a lot from the example we live, but the fact of the matter is that it is ultimately God who gives faith to our kids and leads them to spiritual health.

Paul's words have become more and more real to me as I struggle to raise my kids: "Do not be anxious about anything, but in everything, by prayer and petition, with thanksgiving, present your requests to God" (Phil. 4:6, NIV). Prayer is God's gift to us as we depend on him and his power to keep us on track as moms and dads.

What I give as a parent.

Mark was a teenager who had everything . . . and nothing. I met him when I was speaking on a junior high retreat. From the moment I arrived at the camp, he followed me everywhere. It didn't take long for me to figure out that Mark had some deep needs that were eating him up. I pulled his youth minister aside to find out what was going on with Mark. This is what he told me:

> Mark is longing for the love of an older man. He comes from one of the wealthiest families in our community. All the kids envy him because his father gives him anything and everything he wants. He has the nicest clothes, stereo, and television. Every summer he goes to a prestigious camp in New England. He's got it all . . . except his father's love. What the kids in our group from strong families don't realize is that trading places with Mark wouldn't be much fun at all.

For the rest of the weekend, I went out of my way to pay special attention to Mark. It was a bittersweet moment when I put my arm around him after we won a game of two-on-two basketball. I knew that my arm on his shoulder put a smile on his face because of the emptiness in his heart.

The most fortunate children and teens in the world are the ones who say they live with parents who give them everything. But the "everything" that teens so desperately want and need can't be paid for at the cash register at the local mall. There is no price tag on what they want. When a hundred thousand children between eight and fourteen were asked what they wanted most in their parents, these were the top ten items on their list:

1. Parents who don't argue in front of them.
2. Parents who treat each family member the same.
3. Parents who are honest.
4. Parents who are tolerant of others.
5. Parents who welcome their friends to the home.
6. Parents who build a team spirit with their children.
7. Parents who answer their questions.
8. Parents who give punishment when needed but not in front of others, especially their friends.
9. Parents who concentrate on good points instead of weaknesses.
10. Parents who are consistent.[2]

Parents in strong, healthy families are givers, and by their giving they raise strong, healthy children who find it much easier to make it through the adolescent years of change. Conversely, parents in weak, unhealthy families fail to give their children those things that they really need and abandon their children to be molded and shaped more by their culture than by Dad and Mom.

While my list is not exhaustive, here are the gifts that you need to wrap up and give to your kids every day.

Give them unconditional love. Today the word *love* has been drained of its meaning by those who only refer to it as "made between the sheets." Our children need parents who will help them rediscover the meaning of the word *love* by their demonstration of it in the home. The New Testament word used for the kind of love kids need from parents is *agape,* the same word used to describe God's love for us. Agape is the highest and noblest form of love because it is given in spite of the receiver. There is no condition on the part of the receiver that could turn the free flow of this love on or off. The lover looks past the other person's faults, bad habits, imperfections, and unwillingness to love them back and continues to love. It is a commitment to love the unlovable, even when they don't deserve it.

Have there ever been moments when your children have been unlovable? I asked that question of a group of parents one time and one man shouted out, "Yes, the time between ages twelve and twenty!" Sometimes it is difficult to love our children during the awkward years of adolescence because we may not get anything in return. But true love seeks no return. It just loves. And while your children may not say it or show it, they want and need your unconditional love.

Give them your time. My friend Ron Rand has dedicated his life to encouraging and helping fathers spend time with their children. A pastor, Ron was once like many men who become so consumed by their long list of to-dos that they forget what they must do. He writes:

> Eleven P.M.: two hours later than I'd told Jennifer to expect me. Again. Our sons had been prayed with and tucked in hours before, but not by me. I'd been presiding at a church committee meeting. The night before it had been Evangelism team. And Monday? Absent again. What kind of father was raising my boys? He was busy, distracted, and absent most of the time. Everyone else's needs . . . everything seemed more urgent than being a daddy.[3]

Ron is not alone. There are moms and dads all over America who get so wrapped up in all they are doing that they forsake what they must be doing—parenting.

Juvenile probation officer Fred Green has interviewed hundreds of teens on their way to juvenile detention centers. Most of them talk about family problems and dysfunction. Green has put together a list of ten things that the kids he has interviewed say they wish their parents had done. These kids say: "DO NOT GET HUNG UP ON A JOB THAT KEEPS YOU AWAY FROM HOME. Fathers, keep in touch with your kids somehow. Mothers, cut the heavy social schedule so you can be home to supervise the children."[4]

Give your children unconditional love— even when they don't deserve it!

Ron Rand gives parents good advice when he challenges us to "learn how to spend effective personal time with each family member. Our families need both quality time and quantity time expressed in ways that matter."[5]

Give them your attention. Beth started coming to our church youth group when she was a sophomore in high school. Her parents had divorced when she was young, and her mother had since remarried and had another child. I decided to get to know Beth and went to one of her high school field-hockey games. When the game was over, I started to walk back to my car as Beth joined the rest of her team for an after-game meeting. Just as I was about to get in my car, Beth ran toward me. She threw her arms around me and, with tears streaming down her face, said, "Thanks so much for coming to my game. I've been playing since I was in seventh grade and my parents have never come to see me play." I felt so bad for Beth.

Parents, drop the paper, let the housework go, leave the briefcase at the office, and pay attention to your kids.

Give them boundaries. Healthy families are families with rules and boundaries. Children grow up learning right from wrong and become responsible and obedient. And as they learn to live responsibly within the limits of their freedom, their parents will gradually expand those limits until they are able to live independently.

I once heard it said that raising children and teens is like holding a wet bar of soap: too firm a grasp, and it shoots from your hand; too loose a grasp, and it slides away. A gentle but firm grasp keeps it in your control. One of the greatest gifts we can give to our children is reasonable and loving boundaries.

Give them consistent discipline. Perhaps you've run into the same little boy I've seen in restaurants and department stores. He gets around. He's usually with his mother and grandmother, telling them what to do. They always seem oblivious to the fact that he is out of control, but every once in a while they will lash out at him with some threat you would think might make him behave. "Sit down! Shut up, or I'll rip your arms off," his mother says. In a matter of seconds, he's up to his old tricks, which everyone except his mother and grandmother seems to notice. He keeps it up and keeps it up. His mother keeps on threatening to discipline him, but it never happens. And he knows it never will. If his life continues on this way, this poor boy won't know how to discipline himself and will grow up to have trouble functioning in the adult world. What he needs more than anything else is parents who encourage his good behavior and correct his unacceptable behavior.

When we give our children the gift of consistent, loving discipline, we are helping them to learn self-control. Later, that same self-control will help them make responsible choices in life. That's why Fred Green hears juvenile offenders say that they wish their parents would do the following:

SHAKE ME UP. Punish me when I first go wrong. Tell my why. Convince me that more severe measures will come if I transgress again in the same manner. CALL MY BLUFF. Stand firm on what is right, even when your kid threatens to run away or become a delinquent or drop out of school. Stay in there with him and the bluffing will cease in 98 percent of the cases.[6]

The dictionary defines *discipline* as "training that corrects, molds, and perfects moral character." When your kids look back on their growing-up years, they will thank you that you took the time to teach them that there truly *is* right and wrong in a world that works so hard to teach them otherwise.

Give them two listening ears. The Swiss psychologist Paul Tournier has said, "Every human being needs to express himself. Through lack of opportunity for it, one may become sick."[7] That's a good explanation of what is happening to so many children and teens today. They have so much to say, but nobody is there to listen.

My four-year-old friend Will loves to talk. Whenever I see him at church, he is frantically trying to keep up with his mom and dad. On several occasions I've watched Will tug at his father's trousers in an effort to get his dad's attention. "Daddy, Daddy, I have to tell you something!" Every once in a while his father will glance down from his conversation with another adult to say, "Not now, Will. I'm talking." On one occasion Will wet his pants right there in the hall even though he was telling his father he had to get to the bathroom. Do you know what his father said? He leaned over to Will and asked, "Will, why didn't you tell me you had to go to the bathroom?"

I've met a lot of teenage Wills. They try so hard to get their parents' attention only to hear, "Not now. I'm too busy!" Trouble comes and the parents wonder, *Why didn't you tell me?* But they did try to tell. Eventually, they will make the sad discovery that their parents don't ever have the time—nor do they care to listen. So the kids will go somewhere else to be heard and clam up at home.

Do you want to lead your kids to spiritual health? Listen to them. Drop everything you are doing, be quiet, get in their face, and let them talk. Respond in a way that lets them know that you love them.

Colleen was often late for our youth group meetings. At first I was bothered by what I thought was her apathy about being on time. But I soon discovered that whenever she was late, it was for one of two reasons. Either she had lost track of time while sitting and talking with her parents at the dinner table, or she was out in the church parking lot having a heart-to-heart with her dad. It should come as no surprise that Colleen was a great kid from a great family. Her parents had given her the gift of their undivided attention.

Give them your willingness to admit your mistakes. Anyone who has grown up with a father in the house learns at a young age that there are three things men find it very difficult to say: "I'm lost," "I can't fix it," and "I'm sorry!" You may laugh, but it's more true than it should be.

All of us know when we have done something wrong. But it's hard to admit to ourselves and others that we are capable of making mistakes. We have somehow come to believe that if we don't admit it, nobody will know! But I have learned that if anyone at all is going to notice what I do wrong, it's my wife and children. I'm also learning to swallow hard and go to them to say, "I'm sorry. Would you forgive me?" I'm not as consistent as I should be, but I know that vulnerability is one of the greatest gifts I can give to my children. The most convincing proof for me is the many conversations I've had with teens who are angry and feel cut off from their parents. Many of them have said this: "You know what I can't stand about my dad (or mom)? He (she) thinks he's so perfect. He can never admit when he's wrong."

Give them a spiritual heritage. When I was a teenager, I can remember lying in my bed and hearing the quiet whispers of my parents as they climbed into their bed and turned out the lights. Sometimes I could hear them whispering their prayers before they went to sleep. I would often hear them pray for me.

My parents' bedtime prayers taught me that God occupied center stage in their lives and in our home. Those prayers, combined with years of family devotions, spiritual discussions, and my parents' godly example, gave me a rich spiritual heritage that I hope to pass on to my children and their children.

■ IT'S YOUR TURN

There is a little country airport a few miles from where I live that is home to a parachute club. Every Saturday and Sunday dozens of men and women gather outside a trailer at the end of the runway to get ready for their jumps. Although I've never jumped out of an airplane (and don't plan on doing so—ever!), I enjoy going to the airport and watching a few jumps.

I sometimes wonder if all the time parachutists spend in preparation is really worth it. Before they ever step out of the plane there are classroom lessons, simulated jumps from a small wooden platform to the ground, and numerous equipment checks. I've stood by and watched the concentration and care each jumper invests in untangling their cords and folding and packing their chute. One by one they put them on, checking and rechecking every little latch and buckle. When they are finally ready, they climb into the plane and get ready for a fifteen-minute ride to the correct jumping altitude.

But any question of the value of all the prejump preparations disappears when those little black specks begin to fall away from the plane one by one. One careless mistake or oversight could lead to death. But hours of good preparation pays off in a successful jump that lasts a few short moments.

There is a sense in which this book has been about parachute jumping. It takes years and years of careful concentration and intentional ongoing preparation and planning to raise kids successfully. I believe that those of us who take the time to know and love the heavenly Father, to know and love our kids, and to know how the world is loving and influencing our kids will be rewarded with a successful "jump." Our heavenly Father will help us through the few short years of parenting our adolescents. And as those precious children jump from childhood into adulthood, we will be able to hear them land with a thankful "Yahoo! I made it! I did it! Thanks, Mom and Dad!"

Parenting our children in the nineties isn't easy. The pressures on our kids are big and powerful. The molders and shapers are loud and strong. Their voices will continue to scream into our children's ears, "Come and follow me!" But next to the almighty and all-powerful God of the universe, those forces are like a grain of sand or speck of dust.

Maybe you have some little ones running around your house—it won't be long before those little ones are big ones. Or maybe your little ones are already big ones, and you are watching them take another step toward adulthood each day. Think about them and the many choices and pressures that they face. Are you in touch?

This book has given you a start. And with God's help you can keep up the good work. May God grant you the grace you need to prepare, to pray, to understand your kids and their world, to parent, and to lead your children to him.

GOOD READING FOR PARENTS, TEACHERS, AND YOUTH LEADERS.

Chapter 1: Congratulations . . . You're the Parent of a Teenager!

Encounter with God and *Discovery*, daily in-depth Bible study guides for adults. Available from Scripture Union, 150 Strafford Ave., Wayne, PA 19087 (800-621-5267).

Gordon D. Fee and Douglas Stuart, *How to Read the Bible for All It's Worth.* Grand Rapids, Mich.: Zondervan, 1982.

David Jeremiah and Carole Carlson, *Exposing the Myths of Parenthood.* Waco, Tex.: Word, 1988.

Charles Sell, *The House on the Rock.* Wheaton, Ill.: Victor, 1987.

John Stott, *The Contemporary Christian,* Downers Grove, Ill.: InterVarsity Press, 1992.

John White, *Parents in Pain.* Downers Grove, Ill.: InterVarsity Press, 1979.

Chapter 2: What in the World Is a Teen?

James Dobson, *Preparing for Adolescence.* Ventura, Calif.: Regal, 1989.

Kevin Huggins, *Parenting Adolescents.* Colorado Springs: NavPress, 1989.

Bruce Narramore and Vern Lewis, *Parenting Teens.* Wheaton, Ill.: Tyndale House, 1990.

Cliff Schimmels, *What Parents Try to Forget about Adolescence.* Elgin, Ill.: David C. Cook, 1989.

Earl D. Wilson, *You Try Being a Teenager.* Portland, Oreg.: Multnomah Press, 1982.

Chapter 3: Your Teen's Changing World

Jack O. Balswick and Judith K. Balswick, *The Family: A Christian Perspective on the Contemporary Home*. Grand Rapids: Baker, 1989.

George Barna, *Absolute Confusion*. Ventura, Calif.: Regal, 1993.

George Barna, *The Future of the American Family*, Chicago: Moody Press, 1993.

George Barna, *What Americans Believe: An Annual Survey of Values & Religious Views in the United States*. Ventura, Calif.: Regal, 1991.

Allan Bloom, *The Closing of the American Mind*. New York: Simon and Schuster, 1988.

Charles Colson, *Against the Night: Living in the New Dark Ages*. Ann Arbor, Mich.: Servant, 1989.

Don C. Eberly, *Restoring the Good Society*, Grand Rapids, Mich.: Baker Books, 1994.

David Elkind, *All Grown Up & No Place to Go: Teenagers in Crisis*. Reading, Mass.: Addison-Wesley, 1984.

David Elkind, *The Hurried Child: Growing Up Too Fast Too Soon*. Reading, Mass.: Addison-Wesley, 1981.

Thomas French, *South of Heaven: Welcome to High School at the End of the Twentieth Century*. New York: Doubleday, 1993.

Donna Gaines, *Teenage Wasteland*. New York: Pantheon Books, 1991.

Carl F. H. Henry, *Twilight of a Great Civilization*. Wheaton, Ill.: Crossway, 1988.

James Davison Hunter, *Culture Wars: The Struggle to Define America*. New York: Basic Books, 1991.

William Kilpatrick, *Why Johnny Can't Tell Right from Wrong*. New York: Touchstone, 1992.

Richard Mouw, *Distorted Truth*. San Francisco: Harper and Row, 1989.

Ronald H. Nash, *The Closing of the American Heart*. Dallas: Probe Books, 1990.

James W. Sire, *The Universe Next Door: A Basic World View Catalog*. Downers Grove, Ill.: InterVarsity Press, 1988.

Cal Thomas, *The Death of Ethics in America*. Waco, Tex.: Word, 1988.

Chapter 4: Music: It Affects More Than Your Teen's Ears

Media Update: The Bimonthly Magazine of Al Menconi Ministries. Available from Al Menconi Ministries, P.O. Box 5008, San Marcos, CA 92069-1050 (800-786-8742).

Al Menconi, *Today's Music: A Window to Your Child's Soul*. Elgin, Ill.: David C. Cook, 1990.

Quentin J. Schultze et. al., *Dancing in the Dark*. Grand Rapids, Mich.: Eerdmans, 1991.

Deena Weinstein, *Heavy Metal: A Cultural Sociology*. New York: Lexington Books, 1991.

Chapter 5: Media: What Is It Teaching Your Teen?

Stephen R. Lawhead, *Turn Back the Night: A Christian Response to Popular Culture*. Wheaton, Ill.: Crossway, 1985.

Michael Medved, *Hollywood vs. America*. New York: HarperCollins, 1992.

Quentin J. Schultze, *Redeeming Television*. Downers Grove, Ill.: InterVarsity Press, 1992.

Chapter 6: Leading Your Kids through the Maze of Music and the Media

Robert Laurent, *Keeping Your Teen in Touch with God*. Elgin, Ill.: David C. Cook, 1988.

Paul W. Swets, *How to Talk So Your Teenager Will Listen*. Waco, Tex.: Word, 1988.

Chapter 7: But My Friends Do It!

Chuck Aycock and Dave Veerman, *From Dad with Love*. Wheaton, Ill.: Tyndale House, 1994.

Paul Lewis, *The Five Key Habits of Smart Dads*. Grand Rapids, Mich.: Zondervan, 1994.

Miriam Neff, *Helping Teens in Crisis*. Wheaton, Ill.: Tyndale House, 1993.

Les Parrott III, *Helping the Struggling Adolescent*. Grand Rapids, Mich.: Zondervan, 1993.

Chapter 8: When Love = Sex in Today's World

Books for parents:
P. Roger Hillerstrom, *Intimate Deception: Escaping the Trap of Sexual Impurity*. Portland, Oreg.: Multnomah Press, 1989.

Donald M. Joy, *Parents, Kids, and Sexual Integrity: Equipping Your Child for Healthy Relationships*. Waco, Tex.: Word, 1988.

Josh McDowell, *How to Help Your Child Say "NO" to Sexual Pressure*. Waco, Tex.: Word, 1987.

Josh McDowell, *Teens Speak Out: What I Wish My Parents Knew about My Sexuality.* San Bernardino, Calif.: Here's Life, 1987.

Josh McDowell and Dick Day, *Why Wait?: What You Need to Know about the Teen Sexuality Crisis.* San Bernardino, Calif.: Here's Life, 1987.

Anne Newman and Dinah Richard, *Healthy Sex Education in Your Schools: A Parent's Handbook.* Colorado Springs: Focus on the Family, 1990.

Barry St. Clair and Carol St. Clair, *Talking with Your Kids about Love, Sex and Dating.* San Bernardino, Calif.: Here's Life, 1989.

Mildred Tengbom, *Talking Together about Love and Sexuality.* Minneapolis: Bethany, 1985.

Books for teenagers:
Jim Burns, *Handling Your Hormones: The Straight Scoop on Love and Sexuality.* Eugene, Oreg.: Harvest House, 1986.

Joyce Huggett, *Dating, Sex and Friendship.* Downers Grove, Ill.: InterVarsity Press, 1985.

Mary Ann Mayo, *Caution: Sexual Choices May Be Hazardous to Your Health.* Grand Rapids, Mich.: Zondervan, 1989.

Barry St. Clair and Bill Jones, *Love: Making It Last.* San Bernardino, Calif.: Here's Life, 1988.

Bob Stone and Bob Palmer, *The Dating Dilemma: Handling Sexual Pressures.* Grand Rapids, Mich.: Baker, 1990.

Chapter 9: Living in a Material World

Bruce Baldwin, *Beyond the Cornucopia Kids.* Wilmington, N.C.: Direction Dynamics, 1988.

David Elkind, *Miseducation: Preschoolers at Risk.* New York: Knopf, 1987.

Dr. Ralph Minear and William Proctor, *Kids Who Have Too Much.* Nashville: Nelson, 1989.

Chapter 10: Holding Your Own against Alcohol and Drugs

Discovery (daily Bible study guides for mature teens), *One-to-One* (daily Bible study guides for junior high teens), and *Quest* (daily Bible study guides for ages 7 to 11). Available from Scripture Union, 150 Strafford Ave., Wayne, PA 19087 (800-621-5267).

Stephen Arterburn and Jim Burns, *Drug-Proof Your Kids: A Prevention Guide and Intervention Plan.* Colorado Springs: Focus on the Family, 1989.

Foster Cline and Jim Fay, *Parenting with Love and Logic*. Colorado Springs: Pinon Press, 1990.

Mark S. Gold, *The Facts about Drugs and Alcohol*. New York: Bantam Books, 1986.

Chris Lutes, *What Teenagers Are Saying about Drugs and Alcohol*. Wheaton, Ill.: Tyndale House, 1988.

Joel C. Robertson, *Kids Don't Want to Use Drugs*. Nashville: Nelson, 1992.

Michael J. McManus, *50 Practical Ways to Take Our Kids Back from the World*. Wheaton, Ill.: Tyndale House, 1993.

Frank Minirth, Brian Newman, and Paul Warren, *The Father Book*. Nashville: Nelson, 1992.

Gary Smalley and John Trent, *Leaving the Light On*. Portland, Oreg.: Multnomah Press, 1994.

Chapter 11: Guarding Your Teen's Emotions

T. Mitchell Anthony, *7 Reasons to Keep on Living*. Tulsa, Okla.: HIM Publications, 1985.

John Q. Baucom, *Fatal Choice: The Teenage Suicide Crisis*. Chicago: Moody Press, 1986.

Finley H. Sizemore, *Suicide: The Signs and Solutions*. Wheaton, Ill.: Victor, 1988.

Rich Van Pelt, *Intensive Care: Helping Teenagers in Crisis*. Grand Rapids, Mich.: Zondervan, 1988.

Chapter 12: Pointing Your Teen to Christ

Ken R. Canfield, *The 7 Secrets of Effective Fathers*. Wheaton, Ill.: Tyndale House, 1992.

Jay Kesler, *Ten Mistakes Parents Make with Teenagers and How to Avoid Them*. Brentwood, Tenn.: Wolgemuth & Hyatt, 1988.

Nancy Swihart and Ken R. Canfield, *Beside Every Great Dad*. Wheaton, Ill.: Tyndale House, 1992.

H. Norman Wright, *The Power of a Parent's Words*. Ventura, Calif.: Regal, 1991.

NOTES

Chapter 1

1. John White, *Parents in Pain* (Downers Grove, Ill.: InterVarsity Press, 1979), 14–15.

2. Ibid., 36.

3. Elena O. Nightengale and Lisa Wolverton, *Adolescent Rolelessness in Modern Society,* working paper for Carnegie Council on Adolescent Development, Washington, D.C., September 1988, 5.

4. "Thinking with Computers," prod. by the University of Arizona, 1991, videocassette.

Chapter 2

1. Judy W. Zylke, "Characterizing Healthy Adolescent Development; Distinguishing It from Possible Disturbances," *Journal of the American Medical Association* 262, no. 7 (18 August 1989): 880.

2. Earl D. Wilson, *You Try Being a Teenager* (Portland, Oreg.: Multnomah Press, 1982), 21–22.

3. Dale A. Blyth and Carol Traeger, "Adolescent Self-Esteem and Perceived Relationships with Parents and Peers," in *Social Networks of Children, Adolescents, and College Students,* ed. Suzanne Salzinger, John Antrobus, and Muriel Hammer (Hillsdale, N.J.: Lawrence Erlbaum Associates, 1988), 188.

4. "Kids Talk about Life," *Boston Magazine,* May 1985, 214.

5. For further reading on identity development, self-concept, self-evaluation, self-control, and self-valuation, read Dr. Keith Olson, *Counseling Teenagers* (Loveland, Colo.: Group Books, 1984), 28–32.

6. "Kids Talk about Life," 214.

7. Cliff Schimmels, *What Parents Try to Forget about Adolescence* (Elgin, Ill.: David C. Cook Publishing Co., 1989), 179.

Chapter 3

1. Surgeon General Antonia C. Novello, "Health Priorities for the Nineties," *Vital Speeches of the Day,* LVIII, no. 21, 15 August 1992, 666.

2. National Association of State Boards of Education, *Code Blue: Uniting for Healthier Youth.* (Alexandria, Va.: 1990).

3. Lance Morrow, "Childhoods End," *Time,* 9 March 1992, 23.

4. "Study says 1 of 5 High Schoolers Carries a Weapon to School," *Lancaster (Pa.) Intelligencer Journal,* 11 October 1992, A-3.

5. "You Don't Kill Him He Can Come Back and Get You," *Youthworker Update,* VI, no. 10, June 1992, 1.

6. "1991 School Violence by the Numbers," *USA Today,* 18 November 1992, 7A.

7. "Bullying to Battering," *USA Today,* 18 November 1992, 7A.

8. Ronald Henkoff, "Kids Are Killing, Dying, Bleeding," *Fortune,* 10 August 1992, 63.

9. David Blankenhorn, "The Good Family Man: Fatherhood and the Pursuit of Happiness in America," working paper for Institute for American Values, symposium on fatherhood in America, W.P. 12, New York, N.Y., November 1991, 16.

10. Henkoff, "Kids Are Killing," 63.

11. David Elkind, *The Hurried Child: Growing Up Too Fast Too Soon* (Reading, Mass.: Addison-Wesley, 1981).

12. David Elkind, *All Grown Up & No Place To Go: Teenagers In Crisis* (Reading, Mass.: Addison-Wesley, 1984).

13. Neil Postman, *The Disappearance of Childhood* (New York: Delacorte Press, 1982).

14. Valerie Polakow Suransky, *The Erosion of Childhood* (Chicago: University of Chicago Press, 1982).

15. C. John Sommerville, *The Rise and Fall of Childhood* (New York: Vintage Books, 1982).

16. *Code Blue.*

17. Dan Coats, "America's Youth: A Crisis of Character," *Imprimis,* 20, no. 9 (September 1991): 2.

18. Jerrold K. Footlick, "What Happened to the Family?" *Newsweek Special Edition,* winter/spring 1990, 15.

19. *Code Blue.*

20. Barbara Kantrowitz and Pat Wingert, "Step by Step," *Newsweek Special Edition,* winter/spring 1990, 30.

21. J. O. Balswick and K. Morland, *Social Problems: A Christian Perspective* (Grand Rapids: Baker, 1990), 164.

22. Frank F. Furstenburg, Jr., and Andrew J. Cherlin, *Divided Families: What Happens to Children When Parents Part* (Cambridge, Mass.: Harvard University Press, 1991), 11.

23. Overheard, *Newsweek*, winter/spring 1990, 11.

24. Judith Wallerstein and Sandra Blakeslee, *Second Chances: Men, Women and Children a Decade after Divorce* (New York: Tickner & Fields, 1989).

25. *Code Blue.*

26. David Elkind, *Miseducation* (New York: Knopf, 1987), 24.

27. Mark Robichaux, "Business First, Family Second," *The Wall Street Journal*, Friday, 12 May 1989, B-1.

28. "Intervarsity Staffworkers Respond to the Crisis," *Intervarsity*, spring 1989, 14.

29. Walt Mueller, "Let's Tell the Truth about Sex," *Headfirst Ministries Newsletter*, spring 1992, 1.

30. "27% of Students in High School Consider Suicide," *Lancaster (Pa.) Intelligencer Journal*, 20 September 1991, A-1.

31. *Code Blue.*

32. George Barna, *The Barna Report 1992–93* (Ventura, Calif.: Regal Books, 1992), 36.

33. "What Parents Don't Know," *Parents & Teenagers*, February/March 1989, 2.

34. "Times Have Changed: 1991 Teen MRI Study," ad in *American Demographics*, February 1992, 7.

35. Elkind's thesis is covered by his books *The Hurried Child* (Reading, Mass.: Addison-Wesley Publishing Company, 1981) and *All Grown Up & No Place To Go* (Reading, Mass.: Addison-Wesley Publishing Company, 1984).

36. George Michael, "I Want Your Sex" from the album *Faith*, CBS Records, 1987.

37. Barna, *Barna Report*, 44.

38. Tom Sine, "Will the Real Cultural Christians Please Stand Up," *World Vision*, October/November 1989, 21.

39. James Youniss and Jacqueline Smollar, *Adolescent Relations with Mothers, Fathers, and Friends* (Chicago: University of Chicago Press, 1985), 49ff., 68ff., 87.

40. Merton Strommen, *The Five Cries of Youth* (San Francisco: Harper and Row, 1974), 34.

41. Merton P. Strommen and A. Irene Strommen, *The Five Cries of Parents* (San Francisco: Harper and Row, 1985), 68.

Chapter 4

1. Quentin J. Schultze et al., *Dancing in the Dark* (Grand Rapids: Wm. B. Eerdmans, 1991), 87.

2. From the 1980 study "The Teen Environment: A Study of Growth Strategies for Junior Achievement," *Adolescent Sexuality Research Digest* (Dallas: Josh McDowell Ministries, 1987), 25.

3. Schultze et al., *Dancing*, 12–13.

4. Ibid., 99.

5. Terry Lawson, "Wan Madonna Faces Press and 'Prejudice,'" *Lancaster (Pa.) Sunday News*, Sunday, 17 January 1993, H-6.

6. David Fricke, "Red Hot Chili Peppers Naked Truth," *Rolling Stone*, 25 June 1992, 29.

7. Laura Parker, "Florida Jury Acquits Rap Group," *Philadelphia Inquirer*, 21 October 1990, A-1, 10.

8. Elizabeth F. Brown and William R. Hendee, "Adolescents and Their Music: Insights into the Health of Adolescents," *Journal of the American Medical Association* (22 September 1989): 1661.

9. L. Greeson and R. Williams, "Social Implications of Music Videos for Youth: An Analysis of the Content and Effects of MTV," *Youth and Society*, 18 December 1986, 177–89.

10. David Browne, "Snoop's Doggerel," *Entertainment Weekly*, 10 December 1993, 75.

11. Michael Goldberg, "Madonna Seduces Seattle," *Rolling Stone*, 23 May 1985, 20.

12. "Talking with Madonna: The Unbridled Truth," *Newsweek*, 2 November 1992, 102.

13. Owen Gleiberman, "American Hot Wax," *Entertainment Weekly*, 22 January 1993, 40.

14. Ice-T, "The Pickup Artist: Ice-T Reveals the Secrets of Social Intercourse," *Details*, July 1992, 46.

15. Bill Zehme, "Some Guys Have All the Luck," *Rolling Stone*, 11 July 1991, 48.

16. *Media Update,* March/April 1990, 14.

17. Lisa Schwarzbaum, "The Rapping and Unwrapping of Marky Mark," *Entertainment Weekly,* 15 January 1993, 20.

18. Heather Keets, "Shaker Heights," *Entertainment Weekly,* 18 March 1994, 64.

19. Kim Neely, "Is the World's Most Explosive Band about to Self-Destruct, or Is It Just Trying to Grow Up in Public?" *Rolling Stone,* 5 September 1991, 102.

20. Kim Neely, "As the Crowes Fly," *Rolling Stone,* 24 January 1991, 51.

21. Michael Goldberg, "ZZ Top," *Rolling Stone,* 24 January 1991, 13.

22. Kim Neely, "Billy Idol Turns on the Charm," *Rolling Stone,* 1 November 1990, 25.

23. "Caught in the Act," *Lancaster (Pa.) Intelligencer Journal,* 15 January 1993, back page.

24. "Discriminated Derriere," *Lancaster (Pa.) Intelligencer Journal,* 23 January 1993, back page.

25. Katherine Turman, "Revolution Rock," *Spin,* November 1993, 70.

26. Chris Mundy, "Nirvana," *Rolling Stone,* 23 January 1992, 39.

27. *Implications,* 4, nos. 1 and 2, summer 1991, 2.

28. Brown and Hendee, "Adolescents and Their Music," 1659.

29. Peter G. Christenson and Donald F. Roberts, *Popular Music in Early Adolescence,* working paper, Carnegie Council on Adolescent Development, New York, January 1990, 17–18.

30. *Implications,* 2.

31. Ibid.

32. *The Recording Industry Association of America 1991 Consumer Profile.*

33. Ibid., 56.

34. *Entertainment Weekly,* 29 January 1993, 29ff.

35. Neil Straus, "Music Biz Rebounds in '93," *Rolling Stone,* 10 Feburary 1994, 13.

36. "The High Cost of Rockin'," *Youthworker Update,* December 1988, 4.

37. Howard Polskin, "MTV at 10," *TV Guide,* 3 August 1991, 4.

38. Schultze et al., *Dancing,* 204.

39. "The Sayings of Chairman Bob," in Schultze et al., *Dancing in the Dark,* 192.

40. Lee Winfrey, "All Day, All Decade, MTV Rocks U.S.A.," *Philadelphia Inquirer,* 4 August 1991, H-1.

41. "How MTV Has Rocked Television Commercials," *New York Times*, Monday, 9 October 1989, D-6.

42. Ibid.

43. Christenson and Roberts, *Popular Music*, 36ff.

44. Kim France, "Wild Cherry," *Spin*, January 1993, 43.

45. Kim Neely, "Homestyle," *Rolling Stone*, 4 February 1993, 34.

46. Brown and Hendee, "Adolescents and Their Music," 1661.

47. Chris Heath, "Enigmatic for the People," *Details*, February 1993, 67.

48. Ibid., 65.

49. David Fricke, "Teenage Culture on the Skids," *Rolling Stone*, 22 August 1991, 62.

50. Karen Thomas, "A Role Reversal: Madonna as Child," *USA Today*, 8 September 1992, 2D.

51. S. Robert Lichter and Daniel Amundson, *A Day of Television Violence* (Washington, D.C.: Center for Media and Public Affairs, 1992), 27.

52. Michael Medved, *Hollywood vs. America* (New York: HarperCollins, 1992), 192.

53. Brown and Hendee, "Adolescents and Their Music," 1661.

54. Ibid.

55. "Gangsta Wars," *Entertainment Weekly*, 18 December 1992, 6.

56. Robert Oscar Bakke, "The Kids Want to See Action," *Eternity*, January 1985, 23.

57. "Rap Rage," *Newsweek*, 19 March 1990, 59.

58. Tipper Gore, *Raising PG Kids in an X-Rated Society* (Nashville: Abingdon Press, 1987), 89.

59. "Wild Thing," *New Statesman and Society*, 7 July 1989, 46.

60. Bob Morris, "Higher Ground," *Details*, February 1993, 28.

61. David Fricke, "An Earful of Wax," *Rolling Stone*, 18 April 1991, 104.

62. Deena Weinstein, *Heavy Metal: A Cultural Sociology* (New York: Lexington Books, 1991), 89.

63. Ibid.

64. DeAnthony Darnell, "America's Most Blunted," *The Source*, January 1993, 92.

65. Mike Gitter, "Danzig," *Rolling Stone,* 18 February 1993, 29.

66. *Implications,* 5, no. 2, fall 1992, 20.

67. Schultze et al., *Dancing,* 165.

68. Anton LaVey as quoted by Jerry Johnston, *The Edge of Evil* (Waco, Tex.: Word, 1989), 159.

69. Anton LaVey, *The Satanic Bible* (New York: Avon Books, 1969), 25.

70. *Webster's New Collegiate Dictionary,* 10th ed., 963.

71. "Madonna Says Sinead Went Too Far with Pope," *Lancaster (Pa.) Intelligencer Journal,* 19 October 1992, back page.

72. Legs McNeil, "Sinead," *Spin,* April 1990, 58.

73. Edna Gundersen, "Stage Image No Indication of True Self," *USA Today,* 9 October 1992.

74. Cal Thomas, *The Death of Ethics in America* (Waco, Tex.: Word, 1988), 105.

75. Hits and the Pits, *Entertainment Weekly,* 1992 Year-End Special, 9.

76. Michael Azzerrad, "Inside the Heart and Mind of Kurt Cobain," *Rolling Stone,* 16 April 1992, 39.

77. Ibid.

78. Mike Yaconelli and Jim Burns, *High School Ministry* (Grand Rapids: Zondervan, 1986), 37.

79. "Our Lives, Our Music," *Rolling Stone,* 26 November 1992, 50.

80. Al Menconi with Dave Hart, "Today's Music: A Window to Your Child's Soul," *Media Update,* May/June 1990, 1.

81. Ibid.

82. Brown and Hendee, "Adolescents and Their Music," 1659.

83. *Implications,* 4, nos. 1 and 2, 15.

84. Ibid.

85. David Fricke, "R.E.M.," *Rolling Stone,* 5 March 1992, 47.

86. Ibid., 49.

87. Stephen Parolini, "Music, Movies, Misc.," *Parents & Teenagers,* October/November 1989, 30.

88. David Browne, "Turn That @#!% Down!" *Entertainment Weekly,* 21 August 1992, 22.

89. David Browne, "Stark Raving Fad," *Entertainment Weekly,* 9 April 1993, 23.

90. *Implications,* 5, no. 2, 21.

91. "The Word on the Street Is Heard in the Beat," *Newsweek,* 11 May 1992, 53.

92. Alan Light, "Rappers Sounded Warning," *Rolling Stone,* 9 July 1992, 17.

93. "Who Buys Gangsta Rap Albums, Anyway?" *Youthworker Update,* April 1994, 4.

94. "Rap's Reformation," *New Statesman & Society,* 2 November 1990, 27.

95. William Shaw, "A Gangsta's Tale," *Details,* February 1993, 103.

96. Lynn Minton, "Is Heavy Metal Dangerous?" *Parade,* 20 September 1990, 12.

97. Mikal Gilmore, "Heavy Metal Thunder," *Rolling Stone,* 11 July 1991, 52.

98. Weinstein, *Heavy Metal,* 31.

99. Parolini, "Music, Movies, Misc.," *28.*

100. Browne, "Turn That Down!" 20.

101. Ibid.

102. Gilmore, "Heavy Metal Thunder," 124.

103. Weinstein, *Heavy Metal,* 50.

Chapter 5

1. Rosalind Silver, "Media Culture: Why We Can't 'Just Say No,'" *Media and Values,* winter 1992, 2.

2. Neil Postman, *Amusing Ourselves to Death* (New York: Penguin Books, 1985), 10.

3. Quentin J. Schultze, *Redeeming Television* (Downers Grove, Ill.: InterVarsity Press, 1992), 43.

4. George Comstock, *Television in America* (Beverly Hills: Sage, 1980), 123.

5. Ira Wolfman, "Cosby vs. The Simpsons: Is TV Programming Your Family?" *Family Circle,* 16 October 1990, 80.

6. George Dessart, "Of Tastes and Times," *Television Quarterly,* XXVI, no. 2 (1992), 41.

7. Comstock, *Television,* ix.

8. Nancy Ten Kate, "TV Dynasty," *American Demographics,* January 1991, 16.

9. Jane Delano Brown et al., "The Influence of New Media and Family Structure on Young Adolescents' Television and Radio Use," *Communication Research,* 17, no. 1 (February 1990): 72.

10. Kate, "TV Dynasty," 16.

11. Comstock, *Television*, 4.

12. Pete Hamill, "Crack and the Box: Television Helps Pave the Way to Addiction," *Media & Values,* spring/summer 1991, 5.

13. Judith Waldrop, "Television Viewing," *American Demographics Marketing Tools,* February 1993, 16.

14. Brandon S. Centerwall, "Television and Violence: The Scale of the Problem and Where to Go from Here," *Journal of the American Medical Association* 267, no. 22 (10 June 1992): 3059.

15. Hamill, "Crack and the Box," 5.

16. "Study Shows TV Major Influence in Children's Lives," *National Coalition on Television Violence News,* 13, no. 1–4, January–April 1992, 9.

17. "Teens and TV," *Newsweek Special Issue,* summer/fall 1990, 36.

18. "TV Major Influence," 9.

19. Comstock, *Television*, 59.

20. Schultze, *Redeeming Television*, 46.

21. Ibid., 62.

22. Comstock, *Television,* 57.

23. Ibid.

24. Claudia Montague, "How Viewers Feel about TV," *American Demographics,* March 1993, 18.

25. Schultze, *Redeeming Television*, 77.

26. Richard Reeves, "The Networks Prefer the Low Road," *Philadelphia Inquirer,* 9 March 1989, A-23.

27. Schultze, *Redeeming Television*, 129.

28. Neil Hickey, "How Much Violence?" *TV Guide,* 22 August 1992, 18.

29. "Put It on TV," *Lancaster (Pa.) Intelligencer Journal,* 10 March 1993, back page.

30. Martin Kihn, "Does Crime Pay?" *US,* August 1992, 22.

31. Dana Kennedy, "Scandal Inc.," *Entertainment Weekly,* 4 March 1994, 20.

32. National Association of Elementary School Principals, *Taming the Tube,* an undated report, Alexandria, Virginia.

33. Diane Duston, "Network and Cable TV Tie in Program Violence War," *Huntsville Times,* 28 January 1993, C7.

34. Parker Page, "Quiz and Questions Probe Impact of Violence," *Media & Values,* fall/winter 1991, 22.

35. S. Robert Lichter, Linda S. Lichter, and Stanley Rothman, *Watching America* (New York: Prentice Hall Press, 1991), 187.

36. Deborah Prothrow-Stith, *Deadly Consequences* (New York: HarperCollins, 1991), 39.

37. Ted Baehr, "The Christian Film and Television Commission: Why, What, & How," *Religious Broadcasting,* December 1991, 22.

38. "Sons of Violence," *Psychology Today,* July/August 1992, 13; "Does TV Violence Cause Real Violence?" *TV Guide,* 22 August 1992, 11.

39. Centerwall, "Television and Violence," 3061.

40. Barry S. Sapolsky and Joseph O. Tabarlet, "Sex in Primetime Television: 1979 versus 1989," *Journal of Broadcasting and Electronic Media,* 15, no. 4, fall 1991, 514.

41. "As the World Turns," *Psychology Today,* September/October 1992, 12.

42. Lichter, Lichter, and Rothman, *Watching America,* 26.

43. Josh McDowell and Dick Day, *Why Wait?: What You Need to Know about the Teen Sexuality Crisis* (San Bernadino, Calif.: Here's Life Publishers, 1987), 40.

44. Lichter, Lichter, and Rothman, *Watching America,* 26.

45. Sapolsky and Tabarlet, "Sex in Primetime Television," 514.

46. "Defend Family Values: Turn Off TV November 13," *Morality in Media,* September/October 1992, 3.

47. Casey Davidson, "It's a Dirty Job," *Entertainment Weekly,* 23 October 1992, 9.

48. "Defend Family Values," 3.

49. The Week, *Entertainment Weekly,* 12 February 1993, 45.

50. Michael Kaplan, "You Get What You Pay For: Everything You Wanted to Know about Cable Sex," *US,* August 1992, 80.

51. *Focus on the Family Citizen,* July 1989, 8.

52. Barbara Hansen, "TV's Reflection of Life," *USA Today,* 6 July 1993, 3D.

53. Benjamin Svetkey, "Was It Good for You?" *Entertainment Weekly,* 23 October 1992, 24.

54. Tim Sommer, "It's a Family Affair?" *Spin,* 67.

55. David Blankenhorn, *The Good Family Man: Fatherhood and the Pursuit of Happiness in America,* working paper, Institute for American Values for the symposium on fatherhood in America, W.P. 12, November 1991, 9.

56. Lichter, Lichter, and Rothman, *Watching America,* 12–14.

57. Ibid.

58. *The Mediator,* 8, no. 1, 1.

59. J. Francis Davis, "The Power of Images: Creating the Myths of Our Time," *Media & Values,* winter 1992, 5.

60. Ibid., 6.

61. Michael Warren, "Storytellers Shape Spiritual Values," *Media & Values,* winter 1992, 19.

62. "Young People and Alcohol," *Pennsylvania Issue,* 80, no. 2, fall/winter 1992, 1.

63. Lichter, Lichter, and Rothman, *Watching America,* 301.

64. Quentin J. Schultze et al., *Dancing in the Dark* (Grand Rapids: Wm. B. Eerdmans, 1991), 220ff.

65. Ibid., 212ff.

66. Michael Medved, *Hollywood vs. America* (New York: HarperCollins, 1992), 3.

67. "Ready, Cassette, Go," *TV Guide,* 22 August 1992, 5.

68. *Implications,* 5, no. 2, fall 1992, 18.

69. Ibid.

70. Josh McDowell Ministry, *Teen Sex Survey in the Evangelical Church: Executive Summary Report,* 1987, 15.

71. Mike Yorkey, "Christian Film Critics Urge Moviegoers to Seek Guidance," *Focus on the Family Citizen,* January 1989, 7.

72. Schultze et al., *Dancing,* 222.

73. Lin Johnson, "Sex and the Media," *Jr. High Ministry,* May/August 1990, 30.

74. Medved, *Hollywood vs. America,* 186.

75. Vincent Canby, "Now at a Theater Near You: A Skyrocketing Body Count," *New York Times,* 16 July 1990, C-11.

76. Ellen Blum Barish, "The Thrill of Chills," *Current Health 2,* March 1992, 24.

77. Schultze et al., *Dancing,* 234.

78. Ibid.

79. Medved, *Hollywood vs. America,* 25.

80. Ibid., 50.

81. Susan Campbell, "Hidden Hooks in Children's TV Ads," *Philadelphia Inquirer,* 2 December 1990, H-7.

82. Christopher Power, "Getting 'Em While They're Young," *Business Week,* 9 September 1991, 94.

83. Carrie Goerne, "Marketers Try to Get More Creative in Reaching Teens," *Marketing News,* 5 August 1991, 2.

84. Schultze, *Redeeming Television,* 46.

85. "Teens and TV," 36.

86. Waldrop, "Television Viewing," 17.

87. Goerne, "Marketers Get Creative," 6.

88. Andrew Sullivan, "Flogging Underwear," *New Republic,* 18 January 1988, 22.

89. Edward Sozanski, "The Power of Photos in Advertising," *Philadelphia Inquirer,* 22 January 1989, C-1.

90. Jay F. Davis, "How Advertisers Sell Addiction," *Media & Values,* spring/summer 1991, 29.

91. Teresa Riordan, "Miller Guy Life," *New Republic,* 27 March 1989, 16.

92. Ibid.

93. Jean Kilbourne, "Deadly Persuasion: 7 Myths Alcohol Advertisers Want You to Believe," *Media & Values,* spring/summer 1991, 11ff.

94. Joseph R. DiFranza et al., "RJR Nabisco's Cartoon Camel Promotes Camel Cigarettes to Children," *Journal of the American Medical Association* (11 December 1991): 3149ff.

95. Paul Kurnit, "10 Tips from the Top Agency," *Advertising Age,* 10 February 1992, S-10ff.

96. Paul Gullifor, "Family Communication Patterns and Adolescent Use of Radio," *Journal of Radio Studies* 1 (1992): 1.

97. "Study Details Teen's Heavy Use of Radio," *Broadcasting,* 1 July 1991, 27.

98. Jane Delano Brown et al., "Adolescents' Television and Radio Use," 73.

99. Ibid., 72.

100. "Teens' Heavy Use of Radio," 37.

101. "Where the FCC Draws the Line," *Broadcasting,* 2 November 1992, 56.

102. Carrie Borzillo, "KACE Clears Air of 'Negative' Songs," *Billboard,* 30 October 1993, 78.

103. David Wharton, "Sassy Magazine's Editor Is 29 Going On 16," *Sunday News,* Lancaster, Pa., 17 January 1993, G-5.

104. Teenager Research Unlimited Syndicated Study, 1986, 69.

105. David Lynn, "Teenzines," *Youthworker,* fall 1992, 113ff.

106. Paul Smith, "Mothers Fight a Sleazy Teen Magazine," *Focus on the Family Citizen,* July 1988, 4.

107. "Public Outcry Needed," *Concerned Women,* August 1988, 20.

Chapter 6

1. February, *Rolling Stone,* 13 December 1990, 43.

2. "Top Figures Regarded by Kids as Heroes," *TV etc.,* 2, no. 2, March/April 1990, 2.

3. Quentin Schultze, *Redeeming Television* (Downers Grove, Ill.: InterVarsity, 1992), 167.

4. "Turn It Off," *AFA Journal,* May 1989, 9.

5. Tom Hess, "The Quiet Man Who Tripped Up Donahue," *Citizen,* 16 November 1992, 3.

6. "Study Shows TV Major Influence in Children's Lives," *National Coalition on Television Violence News,* 13, nos. 1–4, January–February 1992, 9.

Chapter 7

1. David G. Perry, Sara J. Kusel, and Louise C. Perry, "Victims of Peer Aggression," *Developmental Psychology* 24, no. 6 (1988): 807ff.

2. Donald M. Joy, "Adolescents in Socio-Psychological Perspective" in Roy B. Zuck and Warren S. Benson, *Youth Education in the Church* (Chicago: Moody Press, 1978), 95.

3. Eugene Roehlkepartain, ed., "How Much Time with Friends," in *Youth Ministry Resource Book* (Loveland, Colo.: Group Books, 1988), 37ff.

4. See David Elkind, *All Grown Up & No Place to Go* (Reading, Mass.: Addison-Wesley, 1984).

5. James Youniss and Jacqueline Smollar, *Adolescent Relations with Mothers, Fathers, and Friends* (Chicago: University of Chicago Press, 1985), 94.

6. Lynn Minton, "Fresh Voices: 'How Do You Resist Peer Pressure?'" *Parade,* 25 March 1990, 16.

7. "Peer Pressure," *Youthworker Update,* February 1987, 3.

8. Robert Laurent, *Keeping Your Teen in Touch with God* (Elgin, Ill.: David C. Cook, 1988), 86.

9. Elkind, *All Grown Up,* 24.

10. Bob Greene as quoted in "Party Line," *Youthworker Update,* June 1988, 1ff.

11. "Quest for the Perfect Body," *Youthworker Update,* September 1988, 2.

12. Jolene Roehlkepartain, "Danger! Steroids," *Parents & Teenagers,* June/July 1989, 19.

13. Bill Barol, "Anatomy of a Fad," *Newsweek Special Issue,* summer/fall 1990, 41.

14. Joanne B. Eicher, Suzanne Baizerman, and John Michelman, "Adolescent Dress, Part II: A Qualitative Study of Suburban High School Students," *Adolescence,* 26, no. 103, fall 1991, 679ff.

15. "Peer Pressure: Asset or Liability?" *Search Institute Source,* IV, no. 3, September 1988, 2.

16. Joe Schwartz, "Teenager Attitudes," *American Demographics,* August 1987, 43ff.

17. A. J. Hostetler, "Teen Killed for Pair of Gold Earrings," *Lancaster (Pa.) Intelligencer Journal,* 24 October 1991, back page.

18. "Asset or Liability?" 2.

19. "Pressure to Try Alcohol or Marijuana," *Youth Ministry Resource,* 41.

20. Susan Dodge, "Substance Free Housing at U. of Michigan Offers Students a Voluntary Haven from Drugs, Alcohol, and Peer Pressure," *Chronicle of Higher Education,* 13 March 1991, A-31.

21. Josh McDowell and Dick Day, *Why Wait?: What You Need to Know about the Teen Sexuality Crisis* (San Bernadino, Calif.: Here's Life Publishers, 1987), 98.

22. Lee Shilts, "The Relationship of Early Adolescent Substance Use to Extracurricular Activities, Peer Influence, and Personal Attitudes," *Adolescence,* 26, no. 103, fall 1991, 615ff.

23. McDowell and Day, *Why Wait,* 105ff.

Chapter 8

1. "In Defense of a Little Virginity," *Focus on the Family,* 1992.

2. "Teenage Girls Take AIDS Risk for Gang Initiation," *Lancaster (Pa.) Intelligencer Journal,* 27 April 1993, A-3.

3. "What World's Teenagers Are Saying," *U.S. News & World Report,* 30 June 1986, 68.

4. Dale Mezzacappa, "Survey Finds Most Philadelphia 10th Graders Have Had Sex," *Philadelphia Inquirer,* 24 January 1989, A-1.

5. Nancy Gibbs, "Teens: The Rising Risk of AIDS," *Time,* 2 September 1991, 60.

6. Robert Byrd, "Most High School Kids Aren't Virgins, Survey Finds," *Johnstown (Pa.) Tribune Democrat,* 4 January 1992.

7. Josh McDowell and Dick Day, *Why Wait?: What You Need to Know about the Teen Sexuality Crisis* (San Bernadino, Calif.: Here's Life Publishers, 1987), 23.

8. Robert Coles and Geoffrey Stokes, *Sex and the American Teenager* (New York: Harper & Row, 1985), 72.

9. "Teen Sex in America," *Youthworker Update,* December 1991, 4.

10. "Selected Behaviors That Increase Risk for HIV Infection among High School Students—U.S., 1990," *Journal of the American Medical Association* 267, no. 18 (13 May 1992): 2449.

11. Ibid.

12. Sharon Sheppard, "Teen Sex Survey in the Evangelical Church," *Christian Parenting Today,* November/December 1989, 70.

13. David Van Biema, "What's Gone Wrong with Teen Sex," *People,* 13 April 1987, 112.

14. Joseph P. Shapiro, "The Teen Pregnancy Boom," *U.S. News & World Report,* 13 July 1992, 38.

15. Mona McCullough and Avraham Scherman, "Adolescent Pregnancy: Contributing Factors and Strategies for Prevention," *Adolescence,* 26, no. 104, winter 1991, 809.

16. "Teenage Pregnancy," *Search Institute Source,* 1, no. 1, November 1985, 1.

17. Julie Stacey, "Children Bearing Children," *USA Today,* 22 February 1994, 2A.

18. McCullough and Scherman, "Adolescent Pregnancy," 809.

19. "Abortion in the U.S.," *Christianity Today,* 11 January 1993, 37.

20. Dinah Richard, *Has Sex Education Failed Our Teenagers?: A Research Report* (Pomona, Calif.: Focus on the Family Publishing, 1990), 24.

21. National Association of State Boards of Education, *Code Blue: Uniting for Healthier Youth* (Alexandria, Va.: 1990).

22. Kathleen McCoy, "It's 4 p.m. Do You Know What Your Teens Are Doing?" *Family Circle,* 14 May 1991, 51.

23. "A Little Virginity."

24. Barbara Kantrowitz, "The Unhealthy Facts of Life," *Newsweek Special Issue,* summer/fall 1990, 57.

25. McCoy, "It's 4 p.m.," 51.

26. "A Little Virginity."

27. McCoy, "It's 4 p.m.," 5.

28. Antonia Novello, "Health Priorities for the Nineties: The Quest for Prevention," *Vital Speeches of the Day,* LVIII, no. 21, 15 August 1992, 668.

29. Barbara Kantrowitz, "Teenagers and AIDS," *Newsweek,* 3 August 1992, 45.

30. Center for Disease Control, *Quarterly HIV/AIDS Surveillance Report,* 31 March 1993.

31. "Staying Current: Straight Talk about HIV/AIDS," *Update,* VI., no. 2, spring 1994, 1.

32. Kantrowitz, "Teenagers and AIDS," 46.

33. "Sex in the 90's," *Spin,* April 1993, 16.

34. "The Root Problem," *Religious Broadcasting,* January 1987, 18.

35. "Teen Sex in America," 4.

36. Tony Campolo, "Sex Ed's Failure Rate," *Christianity Today,* 3 February 1993, 22.

37. "Sex Education: A New Philosophy for America," *The Family in America* (Mount Morris, Ill.: The Rockford Institute Center on the Family in America, 1989), 3.

38. Ibid., 4.

39. Richard, *Has Sex Education Failed?* 52.

40. Letter to Concerned Women for America from Alana Myers, no date.

41. "A Little Rape Is Alright," *Youthworker Update,* June 1988, 3.

42. Sharon D. White and Richard R. DeBlassie, "Adolescent Sexual Behavior," *Adolescence,* 27, no. 105, spring 1992, 189.

43. "Dear Diary," *Psychology Today,* May/June 1992, 18.

44. White and DeBlassie, "Adolescent Sexual Behavior," 185.

45. "The Younger, the Sooner," *Youthworker,* spring 1987, 122ff.

46. White and DeBlassie, "Adolescent Sexual Behavior," 187.

47. McCoy, "It's 4 p.m.," 51.

48. White and DeBlassie, "Adolescent Sexual Behavior," 185.

49. Josh McDowell, "Teens Speak Out," in *What I Wish My Parents Knew about My Sexuality* (San Bernadino, Calif.: Here's Life Publishers, 1987), 130.

50. Jolene Roehlkepartian, "A Shift in Teen Dating Habits," *Parents of Teenagers,* March/April 1993, 35.

51. Kim Painter, "Fewer Kids Save Sex for Adulthood," *USA Today,* 5 March 1991, 1D.

52. Ibid.

53. White and DeBlassie, "Adolescent Sexual Behavior," 184.

54. "Where Christians Learn," in *Youth Ministry Resource Book* (Loveland, Colo.: Group Books, 1988), 52.

55. Merton P. Strommen and A. Irene Strommen, *Five Cries of Parents* (New York: Harper & Row, 1985), 72.

56. John Vertefeuille, "Lowering the Odds of Sexual Promiscuity," *Youthworker,* summer 1989, 37.

57. Carl Henry, speech at Southern Baptist Convention, *Vital Speeches of the Day,* 15 May 1992, 479.

58. Joan Kahn and Kathryn London, "Premarital Sex and the Risk of Divorce," *Journal of Marriage and Family,* November 1991, 845–55.

59. Arland Thornton and Donald Camburn, "Religious Participation and Adolescent Sexual Behavior and Attitudes," *Journal of Marriage and Family,* August 1989, 651.

60. McDowell and Day, *Why Wait,* 333ff.

61. Ann Wharton, "How to Teach Teens about Abstinence," *Focus on the Family Citizen,* June 1988, 5.

62. "From a 15-Year-Old Girl, a Lesson about Sex and Contraception," *Philadelphia Inquirer,* 5 October 1990.

Chapter 9

1. Rory Glynn, "Bargains, Flops in the World of Sports," *USA Today,* 5 March 1991, 2C.

2. George Barna, *The Frog in the Kettle* (Ventura, Calif.: Regal, 1990), 33.

3. *Webster's New Collegiate Dictionary,* 10th ed., 717.

4. Joseph Spiers, "Will the Busters Be Spenders?" *Fortune,* 4 May 1992, 26.

5. David G. Myers, "Who's Happy? Who's Not?" *Christianity Today,* 23 November 1992, 25.

6. William Ecenbarger, "A Nation of Thieves," *Philadelphia Inquirer Magazine,* 29 November 1987, 22.

7. James U. McNeal, "Growing Up in the Market," *American Demographics,* October 1992, 46ff.

8. Christopher Power, "Getting 'Em While They're Young," *Business Week,* 9 September 1991, 94.

9. Doris L. Walsh, "Targeting Teens," *American Demographics,* February 1985, 21.

10. Ibid., 22.

11. Ibid.

12. Carrie Goerne, "Marketers Try to Get More Creative in Reaching Teens," *Marketing News,* 5 August 1991, 2.

13. Steven Waldman and Karen Springen, "Too Old, Too Fast?" *Newsweek,* 16 November 1992, 87.

14. "Parents Differ about Allowances," *Youthworker Update,* January 1992, 3.

15. Waldman, "Too Old?" 81.

16. Ibid.

17. John Schwartz, "Stalking the Youth Market," *Newsweek Special Issue,* summer/fall 1990, 35.

18. Barna, *Frog in the Kettle,* 38.

19. "Protoadults Crave Independence That Comes with Wheels," *Youthworker Update,* March 1990, 1.

20. Annetta Miller, "Work and What It's Worth," *Newsweek Special Issue,* summer/fall 1990, 30.

21. "Religious Faith Firm Foundation for Charity," *Christianity Today,* 19 November 1990, 63.

22. "Cutthroat Execs in Training," *Youthworker Update,* October 1989, 3.

23. Ron Harris, "For Too Many Youths, Clothing an Obsession," *Philadelphia Inquirer,* 23 November 1989, I-7.

24. Rick Telander, "Your Sneakers or Your Life," *Sports Illustrated,* 14 May 1990, 36–49.

25. Kenneth S. Kantzer, "Ron Sider Is Mostly Right," *Christianity Today,* 8 October 1990, 21.

26. Tom Sine, "Will the Real Cultural Christians Please Stand Up," *World Vision,* October/November 1989, 21.

27. Robert Wuthnow, "Maladies of the Middle Class," *Princeton Seminary Bulletin,* XIII, no. 3, November 1992, 296.

28. "Harper's Index," *Harper's Magazine,* 277, no. 1661, October 1988, 15.

29. Otto Friedrich, "Flashy Symbol of an Acquisitive Age," *Time,* 16 January 1989, 54.

30. "I Want An Office—Now!" *Youthworker Update,* June 1992, 1.

31. C. S. Lewis, *The Screwtape Letters,* Letter 28.

32. Rodney Clapp, "Superkids and Superparents," *Christianity Today,* 18 September 1987, 14.

33. "Maybe Chocolate Cheesecake Would Have Done the Trick," *Youthworker Update,* May 1990, 6.

34. Cliff Schimmels, *What Parents Try to Forget about Adolescence* (Elgin, Ill.: David C. Cook Publishing, 1989), 57.

35. Wuthnow, "Maladies of the Middle Class," 291.

36. Brian O'Reilly, "Why Grade 'A' Execs Get an 'F' as Parents," *Fortune,* 1 January 1990, 37.

37. "Welcome to Camp Dow Jones," *Youthworker Update,* September 1989, 1.

38. Bruce Baldwin, *Beyond the Cornucopia Kids* (Wilmington, N.C.: Direction Dynamics, 1988), 11.

39. Ralph F. Minear, *Kids Who Have Too Much* (Nashville: Thomas Nelson, 1989), 10.

40. C. S. Lewis, *Mere Christianity* (New York: Macmillan, 1952), 120.

Chapter 10

1. Antonia C. Novello, "Health Priorities for the Nineties: The Quest for Prevention," *Vital Speeches of the Day,* LVIII, no. 21, 15 August 1992, 667.

2. Louis S. Richman, "Struggling to Save Our Kids," *Fortune,* 10 August 1992, 35.

3. Dean Borgman, "Alcoholism," *Encyclopedia of Youth Studies.*

4. Department of Health and Human Services, Office of Inspector General, *Youth and Alcohol: A National Survey,* RP0799, 1991, 4.

5. Ibid.

6. "Alcohol Use Starts Early," *Parents & Teenagers,* February/March 1989, 3.

7. Ibid.

8. *Youth and Alcohol,* 1.

9. Lewis J. Lord, "Coming to Grips with Alcoholism," *U.S. News & World Report,* 30 November 1987, 56.

10. "Adolescent Chemical Use," *Search Institute Source,* II, no.1, January 1986, 1.

11. David Gelman, "A Much Riskier Passage," *Newsweek Special Issue,* summer/fall 1990, 12.

12. *Youth and Alcohol,* 3–4.

13. Ibid., 6–7.

14. National Association of State Boards of Education, *Code Blue: Uniting for Healthier Youth* (Alexandria, Va.: 1990), 3.

15. Borgman, "Alcoholism," 2.

16. *Youth and Alcohol.*

17. Ibid., 11.

18. *Code Blue,* 3.

19. Insurance Institute for Highway Safety, *Teenager Drivers: Questions and Answers,* fact sheet (Arlington, Va.) April 1992, 2.

20. *Implications,* Spring 1992, 8.

21. Novello, "Health Priorities," 668.

22. Eugene Roehlkepartain, ed., "Alcohol: Leading Gateway Drug," in *Youth Ministry Resource Book* (Loveland, Colo.: Group Books, 1988), 134.

23. George Gerbner, "Stories That Hurt: Tobacco, Alcohol, and Other Drugs in the Mass Media," in *Youth and Drugs: Society's Mixed Messages* (Rockville, Md.: Office for Substance Abuse Prevention, 1990), 57.

24. Ibid., 68.

25. Novello, "Health Priorities," 670.

26. Gerbner, "Stories That Hurt," 68.

27. Novello, "Health Priorities," 671.

28. Joseph R. DiFranza and Joe B. Tye, "Who Profits from Tobacco Sales to Children?" *Journal of the American Medical Association* 263, no. 20 (23 May 1990): 2785.

29. Lloyd D. Johnston, Patrick M. O'Malley, and Jerald G. Bachman, *Drug Use among American High School Seniors, College Students and Young Adults, 1975– 1990,* vol. I (Rockville, Md.: National Institute on Drug Abuse, 1991), 9.

30. "Study: Half of Young Smokeless Tobacco Users Started before Age 13," *Lancaster (Pa.) Intelligencer Journal,* 6 January 1993, A-5.

31. Johnston et al., *Drug Use among Seniors,* 13.

32. DiFranza and Tye, "Who Profits?" 2784.

33. "U.S. Teens Continue to Drink, Smoke," *Lancaster (Pa.) Intelligencer Journal,* 18 September 1992, A-3.

34. Johnston et al., *Drug Use among Seniors,* 15.

35. "Baseball Players' Influence Blamed for Greater Use of Snuff and Tobacco," *Lancaster (Pa.) Intelligencer Journal,* 16 April 1993, back page.

36. DiFranza and Tye, "Who Profits?" 2785.

37. Ibid., 2784.

38. Charles Scriven, "Why the Marlboro Man Wants Your Kids," *Christianity Today,* 8 April 1991, 33.

39. Novello, "Health Priorities," 671.

40. "Youth Who Smoke More Likely to Use Drugs, Study Says," *Lancaster (Pa.) Intelligencer Journal,* 11 March 1994, back page

41. L. D. Johnston, quoted by Lawrence Wallack and Kitty Corbett in "Illicit Drug, Tobacco, and Alcohol Use among Youth: Trends and Promising Approaches in Prevention," in *Youth and Drugs: Society's Mixed Messages* (Rockville, Md.: Office for Substance Abuse Prevention, 1990), 7.

42. "We're Number One!" *Youthworker Update,* January 1988, 4.

43. Johnston et al., *Drug Use among Seniors,* 5.

44. "Adolescent Chemical Use," 2.

45. Johnston et al., *Drug Use among Seniors,* 14.

46. "Parents Underestimate Drug Usage," *Group,* September 1987, 20.

47. Johnston et al., *Drug Use among Seniors,* 29.

48. Ibid., 29.

49. Jean Seligmann, "The New Age of Aquarius," *Newsweek,* 3 February 1992, 67.

50. Johnston et al., *Drug Use among Seniors,* 32.

51. Mark S. Gold, *The Facts about Drugs and Alcohol* (New York: Bantam, 1986), 104.

52. David Browne, "Stark Raving Fad: The Idiot's Guide to What All Those Zany Kids Are Doing," *Entertainment Weekly,* 9 April 1993, 23.

53. Ibid., 29.

54. "Survey Shows More Pre–High School Children Using Drugs," *Lancaster (Pa.) Intelligencer Journal,* 14 April 1993, A-3.

55. Joannie M. Schrof, "Pumped Up," *U.S. News & World Report,* 1 June 1992, 55.

56. Ibid.

57. Craig Neff, ed., "Hooked," *Sports Illustrated,* 24 September 1990, 27.

58. Johnston et al., *Drug Use among Seniors,* 14.

59. Ibid.

60. Ibid., 31.

61. Mike Sager, "The Ice Age," *Rolling Stone,* 8 February 1990, 110.

62. Johnston et al., *Drug Use among Seniors,* 31.

63. "Adolescent Chemical Use," 2.

64. Barbara Goldstein, "Out-of-Control Teen Drinking," *Time,* 6 January 1992, 14.

65. "Why Kids Drink: Peers and Parents," *Youthworker Update,* January 1993, 5.

66. *Youth and Alcohol,* 7.

67. Ibid.

68. Rob Tannenbaum, "The Disciples of Pot," *Rolling Stone,* 28 May 1992, 18.

69. Karen Peterson, "Putting a Cap on Teenage Drinking," *USA Today,* 15 May 1990, 2D.

70. "Why Kids Drink," 5.

71. Drugs and Crime Data Center and Clearinghouse, *Drugs and Crime Facts, 1991,* brochure (Rockville, Md.: 1992), 16.

72. *Youth and Alcohol,* 11ff.

73. Marilyn Elias, "Latchkey Teens More Likely to Drink, Smoke," *USA Today,* 6 September 1989, 1D.

74. *Youth and Alcohol,* 13.

75. Ibid., 13ff.

76. Novello, "Health Priorities," 667.

77. *Youth and Alcohol,* 7.

78. Tim Friend, "Insecure Girls More Prone to Drug Use," *USA Today,* 11 June 1992, 1D.

79. Judith H. Jaynes and Cheryl A. Rugg, *Adolescents, Alcohol and Drugs* (Springfield, Ill.: Charles C. Thomas, 1988), 13–22.

80. Vic Sussman, "How to Beat Drugs," *U.S. News & World Report*, 11 September 1989, 72.

81. "Adolescent Chemical Use," 2.

82. Ibid.

83. *Youth and Alcohol*, 10.

Chapter 11

1. Stephen Fried, "Over the Edge," *Philadelphia Magazine*, October 1984, 97.

2. Philip Bennett, "A Bottle of Wine before the End," *Boston Globe*, 10 November 1984, 21.

3. John Q. Baucom, "The Teenage Suicide Crisis," *Light*, June/July 1987, 4.

4. Diane Eble, "Too Young to Die," *Christianity Today*, 20 March 1987, 19.

5. Ibid.

6. "27% of Students in High School Consider Suicide," *Lancaster (Pa.) Intelligencer Journal*, 20 September 1991, A-1.

7. National Institute of Mental Health, *Suicide Facts*, OM 00-4081, March 1992.

8. Teen Suicide Prevention Taskforce, *Teen Suicide Prevention* (1986): 4.

9. *Gallup Survey on Teenage Suicide*, December 1991, 147.

10. American Psychiatric Association, *Let's Talk Facts about Teen Suicide*, pamphlet (1988): 5.

11. National Association of State Boards of Education, *Code Blue: Uniting for Healthier Youth* (Alexandria, Va.: 1990).

12. Ibid.

13. *Let's Talk Facts*, 5.

14. "Fear of Suicide Pact Causes School in Erie to Cancel Graduation," *Philadelphia Inquirer*, 9 June 1988, B-9.

15. *Gallup Survey on Teenage Suicide*, 9.

16. American Academy of Child and Adolescent Psychiatry, *The Depressed Child*, fact sheet, March 1988.

17. Maureen Culkin Rhyne et al., "Children at Risk for Depression," *American Journal of Nursing*, December 1986, 1379.

18. Brad L. Neiger and Rodney W. Hopkins, "Adolescent Suicide: Character Traits of High-Risk Teenagers," *Adolescence,* XXIII, no. 90, summer 1988, 472.

19. American Psychiatric Association, *Facts about Depression,* 1.

20. National Institute of Mental Health, *What to Do When a Friend Is Depressed,* pamphlet.

21. Dick Polman, "Children in the Thick of a Thinness Fad," *Philadelphia Inquirer,* 11 May 1986, G-1.

22. Ibid.

23. Fried, "Over the Edge," 96ff.

24. Educational Resources Information Center and the Counseling and Personnel Services Clearinghouse, "Teenage Suicide: Identification, Intervention and Prevention," in *Highlights,* fact sheet (University of Michigan: 1985).

25. Dean Borgman, "Child Stress," *Encyclopedia of Youth Studies* (1986): 1.

26. *Gallup Survey on Teenage Suicide,* 4.

27. Ibid.

28. "Drug Use Down, Suicide Up for High Achievers," *Group,* February 1989, 15.

29. Baucom, "Teenage Suicide Crisis," 5.

30. R. E. O. White, "Nihilism," in *The Evangelical Dictionary of Theology* (Grand Rapids: Baker, 1984), 778.

31. "Poll Shows Most Americans Favor Physician-Aided Suicide," *Lancaster (Pa.) Intelligencer Journal,* 4 November 1991, A-3.

32. *Gallup Poll Monthly,* January 1991, 57.

33. "Causes of Depression and Suicide," *Youthworker Update,* November 1987, 5.

34. *Gallup Survey on Teenage Suicide,* 4.

35. Fried, "Over the Edge," 96.

36. *Let's Talk Facts,* 3.

37. Frank E. Crumley, "Substance Abuse and Adolescent Suicidal Behavior," *Journal of the American Medical Association* 263, no. 22 (13 June 1990): 3055.

38. "The Reality of Sexual Abuse," *Rapha Report,* 2.

39. "The Crime of the 90's," *Youthworker Update,* November 1989, 2.

40. "Sexual Abuse," 1.

41. Ibid.

42. Educational Resources, "Teen Suicide Prevention," 5.

43. Walter Byrd, Minirth-Meier Clinic, *Myths about Suicide,* fact sheet.

44. Ibid.

45. Educational Resources, "Teen Suicide Prevention," 5.

46. Kenny Moore, "Ode to Joy," *Sports Illustrated,* 17 August 1992, 30.

47. Neiger and Hopkins, "Adolescent Suicide," 473.

48. Bill Mattox, "Teen Suicide Prevention Programs: The Results Could Be Deadly," in *Policy Perspectives of the Family Research Council,* May 1987, 2.

49. "Faith Is a Bulwark against Suicide," *Youthworker Update,* May 1987, 3.

50. *Gallup Survey on Teenage Suicide,* 10.

51. Ibid., 7.

Chapter 12

1. "Prayer: The 'Rising Tide' in Youth Ministry," *Network News of the National Network of Youth Ministries,* IX, no. 3, fall 1991, 1.

2. "Parental Behavior," *Coral Ridge Encounter,* April 1990, 41.

3. Ron Rand, "A Challenge to Fathers Everywhere," *Princeton Theological Seminary Alumni/ae News,* fall 1988, 6.

4. Fred Green, "What Parents Could Have Done," *Pulpit Helps,* November 1987, 19.

5. Rand, "Challenge to Fathers," 6.

6. Green, "What Parents Could Have Done," 19.

7. Paul Tournier, *To Understand Each Other* (Atlanta: Johns Knox Press, 1962), 17.

For More Information
The CENTER FOR PARENT/YOUTH UNDERSTANDING can pro-
vide you with more information and resources that will help you better
understand the rapidly changing world of your children and teens. We
are committed to helping churches, schools, and community organizations build strong families through a variety of on-site parent seminars
and numerous other resources. If you would like information on our
newsletter, printed and audio materials, or how to sponsor one of our
parent education seminars or parent-teen weekends in your church,
school, or community, please call or write us at:

Center for Parent/Youth Understanding
P.O. Box 414
Elizabethtown, PA 17022
(717) 361-8429

INDEX

Important Resources for Parents of Today's Teens

40 WAYS TO TEACH YOUR CHILD VALUES
Paul Lewis   0-8423-0910-1
Teach kids about life's most important skills and attitudes through these creative, effective ideas.

50 PRACTICAL WAYS TO TAKE OUR KIDS BACK FROM THE WORLD
Michael J. McManus   0-8423-1242-0
Practical examples to help teens deal with the serious issues they face daily.

FAITHFUL PARENTS, FAITHFUL KIDS
Greg Johnson and Mike Yorkey   0-8423-1369-9
Successful Christian parents share methods for instilling values in today's kids.

FROM DAD WITH LOVE
Dave Veerman   0-8423-1333-8
Learn to give your children the priceless gifts of protection, identity, and confidence in your daily parenting.

HELPING TEENS IN CRISIS
Miriam Neff   0-8423-6823-X
A counselor presents facts about and preventive measures for pressures teens face.

PARENTING TEENS
Dr. Bruce Narramore and Dr. Vern C. Lewis   0-8423-5012-8
Guide children through the dependent-interdependent struggles of growing up and leaving home.

PARENTS WHO ENCOURAGE, CHILDREN WHO SUCCEED
Don H. Highlander   0-8423-5005-5
Practical advice for parents and teachers on cultivating the habit of using encouragement—powerful motivation for a child's success.

THE TEENAGE ZONE
John Souter   0-8423-1289-7
Make a child's transition into the teen years a little easier by understanding the changes of adolescence and maintaining a supportive environment.